Antonio

Life of

Gramsci

a Revolutionary

Giuseppe

Fiori

Translated by

Tom Nairn

VERSO

London · New York

First published as *Vita di Antonio Gramsci* by Laterza, Bari 1965
First published in English 1970
This edition published by Verso 1990
© Laterza 1965
Translation © New Left Books 1970

Verso
UK: 6 Meard Street, London W1V 3HR
USA: 29 West 35th Street, New York, NY 10001-2291

Verso is the imprint of New Left Books

ISBN 0-86091-533-6

Typeset in Monotype Ehrhardt
Printed in Great Britain by Biddles Ltd, Guildford

Antonio Gramsci

Titles in the
Verso Modern Classics
Series:

**Karl Kautsky and the
Socialist Revolution
1880–1938**
Massimo Salvadori

The Coming of the Book
The Impact of Printing 1450–1800
Lucien Febvre and
Henri-Jean Martin

Antonio Gramsci
Life of a Revolutionary
Giuseppe Fiori

For Marx
Louis Althusser

Foreword 7
Antonio Gramsci 9
Bibliography 293
Index 299

Translator's Note: *My thanks are due to Remo Bodei, Onofrio Nicastro, Martin Rossdale, and Camillo Pennati of the Italian Institute of Culture, London, for help with this translation. The bibliography has been adapted for this edition with the help of John Merrington and Quintin Hoare.*

Foreword

Gramsci once wrote in a letter to his sister-in-law, Tatiana: 'I received the photos of the children, and you can imagine how happy they made me. It was also very satisfying to see with my own eyes that they really do have bodies and legs; I'd seen nothing but heads for three years and was beginning to worry that they might have turned into cherubim, only without the little wings over their ears.'

The only ambition of this book is to complete the portrait of Gramsci himself in a similar way: to add 'body and legs' to the 'head' we already know – Gramsci the great intellectual and political leader. That is, to show those human factors which made up the 'whole' person, from childhood until maturity, through his days of hunger, of love, and of slow death. It is a portrait of 'Nino' Gramsci, as he was known to close friends.

The book owes much to Gennaro Gramsci, Antonio's brother, whom I remember with affection. He died tragically in a motor accident in Rome, on 30 October 1965, when the book was already written.

Thanks are also due to: Teresina Gramsci, especially for access to a collection of still unpublished letters; Edmea and Carlo Gramsci; Alfonso Leonetti, Elsa Fubini and Renzo De Felice; Leonilde Perilli, for information and documents on the Schucht family; Antonio Gramsci's old friends at Ghilarza, his playmates and school companions; his friends at secondary school and at the Dettòri lycée in Cagliari; his friends from the years in Turin; to everyone else close to him in his struggles and in prison who have agreed to bear witness to the tragic story of his life.

G.F.

The one-storey house where the Gramscis lived in Sardinia is built of reddish lava stone, and stands in the centre of Ghilarza, a big village on the Barigàdu plateau about half-way between Oristano and Maco-mèr. Nowadays a draper and haberdasher called Antioco Porcu keeps shop there. He knew the parents of Nino Gramsci (as everybody here calls Antonio), 'Signor Ciccillo' and Peppina Marcias:

> Francesco Gramsci – but we always called him 'Signor Ciccillo' – came here as a very young man in 1881. He was twenty, and it was his first job: he had come from his home town, Gaeta, to take charge of the local Registrar's office. Like so many other 'continentals' who cross the sea, he was probably thinking of a short stay, the few years of uncomfortable provincialdom one has to put up with at the start of one's career. In fact, he was to spend the rest of his life here. And apart from a few years working in Ales and Sòrgono, he lived right here all the time, in this house where we're chatting now. He died in 1937, fifty-six years after first coming to Ghilarza. Towards the end he even spoke the dialect in his own fashion. Some people had taken to calling him *tiu* Gramsci.

It has been said that Antonio Gramsci was of very humble origins, and this is still widely believed. Antioco now shakes his head before replying:

> Not really. His father, Signor Ciccillo, had a school leaving certificate. He was studying to be a lawyer till his father died and he had to get a job. And Signor Ciccillo's father was a colonel in the carabinieri, I believe. Then on his mother's side too Nino Gramsci came from a respected family: the Marcias family wasn't exactly rich – but not poor either.

On the same subject, Antonio's oldest brother, Gennaro, told me: 'I know. Togliatti once wrote that Nino was of peasant stock, so did reputable biographers, but they were getting away from the truth. . . .'

> Nino himself [he recalls] once mentioned our family background in a letter from prison. I can complete the story for him now. Our great grandfather was a Greek-Albanian Gramsci who fled from Epirus during

or shortly after the popular uprising of 1821, and became Italianized very quickly. A son called Gennaro was born in Italy, the name has been handed down to me. This Gennaro, our grandfather, was a colonel in the Bourbon gendarmerie. He married Teresa Gonzales, the daughter of a Neapolitan lawyer descended from some old Italo-Spanish family which had stayed behind in southern Italy – like so many others – when the Spanish occupation ended. They had five children, father being the last; he was born at Gaeta in March 1860, a few months before General Cialdini's troops laid siege to the town.[1] When the Bourbon regime was gone, grandfather was taken over by the carabinieri, and kept his colonel's rank there. Of the five children, the only girl married a rich Gaeta gentleman called Riccio; one became a treasury official; another was an inspector of railways, after being station-master at Rome; and a third son, Uncle Nicolino, became an army officer. Dad was the least fortunate of the lot: when his father died he was still a law student. He had to get himself a job, and this Sardinian post came up, the Registrar's office at Ghilarza, so off he went. Uncle Nicolino was sent to Sardinia too – first to La Maddalena, then Sassari, and finally to Ozieri, where he was captain in charge of the artillery depot (and he died there). So, father's family was typical of the better-off southern class that supplies the state bureaucracy with its middle-rank officials.

What about Peppina Marcias? 'Our mother,' Gennaro continued, 'was the daughter of a Marcias from Terralba and a Corrìas of Ghilarza. Grandfather on that side was a tax-collector and had a small bit of land. So the Marcias were middling folk, quite nicely off by the standards of our villages: they had a house, some land, enough to live pretty well.'

Peppina Marcias was born in 1861, one year after Signor Ciccillo. She was tall and graceful, a rung higher up the social ladder than most of the other Ghilarza girls, and so likely to attract notice at once ('She dressed like a European,' says an Ales tailor who knew her when she was young). She had stayed at primary school until the third year, and would read whatever she could lay her hands on, even Boccaccio. And this at a time when simply knowing how to read and write was a real distinction, particularly for a woman.[2] Francesco asked for her hand.

[1] In the last days of the Bourbon regime – the Kingdom of the Two Sicilies – its military resistance against Garibaldi's army (advancing from the south) and the Piedmontese army of King Victor Emmanuel II (advancing from the north) was concentrated around Capua and Gaeta, between Naples and Rome. Gaeta was taken by the Piedmontese General Cialdini in the autumn of 1860. (T.N.)

[2] A reliable writer of the period, Vittorio Angius, stated: 'In the whole town those able to read and write number about two hundred.' Ghilarza's population at that time was about 2,200.

But back in Campania his family was upset. His mother especially was put out by the idea that he – son of a colonel, nearly a law graduate – should marry a girl from an obscure lower-class family. They got married all the same: she was twenty-two, Ciccillo twenty-three. The following year, 1884, Gennaro was born. Then, not long afterwards, the family made the move to the Registrar's office at Ales. It was there that the other children were born: Grazietta in 1887, Emma in 1889; and finally, on 22 January 1891, Antonio. He was baptized seven days later.

Were the Gramscis religious? At Bonàrcado, a little village not far from Ghilarza, lives the girl who is spoken of so often and so carefully in Gramsci's prison letters – Edmea, the daughter of Gennaro. Now middle-aged, with greying hair, she is a doctor's wife and teaches in the primary school. About the religious beliefs of Ciccillo and Peppina Gramsci, she says:

> Grandad wasn't much of a practising Christian. But I remember when he was lying helpless at home, in the last months of his life, he often used to enjoy the company of a preacher who visited him during Lent. 'You know you're just like Giosuè Carducci lying there!' the man would say, and he understood it was to raise his spirits a bit.[3] They became friends. They used to spend hours together talking about everything under the sun. Grandad asked to be confessed before he died. . . . Grandmother was more of a regular churchgoer, she used to go to early morning mass every Sunday. Then she fell ill and rarely went out. But even then she always thought about God, especially when Uncle Nino was thrown in prison, and I would hear her repeating: 'Oh God, my God! I want nothing else from you, nothing. But please make me able to bear this . . .!' When she was dying she called me to her, and left me a gift of some images blessed by the priest. . . .

In one of Gramsci's prison letters we also find the following portrait of another member of the close family – Grazia Delogu, Peppina's unmarried half-sister, who lived permanently with the Gramscis and was like a second mother to Antonio:

> Aunt Grazia believed that there once existed a very pious lady called 'Donna Bisòdia', so pious that a place had been found for her in the Lord's Prayer itself. It was actually 'dona nobis hodie', which like many others she misinterpreted as 'Donna Bisòdia' and imagined as a noble dame of the good old days when everybody went to church and there was

---

[3] *Giosuè Carducci* (1835-1907): Famous Italian poet and the dominant figure in Italian culture as a whole in the decade 1880-90. (T.N.)

still some real faith left in the world. One could make up a story all about
this imaginary 'Donna Bisòdia' forever being held up to us as an example.
How often Aunt Grazia used to tell Grazietta or Emma: 'Ah, you're not
a bit like Donna Bisòdia!'

For the christening of Antonio Gramsci, it was not Canon Marongiu,
the parish priest of Ales, who came to the baptistery. This was a
particularly solemn occasion. We read in the parish register that it was
the 'Illustrious and Most Reverend Doctor of Theology Sebastiano
Frau, Vicar-General' who baptized the infant. The godfather was a
Masullas lawyer called Francesco Puxeddu.

There are people who can still remember the celebrations after the
ceremony. Nicolino Tunis, a tailor (retired now he can no longer carry
on his trade) recalls:

> Our two families were very close. My father was a bailiff at the local
> magistrate's court, he and Signor Ciccillo spent a lot of time together,
> and Signora Peppina was quite at home in our house. She was godmother
> to a sister of mine, called Peppina after her. I was ten years old when Nino
> Gramsci was baptized. I still remember it, and the happy atmosphere
> that day, the loads of sweets and good things brought from Ghilarza, and
> the crowds of people who came to fête the child. I was a pal of Gennaro's
> and I used to play with Grazietta and Emma, though they were much
> smaller than I. God knows how often I picked up Nino and held him
> in my arms. He was a fine, fair baby, with light-coloured eyes. He was
> still very small when Signor Ciccillo was transferred to Sòrgono, and I
> never saw him again.

There are no other relics of the Gramscis in Ales. The birthplace
was occupied by a priest called Melis after Ciccillo left it, then it was
taken over as the local headquarters of the Fascist Party for nearly
twenty years, and now the ground floor has been turned into a bar, the
Bar dello Sport. There is a plaque just above the entrance, lost among
the painted tin adverts for aperitifs, digestives and soft drinks. It says:
'Ten years after his martyrdom, this stone was placed on his birthplace
in honour of Antonio Gramsci, by the affection of his fellow-citizens
and the gratitude of all free men.' Before 1947, when a committee set
up in Cagliari decided to do something about honouring Gramsci, few
inhabitants of Ales realized they had had such a distinguished fellow-
citizen.

> He was taken to Sòrgono when he was just about a year old [says Antioco
> Porcu] and there he stayed until he was seven, except for the summer

months. They always came back to Ghilarza in summer. Meanwhile the family had grown: Mario was born in '93, Teresina in '95, and Carlo in '97. They moved back permanently to Ghilarza in 1898, and Signor Ciccillo and Signora Peppina were never to leave it again.

It was a dramatic return. There had been some serious developments in the region's petty political intrigues, which had proved quite disastrous for Ciccillo Gramsci: he had lost his job and ended up in prison. The story had begun with the political elections of 1897.

The historian Bellieni has pointed out that in *fin-de-siècle* Sardinia 'public affairs were scarcely a matter of theoretical debate: the parties were really the personal followings of a few big men'. We have a direct witness to this in the person of Francesco Pais Serra, the parliamentary deputy for Ozieri, whom Prime Minister Crispi asked to carry out an inquiry into economic conditions and law enforcement on the island in 1894. A year and a half later, Pais Serra reported:

> Except in a few centres, and among very few people even there, the terms 'conservative', 'liberal', 'democrat', or 'radical' have no meaning whatsoever. 'Socialism', 'Anarchy', or 'Clericalism' have never been heard of. And yet the parties are very much alive, they are combative, tenacious and intransigent. But they are not political parties, not parties inspired by general or local interests, they are personal parties, family-based cliques in the narrowest sense of the word. . . . Sheltered under the wings of the larger personal factions, one finds microscopic personal factions and cliques in each town, all the more spiteful and violent for having little of moment to quarrel about and being forced to see each other every day. . . . These link themselves up to the grander cliques and receive in return protection and assistance in their little squabbles, help in seeking for personal favours and covering up infractions of the law, and sometimes in getting away with real crimes.

'The old feudal repression,' concludes Pais Serra, 'has given way to this sort of creeping vassalage, whose effects are even worse and more depressing.'

Sòrgono was in the electoral constituency of Isili, where the election of 1897 brought a bitter conflict between two such local chieftains called Francesco Cocco Ortu and Enrico Carboni Boy. Cocco Ortu was one of Sardinia's most prominent citizens, already a member of parliament for twenty years, and twice an Under-Secretary, first at the Ministry of Agriculture and later at the Ministry of Justice. Bellieni describes him as 'the foremost exemplar of the spirit of faction'. But the forthcoming contest was going to be more difficult for this influential man.

His younger rival had a considerable following in his home town of Nuragus, and also in such key centres of the constituency as Tonara and Sòrgono. Ciccillo Gramsci aligned himself with the new man, Carboni Boy.

The battle was a close one, fought mercilessly down to the last vote. But Cocco Ortu was re-elected, and before long he was more powerful than ever: within a few months he had been made Minister of Agriculture, Industry and Commerce in the new Di Rudinì cabinet. We may gather what the attitude of the 'Cocchists', the 'spiteful, violent clique' behind Cocco Ortu, was likely to be from another passage in Pais Serra's report: 'The triumph of this or that political party in Rome matters little . . . All that counts is that the party boss should have influence in the central government, so that he can dominate his following back in Sardinia and behave like a conqueror, distributing favours to the victors and annihilating the vanquished.' Ciccillo Gramsci now found himself in the ranks of the vanquished, and exposed to all the perils inherent in that state, including that of falling foul of 'prostituted justice'.[4]

Some months after the election, a sad event compelled Ciccillo Gramsci to leave Sòrgono for a while: his brother Nicolino, the one in charge of the artillery depot at Ozieri, had died suddenly on 17 December, aged only forty-two. So he went to the funeral, and also to see how Gennaro's studies might be continued, now that he could no longer stay with his Uncle Nicolino. No sooner had he left than a telegram went off from Sòrgono to Cagliari. It was sent by the 'Cocchisti', who took advantage of his being away to suggest that the accounts of the Registrar's office needed looking into. When he returned from Ozieri, Ciccillo learnt that he was to be investigated.

Things were found to be not quite as they should be in his office. There had undoubtedly been some mild misconduct of affairs there. He was suspended and deprived of his salary, and returned to Ghilarza with the family. There, he spent some months of isolation and black depression, tormented by fears of arrest and imprisonment. He was thirty-eight years old, he had just lost his job, and at any moment worse might follow. . . . The carabinieri came for him on 9 August 1898. He learnt that he was to be accused of embezzlement, extortion, and falsification of documents.

---

[4] 'There is no other term possible,' wrote Alfredo Niceforo at this time. 'We felt the greatest disgust, the utmost nausea everywhere in Sardinia, as we saw how the power of parliamentarians and Prefects was used to divert the course of justice.'

He found himself in Oristano prison, where he remained until committed for trial in Cagliari fifteen months later, on 28 October 1899. The trial took place a year later still. At that time embezzlement was the responsibility of the Assize Court, and this was the court which sentenced him, on 27 October 1900. The judgement mentions as a mitigating circumstance the 'slight damage and small value' involved, since the investigator had found only a trifling sum missing. Still, the law took such offences seriously in those days, and even though he was given the minimum, owing to mitigating circumstances, it amounted to no less than five years, eight months, and twenty-two days.

Peppina Marcias was overwhelmed by the disaster, left as she now was with seven children to care for, the youngest still in arms and the oldest (Gennaro) only fourteen. Antonio was seven at the time. Till then the Gramscis had lived a sober, quiet existence; they were not rich but they had always been able to make ends meet without difficulty. They had had money coming into the house regularly each month, a more precious thing than one might think today, in that subsistence economy where exchange in kind still reigned, and there was little money in circulation at all. Now, suddenly, with the imprisonment of Signor Ciccillo and the loss of his salary, the family climate changed. There came a period of the utmost hardship and humiliation. And so, one tragedy came to be piled upon another: because, for some time already, Antonio had been showing signs of physical deformity.

2

It was Nennetta Cuba – mentioned in one of the prison letters – who told me about Gramsci's childhood. She is seventy-eight. A contemporary and friend of Grazietta's, she lived opposite the Gramscis in Ghilarza and was treated like one of the family:

Nino was not always . . . well, a hunchback, let's say it. No, he was perfectly all right when he was little. Perhaps a bit delicate. But otherwise all right, a lovely baby. . . . He was four years younger than I. I always joked about it, and I remember him well before he fell ill, a fine normal boy, curly-haired and fair, with blue eyes. Then he got this sort of bump on the back, I don't know what caused it, and he stopped growing properly. He became under-sized and stayed that way. *Tia* Peppina tried everything to fight the illness, poor thing. She was confused, she used to look so terrified. She would stretch him out and massage him with tincture of iodine for hours on end, but it was no good. The bump got bigger and bigger every day. So they went to Oristano to have him looked at. *Tiu* Gramsci took him to a specialist at Caserta as well. When they came home, the treatment recommended was to keep him hung up from a ceiling beam. They had made him a kind of corset with rings on it. Nino would put this on, then *tiu* Gramsci and Gennaro would hook it up to the ceiling and leave him there hanging in mid-air. They thought this was the right way to straighten him out. But the swelling on his back – and later on his chest as well – just kept getting worse, they never found a cure. Nino stayed very small, even fully grown he wasn't more than one and a half metres tall.

The family believed a fall had done the damage. The youngest of Antonio's sisters, Teresina, told me: 'I've heard mother say so many times that Nino was a lovely baby at first. Then one day they found a swelling on his back, and couldn't understand how it got there. Mother couldn't get over it, she had no peace because of it. Then she had an idea; she called the serving-girl and said: "Did you ever let him fall when you were holding him? Tell the truth now, if you did!" The girl at first insisted she hadn't, but then in the end admitted that she had. Afterwards, none of the treatments were any good.'

Antonio suffered frequently from other ailments besides this physical deformity. He wrote later: 'When I was a child of four I had haemorrhages lasting three days at a stretch which left me quite bloodless and were accompanied by convulsions. The doctors had given me up for dead, and until about 1914 my mother kept the small coffin and little dress I was supposed to be buried in.'

And now there was worse: Ciccillo's imprisonment brought poverty and degradation to a household stricken by grief at the child's ill-health. Peppina Marcias did not give in. Her pride prevented her from asking help from her mother-in-law or her brothers-in-law, from the family that had looked down its nose at her when she was married. Ciccillo's brothers were in good positions, and his sister was married to a wealthy landowner: they were well able to help. But Peppina wanted to manage by herself; she chose to avoid the humiliation of asking for assistance from these relations she scarcely knew.

A woman of strong and combative character (only thirty-seven when her husband was arrested), she confronted the tragic situation with the greatest resolution. First she got together a modest sum of money – enough to pay the lawyers and see to her children's immediate needs – by selling the small landholding she had inherited from her own family. Then she took a lodger, a veterinary doctor called Vittore Nessi. But above all, she worked. 'Our mother was a very good seamstress,' recalls Teresina. 'She made and sold shirts and other articles of clothing. She found time to work by going without sleep.' Long afterwards, Antonio Gramsci looked back on those years of torment and wrote of his mother:

> Would we be capable of doing what Mother did thirty-five years ago? Would we be able to stand alone against such disaster, and save seven children from it? Her life was certainly a great lesson to us, it showed us how important staying-power can be in overcoming difficulties which looked insuperable even to men of great courage. . . . She worked for us all her life, she made unheard-of sacrifices – had she been different, who knows what would have become of us children, perhaps none of us would be here today.

Antonio was now attending the primary school in Ghilarza. Always anxious about his health, his mother did not send him there until he was seven and a half, and then found time to help him with his homework so that he should not get too tired.[1] In his first year he found himself in a class with no less than forty-nine pupils, under a master called Ignazio Corrias. Next year he had another, Celestino Baldussi; and in his third year still another, Luigi Cossu. He was always top of the class in those early years, with a mark of nine or ten out of ten in every subject. 'The school system I went through was a very backward one' – we learn from one of his letters – 'and anyway nearly all my fellow-pupils spoke Italian very badly and with much difficulty, which gave me a great advantage. The teachers had to address themselves to the average pupil, and being able to speak fluent Italian was enough in itself to raise one above the average and make things easy.' But something else made things easy, too: the boy's fierce eagerness to devour any form of printed matter he could get his hands on. 'Sometimes we wouldn't see him for weeks on end,' says one of his old playmates, Felle Toriggia, 'and when I asked him why, he would say he had spent the whole time reading.'

As well as these studious tendencies, he began to show interest in practical activities at about the same time. 'He made himself a special shower-bath,' I learned from the family. 'It was made like this: there was a big metal can attached to a wall-hook. This can could be hung from the kitchen ceiling, and Nino had made lots of little holes in the top part. He would fill it with warm water and pull it up. Then he turned it upside-down by tugging a string, and the water squirted out through the holes.'

The same practical impulse led him to make toys, little boats and carts. 'My greatest triumph' – we read – 'was when one of the village smiths asked me for a paper model of my magnificent two-deck schooner, so that he could make a tin version.' Or again:

I remember the courtyard where I used to play with Luciano [Luciano Guiso, the Ghilarza chemist's boy], and the basin where I manoeuvred my great fleets of paper, cork, and bits of stick and cane, sinking them afterwards with a pea-shooter. . . . I spoke of nothing then but brigantines, frigates, three-masters, schooners, flag signals and topgallant sails. . . .

[1] Antonio wrote to her from prison: 'I remember as if it were yesterday how you used to correct my homework when I was in my first or second year at school. I remember very clearly that I never managed to spell "uccello" correctly, with two "c"s. You must have corrected me ten times at least . . . You made us learn lots of poetry by heart; I still remember *Rataplan*, and another one: "Along the banks of the Loire/Which like a silver ribbon/For a hundred miles/Wends its happy way." . . . I remember too how much I admired the way you used to imitate drum-rolls on the table-top, reciting *Rataplan* – I must have been four or five at the time.'

Only I was always annoyed that Luciano possessed one simple, robust little tin boat that used to sink all my elaborate galleons every time, in spite of their complicated rigging. Still, I was very proud of being able to manufacture them.

He also contrived some gymnastic apparatus for himself. From earliest childhood he was kept going by extraordinary will-power and by a determination to make up in every possible way for his deformity. Every day, methodically, he did a spell of weight-lifting. In the yard of the house where Teresina now lives there are some stone balls. She explained:

They were for dumb-bells. Nino made them out of large boulders. His brothers helped him. They chiselled them out together, then he would spend hour after hour smoothing them down into spheres. He made six of these balls, for three different sets of dumb-bells, all different weights. The rod joining the balls was a broom-handle. Iron was dear in those days, they couldn't afford a metal bar. And anyway the dumb-bell served its purpose well enough, even with a wooden bar. Nino did his exercises regularly, every morning. He wanted to be more robust, to have more muscles on his arms. He would go at it as hard as he could until he was quite exhausted. I remember he once managed sixteen consecutive lifts. . . .

Teresina was visibly moved by her recollection of the episode. She was once the family favourite and, of the three sisters, the one closest to Antonio in intellectual development.[2] She is now seventy and has been widowed for many years since the death of her husband, a postal official called Paolo Palesu. This pale, gentle figure might have stepped straight out from the illustrated pages of some old book: she is shy, retiring, her hair-style and the cut of her black dress recall a bygone era, and her eyes are veiled by sadness whenever those difficult times are mentioned. She used to work alongside her husband in the post office at Ghilarza; since retiring in 1960 she has rarely left the house. 'Of course,' she goes on, 'Nino's unfortunate physical condition could very well have influenced the development of his character. He was rather reserved, he kept himself to himself. . . . But though he wasn't demonstrative – and he really wasn't – he was always very kind and affectionate towards us: I was his little sister, four years younger, and

[2] Gramsci once wrote to her: 'Do you remember how desperately keen we both were on reading and writing, Teresina? I think when you were about ten, and there were no new books around, you once read right through all the legal codes.'

he used to spoil me, he used to spend what little money he had buying me comics. . . .'

Similar accounts are given by other school friends and playmates, with few variations. Nennetta Cuba remembers him as 'reserved, but not boorish'. Felle Toriggia says:

> He was a sad child. But if someone was friendly with him, then he would open up and laugh. . . . One year, I think it must have been 1900 or 1901, we went swimming together down to Bosa Marina. In those days we travelled in ox-carts. During the times we spent together, in the cart or at the beach, I don't think you could say Nino Gramsci was a quiet child. Company always made him more cheerful. Now and then he would be almost gay.

However, he was always conscious of being left out of the more vigorous, aggressive, outdoor games of his playmates. A school friend called Chicchinu Mameli recollects:

> You know what was wrong with him; and this deformity naturally stopped him taking part in some of our games. Boys will be boys, they like fighting and tiring themselves out. Our favourite games were trials of strength and stamina, and Nino could only be an onlooker. This was why he rarely came with us. Usually he stayed at home, reading, or drawing and painting, or making things with wood, or playing away in the courtyard. Or else he would go on long walks. I used to see him a lot with Mario. Gennaro was seven years older, too big to be company for him; and Carlo was seven years younger, too little.

This was the period when he went on excursions up the Tirso valley to San Serafino, to the brooks and gardens of Canzola, or to the house of his Aunt Maria Domenica Corrias at Abbasanta. The wife of a local tax-collector, Signora Mazzacurati, had made him a present of a small collection of books when her husband moved away to another job; among them was a copy of *Robinson Crusoe*. He read it when he was still very small, and it made a deep impression. 'I never used to leave the house without some grains of corn in my pocket and a few matches wrapped in oilcloth,' he wrote, 'just in case I should be cast away on a desert island and left to my own resources.'

He would amuse himself catching lizards, or playing ducks and drakes and listening to the hiss of the stones skimming across the water. He was particularly fond of watching animals:

> Once on an autumn evening, when there was a bright moon shining, I and a friend of mine went into an apple orchard. We hid ourselves in a

thicket, downwind. Suddenly a family of hedgehogs appeared, two big ones and three little ones. They made for the apple trees in Indian file, wandered about a bit in the long grass, then got down to work. Using their muzzles and paws, they rolled all the windfall apples very close together in a clearing. But they still didn't have enough. The biggest one looked inquiringly around him, then climbed up the easiest tree he could spy, followed by his mate. They crept out to a heavily-laden bough, and started to sway rhythmically back and forth. As the motion built up, the bough began to shake more and more violently, and lots more apples fell to the ground. They pushed all these together with the others, and then all the hedgehogs – the little ones as well – rolled over with their spines erect and lay on top of the apples. The apples stuck on the spines, and though the little ones only managed a few, the father and mother each had seven or eight stuck on. As they were heading back for their den, we came out from our hiding-place, put them in a sack, and carried them off home. I kept the father hedgehog and two of the babies for many months in our courtyard, where they wandered about freely.

There is also this other reminiscence:

Once I went with my younger brothers into an aunt's field where there were two enormous oaks and some fruit trees; we were supposed to gather up the acorns and feed them to a little pig. The field was close to the village, but quite deserted, and hidden in a fold of ground. As we came into the field we saw a big fox calmly sitting under one of the trees, with his bushy tail sticking up straight as a flag-pole. It wasn't in the least afraid. It did bare its teeth, but seemed to be laughing rather than snarling. We were very annoyed that the fox shouldn't be frightened of us: it just was not the least bit frightened. We threw some stones, but it hardly moved, and kept on looking at us in this sly, mocking way. Then we put sticks to our shoulders and all shouted 'Bang!' together, still without worrying it much. Suddenly a real rifle-shot rang out somewhere near by. Only then did the fox leap up with a start, and run off very quickly. I can still see him now, a tawny streak flashing along the wall of the field with his tail still erect, then vanishing in the undergrowth.

Then there were the local festivals, the horses that rushed round Sèdilo church in the races held on St Anthony's day, the nougat stalls with their faint, flickering carbide lights, the platforms erected for the dialect verse-speaking competitions. One day, Gramsci was to write to his mother from prison:

When you get the chance, send me some of those Sardinian songs still sung in the streets by the descendants of Pirisi Pirione of Bolotana, and if there are any poetry contests at the festivals write and tell me what the subjects are. Do they still hold the St Constantine's day festival at Sèdilo, and the St Palmerio festival, and how are they nowadays? Is St Isidoro's day still a big thing? Do they still have the flag with the four Moors on it carried round, do the captains still dress up in old soldiers' uniforms? These things always interested me very much, you know; so please write and tell me about them, don't think of them as silly nonsense not worth anyone's attention.

But these images of a carefree life are only one side of the truth. Antonio was deeply disturbed by the terrible poverty in the family after his father's arrest, by the psychological repercussions of this calamity, as well as by his own physical ailment. Theoretically, Gennaro, the oldest son, was the only one who knew all about what had happened.[3] It would have been difficult to keep the truth from a boy of his age, in any case. But possibly fairy-tales and pathetic lies and subterfuges might work for the others – and in fact, Peppina Marcias struggled to the very end to keep the secret within the family. Francesco Gramsci was imprisoned in Gaeta, a few hundred yards from his mother's house. Peppina got him to send letters which she would forward to her mother-in-law with a Ghilarza postmark. The children were told that their father had gone on a long visit to see their grandmother Teresa Gonzales in Gaeta.

But in the small-town world of Ghilarza a flimsy story like this was bound to collapse sooner or later. Given the notoriety of the affair, it was impossible that the children should not encounter oblique references and allusions to it, or overhear adults discussing it among themselves, secure in the belief that the children's attention was elsewhere; impossible, therefore, that they should not come to at least a confused half-understanding of the true reasons for their father's long absence. Thirty years later, in a situation not altogether different, Antonio was to write a letter to Tatiana from prison, referring to his own son:

> I can't think why Delio has not been told that I'm in prison, *and why no one reflected that he might then find out about it indirectly*, that is, in the most disagreeable way for a child, who then begins to doubt the truthful-

---

[3] 'I was in my fourth year at Ozieri school, staying with our uncle Nicolino,' Gennaro told me, 'when Uncle died just before Christmas. But Father fixed things so that I was able to finish the school year at Ozieri. I went home to Ghilarza for the holidays. When school was due to re-open (Dad was no longer there) I learnt from Mother that I couldn't go on studying for the time being, and the reason why not. At that time I was the only one of the seven children to know about Father being in jail.'

ness of those educating him, to think about it on his own account and draw apart. At least, *that was my experience as a child : I remember it perfectly.* . . . So it would be a good thing to persuade Julia [Gramsci's wife] that it is both wrong and – in the last resort – pointless to keep the truth about me hidden from the children. Maybe the first disclosure of the truth could hurt them but this is a matter of carefully choosing the right way to go about it. I believe in treating children as rational creatures with whom it is possible to discuss even the most serious matters. This makes a very profound impression on them, it strengthens their character and above all it avoids leaving their development at the mercy of random environmental pressures and casual, impersonal encounters. It really is very strange how grown-ups forget they were children themselves, and make no use of their own experiences. *For my part, I recall vividly how offended I was at every discovery of a subterfuge, even if it was meant to keep painful facts from me, and how this shut me up within myself and made me withdraw.* By the age of ten I had become a real trial to mother, because of my fanatical desire for frankness and mutual truth, and the terrible scenes and scandals this desire provoked [G.F.'s italics].

As a child the truth was revealed to him in the worst and most crooked way. The resulting trauma was to affect the rest of his life, and was to influence his relationship with his father up to the very end. It led to misunderstandings, to bitterness, to long silences; it was the kind of blow which leaves a permanent mark. As a grown-up, he could still write: '*If she* [his mother] *were to know that I know what I do, and that those events left permanent scars on me*, it would poison the rest of her life . . .' [G.F.'s italics].

Gramsci the man's great tenderness towards his mother was certainly derived in part from his close knowledge of 'the graver mishaps, the harsher tragedies' which she had to endure at this period. Sometimes, when night fell, she would risk leaving the house where humiliation now kept her a prisoner, and creep out of the back door wrapped in a black shawl, avoiding lights and passers-by, till she reached the local church. There, she would huddle in a corner for hours, first of all to pray, then to weep.

3

Gennaro was the first of the Gramsci family to find a job, in 1900 (when he was barely sixteen), and so contribute a little to its depleted finances. Teresina described how poor they were at that time:

> We lived in the direst poverty. Mother was a stubborn woman with lots of energy, and determined to fight back against hard luck. But though she was tireless herself, seven children were seven children, and as we gradually used up the money got from the sale of the Marcias lands, survival became more and more difficult. We managed incredible economies. I remember how Grazietta, Emma and I used to save up the wax that ran off the tallow candles so that we could use it again to make little candles for Nino to read by when night fell.

In those years at the turn of the century, Ghilarza was a place of very limited resources: by no means the most backward part of the island, but not prosperous either. Its poverty was rooted in the primitive character of its mainly agricultural economy:

> The Ghilarza man divides his working time among the grain crops, the vines, gathering firewood, some livestock products, and the maintenance of walls, fences and fields, trying to use only his own labour as far as possible. . . . In addition, the village resources are apportioned so that everyone is more or less a small landholder – hence, there is no labour available for a more productive form of cultivation, and the peasants who are without servants of their own depend upon a system of mutual help and exchange, which they call *a cambios*, or *a manu torrada*.[1]

At the end of 1899, the first steps were taken towards a revision of the old land survey maps, which until then had been mere approximations. As will become clear, this was to have some valuable repercussions within this community of 'low, dark dwellings, ugly crooked streets, traditional costume and patriarchal habits', with its almost prehistoric agriculture and its peasants accustomed to 'drudgery from

[1] Michele Licheri: *Ghilarza : Note di storia civile ed ecclesiastica* ('Ghilarza: Notes on its Social and Religious History'). A monograph printed at the very beginning of this century.

sunrise until sunset'. Among its other effects, it provided a first chance of work and earning for Gennaro, in the local Land Registry.

It was now the summer following Antonio's second year at school. That year his marks had been: three 'tens' (out of ten), one 'nine', two 'eights' and one 'seven'. Hardly evidence of prodigious powers – of the precocious genius portrayed in so many hagiographies – but still, a long way ahead of all the other pupils. So he had the idea of missing out a year:

I had done the second year, and was thinking of doing the final elementary exam that November, which would have enabled me to miss out the third year and go straight into the fourth. I was quite confident I could, but when I went to see the director of studies with my formal request to do so, he suddenly came out point-blank with an unexpected question: 'What about the Eighty-four Articles of the Constitution then – d'you know them?' I had never even thought about them. I had only studied the 'Rights and Duties of the Citizen' section of our textbook. It was a terrible blow. All the more so because on 20 September just past I had taken part in the commemoration march for the first time, carrying a little paper lantern and shouting 'Long live the Lion of Caprera!' (Garibaldi), 'Long live the Martyr of Staglieno!' (Mazzini) along with all the others (I'm not sure now whether we shouted the 'martyr' or the 'prophet' of Staglieno – it might well have been both).[2] There I was, smugly sure of my ability to pass the exam, and so acquire the legal right to become a voter – and all the time I didn't even know the Eighty-four Articles of the Constitution!

So he went through the third year normally, in 1900–01. The following year he had Pietro Sotgiu as a teacher – the one who had asked him about the Eighty-four Articles – and in his final examination he was awarded eleven 'tens', one 'nine' and two 'eights' (in gymnastics and manual work). He was now eleven years old. In the summer of 1902, he went to join Gennaro for a spell of work in the Land Registry office.

He was not really strong enough to go to work at such an early age. But at home things were going from bad to worse, and Antonio and the smaller children were forced to make sacrifices like everyone else in order to obtain money. 'I learnt to look after myself while still a child. I began working when I was eleven, and earned no less than nine lire per month (that meant a kilo of bread a day), for ten hours of work each day, including Sunday mornings. My job was carrying about register

---

[2] 20 September: commemoration of the entry of Italian troops into Rome, in 1870, the last stage of Italian reunification. (T.N.)

books that weighed more than I did, and I passed many nights weeping secretly because my whole body ached from it.' This exhausting routine had severe psychological effects on a child already so physically afflicted. In spite of the special attention given him in the family – the room with the best outlook, the best food available – the whole chain of circumstances, his deformity, the shame of a father in prison, the grim atmosphere in the house, the endless renunciation and sacrifice, all tended to depress him further. He would say of himself later:

> For a very long time, I have believed it was absolutely, fatally impossible that I should ever be loved. . . . When I was a ten-year-old boy I began to feel this way about my own parents. My physical condition was so feeble, I was forced to make so many sacrifices, that I became convinced I was a burden, an intruder in my own family. These are things one doesn't forget so easily, they leave far deeper marks than one would suspect.

Nennetta Cuba said: 'Occasionally he would joke and laugh. . . . But never quite like other children. I never saw him laugh really light-heartedly.'

The next year at school (his fifth, 1902–03) was destined also to be his first real academic triumph. He got: ten for composition; ten in dictation; ten in arithmetic (both written and oral); ten in grammar and reading; and ten in history and geography.

But what next, now that he had finished primary school? Ghilarza was too far away from any town with a secondary school, and Peppina Marcias had no money to send him away to live. So, in spite of all the 'tens' on his primary certificate, Antonio Gramsci suffered the same fate as so many other poor children, from Ghilarza and elsewhere: he had to give up school. The family was not in contact with the Gramscis in mainland Italy: Peppina would never have asked them to look after Antonio, nor – in any case – would Antonio have agreed to go if it had cost his mother her pride. So the only possible solution was ruled out. Antonio had to resign himself to giving up his studies, at least until his father got out of prison. The cost of this act of renunciation was high. He became embittered, and even more isolated and cold. His manner became more biting and ironical: for the first time he began to feel a rebel.[3] Twenty years afterwards, he would write to his wife Julia:

[3] He saw it this way himself years later: 'What was it that stopped me from turning into a stuffed shirt? It was an instinct of rebellion, awakened by the fact that I, who had got ten out of ten in everything, could not go on studying, while the butcher's boy, the chemist's boy, the draper's boy, all the rich men's sons were able to.'

'Because of the isolated existence I have led since childhood, I have become used to hiding my feelings behind a mask of hardness, or an ironic smile. . . . . For long this did me great damage; for long, it made my relations to other people enormously complicated.'

His younger brother Mario was the only one who could get through to him. Two years younger than Antonio, he appears to have been a cheerful, mischievous character.

> He kept us all in stitches [says Teresina] – he was the very opposite of Nino in temperament. Nino was staid, while he was restless, noisy, harum-scarum. Nino said very little; the only way to keep Mario quiet would have been to sew his mouth shut. Sometimes the cat would disappear from the house. It was always Mario – he would carry it round to the baker's and ask him to roast it. I remember once mother shut him up in the house. To make sure he didn't go out, she took his shoes and hid them. Mario took some black polish and painted his feet with it, he was so keen to sneak out all the same. Then mother tried dressing him up as a girl, in one or another of our dresses, just to keep him in the house. And that was the only way of preventing him escaping.

Even Antonio was amused at the antics of this wild, quick-witted brother. They got on well together. Sometimes they entertained one another by trying their hand at poetical improvisation of the sort popular in the local festivals, satirizing the odd quirks of certain village personalities. Antonio's familiarity with the peasant milieu – plus his ironic streak – furnished him with a long series of targets. Long after, during his early prison days, he dedicated a song to those figures of his early childhood. It was based on *La scomuniga de predi Antiogu a su populu de Masuddas* ('Brother Antiogu's excommunication of the People of Masuddas'), a popular satire of the late nineteenth century, and he mentions it in a letter to his mother:

> Do you know what I'd like you to send me? *La predica di fra' Antiogu.* You should be able to get it at Oristano, for not long ago Patrizio Carta had it reprinted at his famous printing works. Since I have so much time on my hands, I would like to compose a poem in the same style with all the illustrious personalities of my own childhood in it: *tiu* Remundu Gana with Ganosu and Ganolla, *maistru* Andriolu and *tiu* Millanu, *tiu* Micheli Bobboi, *tiu* Iscorza, Pippotto, Corroncu, Santu Jancu, etc. It would amuse me a great deal, and in a few years I'll be able to recite it to the children.

Antonio spent what free time he could get from his work at the Registry studying a little Latin. He had not completely given up hope of returning to school when times were better. So he taught himself, in order not to be left hopelessly behind after these two lost years in Ghilarza. Now and then he even took some lessons from someone who had been to secondary school: Ezio Camedda, a hunchback like himself, undertook to pass on to him his small knowledge of Latin. It was scarcely the best sort of preparation for Antonio. Still, it was better than nothing; at least, it distracted him.

At long last, the darkness lifted a little. On 3 January 1904, Signor Ciccillo finished serving his sentence (reduced by three months, thanks to an amnesty). So towards Easter he came home to Peppina Marcias and his children, after more than five and a half years.

Felle Toriggia can remember the evening of his return to Ghilarza:

> We students always used to meet on the bridge at the edge of town. The low parapets made a good seat, and we would stay there for hours chatting. One evening, towards dusk, we saw Signor Ciccillo and Nannaro [Gennaro] coming towards us from the direction of the railway station at Abbasanta. They walked along silently, side by side. As they drew near us, we stopped talking. Signor Ciccillo looked very much older and rather grim. We greeted him and he looked towards us timidly. Nannaro put a hand across his shoulders, and they went on into the town, without saying a word.

Now that he was back, the family could at least regain something of its former peace of mind.

Antonio Gramsci was thirteen, and still 'dragging registers about' in the Land Registry a year after leaving school, when soldiers suddenly fired at a group of miners on strike, and killed three of them. This happened at Bugerru, a big mining centre on the south-west coast of Sardinia, in September 1904; it was the first violent episode of a long-standing crisis which had started (or at least, started to become more acute) about fifteen years previously.

No one could possibly have claimed that the economy of the island was flourishing before 1887. But till then it had at least been saved from total collapse by the export of such agricultural products as wine, olive oil, and cattle to markets in France. Then came the great bank crashes. The Cagliari Savings Bank shut down in 1886; the Sardinian Bank for Agriculture and Industry came close to bankruptcy in 1887; the Agrarian Bank of Sardinia went into liquidation shortly afterwards. The effect of this was to drive Sardinia's small producers back to the local money-lenders, with disastrous consequences – inevitable, given the tiny size and poor resources of most farms.

But even more disastrous was the abrogation of the trade agreement with France, as a result of the higher tariff barriers introduced by the Italian government to protect the big industrial interests of the North. Deprived of its traditional outlets, and affected also by coincidental misfortunes like the phylloxera epidemic, the island's agriculture touched rock bottom. Sardinia lacked above all the manufacturing industries which might have softened this blow to her agrarian economy by absorbing some of her unemployed rural work-force. From this situation there derived four main consequences: intensified exploitation of the Sulcis-Iglesiente mineral basin (not on a scale to provide work for everybody, however); a great rise in emigration; a growth in unemployment and rural 'under-employment' to frightening proportions; and the revival of banditry.

A fifth consequence of the fall in exports was a sharp drop in the price of milk. The cheese manufacturers of Rome, Naples and Tuscany quickly seized this opportunity and built a number of new factories on the island. At first they competed against one another, so that the price of milk began to go up again. This persuaded many Sardinian cultivators that henceforth dairy-farming would be more remunerative than traditional crop-agriculture; so vineyards and grain-fields were rapidly converted into pasture lands. But this in turn provoked a rise in the price of such traditional products as oil, pasta, and vegetables, as the supply of these tended to diminish. The smallholder was worst hit, since normally he could scarcely manage to feed his own family and had little or nothing left over to sell in the urban markets. Then the dairy-farmers too began to feel the pinch. For as the power of the cheese-barons grew, they tended to form corporate organizations for the exploitation of foreign markets, and the bargaining power of the dairymen fell to nothing. Soon, the manufacturers were able to impose the prices they wanted, and to sell their cheese at the high prices of the international market inside Sardinia itself. There was a popular and eloquent saying of the period: *'Chie mandicat casu hat dentes de oro'* ('He who eats cheese has gold teeth').

Besides the cheese manufacturers, the other dominant forces in the island economy were the owners of the mineral extraction rights (mostly foreigners), and the big landowners who had added to their wealth by money-lending:

> The leaders of the revolt against feudalism [writes Camillo Bellieni] – the 'cavaglieris' who followed Angioy and stirred up popular movements when it suited them, became the new landowners once feudalism was destroyed. They took over the lands which had belonged to the old barons with the high-sounding Spanish names, and at once aggravated the system of exactions: their oppressive presence was much harder on the small tenants than the lordly absenteeism they were accustomed to. Far more ferocious than the old estate stewards, their demands were soon so intolerable that the only possible reaction was criminal violence.

Crime again became one of the island's major scourges. Togliatti has told us how in his early years at Turin, Gramsci would try to get his comrades to reflect on 'the trade relations between Sardinia, an island, and mainland Italy or France, and the connexion which could be traced between changes in these relations and facts – apparently quite unconnected with them – like the development of delinquency, for instance, or the spread of brigandage, or of poverty, and so on'. The connexion really was there. Francesco Pais Serra showed it was in 1896, when he pointed out the contrast between the falling crime rate from 1880 to 1887 (the years when trade with France was easy), and the sharp rise which followed the closure of the Marseilles market. Speaking of peasants in general, but with an obvious special reference to Sardinian conditions, Gramsci wrote in 1919: 'The class struggle used to be all mixed up with banditry: it was scarcely distinguishable from taking ransom, from burning down woods and hamstringing animals, from the abduction of women and children, from attacks on town halls. It was a kind of primitive terrorism, with no lasting or effective results.'

However, few were then capable of perceiving the limitations of such anarchic outbursts, the intrinsic sterility of the bandit's individual protest. A halo of legend tended to surround the outlaw. As the myth of the popular hero – the 'avenger' – spread, he benefited from the intellectual support of poets and writers, as well as the practical support of peasants and shepherds always ready to hide him and look after him. The Sassari newspaper *L'Isola* published a clandestine interview by the poet Sebastiano Satta[1] with three bandits, Derosas, Delogu and Angius. This is how Satta depicted Derosas: 'He is proud and impetuous, tender towards whoever he considers part of his family, and devoted to his friends. His fierce pride in not being a mere hired killer, his idea – almost an obsession – of the vengeful mission justifying his fearful crimes, raises him far above the level of a vulgar assassin.' Satta was not the only writer to glorify these 'fine, fierce warriors'. In 1897 the essayist and novelist Enrico Costa published *Giovanni Tolu: Storia di un bandito sardo narrata da lui medesimo* ('Giovanni Tolu: the Life of a Sardinian Bandit, as Narrated by Himself'). Grazia Deledda's early stories contain characters which are like first versions of Simone Sole in *Marianna Sirca*.[2] There was a continual circulation of popular notions from the lower classes up to the intellectuals, where they were imaginatively enriched in literature and returned again to the wider public, more potent than before. Gradually this new barbarous mythology began to oust the old national heroes of the island, Eleonora d'Arborea, Leonardo Alagon, and Giovanni Maria Angioy. Although Gramsci's teacher Pietro Sotgiu continued to make his pupils sing: '*Fulminar la superba Aragona/T'han veduto le attonite genti/Rinnovare gli obliati portenti/Del romano e del greco valor*', they found it

---

[1] *Sebastiano Satta* (1867–1914): lawyer, folklorist, Sardinian nationalist, and the island's most celebrated poet.

[2] *Grazia Deledda* (1871–1936): famous Sardinian woman novelist, author of numerous romantic novels of island life, and winner of the Nobel Prize for literature in 1927. (T.N.)

difficult to feel a lively interest in such deeds.[3] 'I remember we just
couldn't imagine people being "dumbfounded" by the Marquis of
Zuri's heroism,' wrote Antonio Gramsci. 'We liked Giovanni Tolu and
even Derosas far more, and felt them to be more *Sardinian* even than
the great Eleanora.'

The fact is that since no political organization capable of disciplining
and directing revolt existed in Sardinia, banditry was the only possible
form revolt could assume there, however senseless, however bestial and
fruitless it may now appear. Political parties were merely the private
followings of those able to provide the largest handouts. Although Freemasonry aroused some excitement at the time, in practice it was no
more than another disguise for bourgeois intrigues. Radicalism was also
capable of arousing great popular excitement. When Felice Cavallotti
came to the island, for instance, first in 1891 and then in November
1896, and contrasted Crispi's extravagance in the African campaigns
with the miserable sums devoted to Sardinia, he was wildly and enthu-
siastically applauded wherever he spoke.[4]

Yet as soon as he was gone, everything reverted to normal. The
socialist movement was still at its very beginnings in Sardinia (there
were only 128 party members in 1896), and in most places outside the
mining area of Sulcis-Iglesiente was also threatened by a kind of
creeping over-adaptation to local conditions. Camillo Bellieni describes
how in Tempio, 'Socialism signified principally the battle for the
triumph of free thought, and the absolute duty of its warriors not to
have their offspring baptized on any account.' Usually all it meant was
a somewhat grimmer expression and a more visibly fervent radical
spirit on 17 February, the day when it was the custom to honour
Giordano Bruno's martyrdom at the hands of the Church by laying
wreaths in front of his statue. As yet, the 'red sun' had scarcely peeped
above the horizon. The bearers of new ideas were mostly individuals
from the mainland who found themselves in Sardinia by chance.

This was certainly the case in Ghilarza. Like other Sardinian small
towns, Ghilarza had been very much an island within an island until
the 1870s, thanks to the considerable distances between villages, the

---

[3] 'In felling proud Aragon / The dumbfounded people saw thee / Renew the forgotten
prodigies / Of Roman and Greek valour.'

[4] *Felice Cavallotti* (1842–98): leader of the parliamentary 'Extreme Left' radical republicans
after 1886. *Francesco Crispi* (1819–1901): Premier 1887–91 and again in 1893–96. He
repressed the anarchist and socialist movements with great violence at home, and launched
a disastrous colonial campaign in East Africa, which culminated in the Italian defeat of
Adowa (1896) and his own downfall. (T.N.)

few and rough roads (some no better than sheep-tracks), and the self-contained family economy which limited the need for trade between the smaller and the larger towns. Indeed it remained cut off from the modern world longer than most, and had links only with neighbouring villages. 'Foreigners' settled there very rarely. A *Dizionario* compiled in mid-century by Angius informs us that 'the cemetery holds only a few strangers, who died while in prison there'. Later, a railway line to Abbasanta (now joined to Ghilarza) was to lessen its isolation. But in 1899 the town was brought slightly closer to modernity by the arrival of the land-survey squad, mostly young and mostly from northern Italy, a group of officials and technicians sent by the Italian government to different parts of Sardinia to bring the maps up to date. These young men naturally brought with them to Ghilarza a whole flood of new ideas. New customs, more contemporary ambitions, began to stir the town's stagnant atmosphere. And the local young people recruited to work in the Registry at last found new models to emulate, new papers to read, books previously unknown there. The oldest Gramsci brother, Gennaro, discovered *Avanti!* in this way, and grew to like its militant, muckraking style. He listened to tales of the terrible massacre of 1898 in Milan, when masses of defenceless workers had been shot down by the gendarmes of General Bava-Beccaris.[5] He heard too of how the King had at once personally conferred the Grand Cross of Savoy on the General, in recognition of his services. . . . His boyish curiosity lapped up such reports. He was sixteen, this was his first taste of new ideas.

But Sulcis-Iglesiente was the one area really ripe for socialist notions. And there was a socialist active there, busily spreading the doctrine among the miners. This was a northener from a poor background, Giuseppe Cavallera, who had fled to Cagliari at the age of twenty to escape the political persecution of his native Piedmont, and taken a degree in medicine the following year, 1896.

Who were the miners, and how did they live? The agrarian crisis had forced thousands of peasants and shepherds to look for work in mining, the only Sardinian industry capable of absorbing any significant part of the rural unemployed. Their conditions of labour were not very

---

[5] Two months after Cavallotti's death in 1898, a wave of revolt passed across Italy and came to a climax in Milan with violent demonstrations and a general strike. General Bava-Beccaris's pacification ended with 80 dead, 450 wounded, thousands arrested, and the suppression of over a hundred newspapers and of all trade unions, co-operatives and chambers of labour. (T.N.)

different from those of Roman mining slaves. Capital (mostly French or Belgian) was now the master, but the methods of exploitation were unchanged. The peasants who were pressed into mining – like the *gens taillables et corvéables à merci* of pre-1789 France – soon bore on their bodies the brand of this form of profit-seeking. 'The numerous autopsies which I carried out all showed the same things: the miners' lungs were completely blackened by carbon, and their bronchial passages were completely penetrated by oil-lamp smoke' – so read the words of a doctor who testified to a parliamentary Commission of Inquiry sent to Sardinia in the early 1900s. Another doctor told them: 'The workers' spittle is always black.' One extract from the Commission's evidence describes how 'in the washing plant at Seddas Moddizzis work goes on non-stop for eleven hours a day, from six in the morning till five in the evening, and the workers have to eat their pieces of black bread while they work. All they have with the bread is zinc dust'. Doctors in the pay of the mining companies found it simpler not to diagnose illnesses caused by these working conditions. Another testimony records: 'When I got ill, the doctor said I was drunk; then he tried to give me quinine in water, thinking I would refuse it, so that he could suspend me. But instead I was glad to drink it down, for I knew I really was ill. Only then the illness changed and I got terrible headaches. . . .'

Such was life for the some fifteen thousand peasants who had taken to the mines around the turn of the century: terrifyingly long shifts of the most wearying kind of labour, with neither rest-days, nor holidays, nor sick-pay; paid only what and when the mining concessionaires decided (usually every second or fourth month), and compelled therefore to seek credit at food stores either run by the companies directly or leased out to their trusties; housed in barracks, or in hovels no better than animal stalls, and forced to conceal their tuberculosis in order to avoid the sack. It was in these subhuman conditions that Giuseppe Cavallera undertook to try and organize the workers politically.

It was a difficult task, on two counts. In the first place, the old socialist maxim to the effect that 'the State is nothing but the executive committee of the bourgeois class' was in those days anything but a sectarian metaphor. And secondly, these workers were from a background of rural under-employment, new to industrial conditions, and still clinging to old peasant traditions. They were stubborn individualists, reluctant to group together even in self-defence, and too inclined to put up with what was bad for fear of something worse – like losing one's job, for instance. Their natural reaction to such resigned suffering was the riot, rather than any kind of disciplined, patient struggle.[6]

It did not take Cavallera long to discover the role of the State. After the Milan massacre of 1898, he sent some money collected at Carloforte to a fund started by *Avanti!* for the families of the victims. For this, he found himself officially accused of 'unlicensed soliciting of money' and sentenced to six days in jail (but the Cagliari Appeal Court quashed the sentence). In September 1897 he had founded an association among the boatmen who transported the ores extracted at Bugerru; the association was forcibly dissolved in June 1898, in the wake of the Milan shootings, then reconstituted afterwards. In August 1900 he and eighteen others were arrested and accused of the following staggering list of crimes: the formation of their association constituted a 'criminal conspiracy'; the payment of dues was a form of fraud (or at least embezzlement); while to have counselled the setting-up of such a body and the paying of dues was 'extortion'; naturally, they had also intended to 'foment class hatred'. The trial lasted from 17 July to 3 August 1901. Though such charges could hardly be made to stick, Cavallera was sentenced to seven months, of which six were remitted (but then he had spent eleven months waiting to be tried). But he would not give in. After all, one had to take it for granted that the provincial administration, the police, and the army were all mere class instruments, while the judiciary – recruited almost entirely from the propertied class and imbued with its ideology – was a logical part of the same system. So it was silly to be discouraged. When he came out of prison he was only twenty-seven, and his vigour and faith in the socialist cause were undiminished. Giovanni Giolitti (the Prime Minister), who came from the same village of Dromero, described him as a 'firebrand'. But in fact he was a mild young man, always very careful to distinguish between the desirable and the possible, between the imposing of useless sacrifices for unattainable ends and the necessary price workers might have to pay for real progress. He founded the first association of miners at Bugerru, in 1903 (reputedly run by Alcibiade Battelli), and others quickly grew up and flourished at his initiative. He also founded a periodical paper, *La Lega*, edited at first by Efisio Orano and then by a young law student called Jago Siotto. By 1904 he was the leader of a regional federation of miners based on Iglesias. On 4 September of that same year, there occurred the massacre of Bugerru.

---

[6] Velio Spano, a prominent Italian Communist, has recorded Gramsci's rage at 'the glib abstraction which sees a Montevecchio miner as no different from a Fiat worker'.

The workers had been on strike for five days: it was their reaction to the imposition of new hours of work they thought intolerable, but at first nothing indicated the storm that was about to break. Cavallera and Battelli had been negotiating the grounds for a possible settlement of the dispute since the afternoon it broke out, with the two managers of the French company concerned, Achille Giorgiades (Turkish by birth, and a naturalized Greek) and his Swiss assistant Steiner. The troops arrived in the middle of the negotiations: in this and similar respects, Italy had changed little since the days of Di Rudinì[7] and Pelloux.[8] When the soldiers had taken up position all round the company offices, some workers were ordered to get a warehouse ready for them to camp in. They obeyed the order; but to others this looked like scabbing. Stones began to fly. The soldiers fired, killing three of the miners and wounding eleven.

This was the first blood drawn by organized class struggle on the island. It led to a general strike throughout Italy, the largest yet in the history of the Italian working-class movement. In Sardinia itself the protest aroused few echoes, in spite of the very wide popular sympathy with the victims of the Bugerru tragedy: organization was as yet far too weak, a mere embryo. Nevertheless, the incident was a kind of turning-point. Angelo Corsi writes that the death of the three miners 'disturbed and began to awaken the people of Sardinia, even if it did not bring them yet to full consciousness'. It marked the beginning of a transition from the days of banditry to a more effective form of collective struggle, and the blood of the victims appears in retrospect as the consecration of this change. A new chapter of history was beginning.

[7] *Marquis Antonio Starrabba Di Rudinì* (1839–1908): Prime Minister in 1891–92, and then again in 1896–98, he was forced to resign by the Milan uprising of 1898 and was replaced by Pelloux. He was a harsh conservative, although less reactionary than Pelloux. (T.N.)
[8] *Luigi Girolamo Pelloux* (1839–1924): Minister of War in several cabinets under Di Rudinì and Giolitti. An extremely conservative figure, he was made Prime Minister in 1898 to repress the popular forces which had shown surprising strength in the May 1898 uprising in Milan. Pelloux stirred up enormous hostility to himself and the Crown, and resigned in 1900. (T.N.)

After his return from prison, Francesco Gramsci did not at first find life easy. He went out very little and avoided meeting people: he felt shame at the misfortune he had suffered, and he was without a job. He was not to be rehabilitated until much later, and exclusion from public office was a serious obstacle to any return to normal social life as there were very few other jobs. So for a time he lived a segregated existence.

However, the people of the town felt some sympathy for him. Although they tended to be pitiless towards anyone whom they thought merited dishonour, they recognized well enough that Francesco's case was exceptional. There had been political reasons for his downfall, and he had been too harshly dealt with. The suspicion that injustice had been done moved them to some gestures of solidarity. He was admitted to the Literary Society, a very select body which always chose its members with great care. When a mutual benefit society was formed to insure livestock, he was made its secretary. Once he had been rehabilitated, he found that his university law studies came in useful, and he was able to work as a counsellor at the local Magistrates Court. People were glad to provide work for him. He was considered a good sort, and good company. His southern exuberance, his intelligence and charm, made him a welcome guest everywhere at evenings round the card table. Finally, he was to be offered a secretarial job in the Land Registry, and got by tolerably on its small salary for the rest of his life.

Inside the family, things naturally went more smoothly with him at home. But it was still plagued by practical problems, at first because of his forced unemployment, then because of the very modest sums he earned when he did find work. Gennaro was no longer able to help; he had been sent to Turin to do his military service. Mario had left home too after finishing primary school, and was now in a seminary at Oristano. For some time, therefore, Antonio was the only male wage-earner in the family. Carlo was still a child beginning school. Peppina Marcias managed to earn a little with her sewing, and Grazietta and Emma would knit stockings, jerseys and scarves and try to sell them.

It was not until the end of 1905 that Francesco and Peppina, after much thought, decided to continue Antonio's education, whatever new sacrifices it might cost them. He was to go to the secondary school (*ginnasio*) at Santulussurgiu. In his two years at Ghilarza, far from a school desk, the boy had worked a good deal on his own and taken some private lessons. Now, aged nearly fifteen, he thought he should go straight into the third year of secondary school. The school authorities raised no objection: it was a communal school, not a state school, and its rules were more easy-going. So Antonio returned to full-time study, though as we shall see the odd conditions prevailing at his new school made the change less great than one might think.

Santulussurgiu lies eighteen kilometres from Ghilarza. It stands poised on the top edge of a narrow ring of hills, as if built on the lip of a volcano. Around the mid nineteenth century, two landowners called Pietro Ledda and Giovanni Meloni had left their worldly goods to the Pauline Order, on the express condition that they be used for the establishment in the town of a 'Latin grammar school, up to and including Rhetoric'. Should the Order be dissolved, the Communal Council was to take over the administration of the legacy and use it for the same purpose. And in fact, the Pauline Order was forced to give up in 1886, which gave rise to a prolonged dispute between the Commune and the State Commission charged with liquidating the Order's assets, settled only by royal decree in 1901. The communal *ginnasio* started functioning immediately afterwards.

Antonio Gramsci remembered it as 'a very down-at-heel place', as 'a little school where three so-called teachers shamelessly made short work of teaching all five classes'. A look at the minutes of the school governing board will quickly convince one that this was no over-harsh judgement. If anything, it errs on the side of leniency. The school's Director, Francesco Porcu, was forced to admit at the board's session of 4 March 1905 (some months before Gramsci arrived) that: 'Two of the teachers at this institution are without the degrees required for their posts. For two years running they have been allowed to retain these posts, on the understanding that they would attempt to regularize the position. Since they have failed to do so, the time has come to re-advertise the posts for the coming academic year 1905–06.' The jobs were indeed re-advertised, but there was no rush of first-class teachers to apply for them, and in addition a number of those short-listed unaccountably failed to turn up. One who did turn up, Massimo Stara, presented his resignation after only two weeks (he later became secretary of the

Sassari Chamber of Labour). A Milanese teacher was supposed to replace him, and asked for an advance of salary to get to Santulussurgiu. The money was sent, but he never appeared. Antonio did not begin to have lessons in literature from two temporary teachers till 7 February 1906, when the school year was already well advanced. The natural sciences and French were both entrusted to a teacher with a degree in engineering.

Antonio was destined to have such teachers for his whole time at the school. With what effect, we learn from one of the prison letters: 'I showed a very marked aptitude for the exact sciences and mathematics as a boy, then lost them while I was at secondary school, because I had teachers who weren't worth a dried fig.' One of the school governors confirmed this view at a board meeting in September 1906 (Gramsci had done a year at the school by then): 'Unfortunately the results obtained in this school have always been of the poorest kind. . . .' He went on to urge that in the interests of all concerned, 'the governors, acknowledging that this school has never worked properly . . . should close it down for a period of three or four years'. But the motion was rejected. So Antonio Gramsci's education was continued, after a fashion, in fits and starts, up to the fifth year of secondary school. In this, his last year, classes had still not started at the end of December. Teachers were more reluctant than ever to come to Santulussurgiu, and found one excuse after another for staying away, until the Director was at his wits' end. We read in the minutes that he reported:

> We must get the teachers to come, better late than never. . . . On the whole it is better they should come than stay away, for the pupils' sake, since it is now far too late for them to obtain entry to other schools. *And anyway, on other occasions this school has started in January or February*, so the absence of teachers for a few weeks now should not appear too odd . . . [G.F.'s italics].

The teachers' unpunctuality and doubtful talents hardly provided ideal conditions for Antonio to make up for his lost two years in Ghilarza. Neither did the squalid material conditions in which the classes were conducted, particularly distressing for anyone in poor health. According to another of the governors, Dr Giomaria Manca, the Carta-Meloni Communal Secondary School had moved 'from the insanitary convent building once used by the Friar Minors' to a rented house where work went on 'in deplorable conditions', 'in cramped, unhealthy surroundings quite inadequate for the needs of the school'.

Nor did Antonio go home from school to conditions that were much better. He was lodging with a middle-aged peasant woman called Giulia Obinu, in the Su Murighessa quarter. She had previously been the servant of the town doctor, and Antonio wrote of her: 'I paid five lire a month for a bed, bed-linen, and the most frugal of meals.' Giulia Obinu 'had an old mother who was a bit weak in the head, though not quite round the bend, and she was my cook and guardian. Every morning when she saw me get up, she would ask me who I was and what on earth I was doing sleeping in their house, and so forth.' Quite apart from the old lady's lapses, the atmosphere in the house must have been soured by her daughter's character. This ex-servant's main ambition in life was to be rid of her mother: 'She wanted the Commune to send her mother to the local asylum and keep her there at its own expense. Therefore she treated the old lady as abominably and viciously as she dared, hoping to force her into some fearful act of reprisal so that she could be certified as dangerous. I remember the old girl would say to her daughter (who addressed her as *Lei* according to the old custom), "Call me *tu* if you like, but treat me decently!" '

Distracted by such scenes, Antonio would often go off to try and work elsewhere, in the houses of friends. One of these was his classmate Marco Massida, now an accountant, who remembers him as 'a good-hearted, quiet lad, who liked helping his friends. He was always first in everything, and he wrote really marvellous compositions'. (As far as the compositions go, perhaps Massida's affection has clouded his judgement slightly.)

Antonio would make the journey to Santulussurgiu on Monday mornings, in a four-horse cart, two between the shafts and two following behind to change over in mid-journey. He would return on Saturday mornings, sometimes on foot, and not without running some risk in an area where – then as now – bandits were active. Shepherds bring their flocks down from the Barbagie hills to winter there, and it is crossed by a cattle-thieves' trail leading from the pasture-lands of Oristano up towards the hills around Bòrore. But apparently Gramsci never ran into trouble, except for the one episode he was to narrate in a letter to his sister-in-law Tatiana:

I'd like to tell you a Christmassy tale of my youth, which should amuse you and also give you some notion of what life was like in our parts. . . . Once, I and another boy set off on foot one afternoon near Christmas rather than wait for the stage-coach next day, in order to have an extra day with our families. On we plodded, till we were about half-way, in a lonely, completely deserted spot; there was a line of poplars about a hundred yards to our left off the road, and some dense thickets. Then a bullet suddenly whined overhead, ten metres or so above us. We thought it was just a stray shot, and continued on our way. Then there was a second shot, then a third, much closer: we realized we were being shot at and dived into the ditch. We stayed there for a bit, lying flat out. When we tried to get up there was another shot, and so it went on for a couple of hours, with us crawling slowly away, and shots ringing out each time we tried to make the road. Obviously it was a bunch of fellows out for a laugh, who enjoyed scaring us – some joke, eh! It was dark when we got home, very tired and muddy, and we told nobody what had happened, so that our families wouldn't worry. We ourselves weren't really upset about it: we made exactly the same trip when the next holiday came round, at carnival time, and there was no trouble. . . .

Antonio's Saturdays in Ghilarza tended to follow the same pattern. At first everyone would be happy to see him back; then his mother would scold him; finally his father would administer reprimands.

His mother's reproaches concerned the way he habitually treated the weekly provisions they gave him to take to Santulussurgiu – pasta, oil, cheese, and so on. Apparently Nino was given to selling some of it, in order to buy books and newspapers, and his family usually found out. His mother could never forgive him for this, and never tired of warning him of the dire consequences of failing to eat properly – especially for someone as weak as he was.

The fatherly scoldings concerned the subversive literature Francesco Gramsci was appalled to find his son reading. It came from Turin. Gennaro, who before leaving Ghilarza had already tended to sympathize with the new ideas, was now doing his military service in Italy's red capital. As his socialist faith became stronger he looked round him with a novice's fervour for possible new converts, not forgetting his own family. Antonio's taste for reading had grown even more pronounced with the passage of time, and he would ask for Gennaro's newspapers and booklets as soon as he got home on Saturday evenings. Hence the quarrels with his father. He tried to avoid them by making a joke of it: 'Well, Dad, so you really are descended from the Bourbons!' he would say.

It was indeed not pure chance that Francesco bore the name of the last monarch of the Kingdom of the Two Sicilies, Francesco II. He was born at Gaeta not long before the Italian army laid siege to it, and his father – Colonel Gramsci of the Bourbon gendarmerie – was there to the last, stoutly defending the *ancien régime's* only remaining strong-hold against General Cialdini. The story was often told in the family of how grandmother Teresa Gonzales had crossed the enemy lines on foot, fleeing with Francesco in her arms along the coast towards Formia. Francesco's conservatism had other grounds too, besides these family traditions. His brother Nicolino had once been King Victor Emmanuel's military instructor at Caserta, and he had himself once actually met the King. He had never recovered from the profound emotion aroused in him when the august heir to the Italian throne pronounced his name and shook him by the hand. He always kept a photo in his house of the thoroughbred which the future King of Italy had presented to his brother. It perpetually renewed his own pride, and his unshakeable respect for the ruling house.

One may imagine, therefore, his distaste on seeing his young sons so keen to poison their minds with subversive literature. Nor should one forget that in those days the open profession of socialist ideas meant having one's name on a police file, if not worse. 'Signor Ciccillo' was still suffering from the years he had spent in jail, for things no one would ever have bothered about if politics had not been involved, and he was not at all eager to see the Napoleonic hats and inquiring whiskers of the Carabinieri cross his threshold again. But his paternal authority had been somewhat diminished by his brush with the law. To avoid dis-putes, Antonio asked the postman to give him Gennaro's letters and packets directly, without letting his father know. Subsequently, politics were talked about less and less in the family.

There was some political discussion again when Gennaro came back from the army to resume his job at the Land Registry, but it was not open. The family was now reunited again. Mario had come back from his seminary: although he knew it would be a grievous blow to his mother to abandon his priestly vocation, he felt unable to carry on. 'I want to get married,' he said. 'I really don't want to be a priest at all. It's no use. Send Nino to the seminary if you like: he doesn't worry about girls, so *he* could be a priest.'

Nino went to Oristano to take the final secondary-school examinations in the summer of 1908, when he was seventeen and a half. After the two-year break in his school career and the vicissitudes of academic life at Santulussurgiu, it was scarcely to be hoped that he would do brilliantly. In July, he did not even attempt two of his subjects, mathe-matics and science. And the exam in French – the other subject taught by the engineering graduate – was a disaster: he only got 'three' out of ten. However, he did fairly well in the other subjects: 'six' in written Italian, 'seven' in the oral, 'seven' in geography, 'six' in Latin composition and 'seven' in the oral, and – predictably enough – 'eight' in history. In September he sat the subjects omitted in July, re-took the French examination, and was awarded the certificate.

For some time now, Antonio had been drawn more and more to history in his reading. Much later on, he was to recall how passionately he had felt about the subject in a letter to his son Delio: 'I'm sure you will like history, as I used to when I was your age, because history is about the life of men, and everything which concerns men, as many men as possible – all the men in the world, their life together in society, their work, their struggle for a better life. Surely you can't fail to like this more than any other single thing.'

6

In the months of May and June, 1906, when Antonio Gramsci was finishing his third year at the Santulussurgiu school, Sardinia was shaken by a great social tempest. A number of different conflicts suddenly erupted together, shaking the very foundations of the island's society.

On the one hand, there were the new, disciplined struggles of the working-mens' associations; on the other, anarchic outbursts among the rural masses, still without any form of organization and so unable to fix on any goal beyond burning down cheese factories and tax offices. At the same time the old urban cliques continued their intrigues to get control of civic power or to hold on to it: often, hooligan elements infiltrated protest movements and turned them towards pillage or the stoning of harmless shops and shopkeepers. There was also a revival of Luddism among workers whose trades had been damaged by the introduction of machines: the carters of the Cagliari suburbs, for instance, who had been forced to reduce their charges because of the much lower prices for carrying goods on the tramway system, seized the opportunity afforded by the turmoil to set fire to tramway stations and overturn the trams.

Behind it all lay the exasperation of starving masses. And in such conditions any spark, even if originally struck by one of the old political cliques in its struggle against the others (as in Cagliari), could cause a conflagration. The trouble began in Cagliari and spread at once to the mines and the countryside.

Sulcis-Iglesiente was still suffering the ravages of its predatory economy. Mining production had risen, and wages had gone down. In 1905, ore worth 22,885,000 lire had been extracted; the following year, the figure jumped to 25,609,000 lire. At the same time, the miners saw their daily wage drop from an average of 2·54 lire to 2·30 lire; bricklayers dropped from 3·12 to 3 lire; engine-drivers from 3·39 to 3. The workers' wage-claims were supported by the fact that in Tuscan mines the day wage was almost one lira per day higher; but the mining companies invariably opposed such arguments with a thinly-veiled racism. Thus, a representative of the Monteponi Company, Erminio Ferraris, declared in the minutes of the Commission of Inquiry which examined conditions in the mines: 'The productivity of manual labour in Sardinia is very much lower than on the continent. This is because of the tendency towards idleness, the climate, and the general lack of initiative and energy. There are certainly some exceptions to the rule . . . but the average is low, and cannot be put at more than about sixty per cent of the continental norm.' Later, these 'white man's' colonialist tales were disproved by a Sardinian scholar, Giovanni Lòriga, who showed they were no more than a pretext for holding down wages to less than the cost of keeping slaves. He demonstrated that an analysis of the figures in selected Sardinian mines for the four-year period 1904–07 made individual productivity equal to 1665.08 lire – or 281.80 lire more than the average for similar Italian mines. The inconsistency of the employers' argument for cutting wages is obvious.

Worse still, this 'white man' mentality habitually surfaced whenever the miners asked for a more humane form of work discipline. A group of workers at Seddas Moddizzis were sacked for demanding a little more regularity in the payment of wages, two rest-days a month, a ten-hour day, and a one-hour lunch break. Refusals rained down. The employers' position was quite unyielding even towards requests for discussion of the smallest claims. Ferraris's comment on the question of holidays is again most revealing:

> Where a Sunday holiday has been observed for some time, it is quite difficult to find a worker who has managed to put anything aside; whereas one does often find this among workers where labour is continuous, and there is no opportunity for spending. In such mines *one day's rest in every seven is really far too much* because, far from the larger centres of population and with no idea of how to occupy free time, many workers would merely consume their wages, giving way to excessive drinking and so rendering themselves unfit to carry on with their work next day.

The company policy of paying workers irregularly was connected with another stratagem involving company stores, which the workers were compelled to patronize whenever money ran out, they being the only source of credit. The precise method of swindling the miners would vary from one company to the next. One way was to pay the men partly in kind, such goods being (naturally) valued much more highly than those in outside shops. Another way was to pay in cash, but oblige the miners to buy from the company shop, which might be run by the boss himself, or by one of his staff. The most brutal system was where office staff or foremen were in business for themselves, and relied on official connivance to have men sacked if they would not buy at their shop. But in all cases the basis of the operation was the same: the sale of inferior goods at inflated prices. Even postage stamps cost more in the company shops. Wine was 40 centimes a litre, instead of 30 or 35; oil was 1·60 instead of 1 lira; cheese was 2 lire instead of 1·25; and so on.

In this fashion, an entire cycle of exploitation was effected which did not leave even the scraps in Sardinia. No processing industries had arisen alongside the mines. No accessory engineering industries had been created to service them. The re-possession of the miners' miserable wages through the company store system was the last twist to the screw. All that Sardinia derived from the exercise was tuberculosis.[1] And whoever was not already spitting blood was destined to premature old age, or to death or mutilation in work accidents. In one year alone, 1905, there were 2,219 such accidents.

Agricultural workers were not much better off. Small landholders were doubly exposed to disaster: from the weather and from the tax-man. The avidity and ruthlessness of the revenue authorities reached a new peak at this period, and seizure of property was quite common (Alberto Boscolo has pointed out that Cagliari province held the all-Italian record for tax confiscations in the financial year 1904–05). Dairy farmers usually found themselves compelled to seek advances against future milk production, in order to rent pasture land; naturally, the factories dictated the terms of such deals and totally exploited the dairymen. The agricultural day-labourers suffered most from the crisis: their existence became almost impossible as the number of working days was reduced (they might get two hundred days' work a year, with luck), as wages shrank, and as the price of staple goods rose. In 1905–06, they earned between 75 centimes and 1.25 per day (except in the brief periods of intensive farm work, like harvest-time) – a wage that at most bought one kilo of bread, one kilo of potatoes, one kilo of pasta and about a third of a litre of oil per day. Slave of uncertain seasonal employment, undernourished, plagued by the island's chronic diseases (tuberculosis, malaria, trachoma), and usually illiterate as well,

[1] Gildo Frongia, a doctor unconnected with the mining companies, told the Parliamentary Commission of Inquiry: 'Over the twenty years from 1884 to 1905, I found that 35 per cent of the mineworkers died of tuberculosis.'

the rural day labourer was the va-nu-pieds, the poorest of the poor in Giolittian Italy.

The urban masses too were suffering from the general rise in prices. The first signs that they might be near the limits of their patience had come between February and May of 1906. Many different sorts of workers began to organize themselves into associations, and social unrest assumed a more ordered form, and acquired clearer objectives. The dock-workers were first, with three hundred members enrolled in their new union. They demanded that the working day be reduced from fifteen hours to nine, with a rise in wages from 3·50 to 5 lire per day. When the employers refused, a strike was called on 24 February. This was followed by agitation among shop assistants, who were asking for one day off a week. On 6 May, shops did remain closed for the day, and they never again opened on a public holiday. The next day, it was the turn of the bakery workers. Their demand for a reduction in hours from fifteen to twelve was met at once, but others were not; as a result, while some workers prepared to return to work, others attacked the bake-houses to stop them. It should be noted that most of the population was solidly behind these protests, even where violence and sabotage were deplored: political meetings were invariably heavily attended. This success was linked to the astute and unceasing campaign being waged by a local paper, *Il Paese*, aimed at stirring up the discontented as much as possible. The man behind *Il Paese* was a young lawyer called Umberto Cao, leader of the principal faction arrayed against that of the Mayor of Cagliari, Ottone Bacaredda.

As usual, only the haziest political character could be ascribed to the two sides in this battle. Umberto Cao was a gifted young man, already a hardened polemicist, and with a marked sensitivity to the temper of the masses. He is often depicted as essentially an opportunist: an anarchist-monarchist, a social-conservative, an advocate of Sardinian regional autonomy – then a complete separatist when the wind blew in that direction, and eventually a mouthpiece for empty nationalist frenzy. Gramsci did not think much of him. Velio Spano recounts the following episode:

A friend – a boy like myself – once referred to Cao's courageous answer to Mussolini's first speech in parliament after the March on Rome, the famous speech about the 'dingy grey chamber' and the 'billet for legionaries'.[a] We were walking with Gramsci up Via XX Settembre in Rome

[a] After the success of the fascist 'March on Rome', and the formation of the first Mussolini government, Mussolini declared in the Chamber when it reassembled (16 November 1922):

one night. Gramsci took up the point seriously: he seemed to be changing the subject but was actually describing Cao's life for us through two other episodes. The first was the revolution of 1906 in Cagliari: he described how links had been formed between the rural and urban workers, and the intellectuals. His words conjured up a picture of how Cao, the lawyer and philosopher, had made his way through the seething tide of people in revolt, destroying and burning, and mixed with this mass yet lost nothing of his 'dignity', his academic coldness and rigidity. Then Gramsci went straight on to an analysis of Cao's pamphlet on autonomy for Sardinia, which had been the source of *sardismo* for many people, and especially for intellectuals like myself. By this combination of narrative and ideological critique, and without one word of direct judgement on the man, Gramsci had sketched out a portrait of this Sardinian figure for us: an intellectual convinced he was the navel of the universe, endeavouring to be a part of history for his own ends, and yet remaining inevitably cut off from history, and from life itself.

Spano remembers how Gramsci concluded: 'That man never believed in anything but himself.' And Spano points out: 'A year later, Cao went over to Fascism.'

However, Umberto Cao's journalistic campaign of 1906 was founded on facts that were real enough. And it blamed the facts – the intolerable rise in the workers' cost of living – exclusively on Mayor Bacaredda's administration. This is how the discontent was politically manipulated. So the struggle took place on two levels: on the one hand a popular upsurge, and on the other hand a faction-fight carried along on the crest of the wave.

On 12 May a delegation of women tobacco workers asked to see the Mayor, to explain how difficult life had become for them since the rise in prices. Bacaredda told them: 'When mullet gets to costing 2 lire a kilo, I take my hat off to it and buy dry salt cod instead.'[3] When news of the remark about salt cod reached a meeting next morning, people lost their tempers. There was a demonstration at the Town Hall, but things went no further that day, the demonstrators dispersing once some promises had been made about future control of prices. But next morning, when it was found that the market was closed because of a

--- --- ---

'The revolution has its rights. . . . With 300,000 young men armed to the teeth . . . I could have punished all who defamed Fascism and tried to bespatter it with mud. I could have turned this dingy, grey chamber into a billet for my legionaries. . . .' (T.N.)

[3] Ottone Bacaredda was Mayor of Cagliari for over a quarter of a century, having previously attained fame as a writer of bad fiction. His clique knew him as 'Il Padre della Patria', 'Father of the Fatherland'. (T.N.)

brawl between some stallholders and the local tax-man, a crowd gathered and ran to the tobacco factory. The workers came out, and the crowd went on to other factories, to the railway yards and the gasworks, growing in size all the time and led by one of the tobacco women carrying a red flag. A big loaf of bread was stuck on the tip of her flag-staff, symbolically. Now at lava heat, the procession crossed the centre of Cagliari. At La Scafa, government offices were stormed and set on fire. Then the crowd moved to the district round the railway station, where troops had been concentrated. The crowd booed them, there were clashes, stones began to fly, and the soldiers opened fire. Twenty-two people were hit, and two of them died: all were workers, or fishermen, except for one clerk. But the arson and devastation were not over yet. Cagliari continued to be violently shaken by this wave of near-insurrection. Between 16 and 18 May, five thousand more troops, marines and policemen were disembarked, and it began to look like a city under siege.

Now that the spark had been struck, the fire spread far beyond the city. Everywhere the same seething fury turned on the company stores, or the cheese factories, with devastating effect. Soldiers fired on the mobs again and again. On 24 May *Avanti!* asked: 'Why does the government put out official communiqués which talk about the forces of order being attacked, when the dead are always on the other side, among the demonstrators?' Two people were killed at Gonnesa, two at Villasalto (with twelve wounded), one at Bonorva, and another at Nebida. Far from intimidating the crowds, these bloody episodes made things worse. The cheese factories and tax offices at Macomer were stormed, as were the factories at Ittiri and Terranova (today called Olbia), and the tax offices at Abbasanta. The storm was still growing in violence. On 1 June a journalist from the Milan paper *Il Secolo*, Luigi Lucatelli, telegraphed: 'The bestial excesses of the masses do no more than match the unreasonable repression to which they are subjected.'

By early July the hurricane had begun to subside and the repression was already under way. Hundreds of peasants, workers, and intellectuals ended up in jail (among them the socialist leader Efisio Orano), and there were widespread sackings in the mines. On the whole, public opinion remained on the side of the victims of such reprisals. Every steamer brought dozens of magistrates and clerks of the court to Sardinia, to deal with the great wave of pending trials. There were 170 awaiting trial in Cagliari, and the deconsecrated church of Santa

Restituta had to be converted to house the judges and witnesses. The hearings went on from 6 May until 12 June 1907, and the case for the defence was given great prominence in the papers. Gramsci was then sixteen and a half, in his fourth year at the Santulussurgiu *ginnasio*.

Sardinian nationalism drew fresh strength from the repression. In this period generally the split between North and South was getting worse. The regime of tariff protection which was ruining the economy of the South and the islands had indeed favoured the North's rapidly expanding industries. This early twentieth-century boom – which was also very profitable for the Italian exchequer – was accompanied by a kind of separatism in reverse, practised by the Italian State against Sardinia. Luigi Lucatelli wrote, in May 1906:

> As far as laws are concerned, and especially the detestable side of the tax laws, these are all enforced here. . . . But not the rights which law should guarantee. A railway ticket costs the same here as elsewhere in Italy (or even more), yet rail journeys are insufferably slow and uncomfortable. Citizens pay the same taxes here as in Rome, Milan or Turin, yet whenever a state official has been proved stupid or corrupt we make a free gift of him to the Sardinians, so that henceforth he will discharge his duties among them in a spirit of angry resentment at being punished, as well as remaining stupid and corrupt.

Hence, the State came commonly to be considered a hostile entity, a monstrous machine mainly concerned with multiplying methods of strike-repression and breeding armies of tax-officials, Prefects, and police-inspectors in league with the mining companies. *Sardismo* became the dominant sentiment of a whole era. And Antonio Gramsci shared the sentiment strongly. He was to write later: 'I used to think at that time that the struggle for Sardinian national independence was a necessity. *Continentals go home!* – how many times have I myself repeated these words.'

Now nearly eighteen, Antonio Gramsci was soon to make the leap from village to city life. He was to go to the Dettòri lycée in Cagliari. As 1908 drew to a close, the Gramsci parents decided that Gennaro should get himself transferred to the Land Registry offices in Cagliari, and that Antonio should move there too and live with him. Once they got to the city, however, Gennaro did not stay at the Registry for long. Offered a job as an accountant in an ice factory owned by two brothers called Marzullo, which he considered a better opportunity, he left the Registry after only one month.

Cagliari was a small but lively city at this time. It had three daily papers. There was *L'Unione sarda*, which took its line from the Signor Cocco Ortu who had figured so unfortunately in the Gramsci family history; there was the radical *Il Paese*; and the clerical *Corriere dell'isola*. There were also a few periodicals, among them the socialist weekly *La Voce del popolo*. There were two good theatres, the Civico and the Politeama Margherita, where the biggest names in drama and opera appeared regularly. The first *chanteuses* were performing the can-can at the Valdès and the Eden ciné-theatre. Numerous clubs and private societies provided facilities for concerts and lectures. One could see the cinema epics of the period, like *Rocambole, Le Cantiche Dantesche* and *Les Misérables*, at the Iris or the Eden. Nor was there any lack of public meeting places, or restaurants with music and potted palms. For Antonio Gramsci, the abrupt transition from towns like Ghilarza and Santulussurgiu to this new life must have been rather bewildering at first.

Gennaro and he found a room at No. 24 Via Principe Amedeo, a street leading down from the castle rock towards the naval base. They both had to survive there on Gennaro's salary of a hundred lire per month, so life was still difficult. One of his lycée classmates, Renato Figàri, recalls:

> I don't think I ever saw Nino Gramsci in an overcoat. He always had the
> same clothes, a pair of short drainpipe trousers and a jacket too small for

him. On cold days he would turn up at school with a woollen scarf wrapped round him, under his jacket. He had no books of his own, or lacked certain ones. But he always paid close attention to lessons, helped by his very good memory, as well as by his great intelligence. I used to sit on the bench behind his, and watch him taking notes in his tiny writing. Sometimes we lent him books, or the teacher did.

He made an uncertain start at the Liceo Dettòri, and wrote to his father in January 1909:

They've given us the term marks at last. I know I should have done better but it wasn't my fault; because, as Nannaro might have mentioned, I was kept out of school for three days for not bringing the diploma, right when the exam was taking place. So I got nothing at all for natural history, and only 5 for history; the teacher gave me a real talking-to, but I couldn't help it. . . . Anyway, it wasn't too bad, for I can get through natural history with the marks from the second and third-term exams, and it would be funny if I couldn't make up the lost ground in history. Here are the marks: Italian 6/7 [in fact his mark in the Italian oral exam was 8, not 7 – G.F.]; Latin 6/7; Greek 6/7; philosophy 6; mathematics 6; chemistry 8. So you see I did quite well, and you must remember this was the first term and I didn't come from Santulussurgiu very well prepared, especially in Latin, Greek and mathematics.

This letter, full of dialect cadences and syntax, and stylistically clumsy compared to the letters he would be composing not long afterwards, itself suggests how inadequate his preparation had been during the three hazardous years at the Ginnasio Carta-Meloni. However, Antonio had notable powers of recovery from setbacks. In the second term his history mark rose from 'five' to 'seven', and he got 'six' out of ten in natural history. In June 1909 he passed his first-year examination all right, with a record-sheet that was mostly 'sixes', except for two 'sevens' in Latin, and one 'eight' in the Italian oral. He had done a great deal in one year to fill in the gaps left by his earlier schooling.

When he came back from Ghilarza after the holidays he changed lodgings and moved to No. 149 Corso Vittorio, opposite Via Maddalena. His small room there 'had lost all its plaster because of the humidity, and had only one little window which opened onto a kind of shaft that was more like a latrine than a courtyard'. Nevertheless, the change suited him. In a letter of 26 November 1909, written just before starting his second year at the lycée, we read: 'As regards landladies, we're all right: she's an honest woman who never robs us. In fact I'm much better off than last year.' They sent him food from home. He usually ate in his room, or occasionally in a *trattoria* in Piazza del Carmine with Gennaro. Another lodger, Dino Frau, recalls him as being solitary, but not at all misanthropic:

> He lived very much on his own. There must have been six or seven of us there, at Doloretta Porcu's. We were on the top floor, you got there up one flight of very high, steep stairs. Antonio Gramsci used to have to climb them slowly, or he would get out of breath. Then he would shut himself in his room without speaking to the rest of us. I was only in his room a couple of times. It was bare, it smelt of cheese, and there were books and papers everywhere. One evening we were all invited to his room. There was music and singing coming from it. There were lots of people we didn't know, mostly from the country. There was singing, some of them danced. And Gramsci was in the middle, absorbed in performing Sardinian folk-dances to the accompaniment of a harmonium.

He had now recovered from his uncertain start at the lycée, and was studying hard. After a couple of months in the second year (the letter is dated 5 January 1909, but it is clear that Gramsci had automatically put down the previous year by mistake), he wrote home: 'I'm getting on like a house on fire now: it looks as if I might get 7 or 8 in Latin, and though I have nothing in Italian as the teacher is away, all the other subjects are good too.' Then on 31 January he wrote again, to comment on his marks (Latin 7/8; Greek 7/8; history of Greek culture 8; history and historical geography 8; philosophy 6; natural history 6; physics and chemistry 6): 'As you see I got good marks; and I'll do better this term, for I only got the "sixes" through bad luck.' He did nothing but study, allowing himself very few diversions indeed. Claudio Cugusi, now a doctor, relates:

> If by chance we ever bumped into him he would gladly join us. 'Hey, Antonicheddu, you coming too?' I'd say, taking his arm. He was always pleased by such invitations, he liked being one of us. But only for that short stroll in the Corso, from Clavot's patisserie down to the Tramer café, which was where the Cagliari evening walk, the *passillada*, took place in those days. He would never say much, he preferred listening. Then when we all finished up at Su Cau, the billiard hall, he would say goodbye at the door and go off home.

Some compulsion made Antonio stand apart from most ordinary social occasions and forms of enjoyment. Renato Figàri recalls:

> He never smoked while he was at the lycée. He didn't drink. And if any of us were to offer him something he would refuse politely: I've never

known whether it was pride, or because he didn't want to acquire tastes which he couldn't afford. He also came rarely to a club founded by young people, the Vanguard Anti-Clerical Society, which met in a couple of dingy rooms not far from the 'Dettòri', in Via Barcelona. We went there from the lycée and the university, and there were some young professional people too, nearly all with socialist or revolutionary or insurrectionary ideas, and of course full of respect for Giovanni Bovio[1] and Giordano Bruno. We held entertainments there, and amateur dramatics. Every now and then I used to recite the poems of Sebastiano Satta, Ugo Foscolo, and Stecchetti. Gramsci only turned up occasionally at these things. I can't imagine why. . . . His physical condition? No, no. He may have been deformed, but he was not ugly. He had a high forehead, with a mass of wavy hair, and behind his pince-nez I remember the bright blue of his eyes, that shining, metallic gaze which struck one so forcibly. Of course there may have been lots of reasons. We were a bit spendthrift, we tried hard to be dandies, in the fatuous way common at that age. . . . I think it may have been poverty which forced him to lead such a solitary life.

This is probably correct. He felt ashamed of the contrast between himself and his classmates. Until then he had never paid much attention to clothes; now, the way he was compelled to dress humiliated him. On 10 February 1910 he wrote home to his father:

On 26 February the second and third year students are going on a trip to Gùspìni to visit the Montevecchio mines, and so I'll have to go too, and I look really terrible in this worn, shiny old jacket. So will you please send a letter of credit to some tailor for me, so that I can get a suit made . . . I didn't go to school today because I had to get my shoes resoled. During carnival time I didn't go out once, I stayed in my room curled up in a corner, so fed up that Nannaro thought I was ill.

And then a few days later, on the 16th: 'Dearest Dad, you seem to be under the impression that I can live off nothing at all. Nannaro is doing too much for me already, because you really must grasp the fact that one cannot live in Cagliari with what you're sending every month, unless one eats nothing but bread – and little enough of that, at 50 centimes a kilo.' Perhaps he did obtain a little money: but certainly not enough for the clothes. He persisted:

Now I've got to touch on a sore point again: you've done nothing about the

---

[1] *Giovanni Bovio* (1841–1903): writer, jurist and radical politician, linked here with Giordano Bruno as a rather less serious victim of the Church's persecution: he was excommunicated in 1864, after the publication of his 'System of Universal Philosophy' (a version of materialism). (T.N.)

clothes. And yet you yourself said I was indecent when I came home to Ghilarza at Easter. . . . I didn't stir outside the house for ten whole days, so as not to shame you. If I was a sight then, how do you think I look now, after another month and a half? They're not even 'indecent' now, but really filthy and torn. . . . If the Principal sends the school janitor to find out what I'm up to, I shall be forced to tell him I can't come to school because I just don't have any clean clothes to put on.

At the beginning of the second term of this second year, a new Italian master appeared on the scene. He was a small, thin, rather ugly young man of thirty-three called Raffa Garzìa. He frowned incessantly, and appears to have been the very personification of gloom. His irascible temperament gave short shrift to the backward and the swell-headed alike, and he was not at all inclined to tolerate inadequate progress or misconduct. Within a short time, he had transformed a restless bunch of schoolboys into a flock of terrified sheep.

Garzìa already had a small literary reputation. Some ten years before he had published an essay, *Il canto di una rivoluzione* ('Poetry of a Revolution'), which compared Francesco Ignazio Mannu's poem against the Sardinian feudal barons with Parini's *Il Giorno*. He was also the editor of *L'Unione sarda*, which – in spite of its very antiquated printing machinery – was still the largest circulation paper on the island. Garzìa was strongly anti-clerical and inclined towards radicalism, and while he took good care to distinguish his position from that of the socialists, he did not hesitate to discuss them and their ideas in his pages, and sometimes even supported them. The pages were 'his' in the fullest sense: he owned the paper as well. He shared such tendencies with two other teachers at the lycée, both as progressive as he was, or even more so: the Latin and Greek master, Costante Oddone, and the physics master, Francesco Maccarone, a friend of Gennaro Gramsci's and a militant socialist.

Gramsci became Garzìa's favourite pupil at once. He found his essays being read aloud in class as examples of intellectual clarity and good style. Garzìa would lend him textbooks, and other books as well. Though usually brusque with his pupils – as with his printers and journalists – he became gentle towards Gramsci. He would even invite him to his studio on Viale Regina Margherita, where the staff of *L'Unione sarda* held their meetings. At length, the relationship between the two became genuine friendship.

All this time, Gramsci's principal amusement had continued to be reading:

He used to read everything [Gennaro told me]. I came back from my military service in Turin a militant socialist, and at the beginning of 1911 I got a job as treasurer of the Chamber of Labour[2] and secretary of the local Socialist Party. So I used to meet frequently with Cavallera, Battelli, and Pesci, the young leaders of the Sardinian socialist movement, and occasionally Nino would be there too. We had a great quantity of books, papers, tracts, and propaganda material in the house. Nino most often spent his evenings at home, without so much as putting a foot outside the door, and he made short work of reading the books and newspapers.

He had already begun to approach Marx – 'out of intellectual curiosity', as he was to write later, in 1924. His reading list also included Carolina Invernizio, the *Domenica del Corriere*, and (in his own words) 'the socialist journal *Il Viandante*, edited by the revolutionary Tommaso Monicelli'.[3] In a letter to his father he reminded him to 'tell Teresina that she should keep all the articles published in *Tribuna*, and more especially that if at all possible she should send me an article of Pascoli's they published a month or so ago. I'm keeping the *Domenica del Corriere* aside for her, and will send them to her at the first chance'. In a postscript he also asked for the return of Anton Giulio Barrili's *L'olmo e l'edera*, and an issue of *Secolo XX*.[4] He read Deledda too, but didn't like her. Renato Figàri says:

> In Sebastiano Satta's poetry, he liked best the odes to the dead of Bugerru, or those to Giuseppe Cavallera and Efisio Orano. He came once to a poetry reading at the 'Vanguard' club. I said on that occasion that it was up to us young people to support and champion Sardinian writers. Next day he returned to the argument himself. I remember his reproaching Sardinian authors with being too cut off from the realities of the time. Sardinia wasn't all waterfalls, sheep-folds, vendettas, and mothers weeping over their dead sons, he objected. It was also miners working hundreds of feet under the earth for Belgian capital, and getting in exchange not hospitals, not schools and blankets, but military intervention the moment they dared ask for anything at all.

He also followed the *Marzocco* and Prezzolini's *La Voce*, and found

---

[2] *Chamber of Labour*: the 'Camera del Lavoro', a local federation of trade unions. (T.N.)

[3] *Carolina Invernizio* (1858–1916): prolific writer of popular novels. The *Domenica del Corriere*: a Milan popular weekly celebrated for its lurid cover pictures. *Tommaso Monicelli*: an author of children's stories. (T.N.)

[4] *Giovanni Pascoli* (1855–1912): nationalist poet with a romantic sympathy for socialism. *Anton Giulio Barrili* (1836–1908): friend and follower of Garibaldi, author of many serial novels of the kind Gramsci later mentioned in his discussions of popular literature. (T.N.)

his favourite authors in these reviews. His sister Teresina recounts:

When Nino changed his address, the reviews would keep coming to Ghilarza for a while. Then I would be given the job of putting aside in a folder all the articles by the authors he most liked, above all Croce and Salvemini. I can remember Papini and Emilio Cecchi too. Nino had a great admiration for Cecchi. But Croce and Salvemini were always at the head of the list of things he would ask me to cut out and keep for him in the right order.[5]

Studies of the Italian 'Southern Question' were blossoming in this period. And so was Sardinian national feeling, which brought together in a rather ambiguous fashion Giolittian liberalism, socialism, and radicalism. Ever since March 1910, Raffa Garzìa's paper (whose chief sub-editor was Jago Siotto, formerly editor of the early socialist periodical *La Lega*) had concentrated on one principal target: the Luzzatti ministry of 1910–11.[6]

This emphasis largely reflected the influence of Francesco Cocco Ortu, who had been passed over in the formation of this government after being a Minister several times previously. The paper was run at a loss, and so more or less bound to adopt the line of Ortu who subsidized it. His directive now was to concentrate all available fire-power on the 'grande Gigione', as Luzzatti was referred to in the pages of *L'Unione sarda*: his first name, Luigi – 'Gigi' for short – being twisted contemptuously into 'Gigione', meaning a ridiculously bad actor or 'ham'. There was not overmuch concern about where the ammunition came from. Hence, salvoes were fired off from both the right and the left. But the chief source of the paper's polemical exuberance was local Sardinian feeling: indeed, it became the main sounding-board of popular protest on this score, and reasons for protest were scarcely lacking in this backward land whose chief distinction lay in its high

---

[5] *Giuseppe Prezzolini* (b. 1882): editor of the nationalist Florentine review *La Voce*. *Giovanni Papini* (1881–1956): a prolific writer in a Futurist phase at this time, who later made a sensational conversion to Catholicism. *Emilio Cecchi* (1884–1966): art critic and authority on English literature. *Benedetto Croce* (1866–1954): the most prominent and influential of Italian philosophers and literary critics in the present century. *Gaetano Salvemini* (1873–1957): the leader of the *meridionalisti* or protagonists of the South, he was an active socialist from an early age, till he became convinced that socialism would not bring about the emancipation of the South. A bitter opponent of Giolitti and his methods, he later became a leading anti-fascist. (T.N.)

[6] *Luigi Luzzatti* (1841–1927): Italian elder statesman, whose coalition administration of 1910–11 was chiefly notable for its attempt at franchise reform. (T.N.)

ratings for illiteracy, malaria, trachoma, tuberculosis, and death from starvation.

On 23 May 1910, King Victor Emmanuel III and his Queen disembarked at Cagliari from the royal yacht *Trinacria*. They stayed in the city until the evening of the 25th. The King laid the foundation-stone of a public hostel for indigents in Viale degli Ospizi, and the Queen made a gift of 2,800 lire worth of sweets to children in public institutions. Next day, *L'Unione sarda*, though it had given great prominence to the visit – going so far as to publish a photograph of the royal couple, a rare privilege bestowed that year on only one other subject – published an article which was respectful enough to the sovereigns but extremely rude to the government. It was written by Raffa Garzìa:

> The holiday is over. The plumes have fallen to the ground; the flags are rolled up and put away for another day; top-hats and tail-coats have returned to their paternal regime of moth-balls; the policemen who for a few short days afforded Captain Bousquet the satisfaction of having a company to command are back in their offices again; the transport system has been liberated from the feudal yoke and restored to the bourgeois community; all over now, the anxious palpitations and hysterical outbursts of those semi-conscious authorities of ours, drowsing once more over the waters of the port. . . . Peace returns to our city.

But why – *L'Unione sarda* went on to inquire – did the Luzzatti government want the royal visit at all? It would have meant something, had there been some extraordinary new venture requiring consecration, some new state of affairs. 'And what *is* there new in our midst just at present,' concluded Garzìa, 'except for a handful of dust cast brazenly into the eyes of blockheads?' In the event, the sovereigns' visit had created a certain unanimity, but decidedly not the kind of unanimity which the authorities had hoped for. The 'organ of the Sardinian working class', Cagliari's *La Voce del popolo*, dismissed the event in a few lines and never mentioned it again: 'What a display! What a lot of toppers and morning coats, what a lot of beautiful women, what smiles of complacency and moral righteousness! What terrific motor-cars, what wealth, what a lot of flags and soldiers and guards, both in uniform and out of it! Oh look – it's the King!' Even *L'Unione sarda*'s great rival, *Il Paese*, whose usual policy consisted of proclaiming the opposite of whatever Garzìa was saying, joined in the chorus this time. The issue of Sunday 29 May said: 'In spite of Victor Emmanuel III's visit, everything will go on as before in Sardinia, our sufferings will not be lessened in the smallest degree.' It even went so far as to denounce the squandering of money on preparations for the event: 'Whether it was a lot or a little, the sum spent on such ludicrous choreographic displays, such useless and servile parades and vacuous official celebrations was simply thrown away. We say they did not elevate popular feeling: they corrupted it.' Germonio, the Prefect of Cagliari, had invited all the Mayors of the province for Wednesday 25 May, in a circular stating that the King wished to see them. *Il Paese* published the reply sent by the Mayor of Terralba, Felice Porcella: 'Regret unable accept flattering invitation sent by Your Honour, until His Majesty's government deigns take action regarding just but ignored complaints made by mayors, and enacts proper laws at once to assist this poverty-stricken and long-suffering region.' The wind of Sardinian national feeling was blowing again, more strongly than ever.

A few weeks later, when the school year was over, Gramsci went to see Garzìa before returning home. He was nineteen now, and wanted to try his hand at journalism; he had thought of writing brief pieces of local news from his home town during the summer. Raffa Garzìa agreed. They already had a correspondent in Ghilarza, but perhaps Gramsci could write news from another nearby village, Aidomaggiore? The young man left with an assurance that his first journalist's press-card would soon be sent on to him. As indeed it was.

The note Garzìa sent along with the card (dated 21 July 1910) was not in the bureaucratic jargon normally employed in such situations. 'Here's the card you asked for,' wrote the stern critic and teacher of Italian literature, 'your contributions will be very welcome; send us all the news about everything of interest from now onwards, both we and the readers will be grateful. Sincerely and affectionately yours.'

Gramsci's first piece appeared in *L'Unione sarda* five days later, on 26 July, and is certainly his first published writing. It was twenty-five lines of straightforward reporting, written incisively and with humour, and quite free from the self-conscious pretention which has so often marred a provincial journalistic or literary début. It was signed with the abbreviation 'gi', and reads:

> Rumours had been spreading across the countryside that the most startling and fearful things would happen in Aidomaggiore at election-time. The population – obviously ready for any excess – was bent on introducing universal suffrage at one blow, and actually electing its own Mayor and Councillors. Seriously worried by these symptoms, Lieutenant Gay of the Ghilarza Carabinieri moved in an entire army corps: forty carabinieri,

forty infantrymen – fortunately without artillery – and one policeman (who would have been quite enough all by himself). When the polls opened the village was deserted: electors and non-electors alike had done a bunk, for fear of being arrested, and the authorities were compelled to go from house to house and drag out the reluctant voters. . . .

It ended with a characteristically Gramscian twist: 'Poor little almond trees of Aidomaggiore! Infantrymen and phylloxera have much the same effect!'

On 17 November 1910, when Antonio Gramsci had been back in Cagliari for a few weeks at the start of his third lycée year, *L'Unione sarda* carried two very different pieces of news on the same page. One announced the death of Tolstoy; the other, the imminent arrival in Sardinia of the Honourable Guido Podrecca, Socialist Member of Parliament and Editor of the anti-clerical paper *L'Asino*. The second item produced by far the greater effect in Cagliari.[1]

There was still a feeling of general unrest. *L'Unione sarda*'s onslaught on the Luzzatti government had continued. Although it had derived originally from Cocco Ortu's personal spite at being passed over, the objective situation lent it new weight and meaning with each day that passed.

Not only did Sardinia's problems remain unsolved: they were being aggravated by the policies founded on Giolitti's strategy of class alliance in the North at the expense of the South.[2] This strategy was aimed at increasing the profits of the northern industrialists (tariff protectionism was another aspect of the strategy) and buying off the organized working class movement by acceding to many of its demands. The cost of such a strategy inevitably fell on the shoulders of the peasant masses in the Mezzogiorno. And this mattered little enough to those in power. The southern masses were kept out of real political power by their illiteracy, and by the local and personal structure of southern political life. If they objected, or tried to rise, the army was strong enough to crush them.

In Sardinia, the agrarian economy – i.e., most of the island's economic

[1] Podrecca was expelled from the Italian Socialist Party in 1912 and helped found the abortive Reformist Socialist Party. (T.N.)

[2] *Giovanni Giolitti* (1842–1928): Prime Minister 1892–93, 1903–05, 1906–09, 1911–14, and 1920–21. His 'liberal-labour' programme of 1911–14 included a franchise bill extending the vote to all male literates over 21, and to illiterates who had done military service or reached the age of 30. Giolitti, an adroit and ruthless bourgeois politician, practised an 'opening to the left' to forestall the development of socialism. He likewise launched Italy's second major colonial war against Libya (1911–12), to forestall the rise of nationalism. (T.N.)

life – was trapped in a vicious circle. The low level of incomes together with the high level of taxation (people used to call it 'Inland Revenue brigandage') made saving or the accumulation of capital very difficult. But without capital, no real effort to change the structure of agriculture was possible; so the persistence of backward conditions and primordial farming techniques kept incomes down and closed the vicious circle. The number of unemployed was growing. There was a new rise in prices, affecting rents and staple foods, and more especially imported manufactures burdened by customs tariffs. Legislation to help the island had been passed, but what little of it was put into practice was always partial, late, and poorly applied. Even quite marginal demands like that for the abolition of differential tariffs on the railways were not satisfied. Sardinian isolation was aggravated by breakdowns in sea communication – due to the extreme decrepitude of the ships employed in this service – and by the frequent failure of the telegraphic installations, which left the island completely cut off from the rest of the world. Exasperation kept on growing, and was shared by all levels of society. The storm broke in Cagliari at the beginning of the summer: early in July, Mayor Marcello and the whole of his Council resigned in protest at the government's failure to keep its promises.

This mass resignation was followed by others, and *L'Unione sarda* underlined the progress of events with a hammering barrage of exclamatory full-page headlines.[3] All summer long this journalistic battle went on with unabated vehemence. In such an electric atmosphere, it is easy to see why the announcement of Podrecca's visit aroused enthusiasm in the breasts of most citizens, and filled the powers-that-be (especially the clerical ones) with dismay.

He had been invited to Sardinia by the local Socialist Party and the Cagliari Chamber of Labour. The latter, in particular, had become a real meeting-place for workers, tradesmen, and intellectuals. The secretary was a Tuscan trade union organizer called Gino Pesci, one of the group of politically-minded immigrants that had followed Cavallera to Sardinia. Gennaro Gramsci, now twenty-six, would spend a lot of his spare time there, and sometimes Antonio would join him. At that time, young people felt that a visit to the Chamber of Labour was something of an adventure into a forbidden world and exciting

---

[3] e.g. 'Battle Begins with Angry Outbursts', 'Spirited Protests from Cagliari and Province', 'Resignation of Communal Council', 'Mass Resignations from Elected Bodies', 'Great Protest in Defence of Our Rights', 'Down with all Vain Promises', 'Insurrection of the Public Spirit'.

for that very reason, a gesture of defiance that demonstrated one's moral stature. The rooms in Via Barcelona were watched by the police, and going there regularly exposed one to the risk of persecution. In an epoch still marked by romanticism, this aura of secret societies and repression constituted a positive attraction. And now that Podrecca's visit had been announced, there was also the chance of a street battle with the forces of clericalism.

The Socialist deputy was to do a lecture tour. It was to start on Tuesday, 22 November at Cagliari's Valdès Theatre, with a talk on 'The Revolutionary Thought of Richard Wagner'. Then on the 24th, 'Faith and Morality'. At Iglesias on the 26th he was down to speak in the ex-church of San Francesco on 'The Husband of One's Choice'. Finally, on Sunday the 27th, there was to be a big public meeting in Piazza del Carmine, Cagliari, with a speech on 'Working-Class Organization'. Four days before Podrecca arrived, *L'Unione sarda* came out with a strongly anti-clerical item. 'It is rumoured,' said the note, 'that the clericalists intend staging a hostile demonstration at the railway station when the Hon. Podrecca arrives, and others during his lectures.' The paper was up in arms at the prospect. 'This would be an outrage,' it thundered. 'No one can accuse us of being over-sympathetic towards certain methods of the Italian Socialist Movement – nevertheless, we must salute the Hon. Podrecca as a man of ideals, and a brilliant and valorous colleague.'

But the demonstration did not materialize. The editor of *L'Asino* received a triumphant welcome, while at Iglesias, as *L'Unione sarda* put it in its customary inflated style: 'So great was the spell cast by the orator upon the public, that even the clericalists were quite unable to refrain from applauding. . . .' Exaggerations aside, the tour of this popular journalist and politician certainly gave new impetus and heart to the island's left-wing organizations.

At the same time, another alarming phenomenon had occurred to depress public morale, and occasion still more protests against in-competent authority: an epidemic of meningitis. 'The stretcher bearers are hard at work,' cried *L'Unione* on 8 December. The paper's usual rubrics – 'This & That', 'Sardinians in the News', 'Departures', 'Brief Notes' – were joined by another regular section under 'Cerebro-spinal Meningitis'. The leader-writer deplored 'the grave danger we are all exposed to', and went on to attack the 'ineptitude and weakness of the Prefect'. As for the Royal Commissioner appointed to Cagliari after the Council's resignation, the paper complained that 'the Cagliari administration has become merely a sub-section of the Prefecture (and of the Bishopric too, unfortunately). And the government? It keeps its peace. Who raises his voice in Parliament? Nobody. Meanwhile, people go on dying'. Most of the readers shared its sentiments.

On Sunday, 11 December 1910, while this meningitis campaign was in full swing, an assembly of delegates from all the city's associations was held at the Chamber of Labour. It was not concerned with the epidemic. Four days previously, Gino Pesci had sent round a circular to all trade, professional and cultural organizations, in which he pointed out the widespread suffering caused by the continual rise in prices and rents, and said he was persuaded that the only way to reverse the trend was to 'develop an active campaign of agitation like that in many other Italian cities'. The Sunday meeting was a plenary one, and set up a 'Campaign Committee on Prices and Rents'. *L'Unione sarda* approved, and added:

> Prefect Germonio, sound asleep whenever it is a question of combatting the meningitis epidemic, suddenly woke up yesterday full of zeal, and sent a police officer along to the meeting at the Chamber of Labour, although this meeting was solely concerned with economic matters. But Prefect Germonio, who neither knows about nor cares for the vital interests of our citizens, never likes to be caught napping: he took great care to be informed of the names of the 'rabble' who turned up at the Chamber of Labour.

Shortly after, news arrived that the Chief of Police of Bari in south-eastern Italy was to be transferred to Cagliari. He had recently been acquitted by a Commission of Inquiry similar to the one that had condemned Francesco Gramsci. The epidemic was still raging. Prices continued to be impossibly high. All that was needed to inflame passions further was this new proof of the notion which mainland authority entertained of Sardinia as a kind of punishment centre. 'So!' reacted *L'Unione sarda*, 'For Luzzatti, that considerate friend of Sardinia Cagliari and the whole island are no more than a land of punishment and relegation; whenever an official can no longer be tolerated on the continent, because of incapacity or a scandal, the remedy is quickly found: forced residence in Sardinia!'

From 6 to 8 January 1911, elections were held for a new Executive Committee of the Chamber of Labour. The candidates were a railway-man, Salvatore Baine; a stone-mason, Salvatore Crovato; an engineering worker, Luigi Favero; a clerk, Gennaro Gramsci; a marble worker, Luigi Onali; a tailor, Angelo Pischedda; and a boiler-maker, Alfredo

Romani. Gennaro was among those elected, and he was made treasurer. There were some repercussions, naturally, given the close watch kept by the police on trade union leaders. Before long, back in Ghilarza, Francesco Gramsci and Peppina Marcias heard that there had been inquiries into Gennaro's background. They were very upset. Signor Ciccillo was angry and anxious enough to consider going to Cagliari to find out what was going on. Antonio then wrote the following letter to his mother:

> I'm replying at once so that you can stop Dad committing the folly of coming here. You're both afraid because the police are looking for information. But there's really no reason to get steamed up. God knows what you must be imagining: Nannaro in the guard-house, or being marched along by four carabinieri. Don't worry, nothing like that is going to happen. Nannaro took on certain tasks for the Chamber of Labour, so a hitherto unknown name appeared under the noses of the police, and they wanted to find out about this new revolutionary cut-throat who had stepped into the limelight. So they asked for some information about him. All right? You'll see, that's all there is to it, and no harm has been done. There was a strike, and since Nannaro is the Chamber's treasurer the police wanted his address so they could seize the funds and put an end to the strike. But the strike was called off anyway, and the funds were untouched. . . . Another time, keep calm when you hear of things like this, and try to laugh in the faces of the carabinieri, as I've been doing for some time now: poor things, one ought to feel sorry for for them. They're so obsessed by socialists and anarchists that they've no time for robbers and ruffians any more, and go in fear of their own helmets being pinched. . . .

Antonio Gramsci was now twenty. He had adapted himself more thoroughly to the city environment, and we can glimpse a new image through the letters of the period – that of a carefree student given even to noisy theatre-going. 'They thought I was a girl because of my splendid mane of hair waving in the breeze, and were astounded that a woman should make so much din in a theatre, for all they could see was my head, and a hand making a very rude gesture. I didn't mind actually, I was thankful for the attention they showed me.' Or again: 'I drew some fire the other day for my loud admiration of a policeman's splendid whiskers: so I said he should trim them if he didn't want people to talk about them.'

Behind this façade of levity, though, Antonio's life was still a grim one. Without help from home, Gennaro's salary was not enough for both of them. The cost of living had risen, and two people could no longer live on one hundred lire a month. Antonio wrote home to his father: 'Nannaro has made enough sacrifices. He has already been borrowing money, and now doesn't know what to do; I see him get more and more preoccupied every day, and today he had actually decided to send me back to Ghilarza. . . . Only my entreaties were able to persuade him that, if I wrote to you tonight, things would be put right.' He continued his studies at Cagliari, but under the most difficult conditions. Years afterwards he would recall: 'I began by not having coffee in the morning, then I put off having lunch until later and later, so that I could do without having supper. So for eight months I ate only once a day and reached the end of my third year at the lycée in a state of severe malnutrition.'

The class of 1891, Gramsci's contemporaries, were now being called up for military service. Over the whole island, the conscripts numbered 11,632. Of these, well over one half – 7,968 – were exempted from service for reasons of incapacity; and in 2,486 cases the stated reason was malnutrition. It was not to be expected that the socialism of the Italian North, of the reformist trade unions allied to protectionism and in practice indifferent to these tragic conditions, could have much following, either among the deprived masses or among the intellectuals who sympathized with them.

Instead, a kind of 'peasant socialism' based on the ideas of Salvemini began to make headway. We know from his sister Teresina that Gramsci was a keen reader of Salvemini. In *La Voce del popolo* of 13 October 1910, this intransigent *meridionalista* had anticipated part of his address to the forthcoming socialist congress in Milan, and explained the position of his 'dissident reformist' group. They 'did not accept verbal revolutionism, but neither did they intend that reformism should become a mere synonym of parliamentarism, of Giolittian ministerialism, of chronic Freemasonry, and turn the Socialist Party into still another oligarchic body in the service of the more powerful working-class organizations, at the expense of the disfranchised working masses'. In Sardinia, the tendency which corresponded to some extent with Salvemini's was a mixture of more or less radical separatism and a socialism occasionally revolutionary in content – a sort of social-nationalism, deviant both in relation to Marx and to the federalist conceptions of Carlo Cattaneo.[4] It took class struggle

---

[4] *Carlo Cattaneo* (1801–69): Swiss-Italian political theorist of federalism, founder of the monthly journal *Il Politecnico* (Milan), and author of a celebrated history of the Milan insurrection of 1848. (T.N.)

for granted; but the enemy class was rather abstractly and confusingly identified with the wealthy mainlanders – and the industrial workers of the mainland were also considered 'wealthy', or at least privileged. This current of regional socialism was not to acquire real political organization until 1919, when the Partito Sardo d'Azione (Sardinian Action Party) was founded and evolved aims and a precise programme. Till then, it remained mainly a climate of revolt against Italian state centralism.

In March 1911, great celebrations were held in Turin to mark the first fifty years of Italian unity. They could have provided an excellent occasion for a truce, and the assuaging of prickly regionalist resentments. But clearly the great landslides of rhetoric could no longer accomplish this by themselves. Resentment was deep-rooted, and for Sardinians it was actually intensified by the failure to provide cut-rate fares for the Sardinian notables invited to the National Convention on Local Government on 17 March. The Mayor of Cossoine, Agostino Senes, declined to attend with this telegram: 'Will not attend, because huge fare reductions have not been extended to old Sardinia, forgotten by all.' The Mayor of Fluminimaggiore joined him, with the following reply: 'Given great distance and no concessions on voyage from Sardinia and financial difficulties by Commune, impossible attend Mayors Convention. Stop. Nevertheless, repeat, nevertheless, present in spirit as an Italian.' With their different emphases, both these messages fairly represented the Sardinian frame of mind at the time. *L'Unione sarda* called Sacchi, the minister responsible, 'a shabby skinflint'.

What point had Antonio Gramsci's inner development now reached? We know from a letter of 1924 that at this period he believed it necessary to 'struggle for the national independence of the region'. An essay written while in his third lycée year indicates something of his general formation then. His teacher Raffa Garzìa had fallen ill and requested leave of absence. His replacement was a tall, dreamy man called Vittorio Amedeo Arullani, well versed in the Italian classics and politically open-minded, though not of the left. It was for him that Antonio Gramsci wrote an essay on colonialism and the oppressed peoples:

> One day the news is that a student has killed the English Governor of India; or it may be that the Italians have been beaten at Dogali; or that the Boxers have exterminated the European missionaries. Then at once a horrified old Europe calls down curses on the heads of the barbarians, the uncivilized, and a new crusade is proclaimed against these unfortunate

peoples. . . . Wars are waged for trade, not for civilization: how many cities of China did the English bombard, when the Chinese would not buy their opium? Some civilization! The Russians and Japanese massacred each other to capture the trade of Korea and Manchuria.

The piece ends with a passage which clearly indicates the Marxist convictions of the young pupil from the Liceo Dettòri:

The French Revolution destroyed many privileges, it relieved many of the oppressed; but it did no more than replace the power of one class with that of another. Hence the great lesson to be drawn from it: that privileges and social differences are products not of nature but of society, and so can be transcended. Humanity needs another bloody cleansing to rid it of many of these injustices: let not the rulers wait for it, and then repent leaving the masses in their present state of ignorance and ferocity!

This was in 1911 – six years before the fall of the Tsarist regime.

In the final exams at the lycée, Arullani gave Gramsci 'nine' for written Italian, and his other marks were also satisfactory, including the science subjects: he got 'eight' in everything. Gramsci relates:

After my first year at the lycée I never studied mathematics, but chose Greek instead (one had the choice in those days). But in my third year I unexpectedly showed that I had retained remarkable talent for the subject. As it happened, if one did physics in that year it was necessary to know some of the mathematics missed out by those who had opted for Greek. Our very distinguished physics master was Francesco Maccarone, and he derived great amusement from embarrassing us. He gave me some questions involving mathematics in the last practical test of the last term, and told me that my year's average – and so my degree, with or without the exams – would depend upon how well I did. He enjoyed seeing me standing there in front of the blackboard, and gave me all the time I wanted. Well, I was there for half an hour, covered with chalk from head to foot, trying and trying again, writing it down and rubbing it out till I finally 'invented' a proof which he accepted as very good, though it didn't exist in any of the textbooks. This teacher knew my elder brother, and tormented me with his laughter all the rest of the time I was at school: he called me the physicist with a taste for Greek.

9

The Carlo Alberto College offered scholarships at the University of Turin worth seventy lire per month to impoverished and deserving students of the former Kingdom of Sardinia who had obtained a lycée certificate. That year, in the autumn of 1911, thirty-nine such scholarships were being offered. Antonio Gramsci understood at once that without a scholarship his family would find it very hard to bear the extra burden of his university studies. His father was now rehabilitated, and had a permanent job again at the Land Registry – but only as a simple book-keeper, in spite of his certificate in classics and the exams he had passed in jurisprudence. Much more than his meagre salary was required to keep a son at university, when there were still five other children to be looked after. Mario was eighteen and wanted to go into the army or the navy; he had done a few years of school, and might hope to become a non-commissioned officer, or even a full officer later, but in the meantime – until he was old enough to enrol – he stayed at home jobless, a burden on his father's slender finances. Carlo was fourteen, and at school in Oristano. The girls stayed at home, helping out as best they could.

So Antonio's only real hope lay in winning one of the thirty-nine scholarships. If he did get to Turin, Gennaro would still be able to help him a little out of his salary at the ice factory. He had to be selected, first, on the basis of the final lycée examination results; and then, if he was allowed to enter the competition, there would be a long series of written and oral exams in Turin.

Antonio's summer was almost completely ruined. He was weakened by all the meals he had missed in his last period at school. He felt very discouraged, and recollected later: 'I only heard about the Carlo Alberto scholarships at the end of the school year, and one had to do exams in all the subjects studied over all three years at the lycée; this meant making an enormous effort during the three months of the holiday.' He had an uncle in Oristano, a pharmacist called Serafino Delogu, his mother's first cousin; and Serafino had a son, Delio, whom Antonio was fond of, and who needed some private lessons. 'Only Uncle Serafino recognized what a deplorably weak state I was in, and invited me to stay with him at Oristano and tutor Delio. I stayed a month and a half, and only just avoided going mad. I was unable to study for the competition, as Delio took up all my time, and this distraction coupled with my poor state of health quite knocked me out. I sneaked off finally, with only one month left to study in.'

At the beginning of September he heard he had been allowed to take the scholarship exams. Writing to inform him of this, the College secretary added: 'You are one of the only two candidates for the Cagliari scholarship,' and 'from 16 October, at which date you should have arrived in Turin, until the day following the last examination, you will be allowed the prescribed sum of 3 lire per day, plus the second-class fare from Cagliari to Turin (less the equivalent of 300 kilometres).'

So in mid-October, aged twenty and a half (he would be twenty-one in January), Gramsci left Ghilarza to go '*di là dalle grandi acque*' ('beyond the wide waters'), as people used to say then, less affectedly than one might think today. 'I left for Turin in a kind of somnambulistic state,' he recalled later. 'I had 55 lire in my pocket, after spending 45 of the 100 they gave me at home on the third-class fare.' The trip was a lengthy one, and included a stop in Pisa, where Gramsci's uncle Zaccaria Delogu, an army captain, was about to leave for Tripoli. His brothers Serafino and Achille were seeing him off, and Gramsci spent an evening with them on the way.

At last he arrived in the great industrial metropolis. The experience was a stunning one, for somebody 'so very, so extremely provincial, as a young Sardinian was bound to be at the beginning of the century'. In his first letter home, we read that: 'A short walk reduces me to fear and trembling, after just avoiding being run down by innumerable cars and trams.' He was met at the station by a Ghilarza man, Francesco Oppo, an employee at the Pirelli rubber plant, and his first surprise came on arrival at the room which Oppo had found for him. Thanks to the Fiftieth Anniversary Exhibition, there had been a rise in prices, and the room now cost 3 lire a day – as much as the whole allowance being given by the College. He wrote to his father: 'I've had to pay 3 lire a day for this room, unfortunately, and as much or more to eat; but today, when I went to the College to draw the allowance, and recounted my odyssey to the secretary, he was kind enough to find me another little room at only 1.50 lira per day.'

The examinations started on 18 October. According to Domenico Zucàro (who has spoken to other candidates at the same examination) the subject of the Italian essay was 'The contribution of our pre-Risorgimento writers, Alfieri, Foscolo, etc., to the Unification of Italy'. As soon as he knew he had been admitted to the oral part of the examination, Antonio wrote home: 'I've just come back from the University, where I went to see the results of the Italian essay. I got through, thank goodness, but unfortunately cannot feel too reassured by this: there were only five who didn't, out of seventy or more candidates, which means that everyone is very well prepared, and the exam will be more serious than we thought.' He got on well enough in the other written exams too: 21 (out of 30) in history, 23 in Latin composition, 24 in Greek translation, and 25 in the philosophy essay. He sat the oral part on 27 October, and said later: 'I don't know how I got through the exams, because I fainted two or three times.' In the final list of results, he came ninth. Second on the list was the name of another poor student, from another of the Sardinian lycées: Palmiro Togliatti.

They had never met previously. 'The first, fleeting encounter of two rather touchy, unsociable youths' (as Togliatti later described it) did not take place until these examinations at the Carlo Alberto College. They were brought together by their common Sardinian background. Togliatti was the son of a school bursar (deceased in January of that same year) and had been for three years at the Domenico Alberto Azuni lycée in Sassari. In addition, a certain closeness was encouraged by (again in Togliatti's words) 'our common state of dire poverty, as evidenced in the way we both dressed'. However, a closer friendship did not develop between the two students until later on.

Gramsci's first winter in Turin was a critical period, even in his eventful existence. He had taken a little room at No. 57 Corso Firenze, overlooking the Dora river. Friendless and far from home, he now felt the pressures of solitude more strongly than before. He was exhausted by the efforts he had made to win the scholarship, and by the privations he continued to endure. 'In 1911,' he recalled, 'at the time when I was seriously ill as a result of cold and malnutrition, I used to be obsessed by the vision of a colossal spider which would come down from its web every night while I was asleep, and suck out my brain.'

An unfortunate accident made him penniless in the weeks following the examinations. He thought that he would be exempted from the usual University fees. But in fact he had to pay half-fee, and even this concession required the production of a whole range of documents. Until these arrived, enrolment was conditional on paying the whole fee; and until he had enrolled, the College would not pay him the monthly seventy lire of his scholarship. On 4 November Antonio wrote to his father, begging him to pay the whole fee, and added: 'I'm almost broke now, and I've got to pay something to the landlady of this place which I've taken provisionally for one month: so you must send me at least thirty lire, by telegram if possible.' Francesco Gramsci paid the seventy-five lire to the University from Ghilarza on 10 November, and on the 16th Antonio was finally enrolled as a first-year student in the Faculty of Letters: he had chosen the Modern Philology course. The College let him have his first grant immediately afterwards.

For those at home in Ghilarza, the problem was now one of understanding how he could possibly need more than seventy lire to live on. Antonio wrote to them:

> These seventy lire are absolutely insufficient, and I can prove it with facts and figures: in spite of all my efforts, I could not find a room for less than 25 lire, like the one I'm in now. Take 25 from 70, that leaves 45, and with this I must eat, do my laundry (not less than 5 lire, with the washing, ironing, etc.), get shoe-polish, pay for the light, and buy paper, pens and ink for work – which may not sound much, but costs me 40 lire! As regards food, let me tell you a glass of milk is 10 centimes, and for 5 you get only a small bread roll . . . lunch is never less than 2 lire, even at the most modest *trattoria*, like the one where I was eating until a few days ago. There, they gave me a plate of macaroni for 60 centimes, and a paper-thin steak for about the same; so I would stuff down six or seven rolls and come away as hungry as when I went in. . . .

His mother sent him a shawl. As Grazietta wrote on 14 December, it was 'for putting round your shoulders when you're in your room, because though mother laughed at the account of your home attire, at the same time she feels very sorry about your miserable conditions'. Five days before Christmas – his first away from home – Antonio decided to be even more outspoken about the circumstances of his life in Turin. He wrote one of the few letters in which, for once, his usual rather detached chronicler's tone is put aside – a letter in which, instead of saying little about himself and saying that impersonally (as if describing tribulations that didn't concern him), he gives way to his feelings:

I find myself compelled to beg you to send the 20 lire you promised, without fail, before the end of the month. I only got 62 lire from the College this month, of which I've given 40 to my landlady, and I must let her have another 40 shortly. Christmas is going to be a very thin time anyway. I don't want to make it still more depressing by trailing round Turin in the cold looking for another hole to hide in. I had hoped to get an overcoat made this month, with the 10 lire Nannaro sent me. Now God knows how long it'll take me. Think how nice it is to go out and across the city shivering with cold, then come back to a cold room and sit shivering for hours, unable to warm oneself up. If only I'd known, I would not have come here to suffer this glacial existence, not at any price, The worst thing of all is that worrying about the cold prevents me studying, because I either walk to and fro to warm my feet a little, or have to stay huddled in bed, unable to stand the first frost of winter.

The money he asked for arrived on New Year's Day. This can be deduced from a letter written on 3 January 1912. He wrote to his father:

I got your telegraph money-order for fifteen lire the day before yesterday, thank you very much: believe me, I was really in difficulties, and after getting your card on the 26th I had given up hope of receiving the money. I do hope that you won't find yourself in difficulties now, as a result; believe me, I could not have managed without your twenty lire, even after making every possible sacrifice.

But even under such conditions, in a state of total nervous exhaustion, and embittered by his painful loneliness, Gramsci managed to study. He remembered how: 'I lived through the winter without an overcoat, all I had was a lightweight coat suitable for Cagliari. Around March 1912 things got so bad that I did not speak for several months. When I had to speak I got the words mixed up. To make things worse, I was living right on the banks of the Dora, and the freezing river fogs used to turn me to ice.'

One of the professors had taken a liking to him, a young Dalmatian called Matteo Bartoli who taught linguistics. Eight years earlier he had published an essay with the title *Un po' di sardo* ('A Little Sardinian'). Bartoli believed that Sardinian speech had a particular importance in the study of the more remote derivatives of Latin vernacular, hence he was always on the lookout for 'interesting specimens of Sardinian dialect', as Domenico Zucàro puts it. Gramsci spoke Sardinian perfectly, and was one of the few islanders in the Faculty of Letters. This was the origin of the linguist's interest in him; the interest grew into sympathy and then later, as they collaborated more and more closely, into warm friendship. There is a letter from this period to Antonio's father in which he asks him to find someone who can put a list of words into Sardinian – 'in the Fonni dialect, though . . . and indicating clearly the soft *s* (as in the Italian "rosa") and the hard *s* (as in "sordo")'.

He also saw a lot of a teacher of Italian literature, Umberto Cosmo, both at University and outside it, on the long walks they would take together. Cosmo had formerly been a teacher at Gramsci's old lycée in Cagliari:

> When I was a pupil of Cosmo's, I naturally disagreed with him over a number of things, although I still hadn't defined my own position clearly, and was always fond of him. But it seemed to me that I and Cosmo, and many other intellectuals at this time (say the first fifteen years of the century) occupied a certain common ground: we were all to some degree part of the movement of moral and intellectual reform which in Italy stemmed from Benedetto Croce, and whose first premise was that modern man can and should live without the help of religion – I mean of course, without revealed religion, positivist religion, mythological religion, or whatever other brand one cares to name.

A bond of mutual liking drew together the professor and the young student lost in the big city, and it grew stronger with the passage of time. Later on, in the heat of political struggle, there were to be disputes in which Gramsci would let himself be driven to excess by his desire to make a point. But their affection for one another would always survive such polemical skirmishes. Cosmo himself bears this out, in a letter he wrote to Piero Sraffa at the time of Gramsci's imprisonment:

> The university years when I counted G. [Gramsci] and the other G. [Pietro Paolo Gerosa, a catholic from the Canton Ticino, the same age as Gramsci] among my pupils are among my most treasured memories. They were two opposed mentalities, yet they agreed in according more importance to the religious, social and political content of literature than to its artistic side. One thought Cantù was right, the other followed Settembrini; I had to show what was wrong with both of them and stand up for the position of De Sanctis.[1]

Bartoli and Cosmo were the teachers with whom the Sardinian

---

[1] *Cesare Cantù* (1804–95): romantic writer and historian, friend and admirer of Mazzini. *Luigi Settembrini* (1813–76): an early southern fighter against the Bourbon regime, author of the celebrated 'Protest of the People of the Two Sicilies' (1847). *Francesco De Sanctis* (1817–83): the greatest Italian literary critic and historian of the nineteenth century, several times Minister of Education. (T.N.)

student enjoyed most familiarity. But the University as a whole was also destined to leave its mark on him. It was a great school, rich in stimuli, and reflecting clearly the many facets of the Italian culture of the time, sensitive to its new tensions and the need for research and innovation after the 'stifling oppression of the positivist era'. As well as Bartoli and Cosmo, its teaching staff included such names as Luigi Einaudi, Francesco Ruffini, Giovanni Chironi, Vincenzo Manzini, Gioele Solari, Pietro Toesca, Arturo Farinelli, Giovanni Pacchioni, Rodolfo Renier, Ettore Stampini, Achille Loria, and Annibale Pastore: men of many different tendencies and cultural outlooks, some still positivist, like Loria, some drawn towards nationalism, like Pacchioni, near-revolutionaries like Farinelli, liberals such as Einaudi and Ruffini. Given this wide variety, the University's influence upon its students was on the plane of method, rather than that of ideology:

> I remember a lecture-room on the ground floor [writes Togliatti], on the left side of the courtyard as one goes in, where we used to gather from our various faculties, and with our various outlooks, united by a common eagerness to find meaning in our own lives. This was where that remarkable man Arturo Farinelli used to read and comment on the classics of German romanticism. . . . Here was a new morality, which he inculcated into us, founded on the refusal of convention, on a self-denying devotion to the cause with which one's existence is identified, on the supreme law of utter sincerity to one's own nature.

One characteristic trait of Gramsci's adult personality was already emerging. His university studies had more than anything strengthened his taste for research, his liking for exactness: they gave him that 'habit of severe philological discipline', and that 'fund of methodological scruples' which he refers to in a letter from prison. In 1916, he wrote of himself:

> From his own university apprenticeship [the writer] recalls most vividly those classes in which the teacher made him aware of the intense toil of centuries underlying the perfection of the research methods being employed. In the natural sciences, for instance, the great effort it took to free men's minds from prejudices and from philosophic or religious apriorism, to the point where they could recognize that springs of water arise from atmospheric precipitations, and not from the sea. Or, in philology, how the historical method was arrived at through all the trials and errors of traditional empiricism, and how in the work of Francesco De Sanctis – for example – the criteria and basic ideas were all truths slowly winnowed out from a great mass of laborious experience and

inquiry. This was the most vital element in scholarship, the spirit of re-creation which made one able to assimilate great masses of data, the spirit that kindled in us the bright flame of new intellectual life.

For the time being, the young Sardinian immigrant was wholly wrapped up in the University. Outside it, he met only other immigrants, in a restaurant where, according to Piero Ciuffo, 'The proprietor used to chain the knives, forks, crockery and glasses to the table. He wasn't insured against theft, obviously. Sometimes he used to chain clients to the leg of the table too, as an extra precaution'.[2] Among the students, Gramsci had few friends: Cesare Berger, another of the Carlo Alberto scholars, Camillo Berra, and Angelo Tasca, the latter from a socialist working-class family. Tasca was the only political activist.

Three years before, in May 1909 – when Tasca was only seventeen – he had been a co-founder of the first Turin 'Fascio' of the Young Socialist Federation, alongside Giuseppe Romita and Gino Castagno.[3] He would later write of the experience: 'We made up a group of "red cyclists", and went out almost every Sunday morning to spread the word among the peasants, who usually didn't want to know.' They were still heavily influenced by positivism: 'In our great trinity of Darwin, Spencer and Marx, the latter tended to lose out.' However, they were freeing themselves from the dominant positivist trend, little by little. They mistrusted oratory, and preferred serious culture to facile sentiments. At a Young Socialist Congress in September 1912, they were described as the 'culturists' by a Neapolitan engineering student called Amadeo Bordiga. The Turin Fascio was in practice a rallying point for immature 'romantic revolutionaries' and avid readers of Prezzolini's *La Voce* – for a younger generation very different from the older socialists. 'We were nearly all hostile to Podrecca-style anti-clericalism, which was very often all that socialism boiled down to at the local level; our group managed to get a big majority for a motion proposing a boycott of *L'Asino* at a National Congress.' At first, however, Gramsci's relationship with Tasca developed outside this Young Socialist milieu.

He came into closer contact with Togliatti again in the early spring of their first year at university, following a class given by the Professor

[2] Piero Ciuffo was 'Cip', the cartoonist of *L'Ordine Nuovo*, and another Sardinian.
[3] Before being appropriated by the 'fascist' movement, the term 'fascio' had a long history of use on the left, meaning simply 'organized group', or the symbol of such a group, e.g. the Sicilian workers' 'fasci' of 1891. (T.N.)

of Roman Law, Giovanni Pacchioni. Togliatti studied jurisprudence, and unlike Tasca was not yet interested in active politics. Pacchioni now and then liked to hold debates among the students, instead of giving a lecture, and – according to Marcella and Maurizio Ferrara – 'Togliatti chose to discuss the problem of the authenticity or otherwise of the Roman Law of the XII Tables, arguing for its authenticity and criticizing Pais and Lambert. This was his first prepared talk in public, and Gramsci was in the audience. When it was over, the two renewed their acquaintanceship and continued their discussion.' Togliatti recalls the event as: 'The beginning of that long debate with Gramsci which we were to return to so many times, in so many forms, with much more experience and under different circumstances, on the eternal subject of human history, matrix of all that men know or ever will know.'

Those days saw the Italian invasion of Libya: the Italy of the grandiose 'Cinquantenario' celebrations, whose own South was rotten with illiteracy, tuberculosis, corruption, tolerated petty dictatorship, and death from starvation, now attempted to make itself look bigger by occupying an 'underdeveloped' country. Human and material wealth was squandered in a desert. Those who had the sense to resist the patriotic delirium of Corradini and D'Annunzio were derided, as were those who thought that Italy should concentrate on civilizing herself before trying to export civilization to Africa.[4] However well-documented, such ideas were dismissed as defeatist, as revealing what the colonialists contemptuously called the 'stay-at-home' mentality. Such was the climate in which Gramsci and Togliatti began to see more of one another.

'I must say that at that time, as a very young man, his outlook was frankly and proudly pro-Sardinian, even Sardinian nationalist,' states Togliatti. 'He felt very deeply the common resentment of all Sardinians at the wrongs suffered by the island; and for him, too, such resentment turned easily against continentals, and against the Continent itself.' The young Gramsci expressed this feeling in a metaphor:

You must picture Sardinia as a fertile and abundant field, whose fertility is nourished by an underground spring rising from a far-off hill. Suddenly

[4] *Enrico Corradini* (1865–1931): an extreme Italian nationalist who through his review *Il Regno* diffused the conception of Italy as a 'proletarian nation'. *Gabriele D'Annunzio* (1863–1931): poet, novelist, dramatist and aesthete, he was also an exalted exponent of Italian imperialism. (T.N.)

you see that the field's fertility has vanished. Where once there were rich harvests there is now only grass burnt brown by the sun. You look for the cause of the disaster, but you can find it only by looking beyond the limits of your own small field, only by looking as far as the hill the water came from and understanding that kilometres away a wicked egoist has cut off the fertility of your field at its source.

So who was responsible for drying up the spring? Who had condemned Sardinia to backwardness and poverty in this way? As an aid to understanding the full force of the image, it may help to recall the wording of an appeal sent in 1925 by the 'Krestintern' (or Peasant International) to a Sardinian Nationalist Conference at Macomer. Although written mainly by Ruggero Grieco, the inspiration for it came from Gramsci. It claims that:

> Sardinia . . . is one of the relatively rich parts of Italy. . . . It has many and varied mineral resources, iron, silver-bearing lead, copper, antimony, and lithographic stone. It has about a quarter of Italy's pasture-land. Its fishing industry could be a great source of prosperity for the people, so could the cork industry and the salt pans. . . . The people of Sardinia therefore have the economic basis for a reasonable prosperity within their own territory.

This picture is not without some exaggeration. It reflects Gramsci's convictions at this time: deeply impressed by the misery of both the peasant masses and the middle strata of the island's population, he was naturally wondering – who had choked the spring? During his early days in Turin, the Sardinian student gave the answer which island experience had matured within him. 'He used to believe that salvation for Sardinia lay in a struggle against the Continent and the continentals, for her own freedom, her own well-being and progress,' wrote Togliatti.

However, this nationalistic feeling was clearly tempered by socialist tendencies, from very early on. It is Togliatti, again, who recalls: 'When Antonio Gramsci came over from Sardinia he was already a socialist. That he was so, perhaps, is better explained by a Sardinian instinct of rebellion, and the sort of humanitarianism common to young intellectuals from the provinces, rather than by familiarity with any system of ideas.' There was certainly little in the young student's socialism which corresponded to the socialist ideas in vogue around him, still ideologically close to positivist philosophy. Later, he was to write:

> The ideology diffused everywhere among the northern masses by bourgeois propagandists is very familiar: The Mezzogiorno is nothing but a ball-and-

chain impeding the more rapid and civilized development of Italy; southerners are biologically inferior, naturally destined to be barbarians or semi-barbarians; if the South is backward, this is not the fault of the capitalist system or any other historical factor, it is caused by the southern nature, which makes them all slackers, incompetents, criminals, savages – except for the explosion now and then of individual geniuses, who temper this cruel destiny like solitary palm-trees in an arid and sterile desert. The Socialist Party was the main vehicle for diffusing this bourgeois ideology among the workers of the North.

Or again:

The average northern Italian believed that if the Mezzogiorno had failed to progress after being liberated from the shackles of the old Bourbon regime, this must be due not to external causes, not to objective economic and political conditions, but rather to the innate, internal incapacity of the southerners . . . to their organic or biological inferiority, their native barbarism. Such ideas were not only widely accepted, but actually cultivated and given theoretical form by positivist sociologists like Niceforo, Sergi, Ferri, Orano, etc., until they were regarded as scientific *truths*.

A few years before, one of Alfredo Niceforo's books (with a preface by Enrico Ferri) had tried to demonstrate by measuring the craniums of shepherds in the Barbagia district of Sardinia (between Orgòsolo, Orune and Bitti) that this was inevitably a 'zone of delinquency', peopled by men who had sucked in some kind of criminality virus with their mother's milk.

Gramsci's regional patriotism was especially hurt when socialist writers embraced such notions. 'I can say this with complete conviction,' relates Togliatti, 'for it was the subject of our very first conversations together, in the old porch of Turin University, when we arrived from our Sardinian lycées. . . . Gramsci indignantly refuted the current "explanations" put about by hack sociologists who sought the causes of a region's backwardness in "the particular characteristics of its people".' Possibly Gramsci's early distance from the Turin socialist milieu was not unconnected with such facts, for this mileu was at that time mainly absorbed in local, northern issues.

However, there was already something in his general approach which made Angelo Tasca hope he would soon commit himself actively to socialism. One episode reveals this. Towards the end of the first university year, Tasca made Gramsci a present of a French edition of *War and Peace*, and dedicated it with these words: 'To my fellow-

student of today, and my fellow-combatant (I hope) of tomorrow.' It is
dated 11 May 1912.

Gramsci was then studying for his first university examinations. He
was exhausted. On 14 March he wrote home: 'I can't write more, as I
have been feeling unwell for a couple of days, and can neither do anything, nor even think about anything. I can't wait to get away for a
rest, and see whether this wretched headache will get better – it's
tormenting me night and day, it prevents me studying and sleeping, so I
really cannot say that I'm enjoying life at the moment.' He intended to
sit two exams. Later he wrote: 'On 6 July I'm doing the second exam,
then on the 15th I can head for my beloved Sardinia.' But in fact he did
not feel up to doing either of these examinations and put them off until
the autumn.

At home in Ghilarza he was short of money, and thought of earning
some by giving private lessons. His pupil on this occasion, Peppino
Mameli, remembers what happened:

> I had to do my final school exams in Latin and Greek over again, and since
> Nino was back in town for the holidays I took some lessons from him. He
> had an extraordinary gift for teaching. He would put the questions to me –
> always in dialect – and then comment on my answers. His friendly way of
> putting things across made me feel completely at ease. Then after a bit
> we had to give it up. He needed a complete rest, and went off to the
> seaside at Bosa Marina for some time.

In the early autumn of 1912, Gramsci returned to Turin. He changed
addresses, moving nearer the centre to No. 33 Via San Massimo, where
he lodged in the dwelling of an 'embroidery designer', Carlo Gribodo.
His new landlord's profession is on the heading of the paper Gramsci
used for his next letter home: 'I've escaped – no other word for it –
from the place I was in before, because life there had become intolerable, and I've ended up in another house where I'm no better off. So
I'd quit here just as willingly: but to get anything really better I would
have to spend a lot more, and that's impossible.' Via San Massimo runs
across Via Po, and about a hundred yards on the other side stands the
Mole Antonelliana. Angelo Tasca had a mezzanine room at No. 14, on
that same side of the street.

Gramsci did the geography exam on 4 November, and got 30 out of
30; then 27 for the Greek and Latin grammar exam on the 12th; and
finally '*trenta e lode*' (thirty with honours) from Professor Bàrtoli in the
linguistics examination.

He continued to work with Bartoli for a long time after this exam. About two weeks later, he was writing to Teresina and asking her to find out: '. . . if the word *pamentile* exists in the dialect of Logodoro, and if it means *floor*. If the phrase *omine de pore* exists, with the sense of *men of authority*. If the term *su pirone* exists – possibly meaning some part of a scale – and if so, what part? . . . If one says *piscadrici* in the Campidano dialect to mean a fisher-girl, or some kind of sea-bird,' and so on. Months after that, in March 1913, we find him inquiring whether 'Logodoro dialect has the word *pus* with the meaning of *then* (in the sense of 'subsequently') – not *pust* or *pustis*, but just *pus*. . . . Also, does *puschena* exist, and what do *portifale* (arcade?), *poiu* and *poiolu* mean?' He seemed cut out to be a good linguist at this time, and said later that 'one of the biggest intellectual *regrets* of my life is the great grief I caused my old professor at Turin University, Bartoli, who was quite convinced that I was the archangel destined to smite down the neo-grammaticists once and for all.'

In March 1913 Antonio Gramsci was twenty-two and in his second year at the Faculty of Letters. The country was already suffering the consequences of the Libyan expedition: the lower classes naturally suffered most, and the high cost of a war they had not wanted brought about a rapidly spreading malaise. On 19 March, 6,500 car workers went on strike in Turin. Although those who failed to report for work by the 25th were threatened with dismissal, the strike remained solid. Instead of streaming in the gates of Fiat, Spa and Lancia, the workers met every morning in Michelotti Park, on the other side of the Po. Bruno Buozzi and the union leaders would be there, news and information were exchanged, and the day-to-day conduct of the strike was decided on the basis of constant consultation between the rank-and-file and the leadership. 'At first,' says Gino Castagno, 'a little table was borrowed from a nearby inn for the speakers to stand on. Then some enterprising comrades found planks and knocked together a permanent platform in the shelter of a group of large plane trees which looked like a stage backdrop to our meetings.'

April passed, then May. The industrialists continued to refuse the demands, the workers did not weaken, and the great gatherings in Michelotti Park became habitual – while they lasted, perhaps the most striking aspect of the city's social life. Gramsci too was impressed by the phenomenon:

> At certain hours of the morning [relates Togliatti] when we left the class-room and emerged from the quadrangle, walking down towards the Po, we would come across crowds of men very different from ourselves going in the same direction. A whole mass of people was drifting down to the river, and to the parks along its banks. . . . And we would go along with them to where they were going, talking with them and hearing about their struggle. At first sight, they appeared very different from us students – almost like another race. But in reality they were not so different, and not at all another race.

The strike ended successfully on 23 June, after lasting for ninety-six days. Antonio Gramsci was not active in the socialist organizations of the time; but he was not indifferent to what was happening.

His existence was still a lonely one, and plagued by bad health. The holiday period at Ghilarza and Bosa Marina had been of little use to him. Cold, hunger, and the need to follow a strict regime of study if he was not to lose his scholarship – all helped to keep him in a very precarious physical state. Loneliness made things even worse. Kept apart by the deformity which singled him out so sharply, and by an unsociable temperament which made it hard to form friendships, Gramsci still had few ties either in the University or outside it. He saw only one or two fellow students regularly, and would sometimes meet his professor of linguistics, Bartoli, for long discussions about linguistics under the arcades of Corso Vinzaglio, where the professor's house was.

For the rest, he remained isolated, and endured every sort of privation. He never went to shows, or even to cafés. There were only two things which he never gave up: cigarettes and books. Just as he had once sold his provisions at Santulussurgiu in order to buy books, so now, careless of his seventy lire monthly budget, he would go without to obtain the books that interested him. On one occasion, during his second year at university, he purchased a small library of books on Sardinia from the heirs of a certain Marchese di Boyl. It contained Alberto Lamarmora's *Voyage en Sardaigne*, Giuseppe Mannu's *Storia di Sardegna* and his *Storia Moderna di Sardegna dall'anno 1773 al 1799*, as well as 'a big, leather-bound volume (really huge, it weighed at least ten kilos) containing the collected papers of Arborea'.

When he was not absorbed in this or similar reading matter, Gramsci preferred to spend his time at university lectures, often outside his own faculty. Togliatti writes: 'I used to meet him everywhere, wherever there were professors dealing with essential problems in an illuminating way, like Einaudi, or Chironi, or Ruffini. I remember that Gramsci was always there for Francesco Ruffini's famous course on the new conception of Church-State relations, for instance. . . .'

His physical and nervous exhaustion never diminished his intellectual curiosity. But he was rather depressed and cut off from life. For a time he did not reply to letters from home. On 6 May 1913, his mother wrote to him: 'My dearest, this is the fourth time I've sent on letters and postcards, and I'm very upset at being without news of you for so long. I don't know what to think – are you ill perhaps? If you don't answer at once this time, I shall have to inquire through the

College authorities. I'm waiting anxiously.' In July, Gramsci asked the College authorities to take his poor state of health into account, and returned to Ghilarza without sitting the examinations.

There were to be elections that summer, the first since the recent franchise reform. In Sardinia, a free-trade campaign was at its height. It was fostered by the arguments and editorials of such papers as Prezzolini's *La Voce*, Salvemini's *L'Unità*, and *Riforma sociale*. A young Nuoro intellectual, Attilio Deffenu, was trying to give practical expression to this campaign with some form of direct action; he had graduated from Pisa University the year before, with a thesis on 'The Marxist Theory of Capitalist Concentration'. It was at his initiative that a group for anti-protectionist action and propaganda had arisen on the island, and in August a document stating the group's position appeared in certain Sardinian papers and in *La Voce* (No. 35). It was composed by Deffenu and another young journalist, Nicolò Fancello, and was signed by a number of other names: Gino Corradetti, secretary of the railwaymen's union and the Cagliari Chamber of Labour; Massimo Stara, secretary of the Sassari Chamber of Labour (this was the Stara who had been Gramsci's teacher for a few weeks at Santulussurgiu, years before); Giovanni Sanna (later the co-author with Antonio Graziadei of the 'Theses on the Agrarian Question' at the Second Congress of the Communist Party of Italy, in March 1922); Francesco Dore, a future parliamentary deputy; and two young republican lawyers, Pietro Mastino and Michele Saba. The document restated the protest against tariff protectionism, and attributed to its working '. . . arrested development, the growing misery and unemployment of the labouring masses, the high cost of living, the depopulation of the countryside, and emigration. . . . For the sake of certain industries which have shown they do not require protection at all, and certain others which could not even exist or develop without it' – the manifesto continues – 'the economy of the South has been condemned to suffer a slow death.' Especially the Sardinian economy, damaged first of all 'by the high tariffs, which have artificially raised the cost of manufactured goods, machines, and the instruments of production', and then 'hampered in its most profitable forms of trade and export, such as livestock, wine, oil, fruit and cheese', which no longer found an outlet on foreign markets thanks to 'the reprisals of other states against the protectionist policies of our own (as with the closure of the French markets to Sardinian produce)'. Finally, the statement made an appeal for the moral and financial support of all Sardinian progressives in the group's work. Gramsci wrote to *La Voce* from Ghilarza. His name was added to the list of supporters in a later issue of the paper, No. 41, on 9 October 1913. It was the first time that the young Sardinian student had publicly committed himself in a political struggle.

Meanwhile, the electoral battle was raging. Polling day in Sardinia for the island's twelve representatives was 26 October, and for the first time the illiterate were to vote. Hence there had been a precipitous rise in the number of voters in Sardinia: from 42,000 to 178,000, an extra 136,000 who – it was widely expected – would cause nothing less than a political earthquake. 'There was a widespread mystical conviction', writes Gramsci, 'that after the vote everything would be changed utterly, as in a sort of social palingenesis; or so it was in Sardinia, at least.' What was the real situation?

The socialist organizations had been losing ground between the end of 1911 and 1913. They were short of both funds and militants. Some of the most capable leaders, like Giuseppe Cavallera, had left, overcome by discouragement. Even in larger centres like Cagliari, the local Socialist Party section and the Chamber of Labour had had to close down.[1] Given this total vacuum, where until the very eve of the election there was no organization whatever, where no nucleus of political educators had been spreading the new ideas among the illiterate masses, the task of the few enthusiasts who tried to put things right at the last moment was both difficult and complicated. The 'proletarian weekly' *Il Risveglio dell'Isola* ('Island Awakening') had to admit sadly that 'ninety workers out of a hundred listen to us without the faintest understanding of the new message'.

But were the workers always to blame? Did not some some fault lie with the teachers – with their lack of preparation, their remoteness from the popular state of mind, and their reliance on a few weak abstractions? The Sardinian socialism of the time was closer to Podrecca's *L'Asino* than it was to Marx. Its salient characteristic was a crude, bar-room anti-clericalism. *Il Risveglio* said on 6 July 1913, in a piece on an outlaw of the Sàrrabus district: 'Even if Tramatzu was more of a criminal than he is, even if he committed every brutal excess this side of cannibalism, we would still prefer him to the priests.' Two socialists from Domusnovas, Francesco Saba and Giuseppe Onnis, were expelled from the Party, 'one for attending mass, the other for ringing church bells on the St John's Day holiday' (so ran the official pronouncement).

---

[1] Both may have been reactivated with a view to the forthcoming elections by Gino Corradetti, a Sicilian railwayman recently transferred to Sardinia.

Only a minority of leaders had any experience. In the autumn there were to be three socialist candidates: Giuseppe Cavallera (summoned back from his home in Genoa) in the Iglesias constituency, Gino Corradetti in Cagliari, and Massimo Stara in Sassari. Two new figures also came forward for the first time: at Oristano, a reformist called Felice Porcella, and in the Nuoro constituency a progressive Catholic Francesco Dore. How much damage would the wider franchise cause to the old system?

The conservatives were certainly terrified. 'Up to now', Gramsci writes, 'elections had apparently been concerned with very vague issues, since the candidates represented local and personal interests, not national party positions. They were like a cross between elections to a Constituent Assembly and elections for membership of the local hunt club'. There was no trace of argument, as the ideas were bandied about. Votes were simply bought, extorted by intimidation and intrigue, or given as a form of ritual thanks for blessings received. Defamation of character, insinuation and mockery were the usual weapons employed. ('Discovering that a politician was a cuckold explained everything,' comments Gramsci). But now that male suffrage was close to universal, at least a partial change of approach was required. Buying the whole electorate had become rather expensive: it was now four times larger. And after all, the socialists were presenting some sort of political case – however badly – to which some reply was necessary. But what reply? The answer found was fear: a campaign was launched to spread terror of the unknown among the faithful, and among tradesmen and small landholders (who were conscious of being proprietors, however tiny their property).

So a certain real clarification of issues was produced. For many years conservative and populist papers alike, embittered politicians kept out of governments in Rome and local administrators kept short of funds, big landowners angry at high taxation, and workers and peasants oppressed by starvation wages and cost inflation, had all found common ground in Sardinian regionalism. Few had noticed how divergent the real motives behind this protest were, and none had drawn the proper inferences from this divergence. Popular desperation and the spite and vendettas of the ruling class were hopelessly mixed up in the continual, blind assault on government as such. The electoral début of the lower orders, however, began at last to create a watershed separating these different interests from one another, and this was the significance of the 1913 elections. The conservatives stood on one side, workers on the other: the old equivocation of the 'common struggle' for Sardinia dropped away, and confusion was no longer possible.

The Sardinian property-owning class changed targets very swiftly indeed. It now found itself in surprising harmony with Rome, and the socialist organizations became the enemy. Previously it had harnessed popular moods and movements – even supporting trade union actions – in its struggle against inconsiderate central government. Now things were suddenly turned upside down: it was quite happy to use the power, the agents, and the money of central government in a battle against the organized vanguard of the lower classes. The myth of Sardinianism had served its purpose and could be cast aside. Now new topics suddenly filled the pages of the ruling class papers: the youthful martyrs of the Libyan war – sent there to die by the ruling class itself – and unconditional support for rises in the military budget; applause for whoever shot down workers on strike, anywhere; wage claims, depicted as attempts to subvert the 'peaceful accord of capital and labour'; and the vast rivers, the indescribable floods of money which a well-intentioned and friendly government now intended to spend on public works in Sardinia.

The anti-socialist forces gathered round the establishment candidates. At Iglesias, where it looked as if Giuseppe Cavallera might win, the mining company candidate Erminio Ferraris withdrew in favour of Giuseppe Sanna Randaccio to avoid splitting the right-wing vote (in spite of the latter's record of anti-clericalism, the curia obligingly withdrew its *non expedit* against him). During the election campaign in the mining region, voicing any other opinion than the boss's involved risking one's job. Organization became an offence in itself. At Montepone, for instance, nineteen carters out of twenty-four asked for some reduction in the sixteen-hour day, and a rise in their wages (2 lire 60 a day). Although they belonged to no outside organization, the simple fact that the nineteen had signed a written request allowed them to be defined as a 'conspiracy' and the 'chief conspirator' (the first name on the list) was sacked as an example. Everywhere, the struggle took place against a background of such intransigence by the owners. The press and the police openly supported the government candidates. Simply because a socialist was mayor, the local Council at Serramanna was dissolved by official decree. According to the socialist weekly: 'The charges made against our comrade Corradetti are innumerable: he stands accused of inciting class hatred, of instigating civil war, of public defamation of institutions, and of lese-majesty. . . . Every single issue of the *Risveglio* is accused of something or other.' So economic power, the police, the law, and all other available groups capable of exerting pressure were mobilized to the full behind the men of the right.

Nevertheless, they were not entirely successful. New things did happen. Cavallera won in the Iglesias constituency, Porcella won at Oristano, and Francesco Dore at Nuoro. And the whole experience was a decisive one for Antonio Gramsci's political development. He wrote a long letter at the time to his friend and fellow student Angelo Tasca:

> He had been very impressed [says Tasca] by the utter change caused by the participation of the peasant masses in the election, even though they had not known how to make proper use of their new weapon. It was this experience, and his own reflection on it, that finally made Gramsci into a socialist. When he returned to Turin at the start of the following session, I had fresh evidence of just how decisive these events had been for him.

The 1913 elections had made clear to Gramsci the ambiguity of the old Sardinian protest movement and the slogans which he had himself echoed in previous years, like 'National Independence for the Region' and 'Continentals go home!' It was still true that 'kilometres away a wicked egoist has cut off at its source' the fertility of Sardinia. But who was he? Who had in fact choked the well, and condemned the island to backwardness? Was it really the whole Continent?

Now, he began to see clearly that the real oppressors of the southern peasants, of the smallholders and the lower middle classes of his island, were not the workers and industrialists of the North, but a combination of the industrialists with the indigenous Sardinian or southern ruling class as a whole. The evil was also at home, and far removed from the industrial proletariat which he had seen on strike in Turin for ninety-six days earlier that year.

From this time, recalls Tasca, 'Gramsci's links with the socialist movement were mainly with the Young Socialists of the Turin central Fascio.'

When his third university year began in November 1913, Gramsci still had to sit all the examinations for his previous year. He moved again, to No. 14 on the same street, Via San Massimo – the same block of flats as Angelo Tasca lived in. The widowed mother of a student friend, Camillo Berra, had decided to let a room. There is a large central courtyard with a covered gallery on all four sides, and two entrances onto Via San Massimo and Piazza Carlina. Gramsci went to live on the top storey, and was to remain there as Signora Berra's only lodger for nearly nine years, until his trip to Russia in May 1922.

He found study difficult. He had failed again to recover from his chronic mental overstrain during the holidays. What he really needed was a complete change of life – a different diet, some medical attention, and absolute quiet. But without ample funds this was unthinkable. In any case, a prolonged rest and further postponement of the examinations until he was recovered would have entailed the loss of his scholarship, which he could not contemplate either. His father already found it hard to send him occasional small sums to supplement his grant, at the cost of never-ending sacrifices by everyone in the family, and still could not hope to be Antonio's sole support at university. At home, Mario had enrolled in the army cycle corps in December 1911, Carlo was still only sixteen, too young for a regular job, and Gennaro – still at the Marzullo brothers' ice factory in Cagliari – was the only one who could help out a little. Signor Ciccillo continued to support four children on his modest clerk's wages. The loss of the College scholarship would be a disaster, and to avert it Antonio was forced to sit the examinations.

He was very determined; but will-power was no longer enough. He wrote to his father:

> I write to you feeling nothing but rage and utter despair: this has been a day I shall remember for a very long time, and unfortunately it's not over yet. It's useless. I've been working feverishly for about a month and harder than ever these last few days, but now – after a fearful crisis – I have simply

had to make a decision. I do not wish to get myself into an even worse state; and I do not wish to throw away altogether what I'm still hanging on to. I will not sit the exams – because I'm half crazy, or half stupid, or completely stupid – I don't know which – I won't sit the exams in order to be thrown out altogether and completely ruined. . . . Dear Dad, after a whole month's most intensive study I've only managed to make myself dizzy with fatigue and get my old headaches back, more excruciating than ever, and in addition a kind of cerebral anaemia which blots out my memory and ravages my brain, and makes me feel positively insane. I can't get away from it and find peace anywhere, neither walking nor lying on the bed nor (as I do sometimes) rolling to and fro on the floor like a maniac. . . . My landlady called a doctor yesterday, and he gave me an injection of tranquillizer. Today I'm taking opium, but am still shaking all over, and still obsessed by the utter ruin now staring me in the face. A friend has persuaded me I should try to present a medical certificate to obtain exemption: possibly the Professorial Board might agree to let me continue on the scholarship, and take the exams next March.

He did so, and the College accepted the request. The College Board considered his case in their session of 19 February 1914. The minutes (published in 1957 by Zucàro) record that: 'Gramsci Antonio has not been able to sit examinations because of serious illness, as confirmed in a medical certificate from Dr Allasia, which states that Signor Gramsci is suffering from acute neurosis. . . . This student has conveyed his willingness to make up the lost ground by retaking the autumn examinations in March.' An 'acute neurosis' might seem ample justification for failing to sit exams. However, Dr Allasia's certificate did not bring Gramsci the full forgiveness of the Carlo Alberto College. He was to be punished by 'temporary loss of grant, until such time as he should recover his right to the full amount by passing the previously omitted examinations in Greek, modern history (biennial), and another subject of his own choice'.

So, at the very moment that he needed rest most urgently, he was forced to plunge back into work, under conditions rendered even more harsh than before by the loss of his grant money. His father had written to him in November, saying: 'I must urge you to take things a little easier, as overwork is the principal cause of your illness; remember that you are far away from us, and that none of us can come and keep you company.'

Somehow or other – with another great effort of will – Antonio overcame this hurdle. On 28 March 1914 he took the moral philosophy examination, and passed with 25 out of 30; on 2 April he did the modern history exam (27 out of 30). When the Board of Directors met again on 4 April, he still had one exam to sit. Gramsci asked them to renew his scholarship immediately after the third examination, without waiting for their next meeting, and they agreed. On the 18th, he got 24 in the Greek examination, thus reacquiring the right to his full bounty of seventy lire per month. But the extreme effort and suffering of the preceding months had left another deep mark on him. Towards the end of 1915, we find him writing to his sister Grazietta: 'I have had my headache every single day for at least three years now, and always at least one spell of dizziness or vertigo.'

This period of intensive application had also cut him off to some extent from his few friends in the city. After the exams were over, Antonio took to seeing Tasca and Togliatti again, and now spent more time with them. Another student had joined the group in the meantime: Umberto Terracini. He had just enrolled as a law student, and was younger than the others (Gramsci was 23, Tasca was 22, Togliatti was 21, and Terracini was 19). Five years later, after the war, these four would find themselves together again on the editorial board of *L'Ordine Nuovo*. But at the moment only Tasca and Terracini were regularly involved in politics as members of the Young Socialist 'Fascio'. Though he was less involved – like Togliatti, whom Tasca describes as 'more taken up with his studies' – Gramsci felt close to the position of his two near-contemporaries. They had much in common: a keen interest in Croce, for his anti-positivist and anti-metaphysical stance; in Salvemini, who was carrying on his battle against the 'corporative' deviations of northern socialism; and in the youthful revolutionary editor of the socialist daily *Avanti!*, Benito Mussolini.[1]

It is difficult to say whether Gramsci was already a member of the Partito Socialista Italiano (PSI) before 1914, as there is no solid evidence. In April 1964 Togliatti stated in a letter to Alfonso Leonetti:

> As you know, I met Antonio in the autumn of 1911, at the University. For months and months we did nothing but meet and discuss – you remember well what he was like. From all these talks it was quite clear, beyond any

---

[1] Croce defined Mussolini as follows: 'A man of decided revolutionary temperament – which the Italian socialists were not – and considerable acumen, who took over from Marxism its rigidity and intransigence but did not attempt the vain enterprise of reviving socialism in its old form. Instead, with youthful openness to contemporary trends, he endeavoured to instil a new soul into it by adopting Sorel's theory of violence, Bergson's intuitionism, pragmatism, the mystique of action, plus all the voluntarism which was in the intellectual air at that time, and which many thought was idealism – so that he too was called, and willingly referred to himself, as an "idealist".'

possible doubt, that he already had firm socialist convictions. These convictions went back to his Cagliari period, when Gramsci had been in contact with the Chamber of Labour there. What I am not clear about is the year in which he first acquired a PSI party card. . . . I did so in 1914; but Gramsci already had one at that time.

Whatever may be thought of this, there are certainly good grounds for seeing this period as the one where a 'new' Gramsci was born, Gramsci as a 'national' figure. It remains for us to chart the contours of this intellectual turning-point, and of his philosophical evolution towards Marxism. Marcella and Maurizio Ferrara have written:

> The final abandonment of positivism was soon accomplished by both Gramsci and Togliatti. . . . The one sure reference point which remained for them was the work of Antonio Labriola. And his attempts at the explanation and further development of Marxism were at this time read and re-read, studied closely and commented on: works like *In memoria del Manifesto dei comunisti* ['In Memory of the Communist Manifesto'], *Saggi intorno alla concezione materialistica della storia* ['Essays on the Materialistic Conception of History'], and *Discorrendo di socialismo e di filosofia* ['Talks on Socialism and Philosophy]'.

But this was probably not so, at least before the war. It looks very much as if the authors may be attributing to the two young students readings which they only came to later on. The doubt arises from one simple fact: in all his early writings, Gramsci refers to Labriola only *once* (in 1918).

Another memoir of the period has come from Annibale Pastore, the professor of Theoretical Philosophy at Turin. We learn that Professor Bartoli introduced Gramsci to him with the words: 'Give him lots of philosophy, he deserves it. You'll see, he will be somebody some day. He wants to find out more about Marx.' That year (1914–15, Gramsci's fourth year in the Faculty) Pastore was giving a course on the critical interpretation of Marxism. In it he went beyond the conception of Hegelian dialectic as 'fixed in an eternal trichotomy of thesis, antithesis and synthesis', with an 'original discovery' of his own: 'the incubation of material conditions in the womb of existing society, seen as the point of disruption between thesis and antithesis'. Pastore goes on:

> Gramsci grasped the originality of the notion at once, and saw it as a new and critical insight into the meaning of crisis and revolution. He had been a Crocean originally, but was now very restless, without knowing how or why he had to break away. . . . He wanted to understand how culture

developed, for revolutionary reasons: the ultimately practical significance of theoretical life. He wanted to find out how thinking can lead to actions (the technique of propaganda), how a thought can make peoples' hands move, and how and in what sense ideas themselves may be actions. These were the first of my sallies to impress him.... Another very important thing which drew him towards me was my emphasis on experimental logic, on technical innovation, on the transition from *homo sapiens* to *homo faber*, that is, from the logician to the engineer, to the technician, the mechanic, the worker who controls a machine: from mental labour to manual labour. In short, like the outstanding pragmatist he was, Gramsci was concerned above all else at this time to understand *how ideas become practical forces.*

Did Gramsci subsequently forget all about this teacher, who had even given him private lessons? In his articles and notes, and in the prison letters, we often find affectionate references to other professors he had been close to in his time at university, like Bàrtoli or Cosmo; but never to Annibale Pastore, whose lessons may have influenced Gramsci's Marxist evolution somewhat less strongly than the above quotation suggests, or at any rate less immediately and directly. In 1917, the paper *La Città futura* was to show to what extent Gramsci had remained influenced by Croce's historical idealism. It appears therefore that a number of assessments have somewhat accelerated Gramsci's Marxist formation, and predated cultural experiences that belong more properly to his maturity, or at least to a considerably later period.

As far as his university years are concerned, it seems likely that Gramsci's ideas evolved – and transformed the 'Sardinian' Gramsci into a 'national' figure – without any very marked hiatus. Piero Gobetti described him as a man 'come from the countryside to forget tradition, to get rid of the sick, anachronistic heritage of his island and replace it with a single-minded, inexorable drive towards modernity'.[2] He saw the very physical presence of Gramsci as 'the symbol of a rural life renounced for ever, and of the forceful, almost violent imposition of a programme founded on and animated by desperation, by the spiritual hunger of someone who has defeated and betrayed his native innocence'.

But this was not an accurate assessment either. The fact is that Gramsci was alone among intellectuals in a comparable situation

---

[2] *Piero Gobetti* (1901–26): Left-wing liberal and anti-fascist, editor of the brilliant Turin weekly *La Rivoluzione liberale* after the war. He died in France in 1926, from injuries received at the hands of the fascists. (T.N.)

precisely in *refusing* the usual alternatives: that is, either to remain cocooned in regional experience which – however vital – remains limiting when not related to a wider perspective (like Deledda or Satta), or on the other hand to escape from a regional background by assimilating the new way of life *en bloc* and making it the tombstone of one's native experience and sensibility (like Salvatore Farina[3]). Gramsci refused either to shelter within the Sardinian nationalism of his youth, or to let himself be converted passively to the ideology and political outlook of the northern working class – an outlook corrupted at that time by corporative notions no less questionable than the ones prevalent in his isolated homeland. He certainly felt the impulse – as he wrote – to 'overcome the backward way of living and thinking typical of a Sardinian of the early twentieth century, and acquire a way of living and thinking which was national, rather than regional and village-like'. But at the same time he perceived clearly that 'one of the great needs of Italian culture is to overcome the provincialism reigning even within its most advanced and modern urban centres'.

So Gramsci became a socialist without burying his own past. While his socialist viewpoint made him aware of the ambiguity, limits and weaknesses of certain forms assumed by the Sardinian protest movement, so his Sardinian background made him quite naturally conscious of the ideological defects in a working-class movement inclined to see the Mezzogiorno as a 'ball and chain' obstructing civilized progress. Socialism brought him new answers to the questions posed by his early island experience; but, as a Sardinian, he refused to separate the rural problem from the problem of the socialist revolution. 'It was a question,' he writes, 'of leading the workers to overcome their inverted provincialism with its "ball and chain" ideas, deeply rooted in the socialist movement's reformist and corporative traditions.' Tasca and the other avid readers of *La Voce* and Salvemini's *L'Unità* among the militants of the 'Fascio' understood the argument well enough. Tasca wrote: 'Gramsci was a warm champion of the importance of the southern question in socialist politics. We shared his view, and like him made this one of the key points in the political changes we were working for.'

The chance to test the local P S I's openness to such new ideas soon presented itself. As a result of the death of Pilade Gay, the Turin

[3] *Salvatore Farina* (1846-1918): a middle-class novelist, born in Sassari, who spent most of his life on the mainland. (T.N.)

parliamentary constituency of Borgo San Paolo fell vacant, and it was necessary to choose a new socialist candidate. The young militants had the idea of offering the candidature to Gaetano Salvemini. In October 1913 Salvemini had been defeated in the southern constituency of Molfetta-Bitonto by a mixture of violence and chicanery on the part of Giolitti's government.[4] This new move would be a way of affirming the solidarity of the Turin workers with the Puglia peasants deprived of their proper parliamentary representative. With Ottavio Pastore, secretary of the Turin PSI, Angelo Tasca led a debate on this topic in the café-bar of the Casa del Popolo. A formal motion was approved by the local party's executive (which had a large left-wing majority) and the offer was sent to Salvemini, who turned it down. Ottavio Pastore has said that at the time 'Gramsci had not yet begun to be particularly active in the Party'. Nevertheless, the approach to Salvemini must go on record as the Sardinian student's first political initiative in Turin; it was proposed, Gramsci himself recalled, 'by a group which included among its number the future editors of *L'Ordine nuovo*'. The proposal was brought to fruition by private discussion and argument, rather than in the party's public debates. But this does not alter the substantial novelty of the trend which had begun to emerge from Turin, through the efforts of (among others) an obscure young militant of twenty-three who had only recently joined the Party, and was already searching with these others for an original political road to travel.

His circle of friends grew larger. 'We often had occasion to discuss with student friends, in the University porticos', says Tasca, 'but our world, the world into which Gramsci now entered, was composed much more of young office employees and workers, with whom we used to wander about for hours in the evenings, exchanging ideas and giving free rein to all our hopes and enthusiasms, once we had come out of the Casa del Popolo in Via Siccardi.' It was a time for new enthusiasms. Gramsci too offers a description:

> Groups of us would often leave party meetings, and cluster round whoever was the leader of the moment, to pass through the streets of a now silent city, where only a few night people stopped to peer at us. We used to forget ourselves completely, still overflowing with impassioned feelings,

---

[4] Giolitti the great 'liberal' was also the greatest exponent of southern Italian political 'management.' (T.N.)

and the talk would be punctuated with outrageous suggestions, great gales of laughter, and wild gallops into the realm of the impossible, into the world of dreams.

Europe was moving steadily towards catastrophe. On 28 July 1914, four days before the 'useless slaughter' started, the Socialist Party's national leadership and parliamentary group joined in demanding that Italy be 'absolutely neutral'; and Italian neutrality was in fact declared, on 4 August.

However, a lively debate very soon arose among the socialists as to the exact meaning to be given to such neutrality. There was much uncertainty and it is difficult to decide in retrospect whether this derived from *Avanti!* and its editor, Mussolini, or whether the vacillations of *Avanti!* merely echoed the conflicting sentiments there already. The fact was that while many socialists happily accepted an interpretation of the war as essentially a clash of rival imperialist groups, they were nevertheless inclined to look more favourably on republican France and invaded Belgium than on the absolutist 'Central Empires'. On 18 October *Avanti!* published a long article by Mussolini himself, entitled 'From Absolute Neutrality to Active, Meaningful Neutrality'. Reactions were varied, and discordant. In the Turin socialist paper *Il Grido del Popolo* ('Cry of the People'), Angelo Tasca replied to Mussolini on 24 October, and emphasized the need for Italy to stay 'absolutely' neutral. But for some years now *Avanti's* editor had had a considerable following. 'We young people were all enthusiastic about Mussolini,' writes Mario Montagnana, 'partly because he was relatively young, like ourselves, and partly because he had routed the reformists and his *Avanti!* articles appeared strong revolutionary stuff to us.'

Gramsci contributed to the argument with an article in *Il Grido del Popolo* on 31 October (his first published political writing). According to Marcella and Maurizio Ferrara, he 'showed it before publication to Togliatti, who agreed with what he said'. Its title was 'Neutralità attiva ed operante' ('Active, Meaningful Neutrality'), referring back to Mussolini's slogan. However, the intention behind the words was obviously a different one – as the ultimately opposed attitudes of the two men towards the war showed well enough. The young student's argument was aimed chiefly at the reformists. 'They say they are unwilling to *gamble* with war, but they are content to let others gamble, and win. They would like the proletariat to remain an impartial spectator of the events, on the assumption that events work for it – while the adversary, meantime, makes events work for him and actively prepares the terrain for the class struggle.' How can the adversary be checked? Gramsci believed that the revolutionaries should set themselves the task of preparing the conditions most favourable for the decisive social 'dislocation' (or revolution), by exerting a continuous series of pressures upon the various active and passive forces of society. And if the Italian bourgeoisie felt summoned to the war by *its* destiny – here then would be the occasion for another such series of 'wrenches', leading up to the final one:

> So Mussolini is not calling for embraces all round, for a fusion of all parties in national unanimity, since this would be an anti-socialist position. ... Neither does his position exclude the proletariat from seizing public power and getting rid of the ruling class, should the latter falter or show itself to be impotent.

To his interpretation of Mussolini's attitude Gramsci added a prudent footnote: '... if, that is, I have correctly interpreted his somewhat incoherent statements, and developed them along the same lines as he would have done himself.' Later, Gramsci would find it difficult to escape from the accusation of being a war 'interventionist' on the strength of this article: it was consistently interpreted in this light by sectarians.

Once again, he turned to a more solitary existence. In his physical condition, intense activity always had to be paid for by the aggravation of all his ailments. And now he was working for a living, as well as pursuing his studies and engaging in politics. He gave private lessons.[5] In the autumn examination session of his third year he was only able to sit one exam: the biennial test on the literatures of the Romance languages, held on 11 November 1914. He ought to have taken the examinations in Italian literature, Latin, and Sanskrit, in order to satisfy the conditions of his scholarship. When he failed to do so, we learn from the minutes of the College Board at its session of 19 December that 'Professor Bartoli has submitted a statement to the

---

[5] Six years later, in an argument with his professor of Italian literature, Umberto Cosmo – who had described his former pupils as 'pleasure-loving, carefree scholars' – Gramsci wrote: 'He knows very well, since he himself once helped one of them through times of acute financial worry, that these socialist pupils of his lived on grants of seventy lire a month, he knows that if his socialist pupils wanted to acquire books they were forced to scurry from one side of town to another giving private lessons, which he helped them find, because in those days the "master" was fond of his pupils. ...'

Board, to the effect that this student is subject to periodic nervous crises which prevent him from pursuing his studies with proper alacrity'. The Board punished such lack of alacrity by withdrawing Gramsci's scholarship for four months.

There followed a difficult time. Gramsci no longer went to the Casa del Popolo, and ceased writing in *Il Grido*. This isolation plus the severe mental drudgery of his work provoked a further deterioration in his health. He commented later to his sister Grazietta: 'I worked too much perhaps, more than I was really capable of doing.... I worked in order to live, while in order to live I should really have taken a rest, I should have had a good time. In two years, I don't think I either laughed or cried once. I attempted to conquer physical weakness through work, and only made myself weaker than before.'

He was also less close to his family. 'I did not write to my mother for some years, at least two years running, and learned also that it could be painful not to receive letters.' Sardinia, the scenes of his childhood, his family in Ghilarza – little by little they were fading into the background, remote from his present travail. He was forgetting his affectionate arguments with his mother, as when she insisted that putting a little barley in coffee makes it more refreshing, and he would protest, 'But I don't want to be refreshed, I just want coffee!' He rarely thought now of his days watching hedgehogs in the Tirso valley, or of how he had once raised tortoises, falcons and larks, and made sailboats with Luciano, the chemist's son. Nowadays, his head was 'forever filled with pain'.

Still, he did not give up. He stuck to his studies, because it was demanded of him, but also because he demanded it of himself. On 13 April 1915 he took the third-year examination in Italian literature. It was to be the last examination he would ever take: his 'university apprenticeship' was broken off at this point.

He was still in Turin on Monday, 17 May, one week before Italy entered the war, when the city's working class districts rose up in protest at the forthcoming intervention. There was a general strike, and in Via Cernaia and the surrounding streets demonstrators clashed with squadrons of cavalry. A young joiner called Carlo Dezzani was killed by revolver fire. The army broke into the Casa del Popolo and occupied it. Gramsci followed these events, but (as far as we know) did not participate.

Then at last, very slowly, he began to emerge from his deep depression. On 13 November 1915, more than a year after his article on the neutrality question, he published another piece in *Il Grido del Popolo*. It referred to the meeting which had been held in the little Swiss town of Zimmerwald two months before, when representatives had gathered from those European socialist parties still opposed to the war, to reiterate their opposition. *Avanti!* had published the declaration issued from this conference on 14 October, and for the first time thousands of Italian socialist militants saw in print the name of one of the signatories: Lenin. However, this was not the main point of Gramsci's article, which was to comment on the recent Tenth Congress of the Spanish Socialist Party which, it appeared to the young writer, had demonstrated that 'there is still some purely socialist activity going on in Europe':

> For us, small movements can appear great because we relate them to those others which we alone feel, because we are living them, we are them. . . . We feel ourselves to be the molecules of a world in gestation, we feel this great tide rising up slowly but inexorably, the solid cohesion of the infinitude of drops composing it; we feel that in this awareness the International is truly alive.

Towards the end of 1915, writing to his family again after a long period of silence, Gramsci was able to see his time of tribulation as an episode now drawing to a close:

> I should never have detached myself so far from life in the way I did. I've lived right out of this world for a couple of years: it was like a long dream. I allowed all the links which bound me to the world of men to snap off, one by one. I lived entirely by the brain, and not at all by the heart . . . not only as far as you were concerned. . . . It was as if the whole of humanity had ceased to exist for me, and I was a wolf alone in its den.

Now that these sufferings were largely over, the young Gramsci – now twenty-five – slowly reacquired his appetite for living, for political discussion and journalistic work. Articles began to appear in the page *Avanti!* devoted to Turin affairs, and he also wrote regularly for *Il Grido*. In the latter, his pieces included a moving recollection of Renato Serra, a young critic who had been killed in the battles on the Podgora river some months before. Gramsci drew a connexion between Serra and Francesco De Sanctis, 'the greatest European literary critic'.

His return to political work was even more of a turning-point. He had not yet made the decision to give up his university career. But other interests were now eclipsing his academic ones. Socialism came more and more to be the answer to all problems, even to the personal ones which had so greatly harassed him. In fact it was now, at some point between the end of 1915 and early in 1916, that Gramsci the 'professional revolutionary' was born.

He wrote home at this time: 'My life is made miserable only by this feeling I always have of not being able to conquer my weakness, and so not being able to do enough work to both make a living and remain free to work for myself, for my own future, instead of just getting by from one day to the next. If only I always felt well, I tell you I could earn as much as five hundred lire a month. What hurts me is being always on my own, having always to trust others, and live in restaurants, where one spends so much for so very little.' He could have had someone come from Ghilarza to live with him, but was not sure enough of his continued health and earning-power for this. 'Can I undertake the responsibility of making others suffer too? This is the thought which has always stopped me mentioning the possibility of one of you coming to Turin. But now I feel that I really must decide, for I can't go on in this precarious way much longer. I'll write to Mario and see what he wants to do.'

Mario had gone to the war, and Gennaro and Carlo were soon to follow him. Signor Ciccillo and Signora Peppina were left alone with their daughters in Ghilarza. *Tia* Peppina kept on repeating: 'They're going to butcher my boys.' Antonio noted 'how very much more expressive the phrase is in Sardinian than in Italian. She would say "fàghere a pezza" – "pezza" is the name for butcher's meat cut up for sale in a shop, as opposed to "carre", the usual word for human flesh.'

From early 1916 on, much of Antonio Gramsci's life was spent in the Casa del Popolo building owned by the Turin Co-operative Alliance in what was then Via Siccardi (today renamed Corso Galileo Ferraris). Inside the Casa there were the offices of the Associazione Generale Operaio (General Workers' Association), and those of the Railwaymen's Co-operative, the Chamber of Labour, and a number of different unions. There was also a well-equipped dispensary, and on the ground floor a large and very popular café-bar. The Peoples' Theatre once alongside it had been destroyed by police action in May 1915. On the top floor were three small rooms: one was the office of *Il Grido del Popolo*, edited by Giuseppe Bianchi until he was called up later in 1916, and after that by Maria Giudice, a primary school teacher and mother of eight children; another held the office of the Piedmont edition of *Avanti!* (printed in Milan), run by Ottavio Pastore; and in the third was the local headquarters of the PSI, with the Young Socialist Fascio in a still smaller room beside it. Three people looked after *Avanti!*: Pastore, Gramsci, and an ex-waiter called Leo Galetto, a strange, not uncharacteristic journalist given to picturesque wide-brimmed hats and florid cravats.

A new writer now emerged on the pages of these papers, a writer radically different from any known to past readers of the socialist press. Gramsci's name scarcely ever appeared beneath the brief essays and cultural notes, or the short leader-articles commenting on crimes, conferences and shows, which both *Il Grido* and *Avanti!* now published regularly. 'Timidity always forced Gramsci to live impersonally,' Pier Paolo Pasolini has said. If he was referring to this habit of never signing his name, timidity had nothing to do with it. It arose out of scientific disinterest and a repugnance for external show, out of a love of ideas in their own right: Gramsci's aversion to idolatry extended to the cult of names. At the most, one might occasionally see the initials 'A.G.' under his articles, or the pseudonym derived from them, 'Alfa Gamma'. Only a very select circle of readers knew the real name of the new writer. Two and a half years later, in July 1918, when *La Stampa* published a gleeful account of the trial of those involved in the previous summer's uprising, he was called 'Granischi Antonio'. The *Gazzetta del Popolo* knew him as 'Antonio Granci'.

Obscure the name may have been, but many readers grasped the essential novelty of his articles in relation to the prevailing conventions of left-wing journalism. Giuseppe Bianchi had founded a column of Turin news in *Avanti!* under the heading 'Sotto la Mole' ('Under the Mole' – the huge 'Mole Antonelliana', a dome which dominates the Turin skyline). It had been put together by Bianchi himself, or by Pastore and others. When Gramsci took it over, its tone changed abruptly for the better. The notes and comments became satirical gems, showing a marked talent for polemical pamphleteering, all the more remarkable in a country where there was no tradition of pamphlet-journalism. The new style which distinguished them was just as striking: his theatre reviews, no less than his more theoretical pieces, contrasted forcibly with the rhetorical pomposity of the older writers, thanks to the classical purity of his language and his taste for rational argument. His underlying coherence was such that the reader easily saw the link between different topics apparently remote from one another, and how they fitted into a continuing argument. The main-spring of this argument was Gramsci's double conviction that theory which could not be translated into terms of fact was useless abstraction, and that political action not illumined by theory was impulsive and fruitless. It is already possible to see the beginnings of Gramsci's characteristic method – later called 'obstetric' or 'Socratic' – which envisaged mass education as a process of question and answer, rather than of inflammatory harangues from a platform. 'An understanding of the cultural and psychological traits of the leadership of the Turin communist movement necessitates going back to the history of socialist journalism during the war years,' Gobetti said later. Gramsci was the great exemplar of this new socialist journalism, and almost its sole representative during the war.

The most politically active of the 'culturist' group, Tasca, had been called up at the very beginning of the war. So had Togliatti, who was declared unfit for active service, but subsequently volunteered to join the army medical corps. His political activity to date had in any case been slight: some have held that he was not even a member of the Socialist Party before the war started – others, that he left the Party after volunteering for service, and only rejoined again in 1919. Umberto

Terracini, the last of the group, was arrested in September 1916 for distributing pacifist propaganda at Trino Vercellese: he got off lightly with a suspended sentence of one month, but could not avoid being called up. After his training he was refused officer rank for political reasons and ended up as a private on the front line at Montebelluna. Gramsci was left on his own.

The simplistic journalistic populism with which he had to come to terms is very well conveyed by the words of Maria Giudice: '*Il Grido* is still not simple enough, not easy enough, not clear enough. . . . We are more used to reading from the book of life than from books of theory. . . . We know that the masses feel and act not according to how they think or reason, but according to how they feel; when they feel socialist they will act as socialists, *without* all these theories. . . .' This was only another version of Bordiga's refrain: 'Socialists are not made by education, but by the real necessities of the class they belong to.' The older socialist movement in Turin was wholly dominated by ideas like these, until the new generation appeared on the scene. Gramsci refused to let himself be influenced, even while working under the editorial direction of Maria Giudice: he remained a complete *franc-tireur*.

Thus, early in 1916, we find him stressing the necessity of links between revolutionary and cultural activity:

Man is above all else mind, consciousness – that is, he is a product of history, not of nature. There is no other way of explaining why socialism has not come into existence already, although there have always been exploiters and exploited, creators of wealth and selfish consumers of wealth. Man has only been able to acquire a sense of his worth bit by bit, in one sector of society after another. . . . And such awareness was not generated out of brute physiological needs, but out of intelligent reasoning, first of all by a few and later on by entire social classes who preceived the causes of certain social facts and understood that there might be ways of converting the structure of repression into one of rebellion and social reconstruction. This means that every revolution has been preceded by an intense labour of social criticism, of cultural penetration and diffusion.

He concluded with the example of the French Revolution, for which the Enlightenment had paved the way. The ambition of the youthful assistant editor of *Il Grido* and *Avanti!* was to be a source of the culture which the proletariat needed in order to acquire a real awareness of its function in history. From the very outset, whatever his subject,

Gramsci saw himself in this role, and so repeatedly evoked the experience of the Enlightenment with almost missionary zeal, updating the content of that experience to harmonize with the changed ideals of modern proletarian revolution.

Of his work as a theatre critic (he had begun to write on theatre at the age of twenty-five), he was able to say years later, in one of his letters to Tatiana: 'Did you know that I discovered and helped Pirandello's theatre to success, long before Adriano Tilgher? I wrote enough about Pirandello . . . to make a book of two hundred pages, and in those days what I said was really new and original: Pirandello used to be either graciously tolerated, or openly scoffed at.' Even his 'Sotto la Mole' column, daily notes written on whatever pretexts the day provided, appeared worthy of publication in book form to the more appreciative readers of *Avanti!*. Gramsci himself testifies to this:

> In ten years of journalism I wrote enough words to fill up fifteen to twenty volumes of four hundred pages apiece, but it was stuff written for the day it appeared and I always thought it would be dead the day after. . . . In 1918 Professor Cosmo asked me to let him make a selection from among the short editorial pieces I used to do for a Turin paper; he wanted to publish them and write a preface which would certainly have been very friendly towards me, but I would not let him.

Gramsci's ambition to build up a working-class culture now carried him away from his editorial desk in Via Siccardi more and more often. Fellow-militants later recalled his devotion to intellectual propaganda as the most striking thing about him: he never tired of studying ways of conveying political ideas in practice, and his study was methodical. In his dual role of party journalist and ordinary rank-and-file militant, he would go and give talks to study circles in the great working-class districts of Turin. In Borgo San Paolo on 25 August 1916, he gave a lecture on Romain Rolland's novel *Au dessus de la mêlée* (then recently published in Italian translation). On 16 and 17 October he spoke about the French Revolution to groups at Borgo San Paolo and Barriera di Milano; then about the Paris Commune on 17 December. An historical episode, a newly published book, or a new play could all be valid pretexts for the dissemination of ideas.

In March 1917, Emma Grammatica appeared in Ibsen's *A Doll's House* at the Carignano Theatre. The play was coldly received; plainly the public did not like this story of a woman who leaves the husband who has disappointed her. Gramsci saw the reaction as expressing male-centred Latin disapproval of a more advanced moral code 'which perceives women and men as more than just muscle, nerves and skin, perceives them as persons, and perceives the family as more than a merely economic institution, which sees family life as a changing moral world that requires for its fulfilment a fusion of two souls able to give to each other what the partner lacks. According to this conception, woman is more than the female of the species, whose function is to bring up children and drown them in palpitating carnal love – she is also a human creature in her own right, with a mind of her own, her own inner needs, her own human personality . . .'. This was the topic of another of Gramsci's talks, to the womens' study circle at Borgo Campidoglio.

Gramsci's way of looking at the problem of the Socialists' relations with other parties was no less novel. In his account of Gramsci and *L'Ordine Nuovo*, Battista Santhià has described a visit he once made to the editorial office of *Il Grido*, where he found four young people chatting quietly with Gramsci, addressing one another politely as '*Lei*':

> When the lengthy conversation was finally over, I was dumbfounded to learn that the four were young Catholics, and that their opposition to the war was quite different from ours, and founded wholly on pacifism ('We're against all wars,' they kept repeating) and upon biblical precepts. Gramsci suggested I might help them, just to provoke me. I didn't see this right away, and asked naïvely whether he was suggesting I ought to join in their prayers for the granting of a miraculous peace. Gramsci replied dryly: 'All they ever teach you here is a stupid anti-clericalism, quite misguided intellectually and politically. I don't go to church either, because I'm not a believer. But we must recognize that the majority of people are believers. If we carry on ignoring everyone but the atheists, we'll always be in a minority. There are plenty of bourgeois atheists who make fun of priests and never go to church, yet they are anti-socialist, interventionist, and wage war on us. But though these kids go to mass, they aren't industrialists; all they are asking is to work with us to stop the war as soon as possible.'

This rejection of sectarian anti-clericalism and the conception of class alliance were both to be crucial in Gramsci's later thought.

Both at the newspaper office and in his debates and talks Gramsci was engaged in a struggle to disentangle the language and ideas of socialism from the cramping limits an older generation had imposed on them. It took up most of his time, and he had little private life. He still had to give some private lessons, since his salary of fifty lire from

Avanti! was certainly not enough to live on (he worked for nothing on *Il Grido*). In his rare free moments he might see Sardinian friends, like the chief wine expert at the Co-operative Alliance, Corona, or another friend, Mura, who kept a bar in Piazza Statuto; or he might visit the home of Attilio and Pia Carena (she worked as a stenographer on the paper), or spend the evening with Bruno Buozzi, whose family had befriended him. Mostly, however, he chose to pass the time with other young comrades of the Young Socialist Federation.

Towards the end of 1916, Gramsci learned from one of them, Andrea Viglongo, that there was a project afoot to bring out a special pamphlet. He asked if he might write it. And on 11 February 1917, the four-page pamphlet duly appeared, bearing the title *La Città futura* ('City of the Future').

It was wholly the work of Gramsci, although containing also a few extracts from texts by Gaetano Salvemini, Croce, and Armando Carlini, a follower of the idealist philosopher Gentile. This selection of authors indicates clearly the pamphlet's cultural matrix. *La Città futura* may be considered the end-product of Gramsci's intellectual formation so far, and its reliance on idealism is very marked. It defines Croce as 'the greatest European thinker of the present day'. Gramsci himself said, looking back at it subsequently: 'In a short introduction to the extract from Croce's *Religione e serenità* I wrote that just as Hegelianism had been the premise of Marxism in the nineteenth century, and one of the origins of modern civilization, so the philosophy of Croce might be the premise of a renewed, contemporary Marxism for our own generation.' In reality, the section indicated here does not convey this idea. But, Gramsci admitted, 'The problem was touched on only in a primitive and certainly quite inadequate fashion, since in those days the concept of a unity between theory and practice, or between philosophy and politics, was not clear in my mind: *I was still rather Crocean in tendency*' [G.F.'s italics].

The first article in *La Città futura* (censored in several places) was entitled 'Tre principi tre ordini' ('Three principles, three orders'):

Order and disorder are the terms most frequently used in political polemics. The party of order, men of order, public order. . . . The very word 'order' has miraculous power, and political institutions keep themselves going largely by reliance upon this power. The existing social order is presented as a stable, harmoniously coordinated system, and the great mass of people hesitate and lose heart when they think of what a radical change might bring. . . . They can imagine only the present being torn to pieces, and fail to perceive the new order which is possible, and which would be better organized, more vital than the old one. . . . They see only violent destruction, and timid souls reel back from the prospect, afraid of losing what they have, afraid of chaos and helpless disorder. . . .

The article concludes:

Socialists must not simply replace one order by another. Their task is to create order, the only real order. The juridical principle they should aim to satisfy is: *the possibility of the integral fulfilment of the whole human personality, as a right of all citizens.* If this principle were realized, all privileges of the past would fall by the wayside. *It would bring the maximum of liberty with the minimum of constraint.* It would make individual capacity and productivity the law of life and of economics, transcending all traditional frameworks. Wealth would no longer be an instrument for maintaining slavery, but would belong to all impersonally and give to all the means of attaining the greatest possible well-being. Schools would educate intelligence, whoever the intelligence belonged to. . . . Upon this principle must depend all the other principles in the maximal socialist programme. This is not Utopian. It is a concrete universal, it can be willed into existence. It is the principle of true order, socialist order: of that order which we believe will be realized in Italy sooner than in any other country [G.F.'s italics].

In this early pamphlet, many aspects of Gramsci's personality were clearly expressed. The tense energy of a man who felt called upon to take sides and fight:

Like Frederick Hebbel, I believe that 'living means taking sides'. I hate indifferent people. . . . Indifference is a powerful force in history. It operates passively but effectively. . . . Events mature in the shadows, a few hands accountable to no one weave the web of collective living, and the masses know nothing of what happens because they don't mind. . . . I am partisan, I do mind. I feel beating within me the virile awareness of my own side – the life of that city of the future which my side has already begun to build . . . I am alive, I take sides. Hence I detest whoever does not, I hate indifference.

A bitter intransigence towards class enemies:

When debating with an opponent, try to put yourself in his shoes: you will understand him better, and may end by recognizing that there is some truth in what he says, and perhaps a lot. For some time I myself followed this sage advice. But my adversaries' shoes got so filthy that I was forced to conclude it's better to be unfair than risk fainting from the stink they give off.

A strong vein of sarcasm: speaking of intellectuals who desert the socialist movement, he wrote:

> There are dilettantes of faith, just as there are dilettantes of learning. . . .
> For many of them, having a crisis of conscience is like not being able to pay an overdue bill, or deciding to open a current account at the bank.

And aversion to the populist rhetoric of 'toil-worn hands', 'These are worker's hands!' and so on:

> I think it is better if a peasant joins the socialist movement than if a university professor does. But only if the peasant tries to acquire the university professor's experience and breadth of outlook, so that his choice – and the sacrifices it entails – will not be sterile.

La Città futura also shows Gramsci's faith in 'man's tenacious will-power' as a lever of historical change, and a corresponding disgust with the 'scientific superstitions' of positivism, or reformists like the socialist Claudio Treves who worshipped 'natural laws' and the 'inevitable progress of events'. From now on, the young Gramsci's attack on the reformist wing of the PSI was to be unsparing: 'Waiting patiently until we become fifty per cent plus one of the population is for those timorous souls who expect socialism to arrive in the shape of a royal-decree, countersigned by two ministers.'

We can already glimpse the Gramsci of *L'Ordine Nuovo*. And indeed, a note in bold type at the end of *La Città futura* states: 'We have given this document a title which belongs not only to us. Before the scourge of war was unleashed on the world, a group of friends had decided to launch a new socialist review, a review which would be the rallying-point for the new moral energy, the new idealism and [censored word, probably 'revolutionary'] spirit alive in our youth. . . . We believed we could revive the native Italian tradition, the tradition of Mazzini, in socialist terms, fired as we were with youthful faith and generous ardour. The ambition has not been abandoned. It has merely been postponed until those friends the war stole from us return to the rallying-point. Then, such a review will come to exist.'

It was now February 1917. In Russia, the revolution had begun.

At first, it was not easy to understand exactly what had happened in St Petersburg. The objective difficulties in the way of gathering information, plus the censorship, and the tendency of papers like the *Gazzetta del Popolo* to distort news for internal propaganda reasons, all prevented any clear vision of events. On 18 March it was learnt that the

Tsar had been overthrown: there was a provisional government which wanted to continue the war, but also an ultra-revolutionary left-wing group led by Lenin which was working to obtain an immediate cease-fire at any price. Gramsci's first comment appeared in *Il Grido* on 29 April 1917. He declared that 'after reading the newspapers, and all the news which the censorship has allowed to be published' it was still not easy to grasp the real substance of the revolution and determine whether it was liberal or proletarian in character:

> The bourgeois press . . . has told us how the power of the autocracy has fallen and been replaced by another power, they hope by a bourgeois power. They have jumped immediately at the obvious parallel, Russian Revolution = French Revolution, and find that the two events are very like one another. . . . Nevertheless, we are persuaded that the Russian Revolution is proletarian in character, as it has been so far in its deeds, and that it will naturally result in a socialist regime.

A more complete account was published in *La Stampa* on 10 May, including Lenin's slogan 'All power to the proletariat, through the workers' and peasants' councils'. Lenin at once became a fixed target for Italy's conservative press; for the same reasons, the working class now saw him as 'the most socialist' and (in the words of *Il Grido*) 'the most revolutionary of all the major leaders of the Russian socialist parties'.

> The Russian maximalists[1] *are* the Russian revolution. Kerensky, Tseretelli, Chernov [leaders of the March bourgeois-democratic revolution-G.F.] are the present state, the today of the revolution. They have achieved an initial social equilibrium based on a balance of forces in which the moderates have retained much power. The maximalists represent the continuity, the tomorrow of the revolution; it is in this sense that they *are* the revolution. . . . [Lenin] has aroused energies which will not die away. He and his Bolshevik comrades are convinced that socialism can now be realized, at any moment.

Given these responses, and the faith which socialist intellectuals (including Gramsci) and one wing of the Italian working-class movement now had in Lenin's party, the reception accorded Goldenberg and Smirnov by a crowd of forty thousand workers when they arrived in

---

[1] *Maximalist*: the use of the term 'maximalist' to denote the Italian Socialist Party's left or revolutionary wing (and here, by implication, that of the Russian socialists as well) descended from the PSI Congress of 1900, where 'maximal' and 'minimal' programmes were presented. The 'minimalists', or reformists, dominated the PSI after 1900, until the 'maximalists' won control from 1912 onwards. (T.N.)

Turin on 13 August is scarcely surprising. These emissaries of the liberal provisional government had been sent west to establish preliminary contact with the Allied governments. A few days before, Goldenberg had said to the Paris correspondent of *La Stampa*: 'Lenin is no friend of ours, we are his adversaries.' When the delegates from the Kerensky government appeared on the balcony of the Casa del Popolo in Via Siccardi, they were met with cries of 'Long live Lenin!'

Ten days later, there were barricades in the streets of Turin. The immediate cause of the rising had been the disappearance of bread from the shops. But the violent energy with which it was fought – as indicated by the numbers of dead and wounded – had other origins. In the preceding months, opposition to the war had been rapidly intensifying. There was now a widespread popular feeling to the effect that it was better to lose five hundred in a battle for the workers' own cause, than ten thousand against the Germans fighting for the cause of the bourgeoisie. In the factories, where work discipline was actually controlled by army officers and the wartime military penal code was enforced, the resentment of the workers had been growing more acute every day. On such fertile soil, the idea of 'copying Russia' was a natural one, and led inevitably to an attempt at insurrection.

Shooting broke out on the morning of Thursday 23 August. The revolt spread, aimless and leaderless. Trees, tramcars and railway-cars were dragged across the streets as barricades around the main centres of the rising. There was no link between the rebels and the socialist leadership, and no thought-out plan of revolution. It was as if the mob wanted only to loot and destroy. The widespread belief that the troops would fraternize with workers in revolt was disappointed: they reacted by shooting.[2] More than fifty people were killed, and more than two hundred wounded. Then followed a wave of arrests, which deprived the local socialist movement of nearly all its leaders. The task of leading the Turin workers' movement – in so far as this was possible in a city now declared a 'war zone', which meant a court-martial for anything not approved of by the military – now devolved upon an *ad hoc* committee.

Gramsci was one of the twelve on this committee. He had become a leader of the Turin socialist movement for the first time, at the age of twenty-six. On 21 March 1921, he would write in *L'Ordine Nuovo*:

[2] Gramsci believed that the Sardinian Sassari Brigade had taken part in the repression, but this was not so. At that time the Brigade was *en route* for the Bainsizza plateau, and entered the front line on 29 August.

At a very grave and difficult time for the Turin working class, the Party entrusted one of us with tasks of the greatest responsibility: with the political secretaryship of the section when the Party was dissolved and the offices in Corso Siccardi were occupied by the military after the events of August 1917. Then later, after Caporetto, one of us was sent to the Florence conference at which the attitudes and outlook of the Party were decided.[3]

Lazzari and Bombacci for the party leadership and Gino Pesci for the maximalist revolutionary wing had jointly called a clandestine conference in Florence, to be held on 18 November 1917 (Antonio had known Pesci previously, when the latter was secretary of the Cagliari Chamber of Labour at the same time as Gennaro Gramsci was its treasurer). The conference's purpose was to re-emphasize proletarian opposition to the war, even after the defeat of Caporetto. Gramsci subscribed to Bordiga's view that the revolutionary working class might yet intervene effectively in the crisis provoked by the war.

Only four days before, the Bolsheviks had finally come to power (14 November). There was little news available in Italy. On 10 November the *Gazzetta del Popolo* had published an account of how 'a mob of extremists sacked the wine cellars of the Winter Palace and got thoroughly drunk, before being dispersed by force'. Thus, the great historical event was neatly reduced to the dimensions of a delinquent brawl. But Gramsci at once had the intuition that a great turning point had come, in spite of the censorship and the distortions of the bourgeois press. On 24 November he managed to write, in a short introductory note to an article by Boris Souvarine:

> We have received no reliable information on the latest developments in the Russian Revolution. We may not have any reliable information for some time yet. *Il Grido* foresaw, as indeed it was easy to foresee, that the Russian Revolution could not stop at its Kerensky phase. The Russian Revolution is continuing and will go further still.

On the same day the national edition of *Avanti!* carried a signed editorial by Gramsci entitled 'The Revolution against *Capital*'. It was still another – and certainly the most spectacular – indication of Gramsci's persistently idealist outlook, and of his wish to avoid the over-dogmatic interpretations adopted by many other followers of Marx. It was also his first incursion into national journalism.

[3] *Caporetto*; in October–November 1917, the Italian armies suffered a major defeat near the town of Caporetto (north-east of Udine, now in Yugoslavia), which resulted in their being driven back onto the Piave river, with the loss of 10,000 killed, 30,000 wounded, and 300,000 prisoners. (T.N.)

The Bolshevik Revolution is a revolution against Marx's *Capital*. In Russia, *Capital* had more influence among the bourgeoisie than among the proletariat. It demonstrated critically how by fatal necessity a bourgeoisie would be constituted in Russia, how a capitalist era would be inaugurated there, how western-style civilization would flourish there, long before the proletariat could even think of its own liberation, of its own class interests, of its own revolution. But events have exploded the framework within which, according to historical materialism, Russian history should have unfolded. The Bolsheviks have denied Karl Marx, and they have affirmed by their actions, by their conquests, that the laws of historical materialism are less inflexible than was hitherto believed.

The article was full of Hegelian and Crocean ideas:

If the Bolsheviks have denied certain predictions made in *Capital*, they have not thereby denied what is living and immanent in it. They have shown that they are not 'Marxists', nothing more; they have not turned the master's works into an empty compilation of dogmatic axioms. They are living out Marxist thought, the part of it which cannot die, *that part which is the continuation of German and Italian idealism*, and which in Marx himself became contaminated by positivistic and naturalistic encrustations [G.F.'s italics].

Once more Gramsci was rejecting the idea of history as fatalistic development, totally determined by brute economic factors – determinism in the 'positivistic' sense – in favour of man's will as the decisive element in history. It should be added that he had then, and was always to retain, a clear sense of the difficulties attending any great historical upheaval: he kept his distance from those who were so carried away by the euphoria of the moment that they imagined overthrow of the old Tsarist order would in itself bring about social bliss. 'This is bound to be a collectivism of misery, of suffering,' he stated bluntly, but added that in the present situation capitalism would be worse: 'In Russia, capitalism could not accomplish at once any more than collectivism would be able to. Indeed today it would accomplish less, since it would have *at once* to face a discontented, angry proletariat now quite unable to tolerate more years of the pain and hardship that economic crisis would entail.'

Apart from his journalistic activity, the martial-law regime allowed Gramsci few outlets for organizational or propaganda work during his temporary tenure of the local party secretaryship. The record shows only a resolution condemning tariff protectionism, accepted by the provisional party executive. *Il Grido* had brought out a special number on this favourite topic of Gramsci, on 20 October 1917, with contributions by Ugo Mondolfo, Umberto Cosmo, Bruno Buozzi, and also an article by Togliatti – his first for a socialist paper, and the beginning of his active political career (after taking his law degree he had enrolled as a philosophy student, and was now doing an officer-training course at Caserta).

Although there was little scope for activity, Gramsci had set up a discussion circle for young militants: political education continued to be first among his concerns. 'I give one of the youngsters a task', we learn from a contemporary letter to Giuseppe Lombardo-Radice, 'a chapter of Croce's *Cultura e vita morale*, for instance, or Salvemini's *Problemi educativi e sociali*, or his book on the French Revolution or on lay culture, or the *Communist Manifesto*, or perhaps a critical note from Croce's review *La Critica* – something related to the present-day Idealist movement.'[4] A few days later there would be a discussion of the theme selected, most often in the open air. One of the young members of this circle, Carlo Boccardo, told me:

> We used to take long walks along the porticoes, Gramsci ambling slowly in the middle, the rest of us grouped around him. Andrea Viglongo used to come, so did Attilio Carena, Pia's brother, and sometimes Angelo Pastore, Ottavio's younger brother. Gramsci let us talk. We were boys of sixteen or seventeen: as ignorant as our age, and as presumptuous. But Gramsci never lost patience with us, he never acted like a theoretical know-all; he set great store by other peoples' opinions and was a good listener. When he finally said something and summed up the discussion, we usually saw our mistakes and corrected them ourselves. We met like this every evening for a couple of months. I remember New Year's Eve, 1917, when we met at Andrea Viglongo's. Andrea's mother made us a big tray of pancakes to celebrate with. We were in the office of the head of the school where Andrea's father was caretaker. While we waited for midnight we discussed the *Meditations* of Marcus Aurelius. . . . Then we were called up one by one, and the group broke up

Gramsci dedicated a copy of Barbera's 1911 edition of the *Meditations* to the young Attilio Carena when he was called up. It is a pity this has been lost. According to Alfonso Leonetti the dedication took the form

---

[4] It is obvious, once more, how the authors and texts referred to here mirror the young revolutionary's cultural formation: the man for whom Marx was 'a master of moral and intellectual life, not a shepherd chastising us posthumously with his crook', not 'a Messiah who bequeathed us a string of weighty parables, categorical imperatives, and absolute norms outside the bounds of time and space'.

of a series of imperatives ('Thou shalt', 'Thou shalt not', etc.), the 'Ten Commandments' of the discussion circle.

Maria Giudice had been arrested, and Gramsci was now sole editor of *Il Grido* and ran it single-handed. It was soon greatly changed. Attentive to the latest developments in Russia, its twenty-seven-year old editor had a number of Bolshevik texts and documents translated by a Polish comrade, Aron Wizner.

> The little weekly party paper suddenly became an intellectual and cultural review [wrote Piero Gobetti]. It published the first translations of Russian revolutionary writings, and tried to analyse the political meaning of the Bolshevik course. Gramsci's brain was the motor of all this. He saw the figure of Lenin as representing a heroic impulse of liberation: the ideals and motives which made up the Bolshevik myth were in hidden ferment in the mind of the masses and should function *not as a model for the Italian revolution, but as an incitement to free initiative from below* [G.F.'s italics].

Not a model to be followed mechanically, then, but a lesson, a stimulus to rethink the historical and socio-economic realities of Italy: Gramsci continued to reject the concept of politics as an abstract, normative science, 'outside the bounds of time and space'.

His first task when he had come to the big city had been the overcoming of a 'village-like' way of living and thinking. Now, he was engaged on overcoming national horizons too: or as he put it, referring to himself in the third person: 'He confronted the national way with European ways, Italian cultural needs and trends with those of Europe (to the limited extent possible, given his personal situation, but always with a strong sense of the task's vital importance).' And, just as the originality of this once 'arch-provincial' youth had consisted in his absorption of the national culture without repudiating his Sardinian inheritance, so now his originality as an exponent of Italian culture lay in an effort to absorb the lessons of Europe and of the Leninist revolution without forgetting for an instant the very different features and problems of his own country. Gramsci's 'autonomism' – his desire to establish the concrete historical conditions of Italian society and the Italian class struggle – was evident in every issue of *Il Grido*.

The last issue appeared on 19 October 1918. In his farewell message to readers, Gramsci claimed with good reason that under his care it had been transformed from an 'evangelical propaganda weekly with some local news' into 'a little review of socialist culture, developed according to the theory and strategy of revolutionary socialism'.

Peace had returned. Gennaro Gramsci, who had been a sergeant-major with the 21st Sappers at Monterosso, Montenero and Caporetto, now went back to Cagliari to run a consumer co-operative in Corso Vittorio. The youngest brother, Carlo, went home to Ghilarza after being an officer: for some time he was to experience difficulty in getting a job and re-adapting to civilian life. Mario decided to stay in uniform. Thanks to his schooling at the seminary he had managed to become a sub-lieutenant. He had met a girl from the Lombardy aristocracy, Anna Maffei Parravicini, and they were soon to marry. He would remain a soldier till then, at least. At home, Signor Ciccillo and Signora Peppina had Grazietta and Teresina with them, as well as Carlo. Emma had found a job nearby, as an accountant with the firm building the dam on the Tirso river. Economically things were rather better, and life had become relatively easy. There was even some pride in Nino's success as a big-city journalist, although Signor Ciccillo still could not make head or tail of the dear boy's ideas. As for his weird illusions about changing the world . . . it would have been much more gratifying if he had worked for *La Domenica del Corriere* or the *Giornale d'Italia*, respectable papers written by ordinary people with their head screwed on right. . . . But Signora Peppina – who always read all the articles Nino sent home marked in red ink – reacted mildly to her husband's remarks, cutting them short with: 'Yes, yes, I know, but that's just the way he sees things. . . .'

In 1919, little or nothing was known in Sardinia of Antonio Gramsci's activities. Still, he was not without a certain local fame in Ghilarza and round about. Velio Spano recollects:

One day, on the road from Ghilarza to Abbasanta, a relative of mine pointed out a good-looking girl to me as we approached the village: 'Look!' she said. 'That's Antonio Gramsci's sister.' I'd never heard the name before, so I asked who he was. She was rather vague about it, but said he was a professor, a journalist, and lived on the Continent. Whatever he was, she was certainly proud of it. . . .

From 5 December 1918 onwards, Gramsci worked solely for *Avanti!*, which now had a Piedmontese edition printed in Turin at 3 Via Arcivescovado, on the corner of Via XX Settembre. He was much changed. At twenty-eight he showed little resemblance to the timid, painfully sensitive boy who had come from his island years before, and reacted to the cold city environment by retreat and estrangement. He had finally found work which stimulated him. His anguish over being deformed had grown less. He was even in reasonably good health: at the office he took a child-like delight in showing off the remarkable strength of his hands by squeezing his colleagues' wrists. He had discovered a hitherto unsuspected vitality and liberated energies never tapped before; and in the light of his new-found self-confidence, the old image of a man more cut out for 'ascetic linguistic research' (as Gobetti put it) than for a life of combat faded away.

However, a certain coldness remained: Gramsci was too accustomed to mastering his feelings and hiding them behind a mask of reserve. Though he joked and laughed, the laughter remained somewhat forced and cerebral. His outbursts of rage were more spontaneous than these dry explosions of mirth: anger was the surer safety valve for the painful feelings he had repressed so long, and for his ceaseless efforts of will. In his political writing he shrank from any suggestion of softness. Dramatists and theatre managers awaited his reviews with trepidation. Once, the manager Nino Berrini spent a week pressing attentions on him, in the hope of obtaining a friendly review in exchange: but his notice was as savage as usual. Back-scratching among writers and actors irritated him. The dryness and sharpness of his judgements resulted from an extreme aversion to hypocrisy: he clearly felt one could never risk tempering a judgement with indulgence, without being at least a little insincere.

For some time after the war's end Gramsci was without office in the Turin section of the P S I: the old functionaries had all returned from war or imprisonment. On the new executive committee elected in November 1918, the 'ultra-left' intransigents acquired considerable say (these included Franceso Barberis, Giovanni Boero, Pietro Rabezzana, Giovanni Gilodi, and later on Giovanni Parodi). Gramsci's days were passed mostly in his tiny office on Via dell'Arcivescovado, not far from the Savoy Arsenal. The building had once been a reformatory for young delinquents. After the entrance from the street there was a courtyard, where the Turin Co-operative Alliance had a shoe warehouse; then, on the ground floor of the old reformatory, there was the print-shop, equipped with a rather ancient Mariononi rotary press and half a dozen linotypes. The editorial offices were up a spiral stair on the first floor, seven or eight of them, obtained by erecting a number of rough wooden partitions. Gramsci had an ancient writing desk to himself, with little shelves built onto its back, and lived surrounded by great piles of books and mounds of newspapers and proofs awaiting correction or left over from the day before. Here he wrote, studied, and listened to the people who came to see him, especially in the evenings: workers, factory correspondents, party and trade union secretaries from the city and the surrounding province, university students and teachers, and shop stewards. He would go home very late, always in the company of his younger colleagues: Alfonso Leonetti, a man from Puglia who had come to Turin to teach at the Ugo Foscolo Institute, Giuseppe Amoretti, Mario Montagnana, Andrea Viglongo, and Felice Platone.

Tasca, Togliatti and Terracini had returned to the city. They were discussing their old project of founding a new paper again. Gramsci had studied the October Revolution very closely and was following its later developments with the same care. The first extracts from Lenin's writings were becoming known in Italy, through French reviews or the American review *Liberator*, edited by Max Eastman. *Imperialism* and *State and Revolution* were beginning to be circulated. These helped Gramsci to formulate new answers to the questions accumulated in him by his whole experience as a southern Italian who had had to adapt to a great working-class city. His desire to have a new journal for the expression of such ideas was strongly shared by the others; all were eager for a free debate that could proceed independently of the party's ruling circles.

Piero Gobetti, who knew them very well, wrote a portrait of the founders of *L'Ordine Nuovo*. Angelo Tasca, twenty-seven: 'He came to politics with a mainly literary education, and with the mentality of a propagandist, an apostle.' His was 'a literary socialism, a messianic conception of popular redemption, like the Enlightenment's return to nature', and he 'set against modern civilization his personal dream of petty-bourgeois virtue, of workers who would take to moderate ancestral ways and quietly cultivate their own gardens'. Umberto Terracini, son of a modest Jewish family (not Terracini the diamond-merchants): 'Anti-demagogic on principle, an aristocrat by temperament, disliking impassioned oratory, a subtle mind who was firm in argument and action to the point of being arid and pig-headed.' He was considered 'the diplomat, the Machiavellian' of the group. Palmiro Togliatti, the one who had come to politics most recently, greatly afflicted by anxiety 'which looked like relentless, overbearing cynicism and was *really* indecisiveness; often seen as equivocal, he was perhaps merely struggling in vain against his own hypercritical attitudes'. Lastly, Antonio Gramsci:

> The brain has overwhelmed the body.... The voice has a critical, destructive edge, its irony turns quickly to poisonous sarcasm, dogma lived out with tyrannic logic removes all trace of sympathy from his humour.... His rebellion is sometimes resentment, sometimes the deeper, pent-up rage of the islander unable to open out except in action, unable to free himself from age-old slavery except by infusing the most tyrannical energy into his commands and his propaganda.

What was the new message of which Gramsci, Tasca, Terracini and Togliatti wanted to be the bearers? Were they in complete accord? What idea had they in common, apart from their detestation of Turati, Modigliani, Treves, and the other reformist leaders? 'Alas,' said Gramsci, 'the sole sentiment which united us . . . was associated with our vague yearning for a vaguely proletarian culture. We wanted to act, to *do* something, anything; we felt afflicted and lost, drifting helplessly in the intense atmosphere of those months after the armistice, when Italian society appeared near the point of cataclysm.' They met, they discussed the project, and Tasca found money for it – 6,000 lire. On May 1919 the first issue of *L'Ordine Nuovo* came out: as Gobetti put it, 'the only Marxist revolutionary organ in Italy with any degree of intellectual seriousness'. Gramsci's name appeared on the paper's masthead as 'editorial secretary'. The business manager was Pia Carena, who also did excellent translations from the French (Rolland, Barbusse, Marcel Martinet, etc.).

Initially, the paper was slow to acquire the character Gramsci wished it to have. 'It was nothing but a rag-bag anthology,' he himself complained, somewhat exaggeratedly, 'a collection of abstract cultural items with a strong leaning towards nasty short stories and well-intentioned woodcuts.' Later, his critique grew more precise. Gramsci accused Tasca of rejecting 'the programme of devoting our common energies to the task of discovering the Soviet-type traditions of the Italian working class, and laying bare the real revolutionary vein in our history.' What was the point of the task Gramsci was defending in these words? He had studied carefully the history of the Russian experiment with

'Soviets', or councils, and the development of the factory and farm councils into which the workers and peasants had organized themselves. And he asked himself: 'Is there in Italy anything, any working-class institution, which one might compare to the Soviets, anything of the same nature?... Is there any germ, any first wish or tendency in the direction of government by Soviets here in Italy, in Turin?' The answer was yes. 'There does exist in Italy, in Turin, an embryonic form of worker government: the internal committees.'[1] But how could this elementary form of workers' democracy be developed into an organ of genuine workers' power? Gramsci's central idea was that *all* workers (both blue and white-collar), *all* technicians, *all* peasants – all the active elements in society, in fact – should stop being instruments of the productive process and become its masters, stop being cogs in the capitalist machine and become responsible free agents. The change should occur *whether or not they were members of a trade union, regardless of which party they belonged to and whether or not they were militants*, simply by virtue of their being workers, peasants, etc. In this way, the democratically elected workers' bodies – factory and farm councils, district councils – would assume and exercise the authority which previously belonged to the property-owning classes and their government representatives. At present, the factory internal committees were elected only from and by trade union members: the 'factory councils' based on them would be elected by everyone, by all the workers, including the anarchists and even the Catholics. Gramsci was certainly no rabid anti-clerical.[2]

The function of these factory councils should be different from that of the unions: their task was not to struggle for higher wages and better conditions of work within the factory, shorter hours, hygiene, holidays, and so on. They were there not to bargain with the capitalist over such things, but to take over from him: their task was to be that of running the factory, and controlling every aspect of its life. Was there enough preparation, enough maturity and revolutionary spirit in Italy to make possible such an evolution? Did a revolutionary climate exist – outside Turin, as well as in the city?

The question is still debated to this day. Some blame the defeat of

[1] These 'commissioni interne', or 'internal committees' were factory committees of trade union members, elected from the different shops, sections, etc., in the plant. They corresponded to a factory or works committee of shop stewards in Britain. (T.N.)

[2] The following year, in March 1920, he wrote: 'Italy happens to have the Vatican City and the Pope; the liberal State had to come to terms with the Church's spiritual power; the workers' State will have to do the same.'

the factory-council movement on the indecision of the Italian Socialist Party and the principal union, the Confederazione Generale del Lavoro (General Confederation of Labour); others see the movement as a theoretical framework thought up by a group of youthful intellectuals lacking real knowledge of the terrain where the theory was to be realized, and point out that the only solid ground for it lay in Turin itself. What is certain is that the idea immediately had great impact among the workers in Turin, when *L'Ordine Nuovo* first aired it on 21 June 1919, in an article headed 'Workers' Democracy'. The article was written by Gramsci and Togliatti together, and concluded:

> It is time the phrase 'dictatorship of the proletariat' ceased being merely a formula, a pretext for making revolutionary-sounding speeches. Whoever desires the end must desire the means to that end. Dictatorship of the proletariat means the inauguration of a new, characteristically proletarian state, constructed out of the institutional experiments of the oppressed classes, and in which the social life of those classes will become generalized and strongly organized. Such a state cannot be improvised.

The working class of Turin was not slow to respond to this line of thought. Gramsci relates:

> Togliatti, Terracini and I were invited to speak in study circles and at big factory meetings; we were asked to factory committees to discuss with shop stewards and union delegates. We went ahead: the problem of how to develop the factory committees became the central problem, *the* idea of *L'Ordine Nuovo*. It came to be seen as the key problem of a workers' revolution, as the problem of attaining 'freedom' for the workers. For us and for our followers, *L'Ordine Nuovo* became 'the paper of the factory councils'.

In the meantime, the Allied governments were encouraging counter-revolutionary movements against the newly-born Soviet socialist republics in Russia and Hungary. A great solidarity strike was planned in Italy for 20 and 21 July 1919. Towards the end of March the Sassari Brigade – consisting largely of Sardinian shepherds and peasants – was transferred to Turin to help maintain law and order. In May, Gramsci was again elected to the Turin executive of the PSI, along with a number of other revolutionary hard-liners: all were factory workers except one, Clementina Berra Perrone, a woman office worker. The secretary was Giovanni Boero. Gramsci attached great importance to contacting his compatriots in the Sassari Brigade and persuading them to fraternize with the Turin workers: he wanted to make them see that to shoot down a worker meant shooting down someone fighting for the liberation of the peasants from their own unending slavery.

The task was not an easy one. For one thing, it had to be carried out on two fronts simultaneously, since the Turin masses had retained burning memories of other repressions, and many workers – particularly the anarchists – were thirsty for revenge and had to be disciplined. As for the soldiers – the 'Sassarini', as they were called – their frame of mind is conveyed by a story Gramsci heard from a tannery worker (himself a Sassari man) who had made the first tentative contacts with the Brigade. He approached one of the men, and was warmly greeted; he asked:

> 'What have you come to Turin for?' 'We've come to shoot at some gentlemen who are going on strike.' 'But it's not the gentlemen who're going on strike, it's the workers, they're poor people.' 'Here they're all gentlemen: they wear collars and ties and earn 30 lire a day. I know all about poor people and how they dress. There really are lots of poor people in Sassari, field labourers like us – we used to get 1 lira 50 a day.' 'But I'm a worker, and I'm poor!' 'That must be because you're Sardinian.' 'Well, suppose I go on strike with all the others, will you shoot at *me*?' The soldier thought for a minute, then said, putting his hand on my shoulder: 'Listen, if there's a strike, why don't *you* stay at home?'

'Such was the attitude of the overwhelming majority of the Brigade,' comments Gramsci. 'It contained only a few workers, miners from the Iglesias basin. And yet, only a few months later, just before the strike of 20/21 July, the Brigade was taken out of Turin.' The 'Sassarini' left for Rome in two special trains, at two in the morning on 18 July. A soldier in the unit, Antonio Contini of Bonorva, remembers: 'The people of Turin lined the road and cheered us, the night we left. They were happy because we had been different from the others. We had respected the local people and they had shown respect for us. Not a single shot had been fired, there hadn't been a single incident. That's why they liked us and cheered us.'

Gramsci's first brief taste of prison life occurred two days later, on 20 July. Another political prisoner, the young worker Mario Montagnana, remembers the scene in one of the prison's circular yards:

> I saw at least a dozen prison guards standing round and listening religiously to a little man in a dark suit, who was smiling while he spoke to them. It was Gramsci. After only thirty-six hours in his cell he had managed to conquer and fascinate a number of the warders – Sardinian like himself – by speaking to them in their own dialect, in that characteristic way of his,

simple and popular, yet at the same time full of feelings and ideas and facts. They told one another: 'Say, you know there's a Sardinian in No. so-and-so, a politico . . . Go and have a word with him.' A lot of them went, in spite of the tight discipline. . . . Later some of them accompanied him to the office on his way out, as many as were able to, eager to enjoy more of his conversation. They were proud of any Sardinian who was so intelligent, so well-educated and so sympathetic.

Finally, early in September, came the events which according to *L'Ordine Nuovo* might signal the beginning of a revolutionary movement. At the Brevetti branch of the Fiat complex, the two thousand workers elected delegates from the various shops: the first factory council was born. The central Fiat factory at once followed suit. These moves had been preceded by an intensive propaganda campaign all summer, in the course of which Gramsci and other spokesmen of *L'Ordine Nuovo* had insisted that the traditional institutions of the working class (party and trade unions) were 'no longer capable of containing the new flowering of revolutionary life'; they should be supported by a new network of 'proletarian institutions rooted in the widest possible mass conscious-ness' – i.e. the factory councils. The paper published articles by John Reed ('How a Soviet Works'), by Fournière ('Plan for a Socialist State'), by Gramsci ('The Hungarian Soviets'), by Ottavio Pastore ('The Problem of the Factory Committees'), by Lenin ('Bourgeois Democ-racy and Proletarian Democracy'), and by Andrea Viglongo ('Towards New Institutions'). There was a constant reference to the relevant experience of other countries: the revolutionary-syndicalist Industrial Workers of the World, for instance, inspired by the American Marxist Daniel De Leon, and the English shop-steward movement. From analysis of these movements, from comparison and study of Soviet experiments, from discussion inside the factories themselves, there had arisen the conception of a new form of proletarian self-government, government by the workers associated together regardless of party and trade union membership. And now, the birth of the first factory councils at Fiat meant that theory could indeed be translated into practice.

On 5 October, Georges Sorel wrote in the paper *Il Resto del Carlino*: 'What is happening in the Fiat workshops is more important than all the writings published under the auspices of *Die Neue Zeit*.' Sorel's support for the movement was seized on by those who already accused the *Ordine Nuovo* group of anarcho-syndicalism. Gramsci anticipated such dubious polemical attacks by distinguishing between Sorel himself,

'animated by too sincere a love for the proletarian cause, to the point
of losing contact with real life, and all understanding of real history',
and the syndicalist theory – 'different, perhaps, in the mind of the master
from the version presented by pupils and vulgarizers'. He added:

> Sorel has not confined himself to any one formula, and today, conserving
> whatever was vital and novel in his doctrine – that is, the idea that prole-
> tarian movements must express themselves in their own way and *give life
> to their own institutions* – he is able to follow the creative movement which
> has sprung from the Russian workers and peasants with a perceptive eye
> and an understanding heart, and again address as 'comrades' the Italian
> socialists who wish to follow their example [G.F.'s italics].[3]

Each new issue of *L'Ordine Nuovo* continued to present theoretical
essays, practical proposals, translations from the working-class press of
Russia, France and England, and documents and eye-witness accounts
of factory life and workers' councils in action; there were texts by Arthur
Ransome, Bukharin, Béla Kun, and Jules Humbert-Droz. Then in the
autumn, to this continuing theoretical elaboration of the factory-council
movement there was added a growing debate on the forthcoming
Socialist Party congress.

The first post-war elections were to be held on 16 November 1919.
The Socialist Party held its national congress in Bologna six weeks
earlier, from 5 to 8 October. It was a decidedly left-wing congress: even
those who supported the 'rightist' programme voted for joining the
Third International. None of the three programmes presented was
willing to wear the 'reformist' label. Filippo Turati said he was speaking
for the tendency 'which, in that silly out-dated phraseology we still
employ to insult each other, gets called "reformist" '. So what were the
issues at stake?

On the extreme left, the 'abstentionist' group was headed by
Amadeo Bordiga, who since December 1918 had edited the Naples
paper *Il Soviet*. Its conviction was that the right conceded by the
ruling class to drop a voting-slip into a ballot-box every so often, far
from helping the workers advance their cause, would merely serve to
slacken their revolutionary zeal. Only when the workers got rid of the
illusion that progress was possible through bourgeois representative
institutions would they see the necessity of conquering power; only
then would they decide to sweep all obstacles aside by force. Serrati's
maximalist group agreed that force was necessary 'for self-defence

against bourgeois violence, and for the seizure of power and the consolidation of revolutionary conquests'; but it differed in finding the bourgeois parliament a useful forum 'for the more intensive propagation of communist principles'. There were two other points of difference between Bordiga and Serrati: the name of the party, which Bordiga wanted changed to Italian Communist Party; and the question of party unity, which Serrati wished to preserve while Bordiga favoured the expulsion of anyone who either believed in 'the possibility of proletarian emancipation within the democratic regime' or disowned 'the method of armed struggle against the bourgeoisie to set up a dictatorship of the proletariat'. On the right wing, finally, the idea of electoral abstentionism was contested: according to Lazzari, far from demolishing parliamentary institutions, abstention would merely make it easier for the bourgeoisie to control them. The right also opposed the use of violence as the only road to the conquest of power. In Turin, the *Ordine Nuovo* group had mainly supported Serrati in the pre-congress debates, though the secretary, Giovanni Boero, had taken the abstentionist line along with Giovanni Parodi, and spoken in favour of it at Bologna. The congress voting gave a large majority to Serrati's 'electionist' platform, with 48,411 votes; Lazzari's 'unitary maximalist' line won 14,880 votes; and the 'abstentionists' only 3,417 votes.

The Turin factory-council movement had had few echoes in the deliberations at Bologna. Turati had referred ironically to 'the magical significance' of the term 'Soviet', and to those who wanted to 'award a say even to the unorganized workers, even to blacklegs'. In fact, neither Bordiga nor Serrati agreed with the thesis of *L'Ordine Nuovo*. The controversy had started before the congress, and now grew more intense. Bordiga saw the factory-council movement as the repetition of an old error: namely, 'that it is possible for the working class to win emancipation on the level of economic relationships, while capitalism retains control of the State and political power'. He also accused it of putting a merely corporative organ before the truly revolutionary organ of the proletariat, the class-based communist party. Serrati, for his part, thought that to allow unorganized workers to participate was an aberration: was it not hazardous to credit the 'amorphous masses' with such revolutionary capacity? He also attributed to Gramsci and his friends 'a curious confusion between the *Soviets*, the political organs and governing institutions *of a revolution which has triumphed*, and factory committees, which are *technical* organs of production and industrial organization'. And he concluded: 'The only possible dictator-

ship of the proletariat is a conscious dictatorship of the Socialist Party.'
However, Gramsci's answer to such criticisms – that the revolutionary
process had to be rooted at the point of production itself, in the factory,
and that it was quite utopian to imagine proletarian power as a dictatorship of Socialist Party sections – continued to find wide support in
Turin, even among those who at Bologna had supported groups hostile
to the council movement. Boero and Parodi, for instance, continued to
back Gramsci in Turin though they had voted for Bordiga's 'abstentionists' at the congress. The PSI had a dramatic victory in the Turin
elections, winning eleven out of the eighteen seats in the area; none of
the *Ordine Nuovo* group were candidates.

The council movement continued to spread. By autumn more than
thirty thousand engineering workers had set up factory councils, in the
Fiat works at Lingotto and Diatto, in the Lancia works, in the Savi-
gliano plant, and others. The first coordinated action by these councils
took place a couple of weeks after the elections:

> Acting on a request from the Socialist Party section, which held all the
> ordinary machinery of the mass movement in its control, the factory
> councils were able to mobilize one hundred and twenty thousand workers
> inside an hour, with no advance warning whatever, on a simple factory-
> floor basis. An hour later this proletarian army fell like a landslide on the
> centre of the city, sweeping the nationalist and militarist rabble off the
> streets before it.[4]

Clearly, it was no longer a movement the industrialists could afford to
ignore, as they had tried to do earlier. The chance for a counter-attack
came towards the end of March 1920.

In itself, the pretext was trivial. A new official clock-time was being
introduced throughout Italy, making the day's twenty-four hours run
from midnight instead of from sunset (as in the old *ore italiane* system). At Industrie Meccaniche, one of the Fiat plants, the union
shop stewards asked that the working day should be carried on according to the old system, and that the hands on the main factory clock
should not be altered. The management responded by sacking the
entire works committee. There was a protest strike, and all the Turin
engineering workers came out in solidarity, occupying the factories.
Reaction from the owners was not slow in coming. They began a lock-
out on 29 March, and troops were called to the factories. Then, during

[4] Gramsci, in *Il movimento torinese dei consigli di fabbrica* ('The Turin Factory-Council
Movement'), a report sent in July 1920 to the executive committee of the Communist
International and published later in *L'Ordine Nuovo*, 14 March 1921.

the ensuing negotiations, the owners raised the problem of the new factory councils: they were unwilling to recognize them, and indeed prepared to make some concessions provided they ceased to exist. The conflict sharpened. Now that it centred upon the right of these new institutions of worker power to exist, the Turin revolutionaries suddenly found that the Party and the Confederation of Trade Unions were not giving them the powerful support they had expected.

The Socialist Party was, in fact, undergoing something of a crisis: it had been weakened rather than fortified by its recent great increase in membership. The PSI now had 300,000 members, compared to the 50,000 of 1914, and the Confederation of Trade Unions had two million, instead of the half million or so of pre-war days. Parliamentary representation had grown from 50 to 150 seats after the 1919 elections, an expansion which had created a sense of euphoria but also big new problems of organization. The two principal consequences were, on the one hand, a diffuse revolutionary faith based on the blind presumption that this proletarian onrush would inevitably result in final victory whatever the strategies and techniques employed; and on the other (as Pietro Nenni[5] put it) 'the rise to positions of leadership quite out of proportion to their talents' of 'demagogues without theoretical background or experience'. The intellectually outstanding leaders were all in the minority tendencies on the reformist right or on the far left. These two trends, at least, had defined, coherent positions. One believed that the chances of revolution were disappearing; the other, that the conditions were still objectively revolutionary and that hence the whole party must at once take advantage of them to realize its declared aims.[6] The ambiguity lay in between, in the party centre, where the majority was addicted to paroxysms of verbal revolutionism (unlike the right), but refused to consider seriously what means should be employed to achieve real revolution (unlike the left). As Tasca said, the PSI appeared to be afflicted by a kind of 'monomaniac, inoffensive delirium'. It had acquired 'a parasitic psychology, like that of a future heir sitting at the bedside of the dying man (the bourgeoisie) and thinking that to try and shorten his agony just isn't worth the trouble'. The result was – again in Tasca's words – that, 'While it awaits its inheritance, Italian

[5] *Pietro Nenni* (born 1891): reformist leader of Italian social democracy from before the First World War. (T.N.)

[6] It was a right-winger, Claudio Treves, who most clearly evoked the real balance of forces at this time in his famous parliamentary speech of March 1920 (the 'expiation speech'), where he declared to the Prime Minister Nitti that: 'You are no longer able to impose your order upon us, while we are not yet able to impose our order upon you.'

political life has been turned into a non-stop banquet where the capital of revolution is dissipated in orgies of words.'

The PSI leadership was unwilling to abandon its vacillating course, even now that a possibly decisive trial of strength was under way in Turin. It continued to indulge in its word-orgies, doing nothing to back them up. Meanwhile Gramsci prepared and had approved by the Turin section a nine-point document entitled *Per un Rinnovamento del Partito Socialista* ('Towards a Renewal of the Socialist Party'), for consideration at the Party's national level. This is not the place to discuss the correctness of the document's point of view – whether or not it was right to see the Italian situation as revolutionary and equate that situation with the local one in Turin. It affirmed, at any rate: 'The industrial and agricultural workers are unshakeably determined to tackle the question of the ownership of the means of production *in every part of the country* [G.F.'s italics].' The maximalists of the centre shared this diagnosis, however right or wrong it may have been. But (Gramsci's document declared) they refused to draw the practical consequences:

> The Socialist Party looks on like a spectator at the course of events, it never even passes judgement on them, it never proposes policies the masses can understand and accept, never makes effective use of the revolutionary ideas of Marxism or of the Communist International, never tries to impose a general line that might unite and concentrate revolutionary action. As the politically organized vanguard of the working class, its task should be to develop such common action as will render the workers capable of winning the revolution, and winning it for good.

Instead of this, '. . . it has remained a mere parliamentary party even after the Bologna Congress, paralysed within the cramping limits of bourgeois democracy. . . . It has not assumed that form and distinctive appearance which characterize a revolutionary proletarian party, and only a revolutionary proletarian party'. It was passive towards the reformists.[7] It was out of line with the International: *Avanti!* and the Party's publishing house were ignoring the International's debate on theory and tactics, so that the Party was left out of '. . . this vigorous theoretical debate, where revolutionary consciousness is tempered and unity of thought and action among proletarians of all lands is being forged'.

[7] 'Neither the Party leadership nor *Avanti!* counterposed revolutionary conceptions of their own to the incessant stream of propaganda put out by the reformists and opportunists in parliament and the unions.'

From the foregoing analysis [the document goes on] it is clear what efforts of renewal and reorganization the Party must make, and what indispensable structural changes must now be accomplished. The Party must acquire its own distinctive image: it must cease being a petty-bourgeois parliamentary party and become the party of the revolutionary proletariat. . . . It must become a homogeneous, cohesive party, with its own tactics and theory, founded upon a rigid, implacable discipline. Non-communist revolutionaries must be eliminated from the Party, and the leadership – freed from the need to keep a balance among conflicting tendencies and faction bosses – should devote all its energies to organizing the forces of the working class on a war footing. . . . The Party should put out a manifesto stating explicitly that the revolutionary conquest of political power is now its aim, and inviting the industrial and agricultural workers to prepare and arm themselves. It should make clear the main outlines of the communist solution to their problems, namely, proletarian control over production and distribution, disarming the mercenary armed forces, and control by the organized workers of all local government organs.

The document's key argument was its third point, prophesying the onset of fascist reaction:

The present phase of the class struggle in Italy is the one which precedes *either* the conquest of power by the revolutionary proletariat . . . *or* a terrible reaction on the part of the property-owning class and the governing caste. No form of violence will be spared in their effort to subjugate the industrial and agricultural proletariat; they will endeavour to smash once and for all the workers' organs of political struggle (the Socialist Party) and to incorporate the workers' organs of economic power (trade unions and co-operatives) into the machinery of the bourgeois State.

While these nine points were being drawn up and discussed, the Turin engineering factories remained shut and empty; but they alone were affected. The industrialists continued their resistance, supported by the power of the State:

Today, Turin is an armed fortress [wrote Gramsci in *Avanti!* on 30 April 1920]. It is believed there are fifty thousand soldiers in the city; gun batteries stand ready on the hills, reinforcements are standing by in the surrounding countryside, armoured cars are roaming the streets; in the suburbs reputed to be particularly rebellious, machine-guns are trained on the houses, on all bridges and crossroads, and on the factory gates.

The State feared an insurrection. And possibly the factory owners aimed to provoke it – Gramsci certainly believed this – in the hope of then being able to drown it in blood and break the Turin workers movement for good. Gramsci sensed the desire on the other side to go over to the attack. But it seemed to him that conditions were as yet far from ripe for such a direct confrontation: 'In recent months there has been a remarkable accumulation of revolutionary energy in our city, which now seeks to spill over and spread out at all costs. *It must not spill over into a localized haemorrhage which could at this moment prove dangerous, even fatal.*' There and then, it was much more useful to 'help more intensive preparation *everywhere else in the country*, work for a diffusion of forces and an accelerated development of all the factors which must finally join together in the common task'.[8] A general strike was proclaimed on 13 April. Was this not premature if, as Gramsci thought, the owners were looking for a show-down?

The salient characteristic of the April strike, distinguishing it from all previous protest strikes over wages or against the war, was that this time the workers were not driven by hunger or unemployment, and were not demanding higher wages or better working conditions. They were consciously fighting for control of the production process through the factory councils. But the fight was made more difficult by lack of mass support from the rest of Italy, and in effect was prevented from having a revolutionary outcome by such isolation. The city was 'inundated by an army of policemen, and threatened at every strategic point by artillery and machine-guns'.[9] After ten days, there was a return to work, on negotiated terms, which in practice signified the defeat of Gramsci and the *ordinovisti*.

The political contrast now deepened between Gramsci's group and the leaderships of the PSI and the trade unions. The latter were accused of 'short-sightedness'. An open quarrel developed between the Milan edition of *Avanti!*, which reflected majority opinion in the party, and Ottavio Pastore's Turin edition, which supported the *Ordine Nuovo* line. Serrati accused the Turin leaders of having fallen for the deliberate provocation of the owners at the wrong moment, and then looking belatedly for help from the rest of the Italian working class, 'less strong' and 'less prepared' than the Turin workers. Although up to a point this argument begged a vital question (since after all Serrati and the PSI majority were partly responsible for such lack of strength and preparedness), it was nonetheless unanswerable. The Turin *Avanti!* retorted: 'The proletariat of Turin has been defeated locally, but has won nationally, because its cause has become the cause of the

[8] *Avanti!* (Turin edition), 3 April 1920 [G.F.'s italics].
[9] Gramsci's report to the International, op. cit.

whole working class.' The final bulletin put out by the strike commit₁
ended with the same thought, in different words: 'This battle is over,
but the war goes on.'

The internal crisis of the PSI now rapidly worsened, until reconcili-
ation was impossible among the three main tendencies: reformist,
maximalist, and communist. At the same time, dissension was developing among the communist groups themselves: there was little common
ground between *L'Ordine Nuovo* and Bordiga's *Il Soviet*, while within
the Turin group itself Tasca was now tending to break away from
Gramsci, and Togliatti and Terracini were also moving towards a more
independent position.

Apart from their shared dislike of the reformists, Gramsci and
Bordiga differed on practically everything: on the factory councils, on
the problem of the revolutionary party, and on the question of the
correct socialist attitude towards elections. Bordiga thought that to rely
too heavily on the councils meant devoting too much time to the
creation of the institutions of socialist power, and too little to the
business of acquiring such power in the first place. It was an error, he
declared in *Il Soviet*, 'to raise the question of power inside the factory,
rather than the question of central political power'. As for the revolutionary party, *Il Soviet* had maintained since February 1920: 'In our
view, nothing does so much good as a split. The first thing must be to
put everyone in his proper place. One will know in this way exactly who
is a communist and who is not: there will be no more confusion on this
score. . . . A good split clears the air. Communists to one side, reformists of all persuasions and gradations to the other side.'

Gramsci believed, on the contrary, that a leftwards split was quite
wrong, and that the communist groupings should try harder than ever
to gain influence within the PSI, and eventually to win the whole party
over. The 'abstentionism' of the Bordiga faction was another source of
disagreement. Bordiga thought that the rejection of bourgeois democracy must be absolute: his slogan was 'Not one socialist at the polls!'
On 8 May 1920 Gramsci went as observer to a conference of 'abstentionists' in Florence (part of their attempt to build up a national
organization). He pleaded in vain that the abstentionist principle
should be given up, because 'no political party can be constituted on
such a restrictive basis. It requires wide contact with the masses, which
can only be obtained through new forms of organization' (like the
factory councils). His objection was brushed aside. Gramsci was quick
to express his dry judgement on the proceedings in *L'Ordine Nuovo*:

We have always held that it was the duty of the communist nuclei in the Party not to fall into irrelevant hallucinatory trances (like the 'abstentionist' problem, or the problem of constituting a 'really' communist party), but to work towards creating those mass conditions within which all such particular problems could be solved, as aspects of the organic development of a communist revolution.

So Bordiga's abstentionism, and his plan for a left-wing split of 'pure' revolutionaries, appeared to Gramsci at this point as irrelevant fixations upon over-particular issues.

The disagreement between Tasca and Gramsci arose directly out of the councils' movement. Tasca's idea – tenaciously contested by Gramsci – was to affiliate the councils to the already existing union movement and bring them under the authority of the Confederazione Generale. Many years later, Tasca was to explain, recalling his political apprenticeship in the car workers' strike of 1911–12:

> This was my first direct experience of the workers' struggle, and in it were formed my links with the trade union organizations: links which, naturally, the other future editors of *L'Ordine Nuovo* did not share. This brought about a certain disparity in our outlooks which, however one cares to judge it, certainly underlay the later disagreement and near split of 1920.

This 'near split' was on open display in the columns of *L'Ordine Nuovo*, in the form of a lively and sometimes angry public argument which dragged on from June until August.

In the same period, Gramsci also drew away from Togliatti and Terracini. The executive of the Turin party had contained both *ordinovisti* and 'abstentionists' since the previous February, and it was now thrown into crisis by the latter. The abstentionists resigned in July, as part of a campaign to prevent the PSI participating in the local government elections due in October and November 1920, and – more generally – in order to accelerate the movement towards a split in the Party. A new executive had to be elected, and Gramsci no longer wished to appear on the same platform as Togliatti and Terracini. Like them, he was of course in favour of the PSI taking part in the elections and still opposed Bordiga. But he thought that 'electionism' and 'abstentionism' were both in themselves quite 'phoney programmes', and that the dispute between them was merely serving to sow dissension among the communist groups of the PSI, at the expense of the work they should all have been carrying out among the masses, the work of revolutionary education which alone had any value.

He set up a 'communist education group' as an attempt to bridge the gap between the opposing factions. It proposed that the debate on election tactics should be reduced to its proper, marginal place, and that instead 'with tireless, patient energy, all party gatherings must be led to discuss the fundamental problems of the working class and the communist revolution'; or again, that 'the party section must be made to work usefully at preparing the cadres of the revolution, and the concrete social organization which the latter will have to build up; it must endeavour therefore to give a precise political complexion and outlook to the unions and chambers of labour, by exerting mass pressure upon them'.

But few were willing to follow this line. Only seventeen comrades joined the education group (among them Battista Santhià, Vincenzo Bianco and Andrea Viglongo). Gramsci's isolation emerged clearly in the voting for the new Turin executive. The 'electionists' from whom he had dissociated himself (Togliatti, Montagnana, Terracini, Roveda, etc.) won a majority, with 466 votes, and 186 votes went to the 'abstentionist' candidates (Boero, Parodi, etc.). Gramsci had asked his followers to vote with a blank slip. There were only 31 of them. In August 1920, Togliatti became the new secretary of the Turin section.

The Second Congress of the Third International (Comintern) was held in Moscow beginning on 19 July 1920. The Red Army had decisively defeated the counter-revolutionary armies of Kolchak, Denikin and Wrangel. There appeared to be some chance of the revolution spreading to other parts of the world. But disastrous developments in Europe gave grim warning of the difficulties attending such an enterprise.

In Berlin, an alliance of the military and the social democrats had beaten the Spartacist revolutionaries in January 1919, and killed their principal leaders, Rosa Luxemburg and Karl Liebknecht. Another such alliance had overthrown the Bavarian soviet republic on 1 May 1919. In Hungary, Béla Kun's communist government had been defeated by a counter-revolutionary army of Czechs and Rumanians, and replaced in early August 1919 by an administration led by the social democrat Peidle; but this government proved merely a bridgehead for Admiral Horthy's rise to power, and after 12 August a 'white terror' raged throughout Hungary.

Only one conclusion seemed possible: revolution had triumphed only where the revolutionary party (in Russia the Bolsheviks) had gone ahead on their own, without (or indeed against) the moderate or reformist parties (in Russia the Mensheviks and Social Revolutionaries). Inevitably therefore, the main line of this Second Congress was 'war on social democracy'. The assembly discussed and laid down twenty-one conditions for the admission of socialist parties to the Third International. Among these were that the party name should be changed to 'Communist', and that the reformists should be expelled at once.

There was no representative of the *Ordine Nuovo* group in the PSI's delegation to Moscow, which was made up of 'electionists' and 'abstentionists' united (from Serrati to Bordiga) in their hostility to the 'Turinese' and the factory-council movement. Nevertheless, the proceedings of the congress went more favourably for the editor of *L'Ordine Nuovo* than for the editors of *Avanti!* and *Il Soviet*.

What was known about Gramsci in Moscow at this time? Illuminating testimony on this has come from one of the Third International's functionaries, V. Degott, who went to Italy towards the end of 1919, and four years later published a booklet called *Liberty in Illegality: Memoirs of Illegal Activity Abroad 1918–21* (Moscow 1923).[1] Degott wrote:

> By chance I found myself reading a Turin weekly called *L'Ordine Nuovo*, edited by Gramsci. I found it very interesting. The correct position evident in every line of the paper induced me to ask comrade Viz (Aron Wizner) to invite Gramsci to Rome. He came at once. Here was a marvellous, a fascinating comrade. A little, hunchbacked man with a large head (almost as if it did not belong to him) and penetrating, intelligent eyes. He calmly analyses the situation in Italy. Every thought shows him to be a genuine Marxist. In the city of Turin . . . his paper had a wide following and his influence was great, although Serrati and a Russian comrade known as Nicolini passionately denied this was so.

When Degott returned to Moscow for the Second Congress, he went to see Zinoviev at the Smolny, and gave him 'Comrade Gramsci's report' (the report on the factory-council movement). Then Degott saw Lenin: 'I gave a long account of Serrati. I told him about the colossal work being accomplished by the Turin comrades, under the leadership of Gramsci.'

We can be sure, therefore, that although Gramsci and the *ordinovisti* had been excluded from the P S I delegation to Moscow, they were by no means unknown there, at the summit of the international communist movement. Their position had an immediate echo in the proceedings. The seventeenth clause in Lenin's *Theses on the Fundamental Tasks of the Second Congress of the Communist International* stated explicitly:

> Regarding the Italian Socialist Party, the Second Congress agrees with the substance of the critique of the Party and the practical proposals published by the Party's Turin section in the review *L'Ordine Nuovo* on 8 May 1920, as these fully correspond to all the basic principles of the Third International.

This referred to the nine-point April document mentioned above, *Per un Rinnovamento del Partito Socialista*. In the course of the congress,

[1] This book has never been translated. I owe thanks to Renzo De Felice for information concerning the sections on Italy.

further signs of Lenin's agreement with the Gramscian positions emerged.

Serrati rejected the directive on the immediate expulsion of reformists. In other countries – he did not deny – reformists had allied themselves with the national bourgeoisie during the war, and then betrayed the revolution after it. But it was wrong to transpose this judgement mechanically to the Italian situation; it might fit the French and German social democrats well enough, but it was not valid for the PSI's reformists. The really undesirable reformist elements (like Bissolati, Bonomi, or Podrecca) had been expelled already, at the Party's Reggio Emilia Congress of 1912. It would be most unfair to rank them with such comrades as Turati, Modigliani or Treves, who had respected discipline throughout the war, greeted the Russian Revolution as a great event, and (together with the Party's communist groups) demanded that the PSI adhere to the Third International. A gradual purge of the Party might be advisable, but not a sudden split.[2] The maximalist leader was also thinking, not without good reason, of the risks entailed in breaking the socialist front at the very moment when the reactionary Italian bourgeoisie was busy organizing its counter-attack. He declared at the session of 30 July:

> I believe it necessary to take account of the particular conditions in each country. . . . I ask you, comrades: if we were to return to Italy today and find that the reactionaries had turned upon us, if we found the forces of imperialism drawn up against us, could you – comrades of the executive committee – could you advise us to bring about a split in our ranks in a situation of this kind? No, esteemed comrades, leave the Italian Socialist Party the possibility of choosing for itself the correct moment for purging its ranks. We unite in assuring you that such a purge will occur, but give us the chance of carrying it out in the way most useful to the working masses, to the Party, and to the revolution we are preparing in Italy.

But Lenin remained inflexible on his general judgement of social democracy, and little disposed to distinguish Italian reformists from those of other countries. At the same session he answered Serrati's plea:

[2] In 1926, shortly after Serrati's death, Gramsci was to write of him: 'The essential trait in Serrati's personality as a party man came from his feeling for unity, and for the incessant effort which the preservation of such unity had required, the decades and decades of sacrifice and struggle, all the persecution and years of imprisonment which that unity now signified.'

To the Italian comrades we must say simply that it is the outlook of the
Ordine Nuovo militants which corresponds to the principles of the Communist International, and not the outlook of the present majority among
the leaders and their parliamentary group. . . . Hence, we must say to the
Italian comrades and to all parties which have a right wing: the reformist
tendency has nothing in common with communism.

Three days later it was Bordiga's turn to be the target of Lenin's
critical broadsides. Already, in his pamphlet *Left-wing Communism, an
Infantile Disorder*, Lenin had accused the Neapolitan leader and his
'abstentionist' group of 'drawing the wrong conclusion from their very
just critique of Signor Turati & Co., that any kind of participation in
parliament must be harmful'. He had continued: 'These Italian leftists
cannot produce even the shadow of a serious argument to support
their position. They simply do not know (or are trying to forget) the
internationally known examples of the effective revolutionary utilization
of bourgeois parliaments, in a fashion incontestably helpful to the
proletarian revolution.' Now he repeated and amplified such criticisms
at the congress:

> Comrade Bordiga, it appears, was trying to defend the point of view of
> Italian Marxists; but this fact notwithstanding, he failed to reply to a
> single one of the arguments adduced by other Marxists in favour of
> parliamentary action. . . . Comrade Bordiga, you are well aware that here
> in Russia we have expressed our wish to destroy the bourgeois parliament,
> in practice as well as in theory. But you have forgotten that this is impossible without long preparation, and that in the majority of countries it is
> not yet possible to destroy parliament with one single blow. We are forced
> to carry on the struggle to destroy parliament within parliament itself. . . .
> It is said that parliament is an instrument which the bourgeoisie uses to
> deceive the masses. But this argument can be turned against you, Comrade
> Bordiga, it tends to undermine your own position. How can you make clear
> the true character of parliament to these masses who are being deceived
> and kept in ignorance by the bourgeoisie? How can you denounce this or
> that parliamentary manoeuvre, the position taken up by this or that party,
> if you do not enter parliament, if you remain outside it? For the present,
> parliament too must remain an arena of the class struggle.

The Second Congress concluded its work on 7 August 1920.
Gramsci took new heart from it, although in other respects his personal
situation was at that moment objectively very difficult: he was still next
to unknown outside Turin, still at loggerheads with Tasca and with the

abstentionists, detached from the majority in the Turin section (Togliatti, Terracini, etc.), and under attack from the trade union bureaucracies.

He had got his brother Gennaro to come from Cagliari to look after the business side of *L'Ordine Nuovo* and give him a hand with book-keeping and other such worries which he normally managed rather badly. Having Gennaro by his side, he was able to rediscover something of the secure personal affection he had missed for so long. He also discovered a helpmate, constantly asking advice from his brother and confiding in him things never disclosed to his closest colleagues at work or in the movement. Years afterwards, he wrote in a letter from prison: 'I never thought it would be possible to see my brother again here at Turin. I was very happy, because I have always been closer to Gennaro than to the rest of the family.'

It must not be thought that the setbacks of the summer had weakened his political passion in the slightest degree. He continued his fight for the factory councils and the expansion of the communist groups in the PSI with indomitable energy. *L'Ordine Nuovo* of 21 August carried news of the solidarity Lenin had expressed with the Turin movement, and commented:

The report which the Turin section drew up in April for the Party's national executive was disregarded by the leaders and central bodies of the Party. When it was read in Moscow, however, by the comrades of the Third International executive, it became a basis for judgement of the whole Italian Party and was indicated as a worthy subject for discussion by a special congress. The report was written during the early days of the Turin engineering strike, when a general strike was not even considered remotely possible. . . . Subsequent events went in favour of the capitalists, and the working class was defeated. The efforts made by the Turin section to persuade the Party to set itself at the head of the movement went for nothing. It was merely accused of indiscipline, of irresponsibility and anarchism. . . . This is all past history. . . . Nevertheless, the memory of those passionate days of last April ensures that we, all the comrades of this section and the mass of workers who were involved, will derive a special pleasure from the knowledge that the executive committee of the Third International has passed a very different judgement upon us, a judgement which contrasts with that delivered by the leaders of the Italian Party, and against which we thought at the time there was no appeal: it is the policy of those 'few hotheads from Turin' which has won the approval of the highest authority in the international working-class movement.

The Italian working class was now on the eve of its last revolutionary outburst, the occupation of the factories. In factories throughout the country there had been a campaign of obstructionism since 20 August as a result of the owners' refusal to discuss wage increases with the engineers' union, FIOM (Federazione Italiana Operai Metallurgici). The workers reported each day and stayed in the plants in order to forestall a lock-out, but did no work. The FIOM had no revolutionary aim – its aim was in fact to provoke the new Giolitti government into arbitrating the dispute nationally. (Giolitti had returned to power in June with a programme of reforms, in the face of warnings and threats from the employers).

But in Turin the action soon turned from demonstration into revolution. A lock-out was proclaimed by the manufacturers on the night of 31 August, and the next morning the workers moved in to occupy the factories permanently. All power was assumed by the factory councils. In the central Fiat plant a socialist worker, Giovanni Parodi, occupied the desk and chair of Agnelli, head of the Fiat dynasty. It was decided to end the obstructionist campaign and begin work again under the direction of the councils. At Fiat-Centro, production of around 37 cars per day was maintained, compared to the 67-8 of normal times – in spite of the desertion of nearly all the technicians and white-collar workers. Turin became the focus of widespread interest, even outside Italy:

> The social hierarchy has been smashed [said the Piedmont *Avanti!* on 5 September], the standards of history have been turned upside down: the *labouring, instrumental* class has become the *ruling* class. . . . It has found within itself representatives . . . men capable of taking over all those functions which transform an elementary, mechanical assemblage of people into an organic structure, a living creature.

The experiment aroused great curiosity and respectful attention, often in circles far removed from socialism, among people who did not necessarily agree with what it stood for. In a letter to Ada Prospero (his future wife), Piero Gobetti felt compelled to say, on 7 September:

> So here we are in the middle of a revolution. I am following with sympathy the efforts of the workers, who really are constructing a new order. I don't feel within myself the force to follow them in practice, at least not now. But I think I see that things are becoming clearer, bit by bit, and that the greatest battle of the century is beginning. In which case, my place would be with whichever side has the most dedication, the most spirit of self-

sacrifice. . . . We are witnessing a truly heroic event. Certainly, it may yet be drowned in blood; but if so, it would be the beginning of our decadence. . . .

During the occupation L'Ordine Nuovo suspended publication, as it had done during the April strike: Gramsci and the others were constantly in the factories, beside the workers, discussing the innumerable problems of running a factory without technicians, trying to resolve practical questions on a basis of common agreement and collaboration. The new challenge led to disagreements being put to one side: Tasca, Gramsci's 'communist education group', the 'Bordighiani', and the leadership of the section found themselves together again on the crest of the revolutionary wave. Even so, in some of the factories extremism was acquiring a new force and direction which could not fail to preoccupy Gramsci. The desire for an immediate break with the PSI and the formation of a new, communist party was growing.

Gramsci had not altered his views on this question since his article of 3 July, where the idea of the 'pure' communist party was denounced as an 'hallucination'. He still thought that the vital task was communist propaganda at the grass roots, directed towards eventual take-over of the PSI from within. When he heard of moves in favour of a split in certain factories, he went to visit a comrade from his own group in the Spa car factory. It was the evening of 11 September. The guard at the gate failed to recognize the editor of L'Ordine Nuovo and ran to tell the shop-stewards (who were having a meeting in the union office) that 'some under-sized comrade with very long hair' was asking to be allowed in. Gramsci was admitted at once and, after a long tour round the workshops and some conversations with the workers there, at last found a chance to take Battista Santhià to one side. Santhià himself has recorded the dialogue:

GRAMSCI: Have you heard about the move at Fiat-Centro to break with the Socialist Party and found a communist party?
SANTHIÀ: I don't know much about it. But anyway, I agree that the Socialist Party should only be given up after adequate preparation. We've got to leave it as a majority, not as a small minority of dissidents.

My reply didn't surprise Gramsci [Santhià goes on]. We had discussed the problem more than once since the April strike, the Party's behaviour had destroyed whatever hope we had of making the national leadership follow the line of the Third International. Gramsci was convinced of this too, but he knew that the real problem lay in winning over the workers inside the Socialist Party.

It was for this reason that he was unable to approve the plan for an immediate break now being promoted by the 'Bordighian' factory council at Fiat-Centro.

> The outlook of many communist comrades at that factory was worrying [continues Santhià]. They had been poisoned by the worst sort of maximalism, and were more easily swayed by specious slogans than by serious ideological considerations. Comrade Parodi was above criticism. But it was not easy just then to counteract the rising tide of exasperation, as people felt the revolutionary movement in the factories losing its impetus and grew more and more angry.

The conversation ended with Gramsci's suggesting to Santhià, 'very delicately and tactfully', that he might contact Parodi on the matter.

The mission turned out to be fruitless. In Santhià's words again: 'On 20 September, what had been simmering ever since the 13th or 14th finally exploded at Fiat-Centro. The communist comrades of the abstentionist group decided to break off all relations with the reformist leaders of the unions and the Socialist Party, and asked everyone else to withdraw from the PSI at once and help give birth to a communist party.' New day, Bordiga's followers in Turin requested the abstentionist national committee (in the words of *Il Soviet*) 'to begin work on the creation of the Communist Party, as the Italian section of the Communist International, and call a national congress immediately to constitute it'. Bordiga himself was slightly more cautious than this suggested: he believed it would be more advisable to do battle at the forthcoming national congress of the PSI, hence the national committee turned down the proposal from Turin. The leaders of the Turin PSI section also took up position against the Bordiga group at Fiat-Centro. *Avanti!* condemned their action on 22 September: 'This is no matter of playing a game to see who gets there first, it is a matter of making sure that the Communist Party starts life as the one great organ which the proletariat can have faith in, as a body capable of uniting all the forces of revolution.'

Meanwhile, the occupation of the factories was moving towards failure. Once more, mass support for a revolutionary onslaught had proved weaker outside Turin, and the trade union leadership was now merely searching for an honourable way out, assisted in doing so by Premier Giolitti's attempts at mediation. No other course was possible, given the passivity of large sectors of the working class. Ludovico D'Aragona relates:

We had some plants where the workers gave evidence of real awareness and maturity; others, where the workers knew how to get the firm working again in the same way as it had worked before, when the capitalist boss was there to run things; and still others where, for a whole variety of reasons not necessarily related to their state of political consciousness – shortage of raw materials, lack of leaders and technicians, etc. – the workers could not make the factory function at all. There were also some places where the workers simply deserted, and we were forced to transfer workers from other plants in order to maintain a small nucleus and give the impression the workers were still in charge.

Gradually, the tide of revolution fell back. The workers had as good as lost, and were forced to give up the factories. They returned to work at the beginning of October, on the basis of a compromise laid down by Giolitti which – though it displeased the owners in certain respects – also signified the final defeat of the factory-council movement.

In a letter to Zino Zini of 10 January 1924, Gramsci was to say: 'At that time [1919–20], with the socialist party we had, with the working class still seeing things through rose-tinted glasses and preferring songs and brass bands to sacrifices, we were bound to have counter-revolutionary movements destined to sweep us away, whatever revolution we had achieved.'

The local elections of 31 October and 7 November were now close. At the Turin general meeting of the Socialist Party the names of Togliatti and Gramsci were put forward as possible candidates. Tasca has described how, 'when Gramsci's name was heard there was a great outburst of protest in the assembly'. He was accused of having written an 'interventionist' article in 1914 ('Neutralità attiva ed operante', see page 96). 'It should not be forgotten,' continues Tasca, 'that at this time the Socialist Party had decided not to allow as a candidate anyone who had in any way whatever supported the war. . . . But there were also other factors at work.' This can scarcely be doubted, if one thinks of the very different reception afforded Togliatti's candidature, even though the latter had enrolled as a volunteer. What were the other factors? Tasca goes on:

During the period 1916–18, and also later when *L'Ordine Nuovo* was going, Gramsci had been the scourge of the Party's temporizers, and had exposed the vain pretentions of quite a few more or less prominent figures. A great deal of resentment had been stored up against him in Turin. . . . To this must be added the fact that Gramsci was no great public speaker, and so was really known and liked only within a restricted circle of intellectuals and workers.

The attack came mainly from the right. But one must inevitably suspect that certain other differences which had been put aside during the occupation of the factories were now re-emerging. Togliatti (still secretary) and Terracini could have used their influence over the large majority of the section they represented to repel the assault on Gramsci. They chose not to do so and he remained excluded from the list.

This was not the only bitter blow Gramsci had to suffer. On 5 November a telegram had arrived from Ghilarza, telling him that his sister Emma (the one who had gone to work with the Tirso dam construction company) was seriously ill. Antonio left for Sardinia at once: he had guessed the worst. The dam was being built in a malarial area and she had caught the fever in its most malignant form. When he arrived home she was already buried.[3] Now that he was back in Ghilarza he stayed a few days. But he was restless. Often, Signora Peppina would come across him deep in thought, and she was terrified by his thinness and obvious exhaustion: his haggard white face was at once boyish and yet worn out, like an old man's. He was now twenty-nine years old.

He returned to a Turin raging with debate on the forthcoming Socialist Congress. There were changes on the left. The 'abstentionists' were now the 'ex-abstentionists', since the International's Twenty-One Points entailed giving up total opposition to parliamentary action. The 'electionist' title had also become meaningless since the end of the battle over electoral participation. These two groups, Gramsci's communist education group, and the other left-wing socialists, had plastered over their basic disagreements in a common loyalty to the theses of the Comintern. They had called a meeting in Milan during the first fortnight of October, and launched a new manifesto-cum-policy statement. It had been signed by Bombacci, Bordiga, Fortichiari, Gramsci, Misiano, Polano, Repossi, and Terracini, on behalf of all the participant groups. This document was ratified by a subsequent assembly held at Imola on 28 and 29 of November; thenceforth the alliance of communist groups was known by the name of the town. Bordiga and his group predominated, being alone in having a really national organization. In 1923 Gramsci wrote to

---

[3] Emma Gramsci's name is recorded on a plaque in memory of all those who died during the execution of this project, situated just by the entrance to the dam.

Togliatti: 'Because of the antipathy we felt during the period 1919–20 towards setting ourselves up as a faction, we remained isolated, almost a collection of individuals, while on the other side, among the abstentionists, their tradition of factional organization and common activity left a deep imprint whose theoretical and practical effects are still visible in the Party's life today.'

Already at Imola (and even before) it was clear there were two diametrically opposed conceptions of what the new party should be like. One saw it as a sect consisting of a small number of intransigent revolutionaries whom the masses would then follow into revolutionary action; the other saw it as a party *of* the masses, 'not a party which uses the masses to produce a heroic imitation of the French Jacobins'. Hence there were also two opposed views of the PSI: the first was for a split (Bordiga), the second for working within it (Gramsci). Even after the launching of the new manifesto-programme, Gramsci had accused the reactionaries of wishing to strike at Turin because it was 'the seat of a precise political doctrine that threatens *to win over the majority of the Italian Socialist Party*, threatens to *transform the Party* from an organ which perpetuates the death-throes of capitalism to an organ of struggle and revolutionary reconstruction.'[4] And the following week, in a note headed 'The Communist Faction', he declared: 'The communists intend to organize themselves on a wide basis, *they intend to win the leadership of the Socialist Party and the Confederation of Unions*'.

However, Lenin was by now closer to Bordiga's position than to Gramsci's. In *L'Humanité* of 14 October Serrati had written: 'We are all agreed on the Twenty-One conditions set out in Moscow. *The problem is applying them.* I say again that the party must be purged of all its noxious elements, and I myself have proposed the expulsion of Turati. But we must not lose the mass of members in the trade unions and the co-operatives. The others want *a radical split*. This is what the dispute is about.' A reply from Lenin appeared in *False Discourses on Freedom*, composed between 4 November and 11 December, where he objected that:

> Serrati fears the split may weaken the party, especially in the unions, in the co-operatives, and in local government. The communists, on the other hand, are afraid of the revolution being sabotaged by the reformists. If one has reformists within one's own ranks, *it is impossible* to win a proletarian

[4] *L'Ordine Nuovo*, 17 October 1920 [G.F.'s italics].

revolution, *it is impossible* to defend it once it is won. Hence, Serrati is willing to jeopardize the fate of the revolution rather than risk offending the Milan city council.

So far Gramsci wholeheartedly agreed with Lenin's thesis. But the latter goes on:

> In Italy, decisive battles for the conquest of State power are at hand between the proletariat and the bourgeoisie. At such a moment, not only is it absolutely indispensable that reformists of Turati's kind be removed from the Party, it may even be desirable to remove excellent communists from positions of responsibility – that is, those who are liable to waver or show uncertainty over the question of 'unity' with the reformists. Let me give you a striking example. . . . On the eve of the October Revolution, some well-known Bolsheviks and communists like Zinoviev, Kamenev, Rykov, Nogin and Milyutin showed a tendency to worry about the risk of the Bolsheviks becoming too isolated, about whether unleashing an insurrection was not too risky, about being over-intransigent towards a certain sector of the Mensheviks and Social Revolutionaries. Conflict over such points became so acute that these comrades ostentatiously resigned from all their functions and ceased work in the Party and in the soviets. But after a few weeks – or a few months at the most – all these comrades recognized their mistake and returned to their highly responsible posts in the Party and in the soviets. . . . And now Italy finds itself in a *precisely similar situation*. . . . under such conditions, the Party will not be weakened but *strengthened* a hundred times over when the reformists are weeded out from its ranks, *and when the leadership decides to remove such doubtless excellent communists as Baratono, Zannerini, Bacci, Giacomini, and Serrati from their high posts* [G.F.'s italics].

Here was clear authority indeed for Bordiga's strategy of a left-wing split. It has been suggested that it was Lenin's encouragement for this strategy which now inclined Gramsci to give in and subordinate himself to Bordiga. Or is this suggestion groundless, as others have protested? It is a fact that Gramsci only came to accept the split as inevitable after the appearance of *False Discourses on Freedom*. On 18 December, less than a month before the Livorno Congress, he wrote in terms which accepted the leftward split for the first time:

> It would be silly to whine uselessly over what has happened and cannot be remedied. Communists are and should continue to be cool, level-headed reasoners; if everything (in the PSI) has fallen to pieces, then it is necessary to reconstruct everything, to reconstruct the Party. From this day onwards

we must consider and love the communist faction as a Party in its own right, as the solid foundation of the future Communist Party of Italy.

As the revolutionary wave receded, the counter-wave of reaction gathered force. At the local elections of 31 October–7 November 1920 the PSI repeated its good performance of the previous year, winning a majority in 2,162 communes out of 8,000 (including Milan and Bologna), and in 26 of the 69 provinces. On 21 November, while the new socialist mayor of Bologna was appearing on the balcony of the town hall, the Palazzo d'Accursio, to receive the acclamation of the crowd, a group of fascists suddenly appeared and shot at random into the people on the square below. Hand-grenades were thrown into the crowd from one of the lower windows of the Palazzo itself. The massacre claimed sixty-eight victims: ten dead and fifty-eight wounded. A month later, in similar circumstances, the fascists attacked Palazzo Estense, the town hall of Ferrara: this time three of their number were killed by the 'red guards'. The fascist punitive expeditions promptly multiplied in number and ferocity.

Serrati was now more preoccupied with defence than with attack, and these incidents had strengthened his argument in favour of keeping the Italian socialists united, for the time being. On 16 December he wrote to Lenin:

> We do not wish to defend the reformists. We wish to defend the Party, the working class, and the revolution from an insane mania for destruction and demolition. We wish to defend the unity of the Italian socialist movement in order that it may be able to face the difficulties and sacrifices which lie ahead in the work of reconstruction. The Italian bourgeoisie has already launched its campaign of reaction. . . . Today, we are facing the counter-attack it has mounted in answer to the continuous attack delivered by the working class from Armistice Day up to the present. Italian capitalism has behind it the power of the State, of the police and the judiciary, the power of an army it can still rely upon, and it is not disposed to give up the struggle: it is carefully organizing its forces and closing its ranks. The last local elections, and a number of recent incidents in certain Italian cities, have shown that the ruling class will stop at nothing in order to impose an absolute barrier to all further advance by the working class.

If this was the new situation in Italy – a bourgeois counter-offensive demanding united resistance rather than fragmentation into several different parties – it seemed appropriate to Serrati to quote from a writing of Zinoviev's, before concluding: 'We are not centrists, we ask only that the Third International should apply its own standards to us, as it does to others; that it should allow us to be the judges of a developing situation and of the measures that situation requires, so that the Italian socialist movement may defend itself.'[5]

One month later, on 15 January 1921, the Seventeenth National Congress of the Italian Socialist Party opened in Livorno. The result was not what Lenin expected: the majority of the Italian working class failed to come over to the positions of the 'pure' communists.

> We are defeated [wrote Gramsci in 1924] because the greater part of the politically organized proletariat thought we were wrong, and refused to follow us, even although we had the very great authority and prestige of the Comintern on our side, and had placed our trust in it. We had not been able to conduct a systematic campaign, we had not been able to reach all the vital nuclei and militants of the Socialist Party and set a debate going on the right lines; we had not known how to translate the significance of each of the events of 1919–20 into a language understandable to every peasant and every worker.

The way in which the communist faction waged battle bore the mark of Bordiga's direction. Gramsci did not even speak at the congress. Serrati retained control of the leadership, with 98,000 as against the 58,000 'pure' communists and the 14,000 reformists. On the day following the vote, 21 January 1921 – it was also the day before Gramsci's thirtieth birthday – the minority of communists met in the San Marco theatre at Livorno and constituted the new 'Communist Party of Italy'.[6]

The new party was completely dominated by Amadeo Bordiga, who had thus finally (and with the support of the International) realized his 'irrelevant hallucination', as Gramsci had referred to it only the previous July. Gramsci's own conversion to the new truths had come too late, and he had to accept a secondary role at first. Indeed, he was nearly left out of the new party's first central committee. There was a bitter fight against his inclusion. Certain of his new party comrades did not disdain to employ the shoddy polemical tricks first used by his PSI adversaries. Togliatti relates how 'some of the delegates opposed Gramsci and brought up the stupid story first circulated by the reformists and maximalists during the pre-congress debates, to the

[5] The quotation from Zinoviev runs: 'The Communist International naturally has no intention of foisting the same form on all parties. . . . The Communist International certainly acknowledges that there are local developments which must be dealt with according to the needs of the different parties themselves.'

[6] This was the 'Partito Comunista d'Italia' (PCdI), as distinct from the present, renamed 'Partito Comunista Italiano' (PCI) (T.N.)

effect that he had once been an interventionist – or even that he had fought bravely at the front'.

The central committee finally chosen contained eight from the *Il Soviet* group (Bordiga, Grieco, Fortichiari, Repossi, Parodi, Polano, Sessa and Tarsia), five left-wing maximalists (Belloni, Bombacci, Gennari, Marabini and Misiano), and only two from the *Ordine Nuovo* group (Terracini and Gramsci). Gramsci was not elected to its executive committee, which consisted of Bordiga, three of his followers (Fortichiari, Grieco, Repossi) and Terracini.

The Communist Party of Italy was born as a sect, and was to bear the marks of this birth for a long time to come. Gramsci wrote later of these events:

> The reactionary forces intended to thrust the workers back into the state they had known during the early days of capitalism, when they were dispersed, isolated, a collection of individuals without any consciousness of class unity, or any aspiration towards power. The Livorno split (which detached the greater part of the Italian proletariat from the Communist International) was without any doubt the greatest single victory won by these reactionary forces.

15

For some time after the Livorno Congress Gramsci went through a period of relative 'inertia'; or so a number of commentators have suggested (Piero Gobetti, for instance). Was this really so?

From 1 January 1921, *L'Ordine Nuovo* had begun to appear as a daily paper, and Gramsci was still editor. He was earning 1,100 lire a month, a considerable income for those days, but had not given up his modest student's room with the Berra family in Piazza Carlina. Every day, at about 2 or 3 o'clock in the afternoon, he would get up and set off for work, escorted by a colossal bodyguard, Giacomo Bernolfo, an ex-artillery sergeant who was supposed to protect him from possible fascist attacks (sometimes Bernolfo was replaced by an out-of-work Ghilarza man, Titino Sanna). They would go to Via Po, or to a milk bar in Via Santa Teresa – near the junction with Piazza Solferino – where Gramsci breakfasted. Or else (more often) they would go to the home of Pia Carena, where Gramsci would spend some time before going on to the newspaper offices in Via dell'Arcivescovado. There Gramsci would work steadily with only a short break for a meal in the evening, until dawn of the following day, and go home as the first cafés opened along Via Roma and Via Po.

Times were difficult. An unceasing struggle had to be waged against intimidation and violence, in an atmosphere like that of a besieged fortress, and Gramsci was always in the forefront, a source of courage and new heart to his comrades. They recall him as a reliable guide and counsellor, inspiring others by his tenacious resistance to the rising tide of barbarism.

As general conditions in Italy had changed since the immediate post-war period, so had those of Gramsci's journalistic work, and not only because of the change-over from weekly to daily. There were now two other communist dailies: in Trieste *Il Lavoratore* ('The Worker'), edited by Ottavio Pastore, and in Rome *Il Comunista*, edited by Togliatti. The net result of the breaking up of the old Turin editorial group was thus, as Gobetti put it, 'three unreadable newspapers'. A harsh judgement certainly (especially as far as *L'Ordine Nuovo* was concerned), but not without some foundation. Although it had retained a certain liveliness which distinguished it from most of the party press, the daily version of *L'Ordine Nuovo* no longer had the freshness of the weekly. It was now an official party paper, obliged to follow Bordiga's party line, and this lack of independence was damaging. The theoretical boldness, the imagination and creative *élan* which had once distinguished it were now much less in evidence. Within the newly-formed party, for a variety of reasons which are not all easily explained, Gramsci accepted the subordinate role assigned to him by Bordiga.

It was to be some time before the underlying quarrel between them came out into the open again. Writing to Gramsci in February 1924, Togliatti was to say: 'I will not hide my opinion that many of the things you are now saying should have been said openly long before, in public, to the Party, and not in private conversations which were only heard about at second or third hand. Inside the central committee elected at Livorno you represented the group which had different ideas from those of Bordiga.'

However, in 1921 Gramsci plainly thought he had good reasons for keeping quiet and refusing to combat Bordiga's sectarian views openly. Not the least of these reasons was – we must assume – the great prestige then enjoyed by the leader of the new Communist Party of Italy, both among militants and in Comintern circles. The International's approval derived from Bordiga's apparent renunciation of left extremism. At the Third Comintern Congress Lenin spoke of the Livorno split to the PSI delegate, Lazzari:

> You had 98,000 votes, yet you chose to remain aligned with 14,000 reformists rather than take the road of the 58,000 communists. Even if the latter had not been real communists, even if they had only been followers of Bordiga – *and we know this is not so, since after the Second Congress of the International, Bordiga loyally declared he would renounce all anarchism and anti-parliamentarism* – you should still have gone with them [G.F.'s italics].

So Bordiga had been absolved by Lenin, and in Italy disagreement with him could easily seem inopportune, a threat to the solidarity of the revolutionary front. Moreover, the new climate created by the wave of fascist reaction made candid internal debate seem inadvisable. Unity now looked like the condition of staying alive and continuing the fight. As Gramsci wrote in 1924:

After the split at Livorno, we entered into a state of emergency. This is the only justification possible for our attitudes and actions after Livorno. . . . We had to organize ourselves into a party in the throes of a civil war. . . . No sooner were our new groupings established than we had to turn them into guerrilla detachments, into units fit for the most difficult, atrocious guerrilla war any working class has ever had to fight.

Could Gramsci have sustained his opposition to Bordiga's sectarianism in this atmosphere? And even had he wanted to, what real force did he have behind him? Would the mass of communists have followed him? A very recent test had made it look more than doubtful. In the first political elections held since the founding of the PCdI (on 15 May 1921), Gramsci had been defeated. The Turin communists had voted for Misiano and Rabezzana rather than him. It must also be presumed that he was not yet considered quite fit for party leadership in Comintern circles. The judgement of Degott (who esteemed Gramsci highly, as we saw previously) is probably indicative of this:

Gramsci is much deeper than the other comrades and is capable of analysing situations correctly. He has an acute understanding of the Russian Revolution. But he has little direct influence over the masses. In the first place he is no orator; and secondly, he is youthful, small in stature, and hunch-backed, all things which affect audiences unfavourably.

During this period, Gramsci sank back once more into a state of extreme physical and nervous debility. This was aggravated by family worries. There was trouble with Gennaro, who was refusing to marry the girl he had had a child by. More seriously, his younger brother Mario had joined the reactionaries: he had become the first secretary of the Fascist Federation of Varese.

Gramsci went to see him. Since marrying Anna Maffei Parravicini, Mario had left the army and joined a business firm. Antonio had a long talk with him about his reasons for becoming a fascist, and said quietly: 'Does it really seem right to you? Think about it. You're a good lad and you have your wits about you, I know you'll think twice.' Six years after this visit he wrote to his mother: 'When I went to visit Mario at his home a few years back, I think I formed an accurate picture of the milieu in which he is seen as some kind of hero. But it's better to say nothing about all that. Anyway, Mario is my brother, and I like him in spite of everything. I hope he's settled down now, and minding his own business more than he was.'

So Gramsci had a number of different anxieties to contend with, of varying degrees of seriousness. Nevertheless, Gobetti's description of him at that time as 'sterile in ideas and activity' seems somewhat arbitrary.

On the plane of ideas he continued his analysis of the play of forces in Italian society with the same originality and concreteness as before. He reached a better understanding of the real character of fascism, the reactionary vocation of its leaders and principal supporters, the sheep-like stupidity of the petty-bourgeois forces which had risen to follow it, and above all the peril it represented. This peril was still underrated by most communists. In 1921-22, there were many 'Don Ferrantes' who obstinately denied the existence of the plague and its contagion, only to die of it later.[1] The Party's official line was simple: no fascist or military dictatorship was possible in Italy. Gramsci did not share this view, but confined himself to venting his disagreement in private. He was restricted by his formal acquiescence to ideas he did not share, by his refusal to criticize overtly Bordiga's line and all the 'trivial and loutish attitudes that went with it'.

On the plane of action, he devoted himself to the paper. He was very exacting with his writers and refused to tolerate carelessness, super-ficiality, or sloppy writing (even in the least important items) and would often lose his temper and order things to be redone. One of his colleagues, Alfonso Leonetti, recollects his outbursts on certain evenings, when the page-proofs arrived. 'This isn't a newspaper,' he used to shout, 'it's a sack of potatoes! Agnelli can call all his workers together tomorrow and say: "Look, you see! This lot can't even put a newspaper together, yet they want to run the State!" We've got to stop his saying this, but how *can* we if we turn out a paper that looks like a sack of potatoes!'

Gramsci's acceptance of Bordiga's position (which was in any case formal and negative, in the sense that it meant only abstaining from public criticism) did not prevent him from expressing other central ideas of his own. Among these was his conception of 'openness' towards non-communist and Catholic workers and intellectuals. He entrusted the theatre criticism on *L'Ordine Nuovo* to a liberal, Piero Gobetti. In the spring he accompanied one of the Fiume expedition legionaries to Gardano to visit D'Annunzio, though it appears that this

[1] *Don Ferrante*: a character in Manzoni's *The Betrothed*, the archetype of the scholar who lives in his library and proves the impossibility of things which are actually happening (in the novel, a plague). (T.N.)

meeting did not take place.[2] He always paid the closest attention to developments among the left-wing Catholics organized in the Miglioli wing of the Partito Popolare.[3] And he continued to fight the anti-clericalism deeply rooted in certain strata of the Piedmontese working class. Andrea Viglongo told the author:

> I remember a diocesan conference with about two hundred thousand participants; Gramsci wanted us to do something on it. 'It's part of the news,' he said, 'people are involved in it, we can't just ignore it.' So I wrote a short account of it which *L'Ordine Nuovo* published with a headline over two columns. Another time I happened to write a bitter attack on the anti-clericals, with passages like: 'Anti-clerical pornography, which by a curious coincidence flourished at the same time as Prampolini's evangelistic campaign, was produced by the total lack of moral sensibility characteristic of the rationalist socialism of twenty years ago. . . . For us young people *L'Asino* is like the symbol of that socialism: masonic, parliamentarist, and petty-bourgeois'.[4] Gramsci read the piece and approved it, putting it on the front page of the issue of 27 August 1921, as an editorial. There were shrieks of anguish from some working-class groups, at Borgo San Pàolo for instance. But Gramsci took them calmly. He told me: 'That editorial went down very well!'

In the meantime, some divergence of view had begun to develop between the International and Bordiga's leadership of the PCdI. Before the Livorno split Lenin had declared: 'To be able to lead the revolution to victory, and defend that victory, the Italian Party must take *a certain leftward step* (but without tying its hands, *and without forgetting that, subsequently, circumstances might very well call for some rightward steps*)' [G.F.'s italics]. The 'leftward step' had happened: it was the split at Livorno. But now circumstances were calling for 'some rightward steps' – that is, for an alliance with the Socialists in some kind of 'common front' against the reactionary onslaught. Such was the news which arrived from the Third Congress of the International, held

[2] D'Annunzio led an expedition to occupy the port of Fiume (now Rijeka, in Yugoslavia) in September 1919, to prevent the city being detached from Italy by the peace treaty. He and his 8,000 'legionaries' (mostly army deserters) remained in occupation until January 1921, when he was driven out by the Italian army on orders from the Giolitti government. (T.N.)

[3] *Partito Popolare*: the first mass Catholic party in Italy, launched in January 1919 under the leadership of Don Sturzo and Alcide de Gasperi, and the ancestor of the present ruling Christian Democratic Party. The 'Popolari' had a left wing led by Miglioli which was particularly important in agricultural areas. (T.N.)

[4] *Camillo Prampolini* (1859–1930): socialist reformist leader active in the organization of agricultural workers in Emilia. (T.N.)

in Moscow in June and July 1921. It had been recognized in Moscow that the workers' movements were retreating before the counter-attack of the right, particularly in Italy; under these conditions, the prime objective of the working-class could no longer be the conquest of power and proletarian dictatorship – it was now necessary to defend democratic liberties alongside the socialists.

But in Italy, where conflicts had been so exacerbated by the split, the Bordighists stubbornly resisted the new course. Lenin noticed this and issued a reproof. On 14 August 1921 he wrote that certain communist parties, including the Italians, 'had *a trifle exaggerated* the fight against centrism, had gone *a trifle over* the limit beyond which this fight becomes a kind of sport'. In truth, Bordiga and his group had exaggerated much more than 'a trifle'. And now that the International had altered its line – only a few months after Livorno – it seemed to them that to form an alliance with the socialists would be as good as admitting that the split had been a mistake. Gramsci said later:

> Lenin summed up what should have been the meaning of the split when he said to comrade Serrati: 'Separate yourselves from Turati, and then form an alliance with him.' We should have adapted this formula to the split which took place, in a form different from the one foreseen by Lenin. That is, we should certainly have separated ourselves from reformism, and from maximalism (which represented, and still represents, no more than typical Italian opportunism in the working-class movement). It was indispensable and historically necessary to do so. But afterwards, and without giving up our ideological and organizational struggle against them, we should have attempted to build an alliance against reaction. To the leadership of our Party, however, every attempt by the International to make us adopt this line appeared as an implicit disavowal of the Livorno split.

So he wrote in 1926. But his dissent from Bordiga on this question had been much less explicit during the months before the Second Congress of the Communist Party of Italy, held in Rome in March 1922.

Bordiga's tendency towards a closed sectarianism rather than the kind of wide-ranging mass action which alone could have stayed or defeated fascism was shared by most of the Party's leaders, not excluding Togliatti and Terracini. Togliatti himself has admitted this:

> The most surprising and thought-provoking thing was that even comrades like Terracini and myself – who had once followed Gramsci's leadership in a completely opposite direction, and contributed both to the genesis of very different ideas and to their inspired realization in great actions – even we ended by capitulating to a sectarian conception of the Party.

Tasca and others of the right-wing minority opposed Bordiga. Within the majority, Gramsci alone 'did not suppress his criticisms', Togliatti goes on, 'but for long these were given only in personal conversation, and led to no debate in the central committee; they were not voiced at a general meeting of the Turin section until the very eve of the congress'. At this congress, Bordiga's platform rejected the 'common front' strategy, and the line laid down by the International. Apart from the right-wing minority, nobody objected. Gramsci says:

> At Rome we accepted Amadeo's theses because they were put forward as a statement of views to be presented at the forthcoming Comintern congress, and not as a basis for action. We believed that in this way we could keep the Party united around its basic nucleus; we believed this concession was due Amadeo in view of the very great role he played in the Party organization. We do not regret this: politically, it would have been quite impossible to lead the Party without the active participation of Amadeo and his group. ... Then we retreated from this position, and tried to make the retreat as orderly as possible, without further crises or threats of splits in the movement, without adding new disruptive stresses to those already created by the defeat of the revolutionary movement.

There were just enough reservations in this position on Bordiga's line to win Gramsci favour within the International – and just enough acceptance of the line to avoid making an enemy of Bordiga. So it was natural that Gramsci should be nominated as the next representative of the Italian Party on the Comintern's executive committee in Moscow (he had already travelled on behalf of the International to Lugano and Berlin in January and February 1922).

He left towards the end of May 1922. He was leaving Turin after eleven years, and also giving up the editorship of *L'Ordine Nuovo*. There was intense emotion at the leave-taking ceremony in the offices on Via dell'Arcivescovado. However, he was leaving for great events in his political life, through what he was to learn in the presence of the Russian Revolution and its protagonists; and in his personal life, through his meeting with Julia Schucht and the fulfilment this would bring him.

Gramsci arrived in Moscow in a state of acute depression. He was ill. And he was paying now for the great political and personal tensions he had recently gone through, as well as for a period of intensive work almost beyond the powers of anyone already suffering so much from ill-health, malnutrition and psychological traumas. It quickly became evident to his new colleagues that he could not carry on as he was, and early in the summer Zinoviev – then President of the International – suggested that he go to the Serebranyi Bor ('Silver Wood') sanatorium on the outskirts of Moscow for a time. Gramsci was displaying nervous tics, and was subject to convulsive trembling and 'ferocious-looking' fits. 'Many very kind people who came to look after me and keep me company,' he later admitted, 'told me afterwards they'd been scared stiff. They knew I was Sardinian, and thought I might have been on the point of knifing someone!'

One of these 'very kind people' was a woman some years older than himself who spoke Italian perfectly, Eugenie Schucht. She was herself suffering from a severe nervous complaint, which made her unable to walk. Thanks to her knowledge of Italian and Italy, they communicated easily and soon became friends; Antonio learned much about her, and about her family's long stay in Rome. She had been born in Siberia, while her father, Apollo Schucht, was in exile there for anti-Tsarist activity. Two other sisters were born after her, Nadina and Tatiana. In about 1890 the family had moved to Montpellier in France, and then to Geneva. During their emigration Anna Schucht was born, then Julia in 1896, then (sixth and last) Victor, the only boy. After the turn of the century the family went to Rome. Apollo Schucht was a cultivated man of Scandinavian origin, with a wide knowledge of French literature and music, and he had inherited enough from a family of higher state officials to live comfortably. The girls all studied. Nadina took two degrees, and then returned to Russia, to Tiflis, where she married; Eugenie went to the Fine Arts Institute in Via Ripetta; Anna and Julia were both musically inclined, and studied the violin at the music school attached to the Santa Cecilia Academy. All passed their later childhood and early youth in Rome, living first in Via Monserrato, then close to the Colosseum in Via Buonconsiglio, and later in Via Adda. All this time Apollo had no regular job, except for one spell of teaching officers Russian at the Ministry of War.

In the autumn of 1913 the family started to break up. Eugenie and Anna were the first to leave Italy: they went to Warsaw, where Eugenie taught in a Jewish school and, two years later, Anna married Theodor Zabel. A few months after them, Julia left – she had obtained her music diploma – and was followed by her mother. Apollo and Victor went to Switzerland. On 29 September 1915, Apollo wrote to Leonilde Perilli, a Roman friend of his daughters: 'I got a letter from Moscow today – Eugenie has found herself a little job. Julia hasn't found one yet. Anna is going to live with her husband's mother, while he is in a camp near Moscow.' Early in 1916, Eugenie, Anna, Julia and their mother were living together at Ivanovo Vosniesensk, a small textile town about one hundred kilometres from Moscow. Then in December of the same year the family was together again in Moscow, all except Nadina (of whom no more had been heard) and Tatiana, who had stayed in Italy, and they were still there at the time of the October Revolution. Afterwards, Julia, her father and mother, and Anna and Theodor Zabel returned to Ivanovo.

When Eugenie met Gramsci, her family was still at Ivanovo. They used to come and visit her regularly in Serebranyi Bor. Gramsci saw Julia for the first time about the middle of July 1922. For some time, Eugenie had been displaying an evident affection for him, but he was much more struck by the younger sister, Julia. She was tall and fair, with large, sad eyes in a beautiful oval face, and shoulder-length hair. At twenty-six, she was five years younger than he. After seven years in Russia, she was still nostalgic for Italy and had never ceased regretting her departure from Rome. When she was nineteen and on her way home to Russia, she had written back to Nilde Perilli from Tsarikov: 'I am in Bulgaria. I've come closer to Russia, but gone farther and farther away from Italy, from Rome. . . .' And in September of that same year, from Moscow: 'It is cold here already. Sadness comes over me when I think about Rome . . . when I think that this day is the 15th of September, in Rome.' She now had a job teaching music in the lycée at Ivanovo.

Gramsci was very timid at first. At the age of thirty, he had never yet opened himself up to any woman and was accustomed to keeping the tightest possible rein on his feelings for fear of disappointment. More-over, he was still oppressed by awareness of his physical condition: 'For a long time, a very long time, I have believed it was absolutely, fatally impossible that I should ever be loved.' But now, the sight of Julia disturbed him deeply. He wrote to her after one of their early meetings: 'Did you come to Moscow on 5 August as you told me you would? I waited three days for you. I didn't dare leave the room for fear of missing you like that other time. . . . You didn't come to Moscow, did you? You would certainly have come to see me, at least for a few moments. . . . Will you come soon? Can I see you again? Write to me. Everything you say to me does me good and makes me feel stronger.'

During Julia's visits to her sister, she and Gramsci spent much time together. She found herself fascinated by the young Italian: his limbs were weakly developed, but his blue eyes were filled with tenderness, and his inner life seemed one of extraordinary force and vitality. These early meetings at the sanatorium, and the idyll which developed between them, were to haunt Gramsci for the rest of his life:

> I've been going over it all again in thought, over all the memories of our life together, from that first day I saw you at Serebranyi Bor and didn't dare go into the room because I felt so timid (yes, you made me feel timid, today I smile as I remember it), until the day you went away, on foot, and I went with you as far as the main road through the forest, and stood motion-less there for so long watching you grow smaller and smaller down that road, carrying a bundle across your shoulders on your way back to the wide and terrible world outside.

Through this experience, the young man who had once admitted to living too much by the brain and too little by the heart attained a new sort of inner poise. Until now, the whole of Gramsci's life had been a constant retreat within himself, an unceasing, contradictory struggle between his desire for society and his desire to be strong independently of society, and without any reliance on the feelings of others.

> How many times have I wondered [he wrote to Julia] if it is really possible to forge links with a mass of people when one has never had strong feelings for anyone, not even for one's own parents; if it is possible to love a collectivity when one has not been deeply loved oneself, by individual human creatures? Hasn't this had some effect on my life as a militant, has it not tended to make me sterile and reduce my quality as a revolutionary by making everything a matter of pure intellect, of mere mathematical calculation? I've thought a lot about all this, and it has come to my mind

again these last few days because I was thinking of you, and of how you came into my life and gave me love, gave me what I had always lacked. It was this lack that used to make me cross-grained and spiteful.

He was discovering at last that 'one cannot divide onself into fragments and make only one part function; life is a whole, and each activity is strengthened by all the others; love strengthens the whole of one's existence . . . it creates a new equilibrium, a greater intensity of all other feelings and sentiments'. However, given the circumstances of their lives, this relationship which meant so much to Gramsci was destined to be made up mainly of brief encounters and long, painful separations.

The news from Italy was filled with premonitions of disaster. On 28 October 1922, the 'March on Rome' had taken place, and the following day the King had asked Benito Mussolini to form a government.[1] It was two and a half years since Gramsci had written, in April 1920: 'The present phase of the class struggle in Italy is the one which precedes *either* the conquest of power by the revolutionary proletariat *or* a terrible reaction on the part of the property-owning class and the governing caste.' Now the second of these prophecies was being fulfilled.

Throughout the summer, the fascist bands had sacked and burned chambers of labour and co-operatives, and attacked left-wing town councils and the offices of socialist and democratic newspapers; all over north and central Italy left-wing leaders had been persecuted, imprisoned, beaten up and killed. Now, with the fascists officially in power, the outlook was black indeed. All this had taken place on the eve of the Comintern's Fourth Congress, due to open in Moscow on 5 November 1922. The problem before it was: how should the workers' parties and all democratic parties react to this violent frontal assault? Divided, or – breaking with the past – in some form of united resistance? Zinoviev, Bukharin, and most of the other influential Bolsheviks in the International, strongly advised a common front of working-class parties. Indeed, they thought that a fusion of the communists and socialists was indispensable – especially now that the Socialist Party had expelled its reformist wing, at its Congress of October 1922. But

[1] At the Fascist Party Congress in Naples on 24 October 1922, it was decided to attempt an insurrectionary march on the capital. Mussolini saw leaders of industry and assured them that 'the aim of the imminent fascist action is the restoration of discipline, especially in the factories'. In military terms, the action had little chance of success. However, this was never put to the test because the political ruling class (led by the King) caved in and offered power to Mussolini. The 'March' finally occurred as a victory celebration when Mussolini was already Prime Minister. (T.N.)

Bordiga, and even Terracini, remained resolutely hostile to any such change of position.

Graziadei, addressing the anti-fusionists at a meeting of the P Cd I's central committee, stated: 'The split at Livorno took place, inevitably, too far to the left. I, and many other comrades with me, judged this was unfortunate; you, on the other hand, thought it was right and were happy about it. In this difference of judgement lies the basis of a profound political divergence.' Those who had approved of the leftward split at Livorno were still opposed to any talk of reunion with the socialists. And now, Graziadei's difference of judgement was complicated by another, concerning the nature of fascism. Bordiga and his majority were inclined to lump fascists and social democrats together as common class enemies, as equally responsible for propping up the bourgeois order. Mussolini was no different from Turati: what then was new about one bourgeois party, the Fascist Party, taking over the government from another bourgeois party? For Amadeo Bordiga, all that had happened after the March on Rome was a mere change of administrations. This was what all the ex-abstentionist group believed; and they were not alone. Terracini declared that the March on Rome and the call on Mussolini to form a government were no more than a 'rather acute ministerial crisis'. For his part, Togliatti had already written on 27 July 1922: 'The grim tyrant against which all the living forces of the people must rise up has only one face, but three names: he is called Turati, Don Sturzo, and Mussolini at the same time.'

The real difference between fascism and the traditional democratic parties escaped the leaders of Italian communism; and since they were not aware of fascism's specific dangers, they could not see that a form of bourgeois dictatorship was on the point of supplanting bourgeois democracy for good. Hence, the International's new directives on the need for defensive action and the importance of democratic freedoms were not understood, and neither was the need for alliance or fusion with those forces which – as far as most communists were concerned – still represented nothing but the 'left wing' of the bourgeois political spectrum. Gramsci was one of the few who were able to grasp the real novelty of fascism, the growing peril it represented, and the rightness of the defensive tactic proposed by the International.

He came out of the sanatorium for the Fourth Congress, somewhat recovered but still far from well: 'At the Fourth Congress I had only been a few days out of the sanatorium, after a six-month stay which had stopped me getting any worse and prevented a possible paralysis of the legs that might have immobilized me in bed for years, but which had otherwise helped little. I was still suffering from exhaustion, and found work impossible because of insomnia and amnesia.' He was at once approached by Mátyás Rákosi. Gramsci had a very low opinion of him, judging him to be 'a fool', and 'without a single ounce of political intelligence'. But now 'with that diplomatic delicacy so characteristic of him, he assaulted me. He asked me point-blank why I didn't become leader of the Party and eliminate Bordiga, who would be expelled from the Comintern if he persisted with his present line'. Although disagreeing with Bordiga, Gramsci was still to some extent influenced by his powerful personality, and he feared that a rupture might lead to the dissolution of the Party altogether:

> My attitudes on the question were not my own, they were always influenced by concern over what Amadeo might do if I became an opponent: he would have withdrawn, provoked a crisis, he would never have adapted himself to any compromise. . . . If I had led the opposition, the International would have backed me – but with what consequences at that time, when the Party was holding together with great difficulty in a civil war, and under fire every day from *Avanti!*, which exploited every sign of disagreement in the hope of breaking us up?

He rejected Rákosi's proposal:

> I said that I would do all in my power to help the International solve the Italian problem, but that I did not believe it possible to replace Amadeo without much preparatory work inside the Party. Replacing Amadeo, in the Italian situation, meant much more than finding one other cadre to take his place; in terms of general capacity for work, he is worth three at least.

The debates on fusion dragged on interminably. On one side, Tasca supported the International's demand for immediate fusion with the socialists. On the other, Bordiga continued his tenacious resistance, and asked that any final decision on the question be at least postponed. 'I was walking on hot coals,' says Gramsci, 'not the sort of work most suitable to my condition of chronic enfeeblement.' He got out of it by 'wriggling like an eel' (as he put it himself). Within the Socialist Party there had arisen an organized faction which supported the Third International's policy (the *terzinternazionalisti*, or *terzini*). Gramsci brought out a compromise proposal, to the effect that the communists should proceed at once to merge with the *terzini* faction, rather than with the PSI as a whole. This won acceptance. ('Quite involuntarily, I

won myself the reputation of being infernally cunning', he said later.)
A fourteen-point statement of the conditions for fusion was drawn up,
and a joint committee was appointed to take charge of the operation.
Bordiga was nominated, but refused to participate, and Gramsci took
his seat on this committee; the others were Scoccimarro and Tasca for
the communists, and Serrati and Maffei for the socialists.

Gramsci did not return to Italy, however. Serrati was arrested as
soon as he went back, and Tasca was forced to flee to Switzerland.
While Scoccimarro and Maffei went ahead with the work of re-uniting
the two movements, Gramsci continued to function on the International's executive in Moscow. He was forced to sacrifice much of his
private life to his political duties, about which he was scrupulous, but
he would often return to the sanatorium for a rest, or to visit Eugenie
Schucht. He spent Christmas there in 1922. He wrote later:

> The last time I put up a Christmas tree was in 1922. It was to amuse
> Eugenie, who wasn't able to get out of bed yet, or at least couldn't walk
> without leaning on walls and furniture – I can't remember whether she was
> up or not. I remember the little tree standing on the bedside table, covered
> in wax tapers which were all lit at once when Julia came back from a
> concert she had been giving for the other patients while I had stayed to
> keep Eugenie company.

His meetings with Julia tended to be fleeting, because of politics. On
13 February 1923 he wrote to her: 'I'm not sure yet if I can come on
Sunday. They are calling meetings repeatedly, at the most unlikely
hours, and I should hate to miss seeing you without letting you know in
advance.' The lovely young music teacher was now too close to him:
'I must, I absolutely must have you go on loving me . . . for me, all this
has been serious, very serious.' Since knowing her, he had had 'the
greatest, the most beautiful, the most powerful reason in the world' to
distract him from worries and struggles which would once have
absorbed every ounce of his physical and intellectual energy.

This ultra-disciplined functionary of the Moscow headquarters
which manipulated the strings of revolution across half the world had
not chosen the ideal moment to try and tear himself away, to stop being
a 'cave bear' and start being a lover. Once a telegram came from Italy,
warning him that a warrant had been issued for his arrest and advising
him not to return home. The messengers went with it to the Lux (the
Gorky Street hotel where he lived) early in the morning. He was not
there, and none of the other Italians had any idea where he might be: he

had left no word. They went the rounds of Moscow by car, but could find no trace of him. Now deeply worried by his disappearance, they called in the Soviet secret police to help them. When Gramsci finally turned up at the Lux he was greeted (as he put it) 'like someone who had returned from the dead'. All he had tried to do was be a lover for one night, rather than a politician. Such were the conditions under which Antonio and Julia passed the brief season of their greatest happiness together: torn between their duties in two different cities, and hurrying from one to another to share their few moments of freedom. Then even this intermittent bond was broken off.

In Italy the situation had deteriorated still further. The International was now seriously concerned at the state of the Communist Party of Italy, weakened by another wave of arrests (Bordiga and Grieco had been in prison since 3 February 1923) and virtually paralysed by the sectarian attitudes of its remaining leaders. Gramsci described the situation as follows:

> After the arrest of Amadeo and Ruggero [Grieco] we waited in vain for about a month and a half for any news at all about what exactly had happened – how far police action had gone in destroying our organization, and what measures the remaining cadres still at liberty had been able to take to restore organizational links. Instead, there was only one letter sent right after the arrests, which had stated that everything was destroyed and all the central organs of the Party would have to be reconstituted, and after it nothing but polemical missives on the problems of reunification, written in a style which appeared all the more arrogant and irresponsible because in his first communication the author had quite clearly conveyed the impression that henceforth the entire Italian communist movement was to be identified with his own person. . . . Thus, the question of what the leadership of our Party was really worth was posed in the most brutal fashion. There was bitter criticism of the letters, and I was asked what suggestions I had for action. . . . I too had been badly shaken by the letters. . . . So finally I was compelled to admit that, if the situation really was what it appeared to be on the strength of the evidence we had received, then the best thing would be to give up the existing leadership as a bad job, and reorganize the Party from outside with cadres nominated by the International itself.

And so in June 1923 the executive of the International took a decision to liquidate the old Bordiga majority leadership, and appointed Togliatti, Scoccimarro, Fortichiari, Tasca and Vota as the new executive of the Communist Party of Italy. Fortichiari (an ex-abstentionist) refused the nomination, and was replaced by Gennari, an opponent of the Bordiga group. Then on 21 September the whole executive, surprised by the police in a worker's house on the outskirts of Milan, was arrested *en bloc*. After this, it was decided to ask Gramsci to move to Vienna, where he would be able to follow the Italian Party's problems more closely. In this way, the young Sardinian passed from the relative isolation of his final period in Turin to the maximum possible responsibility. At the age of thirty-two, he was effectively the leader of the Italian communist movement, at least in the eyes of the International.

He left Moscow for Vienna at the end of November 1923, after having been with the International executive for one and a half years. They had marked a major turning-point in his life. He was depressed by the thought of leaving Julia; but she for her part had always known very well what sacrifices she might be called on to make by the nature of Antonio's life. Some months later, on 7 June 1924, he wrote to his mother: 'My companion shares my ideas completely; she isn't Italian, but she lived for a long time in Italy and studied at Rome. She's called Julia (Julka, in her own language) and she has a degree from the music lycée. She is courageous and has a strong character. You will all like and appreciate her when you get to know her. Next summer or autumn I hope to come with her to Sardinia for a few days.'

17

Angelica Balabanov had obtained an Austrian residence permit for Gramsci.[1] In Vienna he lived in a street far from the centre of the city, in an unheated room, furnished with a bed he described as 'very German, very hard, very uncomfortable, with an eiderdown quilt instead of sheets and blankets, which keeps slipping off in every direction, so that I'm always waking up with either a foot or a shoulder frozen stiff'. His landlady was a Jew converted to Catholicism, who had subsequently given up her second religion when she married a communist, Joseph Frey. Now, however, she had slipped back into religious practices, and was much given to recalling the days of her dear dead Emperor Franz Joseph and cursing the Party which obliged her to keep a foreigner under her roof – especially one that might get her into trouble with the police. Gramsci changed lodgings after a few months. He only went out to eat, or to attend organizational meetings and talk to contacts. He did not like the city: 'The snow covers the streets, the landscape is a blur of white shapes, it reminds me of the Cagliari salt-pans (not forgetting the convicts who used to work them). Vienna seems very sad and depressing compared to Moscow. Here there are no sleighs jingling cheerfully along the white streets, only the dreary rattle of tramcars. Life goes by, sad and monotonous.' For company he had a secretary, Mario Codevilla, who suffered badly from tuberculosis and was not in any case very bright: 'I'm always alone. The fact is that my companion here never permits conversation to rise above the level of commonplaces.' Gramsci was very anxious that Julia should come to join him as soon as possible.

Such was the theme of his letters: 'I'm leading a very isolated existence, and it can hardly be otherwise, at least for a while. I feel your absence physically, like a great emptiness all around me. Today I understand better than yesterday, and yesterday I understood better

[1] *Angelica Balabanov*: a Russian exile who chose Italy as her country of adoption before the First World War and participated in the socialist movement; author of a celebrated description of the young Mussolini. (T.N.)

than the day before, how much I love you and how it's possible to love someone more each day. When will it be possible for you to come and live and work here beside me?' He returns to the subject insistently, again and again:

I have thought that I may be too much of an egoist in asking you to come to me, asking you to give up the life you're used to just to be with me – far away from the interesting, active life going on round you, and which is there in the very air you breathe, even if your own personal work is mechanical and uninteresting. I have thought that I may want you close to me just because I am too much alone, and this solitude has depressed me.... My dear, you must come. I need you. I can't go on without you. ... It's like living in mid-air, out of touch with reality. I think always with infinite longing of the times we spent together, in such close intimacy, yet with such a vast outpouring of ourselves.

But Julia did not come to join him. She was unwell – suffering, in fact, the first symptoms of the psychic crisis which in later years, during Antonio's imprisonment, would drive her to the threshold of insanity. To justify her failure to come to Vienna, she said she could not leave her family. Antonio persisted: 'I have thought about your family too: but couldn't you come for a few months? ... How wonderful it would be to have another spell of living together, to enjoy every day, every hour, every minute. ... I can almost feel your cheek against mine, and my hand caressing your head, telling you how much I care for you even while my lips are silent.' Something of Julia's condition filtered through her letters but no more than a faint echo.

I get the impression you are always serious, downcast [he wrote on 21 March 1924]. Another reason for wanting you by me: I think I could find lots of ingenious ways to cheer you up and make you smile again. I'd make you clocks of cork, papiermâché fiddles, and wax lizards with two tails – in short I would make full use of my repertory of Sardinian folklore. I'd tell you stories of my wild and woolly childhood – so different from your own – each tale more fantastic than the last. Then I'd embrace you, and kiss you again and again to feel you all alive inside me, life of my life, which is what you are. ...

Julia stayed in Moscow. She was expecting a child. To begin with she had no more than hinted at the fact to Antonio. He answered: 'I felt a shock of emotion reading your letter. You know the reason. But your words were very vague, and left me overcome with desire to hold you in my arms and feel for myself the new life uniting our two lives even closer than before, oh my dearest, dearest love.' But the first mention of her condition was followed by weeks of silence. On 29 March 1924, Antonio wrote to her:

> On 24 February you said that you were going to be a mother. The words filled me with delight. I felt I could desire nothing more than this; I thought that it would lend you strength, and help you to overcome the crisis which I felt was latent inside you, and all bound up with your past, your childhood, and your whole intellectual development. I thought that it might allow you to love me even more completely.... Your love has strengthened me, it has truly made a man of me – or at least, it has made me understand what it is to be a man, and to have a personality. I don't know if my love has had similar effects on you: I believe so, for I clearly feel a creative force at work in you, as it is in me. During that brief period when we were utterly happy, I did think very definitely that our happiness would be completed if you were to have a child. But you have only hinted at the fact in passing, and then said no more about it.

During the Vienna months, political disorientation added to the pain of this break with Julia. Gramsci found it hard to keep properly informed or follow events in Russia and Italy. Since early in 1922 Lenin had been paralysed in the legs and the right arm, and in March 1923 he had lost his power of speech. A bitter factional struggle was developing within the Russian Party. Eight days before Lenin's death, Gramsci wrote: 'I don't know yet the precise terms of the debate which has been going on in the Russian Party. All I've seen is the Central Committee resolution on party democracy, none of the others. I don't know Trotsky's article, nor Stalin's either. I can't understand the attack launched by the latter, it seems very irresponsible and dangerous to me. But possibly I'm being misled by my ignorance of the sources.'

In Italy confusion had reigned in the Party for over a year now. A battle was raging between the right-wing minority (Tasca, Vota, Graziadei) and the majority faction (Togliatti, Scoccimarro, Terracini – Bordiga being in prison, and no longer on the executive). The International's strategy had been successfully resisted all this time by the majority, which was still in the grip of its old sectarianism. At a central committee meeting on 9 August 1923, Tasca had reported:

> The minutes of a meeting held by the comrades of the majority have come into my hands, and from these it emerges clearly that although comrade Palmi [clandestine name of Togliatti] and others expressed a wish to collaborate with the International, after suitable explanations of the past and present position assumed by the majority, comrade Urbani [Terracini]

on the other hand expressed the view that one should accept the International line formally, and then go on working on the old lines behind the scenes.

The fact of those minutes having 'come into the hands' of Tasca is itself significant, and indicates the climate prevailing in the Party. Togliatti says: 'The faction-fighting which went on throughout the Party had as one of its most constant features a search for letters and documents which might be used to damage and discredit the other side.' In this poisonous atmosphere of habitual intrigue and deceit, a new proposal put out by Bordiga from his prison cell was now being discussed. Extreme as Bordiga's views may have been, he was certainly never hypocritical: invariably, he showed himself ready to assume full responsibility for them and all the consequences they might entail, even such disagreeable ones as loss of power. It was natural, therefore, that he should propose that the Communist Party of Italy break with the International. His idea was to circulate a manifesto to this effect, signed by all the Party's leaders (except Tasca and the right-wingers).

Of all those called upon to sign this document, Gramsci was the only one to condemn it out of hand. Leonetti supported him, but for different reasons. Terracini and Scoccimarro agreed with it. Togliatti was undecided. He saw Bordiga's proposal as 'flowing from a rigorous, or even over-rigorous logic' – 'The International's policy would tend to tie us to the PSI in the same way as we were tied before Livorno, or even more so.' But on the other hand, he could not deny the many risks involved in a formal break:

In practice, given the conditions prevailing, to follow Amadeo would mean engaging in open struggle with the Comintern; and to be outside it would mean losing its very powerful material and moral support, while we ourselves would be reduced to a very small group held together almost entirely by personal ties. We would very soon lose all real influence on the course of the political struggle in Italy, and might be completely annihilated.

The strong exception Gramsci took to this document was not confined to its formal aspect. From the earliest days of his political career he had been the protagonist of 'dialogue' and 'openness'. Sectarian mumbo-jumbo and exclusiveness disgusted him. He had always fought them, long before the Livorno split, and then opposed the sectarian direction of the split when it took place. So the subsequent 'rightward step' counselled by the International could not but win his approval: 'I am quite unconvinced that the line promoted by the Fourth Congress is mistaken, either in general or in particular.'

He now had to face the two urgent, closely-related problems posed for him by the manifesto: how to dissuade Bordiga from going ahead with it; and how to bring together a new leadership group willing to adopt the International's strategy.

Gramsci had few illusions about Bordiga changing his mind: 'He is such a vigorous personality, and so profoundly convinced he is right, that it would be absurd to think of snaring him into some compromise. He will go on fighting and putting forward his own view at every available opportunity.' Or again: 'I'm convinced he is immovable, and I think he would rather leave the International and the Party altogether rather than go against his own convictions.' So what attitude should be taken towards him?

> I too think the Party cannot do without his collaboration; but what are we to do? . . . His very nature, stubborn and inflexible to the point of absurdity, obliges us to think none the less of building up a party and leadership without him, or against him. I believe that we can no longer afford to compromise on questions of principle, as happened in the past: better have a clear, frank argument which goes right to the bottom of things, and helps the Party by preparing it for any eventuality. Naturally the question isn't closed: this is just what I think at the moment.

The point was – with whom could any such new leadership be established? At the end of January 1924 Gramsci was still uncertain. He thought the old Turin group around *L'Ordine Nuovo* had now disintegrated too far to be the nucleus for a reconstituted party. On 28 January he wrote to Alfonso Leonetti:

> I can't share your point of view about it being time to reanimate our Turin group associated with *L'Ordine Nuovo*. . . . For one thing, Tasca now belongs to the minority, having taken to its logical conclusion the position he adopted in 1920, at the time of the polemic between him and myself. Togliatti is undecided, as always: he is still under the sway of Amadeo's strong personality, and this is what keeps him in the middle of the road, justifying his own indecisiveness with legalistic hair-splitting. I believe that at bottom Umberto [Terracini] is even more of an extremist than Amadeo, because he has absorbed the latter's ideas without absorbing his intellectual power, or his practical sense and organizing ability. So what could serve to rally this group again? It would only look like a clique reassembled around my own person for bureaucratic reasons. Even the basic ideas which distinguished the activity of the *L'Ordine Nuovo* group

are anachronistic today, or would quickly become so. . . . The outlook is very different today, and one must carefully avoid stressing the Turin tradition or the Turin group too much. It would all end in personal feuds over the right of inheritance to a legacy of mere memories and words.

But circumstances did not offer many possible courses of action. Over the following weeks Gramsci somewhat revised this initial judgement, which may have depended on a passing mood as much as on critical consideration of the Turin experience and its fate.

At New Year 1924, he had written to Julia: 'Pull Bianco's ears for me, and tell him that I'm writing at least half a dozen letters a day.[2] I've never written so many letters in my life as in these last few days.' Letter-writing had certainly never been his strong point. But he kept at it throughout his sojourn in Vienna, and gradually some comrades became convinced; others decided to at least give the impression they had been won over. The new leading group was constituted, still surrounded by uncertainties. But it provided some possibility for political action along the lines laid down by the International. On 1 March 1924 Gramsci wrote to Scoccimarro and Togliatti:

> For a time I was lacking in capacity and will-power and felt unable in the circumstances to take on the responsibility of deciding what form the new political situation should assume. Today, after getting your letter, I've changed my mind: it is possible to get together a group capable of hard work and determined action. I am prepared to put all I can into this group, to the limits of my powers, such as they are. I won't be able to do all that I'd like to do, because I still go through periods of atrocious feebleness which make me fear a relapse into the kind of stupid coma I have suffered from in recent years; but I shall try to do my best nonetheless.

In spite of this poor health, he was also writing for the party press and doing translations. On 12 February 1924 the first number of a new paper called *L'Unità* appeared. In March the third version of *L'Ordine Nuovo* started to appear, this time as a fortnightly. He wrote to Julia on 15 March:

> Will I ever be able to stick my tongue out at you again? We're serious persons now, we'll soon have a child and mustn't set a bad example to the children. You see what new horizons are opening up before us? . . . I'm playing the fool, but I don't feel terribly like doing so. The truth is that I love you, I think of you continually, and every now and then feel you

---

[2] *Vincenzo Bianco*: an Italian political exile living in Moscow. (T.N.)

close, very close in my arms. Strange things happen to me: as soon as I'd received your last letter I began to feel sure you must have arrived in Vienna, and that I would bump into you in the street. I had been feeling low again, and unable to sleep properly, and your letter made me feel enormously better. When I can hold you in my arms again, I think I shall be so overwhelmed it will be painful. Darling Julia, you are the whole of life to me, for I had never felt what life was until I loved you: something huge and beautiful which fills out every instant and every vibration of one's being. I want to be strong today as I never wanted to in the past, because I want to be happy in your love and this wish shows in everything I do. I believe that when we live together again we shall be invincible, we shall find a way of defeating even fascism; we want a free and beautiful world for our child, and we shall fight for this as we have never fought before, with a cleverness we never had before, with a tenacity and energy that will overcome every obstacle in our path.

He finally left Vienna on 12 May 1924. There had been parliamentary elections in Italy on 6 April and he had been elected by a constituency of the Veneto region. Thanks to the immunity guaranteed parliamentary deputies by law, he could return to Italy without fear of arrest. He had been away for two years (the Vienna stay had lasted five and a half months). Soon, he was hearing eyewitness accounts of the terrible events of those years, the killings, the beatings and burnings. His own brother Gennaro had been subjected to fascist violence in December 1922, and Pia Carena had helped him flee to France.[3]

Gramsci quickly saw for himself that the Party no longer existed as a homogeneous structure. There was a division, a lack of contact, between the Party's head and its body, between the new ruling group and the rank and file, which regularly resulted in political paralysis or worse. Indeed, the organism was moved in one direction by its brain (orders from the International or from Gramsci), and in quite another and contradictory way by its limbs. Though Bordiga had been dispossessed by fiat from above, he continued to dominate most of the local federations: the masses were still as susceptible to a certain style of incendiary preaching, and preferred to follow his extremism, his refusal to consider any prospect other than immediate insurrection. Gramsci was able to estimate for himself the balance of power within

[3] Gramsci wrote to Julia: 'It has been a rather melancholy experience to come back to Italy . . . and hear right away from others about how the fascists hunted my ghost in Turin when they heard a rumour I was there and found my brother instead, so he got the beating and bayoneting meant for me, losing one of his fingers and half his blood.'

the Party at a clandestine conference held in the neighbourhood of Como a few days after his return.[4]

This was the first chance for people to stand up openly and be counted, and the count was distinctly unfavourable to Gramsci. There were three motions to be voted on: the first, put forward by the new leadership, was supported by only four comrades of the central committee and three federation secretaries; the second, which came from Tasca and his rightist minority, won four votes in the central committee and six among the federal secretaries; the third came from Bordiga, and won an easy victory, with only one supporter in the central committee but no fewer than thirty-nine votes from the local leaders and the youth movement. That day Gramsci was able to take the measure of the task before him: the task of reconquering and reuniting a movement which was Internationalist at the top and Bordighist at all its lower levels.

But he was not dismayed. In these two years abroad he had changed. He had acquired a different bearing, a new severity of manner, and showed a hitherto unsuspected will to dominate. He saw more clearly than before that the development of ideas required a simultaneous exercise of power in their affirmation, or else they might be lost. He had by no means fully recovered from his illness, and he was still plagued by insomnia. But he turned to work unremittingly at this new task, sustained by that will-power which had enabled him to survive so many other crises in the past.

---

[4] 'We pretended to be employees of a Milanese firm on a tourist jaunt,' wrote Gramsci, 'and we discussed tendencies and tactics all day long except at lunch, when we made fascist speeches and sang the praises of Mussolini in order to avoid raising suspicions and being disturbed at our work, which was conducted in lovely little valleys white with narcissi.'

18

In Rome, Gramsci went to stay as a lodger with a family of Germans, the Passarges, in a house on Via Vesalio (off the Via Nomentana). They knew next to nothing about him, not even that he was a communist deputy.[1] Felice Platone, one of the old *Ordine Nuovo* group, remembers:

> He quickly found his old ways again in that room: discussions, frequent visits, hard work and intense thought. To begin with we never tired of going over the *Ordine Nuovo* days together, as he tried to re-establish contact with his old friends and gather them round him again; he found out all about them, and was impatient to see the 'old' editors of the paper, Amoretti and Montagnana. The restaurant where we used to eat (near Termini station – it had been 'discovered' by Gennari) became a regular meeting-place at once for anyone who wanted to speak with Gramsci. In the evenings we would usually stroll together down towards the Coliseum, or sometimes go to the cinema.

As he had done earlier in Turin, Gramsci paid special attention to the younger people. After the 1924 elections *L'Ordine Nuovo* groups had begun to spring up in Rome. Velio Spano recalls: 'In the first group there were about twenty of us, the oldest not more than twenty-two. We had drawn up a list of subjects, and each time someone would be nominated to lead the discussion. We used to meet in an old warehouse behind Piazza Venezia, where there was nothing but one table and three or four chairs; we gave the best chair to Gramsci and the next best to whoever was leading the discussion. Everyone else usually stood. We always wanted Gramsci to speak, while he wanted to hear us speak.'

Gramsci had been back in Italy less than a month when the Matteotti affair exploded.[2] Public opinion was very disturbed by the socialist

---

[1] 'I try to look like an ultra-serious professor, they hold me in some awe and go to the most exasperating lengths to leave me in peace.'

[2] *The Matteotti affair*: the fascists won the elections of April 1924 (those at which Gramsci was elected) by a large majority, thanks to their new electoral law, and to various forms of

deputy's sudden disappearance. But it had also been intimidated by three years of terrorism, and at first reactions were very uncertain. Gramsci did not hesitate. Giuseppe Amoretti (then editor of *L'Unità* at Milan) recalls what happened:

A policeman turned up at the paper and informed us with a great show of mystery that the socialist deputy Matteotti had disappeared. He told us we should publish only the bare facts and, in effect, keep quiet about the whole thing. Under the diplomatic language, his advice was clearly a threat. 'Suppose we don't, we objected, 'will we end up like Matteotti?' He nodded, as if to say: 'If that's the way you want it. . . .' Then off he went. We didn't know what to do. We felt gravely threatened by the whole apparatus of repression. There was always a bunch of blackshirts standing around outside the door. The newspaper could be wrecked, we would be beaten up again. . . . At this moment we had a phone-call from Gramsci in Rome. He said there should be an attack, and we should lead it. We should take the initiative, and encourage the awakening masses to act for themselves.

L'Unità came out with a full-page headline saying 'Down With This Government of Assassins!' Subsequently, even those sectors of opinion which had so far reacted very ambiguously to the fascist advance rose up in arms. Less than two weeks later, Gramsci wrote to Julia:

I have lived through some unforgettable days, and I'm still living them. The papers give one a quite inadequate idea of what's happening in Italy. We were walking along the edge of a volcano on the point of eruption. Then suddenly, when no one expected it – certainly not the fascists, complacent in their absolute power – the volcano erupted, releasing an immense torrent of burning lava which has spread across the whole country, carrying the fascists bag and baggage before it. Events succeeded one another like lightning with unheard-of rapidity. The situation changed from one day to the next, from one hour to the next, the regime

---

intimidation. When parliament reassembled, the Reformist Socialist Party deputy Giacomo Matteotti made a courageous attack on Mussolini and denounced fascist brutality. He accused Mussolini of being ready to use force if the fascists had failed to win at the polls (at which a great cry of 'Yes, yes!' arose from the fascist benches). As he sat down, Matteotti remarked to friends: 'Now you can prepare my funeral oration.' A few days later he was beaten and stabbed to death by a gang of *squadristi* led by Amerigo Dumini. The body was buried in a wood fifteen miles outside Rome, where it was not uncovered until two months later. At the time, Dumini was on the payroll of Cesare Rossi, Mussolini's press secretary. (T.N.)

found itself under attack from every angle, and fascism was isolated in the country to the point where its leaders became panic-stricken and the hangers-on were deserting its ranks. We worked feverishly, taking decisions, issuing orders, trying to give aim and direction to this flood of popular feeling which had burst its banks. At the moment it looks as if the most acute phase of the crisis is over. Fascism is striving desperately to rally its forces, which are greatly diminished but still on top, thanks to the support of the whole state apparatus, thanks also to the incredible fragmentation and disorientation of the masses. Still, our movement has taken a great step forward: the paper [*L' Unità*] has trebled its circulation, and in many centres our comrades assumed the leadership of the mass movement and attempted to disarm the fascists, while our slogans were acclaimed and repeated in the motions passed at factory meetings. I believe that our Party has become a real mass party in these last few days.

Gramsci's illusions about the effectiveness of the Party were short-lived. Once fascism had recovered from the initial shock, it began to regain ground and prepare for a counter-offensive, helped above all by the sheer disorganization of the masses and – even more – by the inertia of the parliamentary opposition.

The various parliamentary groups, some definitely opposed to fascism and others simply worried by scruples over the government's methods, had been able to agree on only one thing: that they should all withdraw from parliament as a protest. This secession from the Chamber became known as the 'Aventine'.[3] But what real political purpose did the Aventine parties have? The old divisions and mutual suspicions persisted, and the differences of ideology and strategy proved irreconcilable. One wing was in effect semi-fascist, and perfectly willing to support the government if only Mussolini would pay more attention to constitutional niceties; while on the other side were the nineteen communists, devoted to overthrowing the government by appeals to mass action outside parliament altogether. In between were the liberals, who still – despite everything – placed their trust in the King's wisdom and expected him to intervene and solve the problem; and the Catholics of the Partito Popolare, as hostile (or even more hostile) to socialism as to fascism. The disputes of the past years had also created an abyss between the communists and the socialists (the PSI now had a new leadership under Vella and Nenni).

[3] *The Aventine parliament*: the secession of parliamentarians in protest at Matteotti's assassination was named after the Plebs of ancient Rome who once withdrew in protest to the Aventine hill outside the city. (T.N.)

Thus, fascism did not have to face a cohesive front resolved on common action, but a vague consortium of disunited groups quite undecided on action and incapable in practice of much more than verbal indignation. In the days immediately following the Matteotti crisis Gramsci had proposed a political general strike to the Committee of Sixteen, the joint executive of the Aventine parties. But this proposal was turned down, and Gramsci commented on 22 June: 'Big words but no intention of doing anything: incredible fear that we might take the lead, and hence manoeuvres to force us to quit the meeting.'

For months afterwards the Aventine's activity was to consist of little more than abstract affirmations of principle, and a monotonous chain of feeble lamentations. Mussolini was cruelly accurate in defining its policy as one of 'vociferous nagging'. However, it should also be said that the Communist Party's extremism played a part in increasing the reluctance of the other groups to join in any active opposition front. Gramsci's political action was gravely hampered by the fact that he was at the head of a young, badly organized party, weakened and often paralysed by the leftist sectarianism which had always marked it. He could not help being conditioned by this circumstance.

Gramsci was aware that the wave of fascist reaction had driven the Italian working class back into positions which made revolution more difficult; and he drew two obvious conclusions from this: first, the need to recover lost ground before any decisive attack on the bourgeois order could again be contemplated, and second, the impossibility of recovering this ground without building up a wide system of alliances with other anti-fascist forces. Bordiga on the other hand wanted no such alliances simply because he rejected their aim, the restoration of bourgeois democracy: his one and only objective was the dictatorship of the proletariat, to be attained directly, without intermediate phases. Gramsci agreed about the ultimate aim, but refused to make a fetish of the means. His cultural background and outlook were entirely different, and he was little inclined to shelter behind such immutable magic formulae. This was why he had accepted the International's latest policies as appropriate to the Italian situation: first the reactionary tempest had to be weathered, and then when bourgeois liberties had been re-established the final victorious assault of the socialist revolution could be prepared.

But these two distinct elements of the strategy tended to be confused in the actual political action which Gramsci conducted. While he proposed unity of action to the other groups led by Treves, Arturo

Labriola and Amendola,[4] he at the same time indulged in the most
violent polemics against these men, and described them as mere expres-
sions of the capitalist order to be destroyed. In this way, the development of any serious dialogue was rendered very difficult: doubt and
hostility invariably nipped it in the bud. This then was the overall
picture which the Aventino presented: lack of agreement between the
bourgeois–democratic parties and the working-class parties; serious
differences between the Reformist Socialist Party (Turati) and the
main Socialist Party (Vella, Nenni), and between both of these and the
Communist Party; serious differences again within these parties, and
especially within the Communist Party, where the dispute between
Bordiga's faction and the leadership had become more than ideological
and assumed the form of widespread personal defamation and animos-
ity. All this at the very moment when coherent, determined action was
required to thwart the fascists' desperate attempt to survive the crisis
and remain in power.

The only appreciable change brought about by the Matteotti crisis
was a slackening in the regime's repression. Gramsci was able to move
about Rome without trouble – 'because the police are not functioning,
sabotaged like all the other organs of the fascist State. I don't know how
long this can go on. Events are imposing a very difficult test on the
Party after its three years of illegality and defensive organization and
work. It has to resume forward movement again, agitate, come out into
the open: the comrades were not ready for this sudden jolt, and have
shown their uncertainty.' Every week he would hold three or four meetings, either with the leadership or with groups of the rank and file.
'Very interesting meetings,' he commented, 'especially those with the
workers. Talk, discussion, exchange of news and information, problems
that have to be solved, questions of principle and of organization to be
dealt with.' Outside the Party, he seems to have had no contacts.

His father's brother Cesare lived in Rome, a civil servant at the
Ministry of Finance. Gramsci did not go to see him, and wrote to his
mother:

> I've never met Uncle Cesare and don't know where he lives. I won't go
> to see him either at the office or at home (if I should happen to find out
> where he lives). I still recall how terrified he was in 1917, when I was in

[4] *Giovanni Amendola* (1886–1926): a liberal ex-minister and courageous anti-fascist, the
main leader of the Aventine secession. He had already been assaulted by the fascists in 1923,
and died from his wounds after a second beating in July 1925. Claudio Treves and Arturo
Labriola were Reformist Socialist leaders. (T.N.)

Rome as a witness at a political trial, and I went to see him: he was afraid of being compromised, and told me a pack of lies about the police going to his house to look for me, all invented out of sheer fright. He knows I'm in Rome, and he can find me at the parliament building: if he hasn't done so, he must have his own good reasons which I have no wish to discuss, or put to the test.

He was alone. On 7 July he wrote to Julia: 'Dear Julka, the memory of your caresses makes a fever come over me and makes me keenly aware of my sad solitude here. It keeps me from enjoying the beauty of Rome. How I would love to go for a stroll with you so that we could see together, remember together ... I shut myself up in my room: I seem to have become a cave bear once more.' He was suffering from weakness and insomnia again:

Thinking tires me, work reduces me to being a limp rag in no time. How many things I should be doing, and just cannot do. I think of you, and the sweetness of loving you, and of knowing that you are very close as well as very far away. Darling Julia, even far away the thought of you helps me to be stronger. But my life can never become normal again as long as we're separated; loving you has become too much part of my personality for me ever to feel normal again without your presence.

However, the harsh stimulus of the absorbing events he was living through must have left him relatively little time for such thoughts:

The Party has to be reorganized, it is weak and on the whole works very badly. I'm part of the central committee, general secretary, and should also be editor of the Party's paper [*L' Unità*], but don't have enough strength to do this as well. I still can't do much work. One ought really to keep an eye on everything, follow everything that happens. . . . We're short of reliable party workers, particularly in Rome; the meetings I go to are very satisfying in one way, because of the good will and enthusiasm of so many comrades, but in another way they make me pessimistic, because of the general lack of preparation. The situation could not be more favourable for us. . . . Fascism is crumbling, it seems to have gone crazy and lost its bearings altogether. Everything is turning against it. Yet the exploitation of the situation remains relatively slow, because we are still so few, and so badly organized.

This letter was written on 18 August 1924. Gramsci had been a father for eight days, but Julia's letters bearing the tidings had not yet arrived. Three days before he had written to his mother: 'My child should be born just about now, but so far I've received no word, given the great distance which separates me from my companion: I know the doctors said it would be between the 8th and the 15th of August. I'm sure everything will be all right, and hope to have some news next week.' Then on the 18th, to Julia:

Perhaps as I am writing now the child is already born and lies there beside you, where you can caress him after having suffered to bring him into the world. This makes my happiness a little melancholy. How many things there are that I can't know, but would so much like to know. But what does knowing matter, when it wasn't possible to suffer with you. . . . My happiness wears a glum expression and feels rather sad. . . . I wrote and told my mother that we'll soon have a baby: she's very anxious to have news. If you can send photos, let me have two copies: this will certainly give my mother enormous pleasure, she feels family bonds with great passion, in the Sardinian way.

The next day, 19 August, he left Rome for a trip to Milan and Turin.

When he returned to Rome two weeks later, on 3 September, two letters from Julia were waiting. He wrote back:

After reading your letters I don't know what to say. Something serious and melodramatic? I couldn't keep my face straight enough for that. So I just don't know. . . . One gentle caress would say what I mean better than any deluge of words. In the meantime, I approve of all that you've done. I approve of the name too, though it does seem odd to call a three-and-a-half kilo baby without a single tooth in his head Lev ['lion']. But he will be a true lion one day, will he not? . . . Really I don't care a bit what he's called; all I care about is that he is a living child, our son, and that we shall love each other more each day that comes because we see ourselves in him, only stronger and happier. . . . I too can hardly wait to share with you the joy of seeing the different phases of the child's evolving personality. Personally, I am convinced that the day a child puts his foot in his mouth is of prime importance: don't fail to inform me immediately this act is accomplished, symbolizing as it does official possession of the outermost limits of the national territory.

He gave the news to his mother two days later, writing on 5 September:

The baby was born on 10 August, and his mother is well because she wrote to me right away, on the morning of the 11th, and again on the 18th. It weighed three kilos six hundred grammes, had a lot of brown hair, and a well-formed head with a high forehead and very blue eyes – I'm copying his mother's description for you, and she added very poetically that he looked as if he had been a long time in the sunlight already, like a ripe fruit still attached to its tree. He's twenty-five days old already, and must have grown a lot by now. He's called Lev, which means 'lion' in Italian, and seems a bit much for a baby weighing three and a half kilos without a tooth in his head. It's very depressing to be so far from my companion at this time. I am afraid she will have to delay coming here for some time yet: a five-day rail journey is difficult with a new-born baby. She's with her family for the time being. She will send me a picture of the baby as soon as she can, and I'll forward it to you. So you'll be able to see your new grandchild, who at the moment is only able to torment his mother, three thousand kilometres away from Italy. She writes crazy things about him – she says he puts his tongue out at her to make her angry, which seems rather much to me. Don't you agree? But perhaps all mothers see such miracles in their first child.

Later the baby was renamed Delio, after Delio Delogu, the cousin whom Antonio had lived with as a child at Oristano, and who had died very young (he asked his mother: 'Does Uncle Serafino know that I've given the name to my son?').

Gramsci now felt sadder than ever at having to live without Julia: 'Very dismal thoughts creep into my head sometimes. I start thinking of all the time we've spent away from one another, of your intense life and all the things and moments in it which I have been absent from. The worst thing of all is that I can see no early solution to the problem, as it will be very difficult for me to leave Italy for some time to come, and I appreciate all the difficulties in the way of your coming to Italy.' He wanted to help her in some way. But she always believed she should manage by herself when in difficulties, and refused the money he sent. This gave rise to many long arguments:

> But why on earth wouldn't you accept the money that he [Vincenzo Bianco] was supposed to give you? I don't believe that there is anything in this contrary to our principles and standards: it would have given me great pleasure if you had accepted. I often think that there's so little I can do for you and the child, and I would like to do something. I feel that if you knew that something I did had some kind of importance in your life, or helped you over some difficulty, I should be very happy. I should feel then that a new bond had been created between us, something to give us at least the illusion of being close to one another.[5]

[5] In 1931, he would write from prison: 'Why did you refuse so stubbornly the help I sent you through Bianco? And why didn't I assert myself, and make you acknowledge my right to help you? I had received 8,200 lire on my journalistic expense account and put it all into the new paper. How could I allow you to contract debts of 12 roubles while I was paying out so much to the paper, and could quite well have done my duty completely by paying only 50 per cent of it? All this makes me very exasperated with myself, as I was then, and makes me aware of just how incongruous and disgracefully romantic our relationship

He had tried, but without success. On 6 October 1924 he wrote, almost as if to excuse himself:

> Why did I want Bianco to give you something on my behalf? . . . I was thinking of only one thing: that it would make me happy to feel that in some small way I had contributed something to the life you and the child have together – it represented a very small sacrifice, say one packet of cigarettes or one cup of coffee less. Why should I want this so much? I think it must come from the experiences of my own childhood, which were so influenced by material hardship and all the deprivations which we had to undergo in the family – these things create bonds, feelings of solidarity and affection which later on nothing can destroy. Do you believe that the best of communist societies will basically change these conditions of individual existence? Certainly not for a long time to come.

The feeling that such efforts must be made to overcome difficulties was not at all bourgeois, he explained: it was found among the social classes which suffer a basic instability in their existence and are unsure of being able to feed, clothe and shelter their children and old people. 'You believe you're safe from such things because you live in a Soviet state; but you must admit that very many people still live under such conditions even there.' There were Soviet laws which entrusted the care of children to society as a whole as well as to the parents, as she had reminded him. But Antonio thought this was closer to Rousseau than to Lenin: 'When you described how the children are all brought along in a big trolley before being distributed to their mothers to be fed, the scene seemed so real to me that I was tempted to provoke you by suggesting that maybe they give a different infant to the mother each time (given that Soviet discipline is so imperfect, and scarcely likely to reign among the nurses in a children's hospital).' Finally he returned to the underlying cause of his sadness: 'It's a great pity I have not been able to share the anxieties and joys of this time with you; this will always be a great gap in my life.'

The conditions of his work had grown more difficult again. During the Matteotti affair he had thought that the downfall of fascism might be imminent. He gave an exposé on this theme to his central committee, which ran as follows: (1) Fascism had risen to power by exploiting and organizing the petty bourgeoisie, the 'blind, sheep-like stupidity of the lower-middle class, carried away by hatred of the working class. . . . The

---

used to be. It's true you never mentioned the 12 roubles to me, and mocked my "pretensions" to help you, but I feel now that I ought to have found a way of making you accept what you didn't want.'

main characteristic of fascism is its success in organizing the petty bourgeoisie into a mass movement. It is the first time in history this has happened. The originality of fascism lies here, in its having found the appropriate form of organization for a social class which previously had always lacked any structure or unifying ideology. (2) Fascism had kept none of its promises, satisfied none of the hopes it had aroused, alleviated none of Italy's miseries, so 'the middle classes who reposed so much faith in the fascist regime have been overwhelmed by the general crisis. (3) Hence, fascism was under sentence of death:

> The Fascist Party was surprised by the great wave of indignation aroused by the Matteotti crime; it was overcome by panic and lost its head. We know from the three documents written during the panic by Finzi, Filippelli, and Cesarino Rossi, which have come into the hands of the opposition, that the highest chiefs of the movement had momentarily lost all confidence and were making one mistake after another. Fascism entered upon its death throes during this time. It is still propped up by the so-called flanking forces, but these are holding it up much as the rope holds up a man who has just been hanged. The Matteotti crime was the definitive proof that the Fascist Party will never become a normal governing party, and that Mussolini is capable only of striking picturesque poses, not of being a real statesman or dictator. He is no national figure, no Cromwell or Bolivar or Garibaldi, he will go down in history as a quaint phenomenon of our provincial rustic folklore.

In point of fact, the forces which flanked and sustained the fascist movement were not in the least like the rope round a hanged man's neck. Once the movement had got over its first bewilderment, it found it was still being supported by agrarian and industrial capitalism, and quickly began to recover its old aggressiveness. On 31 August, addressing an audience of miners at Monte Amiata, Mussolini declared: 'The day they [the Aventine deputies] stop their vociferous nagging and try to do something – on that day we shall make hay of them, and use it as litter for the camps of the blackshirts.' Fascist violence was reviving once more, as in 1921–22: beatings, killings, the searching and wrecking of offices, newspapers and the homes of known oppositionists. On 5 September 1924 Piero Gobetti was viciously beaten up in Turin and his house burned. (Afterwards his parents went to live in the block of flats between Via San Massimo and Piazza Carlina, where Tasca and Gramsci had once stayed). Then on 12 September a fascist deputy called Armando Casalini was shot and killed in a Rome tramcar by a deranged young man, Giovanni Corvi. To the fascists, things now looked even: Casalini made up for Matteotti. The repression redoubled in intensity. Gramsci was no longer free to move about, as he had been for some months:

> They left me alone for a while, but after the killing of Casalini I was under surveillance again. Once, I was recognized by a fascist from Turin, who pointed me out to a band of his friends; the police began to follow me everywhere, to 'protect' me, and this made all movement very difficult, obliging me to spend money on taxis rather than trams every time I wanted to attend a meeting, so that I could shake them off.

Decisive and energetic action was now clearly called for. On 20 October, the communist deputies proposed that the Aventine should turn itself into an 'anti-parliament' and proclaim itself the sole legitimate representative of the popular will, as against the fascist parliamentary majority now totally dominated by the Fascist Party. The motion was rejected.

During this period Gramsci had been attending a number of local communist congresses in cities throughout Italy. It was during a break in this hectic tour of duty that he managed to spend a few days with his family in Ghilarza. The Sardinian regional party congress was held clandestinely on 26 October 1924, in a field between the Cagliari salt-pans and the village of Quartu. It was a Sunday. Gramsci had arrived the previous evening by train, and spent the night in a lawyer's office only a few hundred yards from the house in Corso Vittorio where he had lodged as a student. He would have liked very much to stroll round and revisit some of the scenes of his youth, but it was too dangerous. The second anniversary of the March on Rome was only three days away, and on Saturday the fascist militia was already everywhere, preparing for the event. He slept on a camp bed in the little office, furnished only with a table and some chairs, and an oil lamp. Next morning at daybreak a young engineering worker, Nino Bruno, from the Costruzioni Meccaniche firm, came to fetch him. Bruno relates:

> He had on a worn, dirty shirt, and no tie. I'd never seen him before, but after hearing so much about him I had imagined a colossus, tall and strong. Instead, there was this little, deformed chap who didn't even bother to keep himself neat; he was unshaven and had a great shock of uncombed hair, and wore a cheap suit with stains on it. I had proposed the place for the meeting, and we went out to make our way there. It was still dark, the roads were deserted. I had chosen a quiet route to take us there, roads right on the edge of town, almost in the country – a long, roundabout

way which wouldn't attract attention. But he showed no signs of fatigue. He was a very cheerful fellow, laughing and joking all the time, talking to me in Sardinian. We arrived at the place, Is Arenas, between Poetto and Monte Urpinu, around seven o'clock. There were already quite a few delegates there, and others kept arriving, a few at a time. There were less than twenty when everyone had come. The congress started right away. It was pomegranate time, and we sat around on the ground; nobody could see us, we were far off all the roads, and hidden among the vines and hedges. Gramsci sat under a tree and made the principal speech. He spoke about Bordiga, then about the need to reorganize the Party, and the propaganda which had to be produced in Sardinia to persuade the peasants, the shepherds and the fishermen to side with the workers elsewhere in Italy. Then there was a discussion. The only speaker favourable to Bordiga was the delegate from Sassari, but he had to leave early to catch the two o'clock train. We had something to eat. Scalas from Oristano had brought some pasta with him, but Gramsci didn't want any. He said he preferred *pane e casu*, bread and cheese, and he also ate some apples and drank some wine. We finished about six in the evening, dispersed, and went singly back to town, all except Gramsci, who was accompanied by somebody else.

Next day, once the congress was over and there was less concern about being followed, they held a lunch at Fanni's, a restaurant in Largo Carlo Felice in the city centre. Afterwards they went for coffee to a bar on Piazza Jenne, where Gramsci was served by a young communist waiter, Giovanni Lay (they were to meet again seven years later, in the prison at Turi). Then at two o'clock he took the train for Ghilarza.

He had not been home since Emma's death in 1902. There had been some changes in the family. Carlo, now twenty-seven, had taken over a shoe shop in the town and was just managing to subsist on that. Teresina was a post office clerk, and she had married Paolo Paulesu, the post-master, some months before. Only Carlo and Grazietta lived at home now, to keep the parents company (Signor Ciccillo was sixty-four and Signora Peppina sixty-three), though they also looked after Gennaro's four-year-old daughter Edmea. There was a great flurry of preparations for the return of Nino. Peppina especially could hardly wait to see and embrace her son again, now thirty-three, a parliamentary deputy, and (to complete her happiness) possessed of a wife and son. Signor Ciccillo was looking forward to the reunion too. A group of old friends went to meet him at the railway station at Abbasanta, among them Peppino Mameli, who later recalled:

He got down from the train and embraced us. Then I noticed him winking, and saw that two other people had got off and were standing there, some distance away, trying very hard to appear inconspicuous and uninterested. Policemen, obviously. Nino stood chatting with us, leaving the carriage door open, and when the station-master blew his horn to announce the departure, he jumped back in the train again. The policemen got on too. The train started. We were standing there waving. Nino opened the door again very quickly and jumped off. I don't know if the policemen even noticed. Anyway the train was moving too fast now for them to get off. Nino had got rid of them.

They set off for Ghilarza. Gramsci's visit of four years previously had been a short one, largely taken up with Emma's recent death, and it had taken place at a very distracting moment in his life: there had been the critical situation in Turin, the defeat of the factory-council movement, the Piedmontese *Avanti!* threatened with closure by Serrati for 'indiscipline', the not always amicable disputes with Togliatti and Terracini, a whole variety of anxious preoccupations and agitated thoughts he could not escape from. . . . It was in fact eleven years since he had spent any time in the town and had a chance to look around.

Nothing seemed changed. Ghilarza looked to him as it had always done, with its squat lava-stone houses, the bluish smoke rising slowly up and eddying above the roof tiles, the smell of orange trees, the clatter of donkey hooves every evening as the peasants returned from the fields; and the Tane sisters, the Cozzoncus, and the Remundu Ganas passing the time of day as usual at the doors of their houses. The only novelty was the first bicycles, just beginning to compete with the donkeys. The older men touched the peaks of their caps in salute as Gramsci passed, and the word soon spread: the son of Peppina Marcias has arrived, Grazia Delogu's nephew is in town.

Then right away the procession of *prinzipales* to the Gramsci house began, the village notables and worthies – 'even the fascists', Gramsci noted, 'they came too, with a great show of dignity and condescension, and congratulated me on being a deputy even though a communist one. The Sardinians are doing well, eh! *Forza paris!* Good for Sardinia!' Gramsci was very amused. 'But a group of workers, peasants and artisans from the local Mutual Aid Society also turned up, in spite of a president who was anxious not to compromise the Society's apolitical reputation, and asked a lot of questions about Russia, how the Soviets worked, about communism, what "capital" and "capitalist" meant, what was our attitude towards fascism, and so on.' Carlo had arranged this meeting, and kept watch outside while it went on. Gramsci later described it to his colleague Celeste Negarville, who says:

> They were very simple, backward men, defeated by a lifetime of toil and misery, and they listened closely to every word he said. But it was not easy to explain what they wanted to know, and Gramsci's singular talent for talking with working people must have served him well. One of the peasants said: 'When we heard they'd made you a candidate at the elections, we decided to vote for you, because we knew you were an honest man. But they told us we couldn't, and we were very sorry about that [Gramsci had been a candidate in constituencies in Piedmont and Venezia Giulia]. But to be quite frank, we weren't sure what party you belonged to on the Continent.' Gramsci explained that he was in the Communist Party, and what the Communist Party was. The peasants thought about it for a bit, then one said: 'But why leave Sardinia, which is so poor, then join up with another lot of poor folk over there?'

Signora Peppina was rather upset by the visits. And Nino himself preferred to remain quietly at home, chatting with his mother and playing with Gennaro's child. He told the family about Julia, how they had met, what she did, and Signora Peppina never tired of listening. 'Her eyes were shining with delight,' Teresina says, 'because she could see Nino was more serene than ever before, happy because of Julia, and because he had a child of his own.' Gramsci spent much time playing with little Edmea (thinking of Delio, perhaps) and she remembers it vaguely: 'He was laughing all the time. We went on great imaginary trips together, with him bouncing me up and down on his knee, and laughing wildly at my tricks.' Antonio wrote to Julia a few days later about these moments of great contentment:

> I've been playing a lot with my four-year-old niece. She'd been scared by seeing some big boiled crabs, so I made up a whole story for her all about 530 wicked crabs under the command of their leader General Chewbroth, with his brilliant general staff (Fieldmistress Bloodsucker, Fieldmarshal Cockroach, Captain Bluebeard, etc.), who were foiled by a little band of good crabs, Fidget, Thudbang, Whitebeard, Blackbeard, etc. The wicked ones pinched her on the legs with my hands, while the good ones came scuttling to her defence on tricycles, armed with brooms and skewers. The whole house echoed to the whir of the tricycles, the thump of brooms, and numerous ventriloquial dialogues among the crabs scampering to and fro everywhere. The little girl believed it all absolutely, and took the story so seriously she thought up new episodes and twists to it herself. So, I relived a little of my own childhood, and found it very much more entertaining than receiving all the village dignitaries.

The holiday lasted ten days, from 27 October to 6 November 1924. The moment for leave-taking came at last. Peppina gave him a traditional Sardinian baby's bonnet from the village of Desulu, to give to Julia for her. As she embraced him when he left, she could not know that it was to be for the last time.

As fascist repression increased, it became more and more evident that the Aventine parliament was quite unable to offer effective opposition to it. On 12 November 1924, five days after Gramsci's return from Sardinia, there occurred the first break between the communists and the Aventine. When the official fascist-dominated Chamber at Montecitorio was reopened after five months' closure, a communist deputy was sent there to make a declaration. This was Luigi Repossi. He found himself alone in an assembly consisting entirely of fascists and their fellow-travellers who intended to 'commemorate' the death of Matteotti officially; but he was not intimidated. In front of the very élite of the fascist *squadristi*, he said: 'Never throughout history has it been permitted the perpetrators of such a crime to commemorate its victims.' Two weeks later the whole communist group left the Aventine and returned to Montecitorio, determined to wage the war against fascism from this more favourable forum.

On that same day, 26 November, Gramsci wrote to Julia:

We're working feverishly at the moment. The political situation is now such that we have to undertake a task which is at once very small-scale and very great in its overall meaning. The working class is awakening and regaining some consciousness of its strength; among the peasants the change is even more striking, their economic situation is terrible. But mass organization is still difficult and the whole party organization of cells and village groups works very slowly. We at the centre must constantly intervene on the spot, stimulating and guiding the work, assisting our comrades and working alongside them. We have become very strong: we're managing to hold public meetings in front of factories, with as many as four thousand workers cheering the Party and the International. The fascists now arouse less fear: after meetings, it has already happened that people organize themselves to attack the houses of fascist chiefs. The bourgeoisie is in pieces, it doesn't know where to turn to find a reliable government, and so is forced to cling desperately to fascism. The other opposition parties are floundering, and the practical effect of their work is merely to demand greater respect for legal forms from Mussolini.

The respect was not forthcoming.

In July, Gramsci had made a report to the central committee of the PCdI, which appeared in *L'Ordine Nuovo* on 1 September:

> Will there be any compromise between fascism and the opposition parties? . . . This is very unlikely. . . . By the very nature of its organization fascism does not tolerate collaboration on an equal footing; all it can use are bond-slaves: there can be no representative assembly under fascism. The fascist regime turns any assembly into an armed camp or into the antechamber of a brothel for the inebriated lower ranks.

The correctness of this judgement was seen on 3 January 1925. For long the legalitarian opposition groups had deluded themselves about the imminent 'normalization' of fascism. Many of them believed that the situation had simply got 'out of hand', that Mussolini was not directly responsible for the wave of violence, and that a gradual expulsion of the 'extremists' from the Fascist Party would bring the civil war conditions to an end. The extracts from Cesare Rossi's memoirs published in Giovanni Amendola's journal *Il Mondo* on 27 December should have been enough to dispel any such hopes. Rossi had formerly been head of the government's press bureau, and had decided to stop being a scapegoat. He wrote: 'Everything which has happened has happened either by the direct wish, or with the approval, of Il Duce himself.' Seven days later, Mussolini brutally cast aside his usual practice of saying one thing and doing another – respecting the constitution in words and at the same time encouraging anti-constitutional violence – and stated in the Chamber: 'I declare here and now, in front of this assembly and of the whole Italian people, that I and I alone assume the political, moral, and historical responsibility for every single thing which has happened. . . . If fascism is a criminal conspiracy, then I am the chief conspirator!' Over the next three days, from the 3rd to the 6th of January, 95 politically suspect clubs or societies were closed down, 25 'subversive' organizations and 120 branches of the 'Free Italy' movement were dissolved by decree, 655 private houses were ransacked, and 111 'subversives' were arrested. The seizure of opposition newspapers became a daily affair.

How did the Aventine react? With another declaration of general principles. On 8 January the constitutional opposition met in an antechamber at Montecitorio and drew up a common statement which said, among other things: 'The mask of normalization and constitutionalism has been dropped. The government is trampling the State's fundamental laws underfoot, suffocating the free voice of the press with unheard-of arbitrariness, suppressing the right of free assembly, mobilizing the armed force of its own party and tolerating or leaving unpunished the deliberate destruction and arson inflicted on its opponents.' But this discovery of fascism's totalitarian ambition was somewhat belated. As an attempt to save Italy from despotism, it was no more than a glass of water cast on the raging bonfire of constitutional rights and freedoms. Mussolini was unlikely to be worried by denunciations at this stage. On 12 January, Gramsci wrote to Julia: 'I believe that here in Italy we are living through a phase of history no other country has known yet, full of the unexpected and the unforeseeable, because fascism has now realized its aim of destroying all the organizations, all the channels through which the masses can express their wishes.'

He was ailing: 'I'm depressed and agitated, and suffering from anaemia even more than from my nerves' (4 December 1924); 'I'm rather tired. For some days now I've been tormented by neuralgia, and so unable to sleep either: my head feels heavy, my mind is muddled' (2 February 1925). Events allowed him no respite, and his unceasing effort had now lasted more than a year.[1] He was writing many articles and – as Felice Platone recalls – travelling from one end of Italy to the other, holding meetings 'to clear up misunderstandings, get rid of prejudices, explain the situation, define lines of action, mobilize people and organizations'. He kept in touch with other militants through the instalments put out by the Party's correspondence school, and had not given up his old Turin custom of impromptu schooling for the younger members in the form of long nocturnal rambles through the city streets. Velio Spano has described them:

> Two or three of us would always accompany him back at night, from the centre of town as far as the Via Nomentana. There was never anything abstract or bookish in the conversation of this extraordinarily cultivated man. . . . He would talk quietly as we went along, building up the argument slowly, piece by piece, with an observation here or there, or more often a question followed by an answer from one of the other comrades.

Among non-communist politicians, he saw Emilio Lussu of the

[1] On 16 January 1925, he wrote to Julia: 'More than a year has gone by since we parted: for me, this has been a year of high-pressure living, and I have not yet been able to sustain the pace.'

Sardinian Action Party most often. They would go and eat together, and Lussu would ask about the Soviet Union while Gramsci inquired about the state of the peasant movement in Sardinia. Distractions were rare – an occasional visit to a cinema or theatre. As he wrote to Julia, he hardly ever managed to escape from 'this desert of pure politics'.

At the end of January 1925 he met Julia's sister, Tatiana Schucht, whom he had been looking for in vain ever since his return to Rome. For many years, Tatiana had been out of touch with her family, having stayed on in Rome as the others departed for Russia one by one. Then the March and October Revolutions had made communication difficult because of the general isolation of Russia, and she had found it hard to keep in contact at all. On 17 August 1921 Julia had written to Leonilde Perilli: 'If this letter should reach you, please try to locate Tatiana and give her our address.' The letter did arrive, but Leonilde had taken some time to track Tatiana down, and when she found her Tatiana had behaved rather strangely. She was in a depressed state, and suspected so strongly that someone had died in her family that she refused to write to them. This extreme fear of having her suspicions confirmed naturally made the suspicion and general depression even more acute. Gramsci was the first person to bring her news directly, and she learned from him of the marriage with Julia.

At this time Tatiana was about forty, four or five years older than Gramsci. She had been beautiful, but was now prematurely aged by the vicissitudes of her life. She earned a living teaching science at the Crandon Institute in Via Savoia. Immediately after the meeting on 2 February, Gramsci wrote to Julia:

I've met your sister Tatiana. We spent yesterday together, from four until nearly midnight, talking about so many things, politics, her life here in Rome, her work and its possibilities. We also went to eat together, and I'm not surprised she's so weak: she eats next to nothing, although she isn't physically ill in any way and appears to be in good health, as she says she is. I think we are good friends already. . . . She's promised to tell me all about her adventures, so that I can tell you about them when I see you. I was very happy to meet her. Because she is very like you, and because politically she's much closer to us than I had been led to believe. . . . The only things she takes exception to are the denial of free expression to the Social Revolutionaries, and the imprisonment of a certain Ismailia (I think it was) and Spiridonova. She would like to work for the Soviet regime, but they've made her believe that the Soviet representatives here in Rome are all corrupt rascals and she'll have nothing to do with them.

She doesn't want people to think that by working with them she is trying to get some of the benefits of the Revolution without having undergone any of the sacrifices.

Antonio and Tatiana saw each other again. But such brief moments of private life were not enough for Gramsci, impatient to be with Julia again and finally see his son. There was to be a meeting of the full executive of the International at Moscow on 21 March 1925, and Gramsci was to lead the Italian delegation. He wrote on 7 February:

> My trip has had to be put off again for a fortnight or so, but I think it will certainly be all right. They're even going to give me an ordinary passport; which may be some small consolation for the added delay. Will we have time to go on some walks together, at the end of March and the beginning of April? . . . You know your sister Tatiana is rather like an anticipation of you: she's like you in many of her features and movements, the music of her voice is like the echo of your own (she would be pleased to know I put 'echo', because she objected to my comparing her voice to yours, which she says is very beautiful). I see her often; she comes to eat with me in the Roman *trattorie*, but I've been unsuccessful in getting her to eat more than usual. . . . She wanted to buy some shoes for you, with the most terrifying heels – I resisted strenuously, insisting that you would certainly never wear such horrors. . . . She wants to buy little shoes for the child too. What a terrible woman, with her mania for shoeing the whole world!

He left towards the end of February 1925. He had not seen his wife since November 1923, nearly a year and a half. And Delio became at last 'a real living child, instead of a faint impression on photographic paper'. Unfortunately the child was in the throes of whooping-cough; Gramsci often took him out for walks in his pram, in the gardens near Tverskaya Yamskaya (now Gorky Street), where the Schuchts lived.

More disturbing than Delio's illness, however, was the condition of Antonio's sister-in-law Eugenie. She had been cured of the grave psychosomatic ailment which had kept her helpless for so long at Serebranyi Bor. But she was plainly still in a highly neurotic state, and it occasionally verged on something worse. Earlier, in the sanatorium, she had been more than friendly towards Gramsci, and now she seemed to consider herself another mother to Delio. Gramsci was greatly struck by something which happened soon after his arrival in Moscow. He and Julia had decided to give a present to the woman doctor who was looking after Delio, and chose a reproduction of Correggio's *Danae*. He signed, as the father; then under Julia's signature Eugenie added her own, and wrote alongside both names 'the mothers'.

Apollo Schucht was very annoyed by Eugenie's behaviour. He would not let Delio call Eugenie 'mother', and continually repeated to the child: 'Delio has only one mother, only one mother, only one!' Gramsci too was upset by the situation, but preferred not to confront it so directly. He was fond of Eugenie; he had known her when she was bedridden, and remembered her sufferings. He could understand how – given her persisting physical incapacity and isolation – Delio had become to her something like a child of her own, her only meaningful link with life and the wider world outside herself. So he reacted humanely. When he left Moscow, it was on the understanding that when Julia and the child came to join him Eugenie should come as well.

He was back in Italy by 28 April. The government was preparing a new law which – according to the official pronouncements – was principally aimed against the Freemasons. However, it contained a more general formulation to the effect that the purpose was 'to discipline the activity of associations, clubs, and institutes, and the participation of public servants in such activity'. It was easy to perceive the wider meaning of the act, which would provide the regime with an instrument for striking at any anti-fascist organization whatever while preserving an appearance of legality. As far as Freemasonry was concerned, Gramsci maintained that fascism was a competitor rather than an opponent; and in this sense, the act's aim was to put the Freemasons in their place and assert the superiority of fascism, after which a compromise would be arrived at. It was other organizations, those with which no such compromise was possible, that would bear the brunt of repression once the law was passed.

On 16 May 1925 Gramsci entered the Chamber to denounce the law's tyrannical implications. It was his parliamentary début. Finally, they confronted one another face to face: the one-time leader of a revolutionary generation, editor of *Avanti!* until 1914, and now at forty-two called 'Duce' by the organized might of the bourgeois counter-revolution; and across the Chamber, the new, younger leader of the leftist opposition. Although they had never had occasion to meet until then, they knew one another well. In 1921, speaking from the opposition benches, Mussolini had said: 'The anarchists define the editor of *L'Ordine Nuovo* as one who pretends to be stupid, pretends to because he is really a Sardinian hunchback, a professor of economics and philosophy with a brain of undeniable power.' Gramsci, for his part, had written in *L'Ordine Nuovo* of 15 March 1924:

In Italy we have the fascist regime, with Benito Mussolini at its head. We have an official ideology which makes the leader into a divinity and declares him infallible, the predestined architect and inspirer of a new Holy Roman Empire. Every day we see printed in the papers hundreds of telegrams of homage to the chief from the vast local tribes that owe him allegiance. We see the photographs: that mask-like visage, rather hardened now, which we once saw at socialist meetings. We know the face: we know that trick of rolling the eyes round in their sockets, whose mechanical ferocity was once designed to make the bourgeois shit with fear, and is now turned upon the workers. We know that fist, forever clenched in a threatening gesture. We know all the machinery and how it works, we understand how it can impress people and stir the viscera of bourgeois schoolchildren – it is genuinely impressive, even on closer inspection. . . .

But who was Mussolini, in fact? 'The concentrated essence of the Italian petty bourgeois, that touchy, ferocious sediment compounded of all the centuries of rubbish deposited on our soil by foreign domination and the rule of priests. He could not be the leader of the proletariat; so he became a bourgeois dictator. The bourgeoisie likes ferocious faces when it needs to put the clock back, and hopes to see the working class trembling with the same terror it once felt itself at the sight of those rolling eyes and that perpetually raised, menacing fist.' Now these two diametrically opposed personalities and temperaments faced one another across the Chamber at Montecitorio.

Gramsci was no resounding orator: his speech gave the impression of coming directly from the brain, not from lungs and throat. In *La Rivoluzione liberale* Gobetti had once written, after the 1924 April elections: 'If Gramsci ever speaks at Montecitorio we shall probably see the fascist deputies quiet and attentive for once, as they strain to hear the inflections of that faint voice, and experience a completely novel intellectual sensation. Gramsci's dialectic does not protest against the swindles and intrigues of bourgeois government, it looks down from the pure heights of the Hegelian Idea and coldly demonstrates their inevitability.' Prophetic words. Velio Spano remembers how, as Gramsci spoke, 'all the deputies thronged round the benches of the extreme left, in order to hear the faint, inflexible voice better. One of the Rome papers published a large picture of Mussolini himself leaning forward with his hand to his ear'. Calmly, Gramsci analysed the class character of Freemasonry, and then that of fascism: 'Given the way in which Italian unity was achieved, given the initial weakness of the

Italian capitalist bourgeoisie, Freemasonry was for long the only real
and effective party the bourgeoisie possessed.' As for fascism: 'The
original, instinctive political line spontaneously taken up by fascism
after the occupation of the factories was summed up in the phrase:
"The rural bourgeoisie must take over from the urban bourgeoisie,
which is not tough enough with the workers".' He then drew his first
conclusion from the analysis:

> Fascism is struggling against the only efficiently organized force the
> bourgeoisie ever had in Italy, in order to supplant it as the main source of
> patronage for official and civil service jobs. The fascist revolution is nothing
> but the replacement of one set of administrative personnel by another.
> MUSSOLINI: Of one class by another, as happened in Russia, as happens
> normally in every revolution, as we shall do methodically. . . .
> GRAMSCI: A revolution is only such when it is based upon a new class.
> Fascism is based on no class which was not already in power. . . .
> MUSSOLINI: Then why is a large part of the capitalist class against us? I
> can mention several very big capitalists who vote against us, who are part
> of the opposition, like Motta, or Conti. . . .
> FARINACCI (Secretary of the Fascist Party): And they are even subsidizing
> subversive papers!
> MUSSOLINI: The big banks are not fascist, as you know very well!

It was easy for Gramsci to retort that fascism was, precisely, engaged
on engineering a compromise with those forces not yet absorbed by the
system:

> Fascism has not yet succeeded in completely absorbing all other parties
> into its own organization. With the Freemasons it first tried the political
> tactic of infiltration, then the terroristic approach – burning down lodges;
> and finally, legislative action, which will lead to numbers of key people in
> the big banks and the upper reaches of the bureaucracy going over to the
> winning side in order to safeguard their jobs. But the fascist government
> will also have to compromise with the Freemasons. What does one do
> with a strong enemy of this sort? First break his legs, then when he is down
> force an agreement with him from a position of evident superiority. . . .
> Hence, we say that in fact this law is directed specially against the organiza-
> tions of the workers. We demand to know why for many months now,
> although the Communist Party has not been declared an illegal organiza-
> tion, our comrades are arrested by the carabinieri every time they are
> found together in groups of three or more. . . .
> MUSSOLINI: We're doing what you do in Russia. . . .
> GRAMSCI: In Russia there are laws which are respected: you have your
> own laws here. . . .

MUSSOLINI: In Russia you're very good at rounding people up. Quite right too!
GRAMSCI: In fact the state security apparatus already considers the Communist Party as a secret organization.
MUSSOLINI: That's not true!
GRAMSCI: Then why are people arrested every time they gather together more than three at a time, without any specific charge, and thrown in jail?
MUSSOLINI: But they get out quickly enough. How many are there in jail? We only pull them in so we can get to know them.
GRAMSCI: It is a form of systematic persecution, which anticipates and justifies the application of this new law. Fascism is falling back on the methods of the Giolitti government, you're doing what they used to do in the South, when they hired thugs to arrest anyone who voted for the opposition . . . so they could get to know them.
A VOICE: There's only been one case. You know nothing about the South.

'I am a Southerner,' answered Gramsci. The continuous interruptions prevented him from developing his argument smoothly. However, he always managed to return to it:

> Since the Freemason movement will go over *en masse* to the Fascist Party and become one of its currents, it is clear that you intend to stop the development of large-scale worker or peasant organization with this law. This is the real point, the real meaning of the law. Somebody in the fascist movement still guards a nebulous recollection of the teachings of his former masters, of the time when he too was a revolutionary and a socialist; he knows that a class cannot remain itself, cannot develop itself to the point of seizing power, unless it possesses a party and an organization which embodies the best, most conscious part of itself. Here is the grain of truth in this muddled, reactionary perversion of Marxist teaching.

But, in the existing situation, was it in any case so certain that breaking up the working-class parties would destroy the strength of the Italian proletariat? To the voice which had cried 'You know nothing about the South', the Sardinian deputy replied more fully:

> In Italy, capitalism has only been able to develop to the extent to which the State has squeezed the peasant population, particularly in the South. Today you feel the urgency of the problem well enough; why else do you promise millions to Sardinia, and hundreds of millions to the Mezzogiorno as a whole? If you were truly serious and wished to do something concrete, you could begin by restoring to Sardinia the hundred or hundred and fifty million which you extort from the island's population every year. You should give back to the people of the Mezzogiorno the money extorted

from them each year in the form of taxes. . . . Each year the State removes from these southern regions a sum which it in no way makes good, neither in services nor in any other way. . . . Such sums are employed by the State to build up the basis of capitalism in northern Italy. Upon this terrain, upon the contradictions of the Italian capitalist system, the workers and peasants will of necessity unite against their common enemy, in spite of the repressive laws, in spite of all these difficulties placed in the way of building large organizations. . . . You may 'conquer the State', you may change the statute book, you may try to stop organizations from existing in the forms they have assumed up until now; but you cannot hope to prevail over the objective conditions which determine your own actions. All you will succeed in doing is force the proletariat to find another outlet from the one hitherto most used. From this forum, we wish to say to the proletariat and the peasant masses of Italy: the revolutionary forces of the nation will never let themselves be shattered, and your dark dream will never be turned into reality.

As he ended, the Chamber was in turmoil. Gramsci's maiden speech was also his final one. He was never to speak again from the parliamentary bench. It has often been said – though there seem to be no direct witnesses of the incident – that Mussolini saw Gramsci immediately afterwards, having a coffee in the parliamentary bar, and went up to him with outstretched hand to congratulate him on his speech. Gramsci continued sipping his coffee indifferently, ignoring the hand held out to him.

Nine days later he wrote to Julia:

Work goes on in a very disordered way, in fits and starts: my state of mind reflects this, as if it wasn't disordered enough already. Difficulties get greater every day, now we have a law against organizations which is the prelude to a systematic police effort to liquidate our party. I made my parliamentary début speaking on this law. The fascists accorded me an unusually favourable reception, so from a revolutionary point of view I started off badly. As my voice is so feeble they all crowded round to listen, and let me say what I wanted, interrupting all the time to make me lose the thread, but not trying really to sabotage the speech. I was amused by their remarks, but couldn't stop myself answering them and so played into their hands, because I got tired and didn't succeed in following through the line of argument I had chosen to pursue.

He was tired. The Roman summer drained him of energy and gave him insomnia. He had to move about with the utmost caution and as little as possible, and saw few friends:

I'm oppressed by solitude more than anything, partly because of the illegal operation of the Party, which forces one to operate individually and independently. I try to get away from this political desert by going often to see Tatiana, who reminds me of you. But there's no real way of making up for your absence. Everything I lay eyes on in the world round about me seems to remind me of you and Delio, and so makes me more acutely aware of my unhappiness. . . . But it doesn't matter. . . . It will pass, because I'm sure that you will come to Italy, and that all our energies will become greater, our personalities will become fuller, as we experience together the development of Delio's life.

Julia and the child rejoined him in Rome in the autumn.

The meeting of the Comintern's full executive in March-April 1925 had confirmed the policy established by the two previous congresses. Dictatorship of the proletariat remained the final answer. But meanwhile, in Italy, an intermediate objective had become mandatory: the recovery of bourgeois-democratic freedoms. And to attain this – in the International's view – it was necessary to form the widest possible alliance of working people and their parties, under the hegemony of the industrial working class and its organized vanguard, the Communist Party. After three years of fascist terror, there had been a revival of popular desire for democratic order in Italy, rather than for a revolution, and Gramsci was aware of this. He still did not doubt that the International's policy was correct, therefore. In *L'Ordine Nuovo* of 1 September 1924, he had written:

> There are many lessons for us in the Matteotti crisis. . . . It has shown us that after three years of terror and oppression the masses have become very cautious and are unwilling to take risks. . . . [This caution] . . . is certainly destined to disappear, and before too long, but in the meantime it exists, and can be overcome only if we go forward cautiously ourselves, taking care at each step, on each occasion, never to lose contact with the working classes as a whole.

Hence the added urgency of the struggle against Bordighism: 'If there are fanatical groups and trends in our Party which wish to force the situation, it will be necessary to struggle against these in the name of the Party as a whole.'

But Bordiga seemed as little disposed as ever to yield. He still rejected all intermediate solutions. There was still no possible alternative to bourgeois dictatorship but proletarian dictatorship. He did not think that bourgeois rule by democratic forms was preferable to bourgeois rule by radical despotism. The advent of fascism had been merely the replacement of one bourgeois group by another. And since all other parties – from the Italian Socialist Party to the Sardinian Action Party – were so many pillars of the bourgeois order, and the Communist Party its only genuine adversary, it followed that the communists had to destroy fascism all on their own, unhampered by impure, contaminating alliances. Intermediate, transitional stages involving reliance on democracy were more pernicious than fascism itself – after all, had not fascism opened the way towards communism, by suppressing all democratic illusions?

This was an abstract diagnosis, quite out of touch with reality. Put into practice, it would have condemned the communists to suicidal isolation and to forms of revolutionary bombast at a time when it was vitally necessary to oppose fascism with concrete actions.

In the spring of 1921, groups of combatants called the 'Arditi del Popolo' had been formed with the aim of encouraging armed resistance to fascist violence. Bordiga was so convinced of the wrongness of alliances that he ordered the communists not to fraternize with the socialists, even on this terrain: the penalty of joining in this armed fight against fascist destruction was expulsion from the Party. And the fact is that scarcely anybody in the party leadership had opposed or contradicted this sectarian decision. Since that period, Bordiga's attitudes had not altered in the slightest. Zinoviev had attempted to win him over by offering him the vice-presidency of the International, but to no avail. In this rigid and combative man a misconceived worship of abstract dogma was stronger than vanity.

There was to be a national congress soon where the balance of forces inside the Party would be established, and Gramsci was making long trips in preparation for it. On 15 August he wrote to Julia: 'I've been away from Rome for some time, and still am. I have to travel to attend meetings, and shake the police off my trail all the time.' Giovanni Farina remembers the words he used at a meeting of militants and party functionaries from the Milan area in the summer of 1925: 'At this time the Italian people are not struggling for the dictatorship of the proletariat but for democracy. Failure to understand this means failure to understand the sense of what is going on under our own noses.' Such terms savoured of heresy to those on the extreme left who still 'saw revolution on every street corner' (as Farina puts it), and encouraged among them the fable of Gramsci's regression towards 'social-democratic' positions.

It was a summer of intensive work. He was missing Julia and Delio greatly:

> I've travelled round a lot recently, and seen places they tell me are very beautiful, landscapes which must be marvellous, since foreigners come such a long way just to gaze at them. I was at Miramare for instance, but to me it looked like some aberration straight out of Carducci; the white towers looked like badly white-washed chimney pots, and the sea all round was dirty yellow because labourers building a road nearby had chucked tons of rubbish into it; the sun seemed no more than a central heating system working out of season. But I reminded myself that all these impressions must be tied up with one's own 'apathy' – to use your mother's term – with the fact that I've lost all taste for nature and the life going on around me, because I'm always conscious of how far away you are, because since knowing you I can feel no joy which is not related to you, which does not cease on the spot if I think that you're not there, that you can't see what I am seeing. . . . Delio came into my life like a bright falling star in August – but then, hasn't the whole story of our love been rather like that?

Other children reminded him of Delio. During his brief visits to Milan he stayed at No. 7 Via Napo Torriani, where *L'Unità* publishing house had its offices. The business manager of the paper, Aladino Bibolotti, lived in the adjoining flat with his wife and two small children. There was always a small room in this flat at Gramsci's disposition when he required it. And Fidia Sassano, another of the *Unità* journalists, can remember how 'in the corridor between the offices he used to crawl about after Bibolotti's children on all fours, when nobody was looking'.

In September he moved to Togliatti's house in Rome for a few days. Here, under his direction, the theses for the Party's Third Congress were composed. The congress was to be held at Lyons in January. The document they composed was a cool and lucid essay on the situation in Italy and the tasks of the Communist Party. It marked a new departure: its scientific rigour contrasted forcefully with the rhetorical polemics which had characterized too many such documents in the past. It analysed the country's social and economic structures, the contradictions of its capitalist order, and the nature and function of fascism in relation to these contradictions; then, the class and political forces which were the motor of proletarian revolution, and those other forces which could be aroused and included in a system of alliances capable of overthrowing fascism. Nothing indicates better the profundity of the document's analysis than its truly prophetic forecast of the future extremes to which fascism would go:

The crowning glory of all the propaganda and all the political and economic work of fascism is its tendency towards 'imperialism'. This trend is the expression of the need felt by the Italian agrarian-industrial ruling class to find an answer to the crisis of Italian society outside Italian society itself. It is a trend which contains the seeds of war, of a war which will ostensibly be fought for Italian expansion, but which will in reality turn fascist Italy into a tool in the hands of one or other of the imperialist groups contending for world domination.

In brief, the Lyons theses provided: a definition of fascism as Italian capitalism's way of achieving stability; a proclamation of the proletariat's hegemonic rôle in the anti-fascist struggle; an analysis of all the mass forces which could be won over to the worker-peasant bloc, with a distinction made between the bourgeois forces which had committed themselves irretrievably to fascism and those others which remained organized, or could be organized, into democratic, anti-fascist formations; finally, an outline of the basic, leading role of the Communist Party and its cellular structure at the head of the working class. The theses were a great advance on anything produced in Bordiga's day, even if they did show (as Togliatti has conceded) some remaining traces of the old sectarianism.

Gramsci was very agitated by the news – which he had only heard at second hand – that Julia was now definitely coming to Rome, and had been found a job there. 'I don't know what to think of this, as I've heard nothing from you about it; I told Tatiana about the rumour, and she was so affected by it she was unable to sleep. She is confident you're coming, in any case, and is waiting anxiously.' Julia and Delio arrived in October with Eugenie. Gramsci had moved in the meantime to Via Morgagni, still as a lodger with the Passarge family, and he rented a furnished flat for the others in Via Trapani. He thought it more prudent not to stay there himself. If she were known to be involved with him, the government might well withdraw Julia's visa.

There had been another clamp-down. At Florence, on the night of 4 October, the *squadristi* had behaved with greater ferocity than ever before: in addition to a large number of attacks on persons and homes, the former socialist deputy Gaetano Pilati and a lawyer called Gaetano Consolo had been killed, the latter in his own home and in front of his wife and children. The life of all opponents of the regime was clearly in peril, and great caution was necessary. On 24 October Gramsci's room in Via Morgagni was ransacked in a police search. Then on 4 November the police uncovered a plot by the former socialist deputy Tito Zaniboni to assassinate Mussolini, by shooting at him from a room in the Dragoni Hotel when he appeared on the balcony of Palazzo Chigi at the celebration of the victory of 1918. The atmosphere became still worse.

Every morning and afternoon Julia would go to her job at the Soviet embassy (she had abandoned her musical career to be with Antonio in Italy). Later on, Gramsci would come to the flat in Via Trapani for supper and stay there until after midnight. They never went out together. Occasionally Julia would go with her sisters or Leonilde Perilli to concerts at the Argentina or Adriano concert halls, but Antonio did not accompany them. He stayed at home and played with Delio.

Delio was now about one and a half, but his father treated him like a small adult and divined in him the most astonishing talents. 'His love of animals [Gramsci said] was put to good use in two ways – in music, where he managed very cleverly to reproduce on a piano keyboard the whole musical scale according to animal noises, from the bears' baritone right up to the high notes of the chickens at the other end – and also in drawing.' The child liked being amused in the same way over and over again: 'The first thing was to put the wall-clock down on the table, and move the hands into all the possible positions; then one had to write a letter to his maternal grandmother with drawings of the animals he had noticed that day; then we would go to the piano and play his animal music, then there would be various other games.'

At home, Eugenie was in charge. She did the cooking and looked after Delio while Julia and Tatiana were out at work. They were all greatly influenced by her and overlooked the disturbing symptoms she was still displaying. Gramsci had thought and worried a good deal about Eugenie's attachment to the child since the trip to Moscow. He had been struck by a newspaper item about a Sardinian family drama in Genoa: a woman suffering from cancer had poisoned herself and her five-year-old grandson, leaving a note saying that she had had to take the child to paradise with her because she could not do without him even there. And he had some reason to ponder such morbid sorts of affection, capable of leading to crime: for some days he had been surprised to hear Delio calling him '*dyadya*', which means 'uncle' in Russian. Only when Tatiana brusquely intervened and took Eugenie to task were things put right. But though worried, Gramsci was careful not to make too much of the situation.

In late January 1926, Gramsci crossed the French frontier clandestinely to attend the Party Congress at Lyons. Going abroad was no simple task, but Gramsci had become used to long mountain treks and meetings in the open air. The previous year he had spoken to Julia of his apprenticeship in snow-trekking, and even in lying out in it overnight'. Delegates had come from all over Italy to Lyons, but 18·9 per cent had to be recorded as 'absent or not consulted' (the Bordighini accused Gramsci and his leadership of rigging the procedures for the designation of delegates, at the level of the provincial congresses).

On 20 January, Gramsci addressed the conference's political commission and continued his polemic with the left on the subject of insurrection:

> There is no country where the proletariat is in a position to conquer power and retain it by itself: it must therefore always seek allies. It must look for a policy which will allow it to assume the leadership of those other classes which have anti-capitalist interests and guide them in the struggle for the overthrow of bourgeois society. The question is particularly important in Italy, where the proletariat is a minority in the working population, and where it is dispersed geographically in such a way that it cannot presume to lead a victorious struggle for power until it has given a clear solution to the problem of its relationship with the peasant class. In the immediate future, our Party must devote itself to the definition and solution of this problem.

It was time to think of long-term political organization rather than of seizure of power via an insurrection, claimed Gramsci's central committee majority. His majority thesis won 90·8 per cent of the votes cast, while Bordiga's left-wing faction was reduced to 9·2 per cent. Bordiga complained to the International that there had been 'irregularities' in the organization of the congress, but his appeal was rejected.

The fascist steamroller was now about to crush out the last remnants of free political life in Italy. The Partito Popolare deputies withdrew from the Aventine and reappeared in the Chamber at Montecitorio; they were attacked and beaten up by the fascist deputies. Next day, Mussolini declared:

> Those who wish to return from the Aventine to this Chamber and be tolerated within it must, first of all, solemnly and publicly recognize the fascist revolution as an accomplished fact, opposition to which is politically

useless, historically absurd, and meaningful only to such as have placed themselves outside the State and her laws; secondly, no less solemnly and publicly, they must acknowledge that the execrable, scandalmongering campaign conducted by the Aventine has been a miserable failure, because there never has been any moral question concerning either the government or the Fascist Party; thirdly, and no less solemnly and publicly, they must disown all those who are carrying on anti-fascist agitation abroad. Once they accept and fulfil these conditions, the outlaws of the Aventine may hope to win our tolerance and re-enter this Chamber. Until they do accept and fulfil them, then as long as I occupy this post – and I intend to do so for a good while yet – they will never re-enter: not tomorrow, not ever!

The 'Napoleonic Year' of the fascist revolution (as Mussolini chose to define 1926) was beginning. Turati's Unified Socialist Party – to which Tito Zaniboni belonged – was dissolved after the discovery of his plot against Mussolini, and his paper La Giustizia could no longer appear. La Rivoluzione liberale had ceased publication in November 1925, and Piero Gobetti had been ordered by the Turin police to stop all publishing and journalistic activity. He left for Paris on 6 February, to die there nine days later, not yet twenty-five. Amendola and Salvemini had also emigrated. A law of January 1926 decreed loss of Italian citizenship for whoever continued to attack fascism from abroad, accompanied by sequestration of their property in Italy or (in the worst cases) outright confiscation. Among those deprived of citizenship were Salvemini and a Catholic journalist, Giuseppe Donati, who had accused the Rome chief of police De Bono of complicity in the murder of Matteotti.

The trial arising out of the Matteotti affair took place at Chieti from 16 to 24 March 1926. The accused were defended by Roberto Farinacci, the extremist General Secretary of the Fascist Party (who was accorded an official reception at the town hall by the judges and authorities). Premeditation was ruled out by the public prosecutor, and the verdict was manslaughter. The three men found guilty were sentenced to five years, eleven months and twenty days (of which four years were remitted under the terms of the previous year's amnesty decree). Two weeks after the sentence, there was still another attempt on Mussolini's life, by a sixty-two-year-old British woman, Violet Gibson (she had been a mental hospital inmate for some time). She shot at him as he came out of Palazzo dei Conservatori on to the Campidoglio in Rome, wounding him slightly in the nose. The fascist reprisals hit at the few remaining free papers, and the offices of *Il Mondo* and *La Voce repubblicana* were sacked. For Gramsci, life became more complicated than ever.

Apollo Schucht came to Rome, a handsome Tolstoyan figure, strongly built and with a long white beard. The armed camp to which he returned must certainly have seemed very different from the peaceful, tolerant Rome he had left eleven years before. But Delio provided the best of reasons for living there. The Schucht family was thus partially reconstituted in Italy – though without Nadina Leontieva, Anna (with her husband in Moscow), Victor, and the mother. For Gramsci, in spite of the prevailing social climate and his semi-clandestine existence, there were a few happy months: he could at least relax in a congenial family environment, and Julia and Delio helped him withstand the extreme pressures of his work.

Julia was now expecting another baby. She did not wish to give up her job at the Soviet embassy or leave Italy, but everything was now conditioned by the growing darkness of the political scene. It was necessary to reckon with the likelihood of being forced to leave Italy sooner or later; while Antonio might very well have to go into exile too, like other opposition leaders. Eugenie argued that it therefore made sense to anticipate the course of events, since the birth of the second child would certainly make things more difficult. Julia let herself be swayed. The change of climate from Rome to Moscow might be harmful to a new-born baby, in any case; and once the family was safely in Moscow, Antonio's freedom of movement would be much greater. The two left Rome in July, letting it be known they intended to holiday at Trafoi, in the province of Alto Adige. Julia crossed the border on 7 August. Twenty-three days later she gave birth to another boy, Giuliano. Eugenie, Tatiana and Delio remained in Trafoi, and Antonio came to join them later in August:

> I had the impression that Delio was much better than in Rome. He looked stronger and more lively. He has also developed intellectually; he has made contact with the outside world and learnt innumerable new things. I think that the stay at Trafoi against this magnificent background of mountains and glaciers is bound to leave a lasting impression on him. We played a lot. I made some little toys for him, and we lit fires out in the fields. There weren't any lizards, so I couldn't show him how to catch them. I think he's at the start of a very important stage in his development, the one which leaves the most lasting memories, because during it one learns to conquer the wide and terrible world outside.

He had wanted to teach Delio a few words of Sardinian: 'I wanted to teach him to sing *Lassa sa figu, puzone*, too ['Leave the fig alone, bird', a title with an obvious *double entendre* – T.N.], but his aunts wouldn't let me.' Delio left with his aunt Eugenie in September. Antonio never saw him again.

In the autumn of 1926, Gramsci sat down to try and write an essay on *'la questione meridionale'*, the Southern Question. It was no new subject for him. It had been the theme of his first political thoughts when he was still a boy at Ghilarza and Santulussurgiu, living in a society of peasants and shepherds. It had continued to dominate his thoughts as a lycée student in Cagliari, where he had read and been influenced by Salvemini. In Turin he had not forgotten the problem, though he saw it more maturely and from a different angle. Eventually, he had come to perceive it as one aspect of a much vaster problem, the problem of proletarian revolution.

His earliest formulation of the Southern Question had been a narrow one, influenced by an ambiguous peasant-populist irredentism. It reflected the Sardinian climate of the period, with its constant stress on the mainland's neglect of the island as the cause of its backwardness: according to it, the *whole* of Sardinia must act to improve the conditions of the peasants and other impoverished strata, and such advance could only come from a regional-national struggle against the 'Continent'. Then Gramsci made his first steps towards socialism and discovered the class character of society; and in Turin, he realized that those who profited from the protectionist regime were not the 'continentals' but the northern property-owning class, the industrial bourgeoisie which was alone in fact 'protected' by the laws afflicting the old southern agrarian economy. Gramsci's support for the anti-protectionist manifesto of 1913 derived from his protest at the role of this parasitic entrepreneurial class. But he had already begun to grasp another, more basic truth: there *was* no Southern Question on its own for which specific remedies could be found independently of the more general 'national question'. That is, there could be no right policy towards the Mezzogiorno so long as the general political life of the nation remained the expression of particular interests. In one of Gramsci's first articles, written when he was twenty-five and had only recently begun to work for *Il Grido del Popolo*, we read:

The Mezzogiorno does not require special laws and special treatment. What it needs is an overall political programme founded upon respect for the overall needs of the country, rather than for particular political or regional tendencies. It is not enough to build a road here or a dam there to make good the damage suffered by certain regions because of the war. What is required – before anything else – is that future trade treaties do not close markets to the products of these regions [Il Mezzogiorno e la guerra – 'The Mezzogiorno and the War', 1 April 1916].

Once the Southern Question had been integrated into a wider national perspective in this way, his consideration of it evolved logically with the general development of his ideas towards socialism, in the period 1919–20: 'The northern bourgeoisie has subjugated southern Italy and the islands, and reduced them to the status of exploited colonies; as the northern working class emancipates itself from capitalist slavery, it will also emancipate the southern peasant masses from their servitude to the banks and the parasitic industrialism of the North' [*L'Ordine Nuovo*, 3 January 1920].

Such was the end of the long train of thought which derived originally from Gramsci's direct knowledge of the peasants and countryfolk of his own region. The deputy who had shouted 'You know nothing about the South!' obviously knew little of Gramsci's past or interests. Yet it is important (and quite surprising) to observe that this aspect of his life and thought was in fact known to few people outside a small circle of friends at that time. The essay he now settled down to write, a few weeks before his arrest, was to surprise a great many people when it was finally published in Paris four years later.

La questione meridionale marks a transition from the journalism of his early years of political struggle to the more meditative style of his prison writings. In the first ten years of journalistic production there are certainly pages which look forward to the great essayist of the *Quaderni del carcere*, the Prison Notebooks. But generally speaking it had been dominated by immediate necessities, by the propaganda and polemic required in the day-to-day political battle: his journalistic pieces were mostly designed as weapons, instruments, to mobilize the working class and lead it into attack. The Gramsci of the 1916–26 period was mainly, though never exclusively, a pamphleteer. His essay on the Southern Question bears the marks of this period, its style and attitudes are sometimes journalistic; but in it he also rises clearly above this level for the first time, and adopts a wider, more philosophic and 'disinterested' point of view – the attitude which was to be characteristic of the Prison Notebooks. The result was an exemplary study of Italian realities, a model of political and social analysis.

In it Gramsci offered a Marxist interpretation of Italy's political evolution over the previous thirty years. After ruling too exclusively and violently at the end of the nineteenth century, the Italian bourgeoisie realized at the beginning of the twentieth that it could no longer go on in the old way. The Sicilian peasant uprising of 1894 and the Milan insurrection of 1896 had given warning that change was indispensable. It was necessary, therefore, to seek alliance with and support from other social classes, and to govern more democratically. There were two possibilities: the bourgeoisie could try to build up a rurally based democracy founded on an alliance with the southern peasantry (which would have entailed a free-trade policy, effective universal suffrage, administrative decentralization, and low prices for manufactured goods); or else it could build up an industrial alliance of capitalists and workers, founded on customs protectionism, limited suffrage, and reinforced state centralization (the price being, naturally, a more lenient policy towards wages and trade union organization).

The ruling class had opted for the second solution: hence the Giolitti regime, and the way in which the Socialist Party of the period had been turned into an instrument of his policies. However, the proletariat had grown restive and reacted against its subordination to this system – so, after about 1910, the PSI had been forced back towards more intransigent positions which had tended to undermine the system's working. This was the point at which Giolitti tried to change tactics: he attempted to replace the implicit alliance between bourgeoisie and workers with an alliance of bourgeoisie and Catholics – who at this stage represented mainly the rural masses of northern and central Italy.

In this changed situation, what should be the first objective of the working class? Gramsci answered firmly that it should be to isolate the bourgeoisie by detaching it from its unnatural allies. The Italian proletariat could only become a dominant, governing class by creating for itself a system of class alliances which would allow it to mobilize the majority of the working population against the bourgeoisie. And this in fact meant, when it won over the peasant masses. But in Italy the peasant problem had historically assumed two distinctive forms: the Southern Question and the 'Vatican question'. Hence, in order to win over the rural masses, the working class had to find its own solution to both these questions: it had to understand the class forces behind them and incorporate these forces into its revolutionary programme. Only if it did this, only if it looked outwards and divested itself of every remnant of the closed working-class corporativism encouraged by the Giolittian regime, would it be able to make itself into a potential ruling class. Otherwise the peasants (the majority of the population in Italy) would remain under bourgeois direction and provide the bourgeois State with a permanent, effective weapon against the workers – an inert mass that would weaken and break every assault upon it.

If this was so, then how could the peasant masses be won over? Southern society, as Gramsci analysed it, was an agrarian bloc consisting of three main social strata. At the bottom lay the great peasant mass, fragmented and amorphous; above them, the small and middling rural bourgeoisie with its attendant intellectual groups; and above it, the big landowners and the 'great intellectuals'. The function of the intellectuals was vital to the maintenance of the system. Those from the middle group, the Southern 'middle class' intelligentsia, were off-shoots of a social stratum whose members had the following well-defined characteristics: they were not peasants and did not themselves work the soil, indeed they regarded the actual practice of agriculture as shameful; they would generally either rent their land or give it out under some form of share-cropping; and their interest in the land was solely in what they could derive from it, enough to live comfortably, send their sons to the university or the seminary, and provide a dowry for their daughters (who were of course supposed to marry either army officers or civil servants). Intellectuals from such a background inherited a bitter dislike of the peasants and regarded them as mere work machines to be driven to the limit, easily replaceable thanks to the chronic overpopulation of the region. But they also had a healthy fear of the peasants, grounded in long experience of their sporadic violence and destructiveness in the past. Hence they were by nature refined hypocrites, who had inherited and cultivated the most sophisticated techniques for swindling the peasant masses. They appeared as democrats when they turned towards the peasants, and then as utter reactionaries when they dealt with the big landowners and the government. Corrupt, disloyal, pettily political in outlook, they formed the link between the southern peasant and the great landed proprietor. The monstrous agrarian bloc which they cemented in this way then functioned, in turn, as the agent and overseer for northern capitalism and the big banks. The sole aim of such a system was preservation of the *status quo*. The big landowners at the political level, and the 'great intellectuals' at the level of ideology (men like Benedetto Croce and Giustino Fortunato), centralized and controlled the inner functioning of the bloc; they were its brain and higher nervous system.

There have undoubtedly been intellectuals – Gramsci continued – who have endeavoured to break out of the framework and look at the Southern Question in new ways. Indeed, the effort to do so (*meridionalismo*) had inspired the most outstanding cultural developments of the twentieth century in Italy, expressed through such organs as Prezzolini's *La Voce* and Salvemini's *L'Unità*. But this trend was always counteracted by the work of the great moderators, Fortunato and Croce, who had successfully contained it within certain political and intellectual limits, and prevented it from becoming revolutionary. It is in this context that *L'Ordine Nuovo* appeared as unique, even though – as Gramsci admitted – it had itself been deeply influenced by the ideas of Fortunato and Croce. *L'Ordine Nuovo* had broken completely with tradition by taking the urban working class as the protagonist of modern Italian history, and hence of the Southern Question as well. The Turin group had tried to function as a link between the northern proletariat and those intellectuals of the Mezzorgiorno who were trying to pose the problem of their region in a new, more progressive way. Of these men, Guido Dorso[1] appeared the most complete and interesting to Gramsci. These were not communist intellectuals. But the point was that the old agrarian bloc would only be broken up by the emergence of a new left-wing intellectual stratum (whether communist or not) which would not serve – as had its predecessors – merely to bind the peasants to the great landowners. Any alliance between the working class and the peasant masses of the South, concluded Gramsci, demanded and would depend upon a transformation of this sort.

The manuscript broke off at this point. Gramsci was prevented from finishing and revising it by his arrest and imprisonment. But even as it stands, as a first sketch for an essay which Gramsci probably intended to extend and develop much further, it is an inspired piece of writing, remarkable both in its method and in the acuteness of its judgements.

---

[1] *Guido Dorso* (1892–1947): the most revolutionary of the *meridionalisti*, and naturally the most sympathetic to Gramsci; associated also with Piero Gobetti and *La Rivoluzione liberale*, he was the author of *La Rivoluzione meridionale* (1925), which maintained that 'the Italian revolution will be the southern revolution'. (T.N.)

The news from the Soviet Union was more and more disturbing. The differences within the Bolshevik ruling group which had emerged even before Lenin's death were now acute enough to have generated a bitter factional feud. Though twice defeated by the 'triumvirate' (Stalin, Zinoviev and Kamenev), over his critique of the Party's bureaucratic sclerosis and over the question of 'permanent revolution' versus 'socialism in one country', Trotsky had not slackened his opposition to Stalin. But now the Secretary General of the CPSU had concentrated immense power in his own hands. The advice dictated by Lenin in his 'will' (December 1922–January 1923) had been conveniently side-tracked:

> Since becoming Secretary General, Stalin has concentrated immeasurable power in his hands, and I am not sure that he will always know how to use that power with sufficient caution. . . . Stalin is too rude, and this defect is becoming unbearable in the office of the Secretary General. I propose therefore that a way be found of removing Stalin from this office, and that a successor be nominated . . . more patient, more loyal, more polite, more attentive to comrades, less capricious, etc.

If Stalin had managed to survive Lenin's severe strictures, he owed it to Zinoviev and Kamenev, who were at that time more concerned to liquidate the opponent they considered most dangerous, Trotsky. They agreed to support the third 'triumvir', and got the central committee of the Party to agree that the 'will' should not be placed before the Thirteenth Congress of the CPSU, and that Stalin should be confirmed in his office. Subsequently, Stalin got rid of Zinoviev and Kamenev. The process of degeneration from proletarian democracy to a regime of autocracy exercised in the name of the proletariat now proceeded rapidly. Within the Politburo, Trotsky, Zinoviev and Kamenev joined to form an opposition group, and were isolated under attack from the right (Bukharin, Rykov and Tomsky), as well as from Stalin and his new group of henchmen elected by the Fourteenth Congress (Molotov, Voroshilov, and Kalinin).

During the summer and autumn of 1926, the personal rivalries and ideological disagreements were complicated by the differing interpretations given to Lenin's NEP (New Economic Policy). The NEP was a system of mixed economy, under which heavy industry was run by the State while smaller industries, commerce and agriculture were entrusted to private enterprise. It had given rise to a contradiction between the working class, which suffered severe privations because of the crisis in industrial production, and the various rural strata who naturally supported a policy of low prices for manufacture and high prices for agricultural goods. In the ensuing controversy, the left opposition group around Trotsky held that rapid industrialization was indispensable to resolve the contradiction and would alone provide a secure basis for the socialist revolution. Otherwise, the weakened condition of the proletariat and the growing strength of the more prosperous peasant class (the *kulaks*) might well open the way to a restoration of capitalism. The debate on this issue now raged in Moscow with a bitterness accentuated by all the resentments and hostilities accumulated in the course of the struggle for power. Stalin had not finally committed himself to Bukharin's pro-peasant policy but was supporting it for the time being. He was inclined to ally himself temporarily with the right wing in order to proceed to the final elimination of Trotsky and the left opposition; and he reckoned, too, that any move towards attacking private property in the countryside would elicit dangerous reactions from the peasants, to be avoided while there was still an open conflict with figures as important as Trotsky, Zinoviev and Kamenev. The showdown between the left opposition and Stalin's majority on the central committee came in October 1926.

Gramsci accepted the views of the majority. He had also opposed Trotsky's line in the dispute over 'permanent revolution' and 'socialism in one country' (in prison he would write a note dismissing the idea of exporting revolution, or 'revolutionary Napoleonism'). In this new controversy, he could scarcely fail to support the majority line, given his own past positions: he had always held that a permanent alliance of workers and peasants was necessary for the stability of any proletarian conquest, and was inclined to see a revival of working-class corporativism in the theses of the left opposition. But what really worried him – quite apart from the substance of the debate – was the manner in which it was being conducted, its fury and bitterness, and the repercussions which the angry split might have upon the revolutionary movement elsewhere, especially in Italy, where it was now engaged in a desperate life-and-death struggle. Were the Russian comrades really unable to take account of this? Were they forgetting their duty towards the proletariat of other countries? On 14 October 1926, he decided to write a frank letter to the central committee of the CPSU, on behalf of the executive of the Italian Party. Independence had always been his strength. He respected no fetishes, and wrote what he felt:

> The Italian communists and all the most advanced workers of our country have always followed your debates with the closest attention. Before every congress, every conference of the Russian communists, we always felt sure that, however bitter the arguments might become, the unity of the Party would not be imperilled. . . . Today, on the eve of your Fifteenth Congress, we no longer feel so secure. We cannot help feeling the deepest anguish. It appears to us that the present attitude of the opposition group and the acuteness of the conflict demand the intervention of fraternal parties. . . . Comrades, during the last nine years of world history you have been the organizers, the motive force of the revolutionary movement in all lands, and the great, the gigantic role you have played has no parallel in the history of human kind. But today you risk destroying your own handiwork, you are degrading and may even annul completely the leading position which the CPSU acquired under the direction of Lenin. It seems to us that your passionate absorption in Russian questions is making you lose sight of the international implications of these questions, and is causing you to forget that *your duty as Russian militants can and must be fulfilled only with reference to the interests of the international working class* [G.F.'s italics].

Gramsci was willing to admit the paradoxical nature of the state of affairs denounced by the Trotsky-Zinoviev-Kamenev bloc: where, that is, the proletariat – supposedly the ruling class – found itself in a markedly inferior material position *vis-à-vis* other strata which were in theory subject to proletarian dictatorship:

> Nevertheless [the letter continues] the proletariat cannot become a ruling class if it is not willing to sacrifice its corporative interests in order to overcome the contradiction. It cannot maintain its hegemony if it does not continue to sacrifice such immediate interests for the sake of the general, permanent interests of its class, even after it has assumed power. Of course it is easy to score debating points in such a situation. It is easy to focus on the negative aspects of the contradiction: 'Are *you* really a ruler, you scruffy underfed workman, in the presence of the "Nepman" with his fur coat and abundance of worldly goods?' . . . This is good terrain for demagogues; and it is hard to avoid demagoguery when the problem has been posed in corporative terms, and not in Leninist terms, not in terms of the

theory of proletarian hegemony, and the real historical position in which the proletariat finds itself. . . . Here is the source of the errors of the left opposition group, and of the dangers inherent in its activities. In its ideology and practice there is a full return to the traditions of social democracy and trade unionism, to those very factors which have so far prevented the western proletariat from organizing itself into a ruling class.

In conclusion, Gramsci made an appeal for unity to both sides of the conflict:

> Comrades Zinoviev, Trotsky and Kamenev have contributed powerfully to our education as revolutionaries, they have at times corrected us with great energy and severity, they have been our teachers. We appeal to them especially, as the group mainly responsible for the present crisis, because we would like to be sure that the majority of the central committee of the CPSU does not intend to go too far, that it does not intend to abuse its victory and take excessive measures.

The letter did not please Togliatti, who was at that time the Italian Party's representative in Moscow. In his judgement it had erred by placing too much stress on the fact of the split itself, and not enough on the problem of the rightness or wrongness of the majority's line. It was necessary – he said explicitly in a letter to Gramsci on 18 October – to express agreement with that line 'without imposing any conditions'. And in any case, what was the point of the appeal for unity?

> There is considerable peril in the position taken up by your letter [he went on] because from now on the unity of the Leninist old guard will not be maintained, or at least not constantly or without great difficulty. In the past the great cement of such unity was the enormous prestige and personal authority of Lenin. And this factor cannot be replaced.

Was it correct to attribute responsibility for the rupture to the *whole* ruling group, without distinguishing more clearly between the majority and the opposition group?

> In the first part of your letter, where you discuss the possible consequences of a split in the Russian ruling group for the western movements, you speak indifferently of the leading Russian comrades, making no distinction between those comrades who head the central committee and those others who are leading the opposition. On page two of the section written by Antonio [Graziadei], you invite the Russian comrades 'to reflect, and be more conscious of their responsibilities'. There is no reference here to any distinction among them. . . . One can only conclude then that the executive of the Communist Party of Italy considers everyone responsible, considers

that everyone must be called to order. True, this attitude is corrected at the end, and it is stated that Zinoviev, Trotsky and Kamenev are the group 'mainly responsible' for the situation. You then add: 'We would like to be sure that the majority of the central committee of the CPSU does not intend to go too far, that it does not intend to abuse its victory and take excessive measures.' The phrase 'we would like to be sure' has a limiting sense, it really means that *we are not* sure. Now, apart from all considerations on the opportuneness of intervening in the debate and placing some blame on the central committee majority, apart from noting that a similar step can do nothing but *benefit* the opposition at the moment, apart altogether from such questions of timing – is it legitimate to place any blame at all on the majority of the central committee?

Togliatti thought not. He was in the most total agreement with the Stalin-Bukharin group, and it seemed right to him that the struggle against the Zinoviev-Kamenev-Trotsky faction should be pushed to the most extreme point. Hence he was unable to subscribe to the letter's appeal against 'excessive measures':

> Inner party life in the Soviet Party certainly has its rigorous side. But so it should have. If the western parties intervene with the Russian leadership against such rigour, they commit a very serious error. . . . Foreign parties are right to be worried by the growing crisis inside the Russian Party, and they are right to do their best to render the crisis less acute. However, it is quite clear that if one agrees with the central committee's line, then the best way to help overcome the crisis is to express one's agreement with this line, without any reservation whatever.

Gramsci did not change his mind upon receiving Togliatti's reply. Togliatti stated much later in a letter to Giansiro Ferrata: 'Gramsci received my letter via one of the Soviet officials in Rome. He probably read it quickly in the Soviet office where it had been sent for him to collect, and he replied at once with a short note dismissing my arguments.' This was the last direct contact between Gramsci and Togliatti. They never met or exchanged letters again.

There was a plenary meeting of the Russian central committee and the CPSU 'Central Control Commission' in Moscow from 23 to 26 October. Gramsci's plea against 'excessive measures' naturally had no effect. By now the Stalin-Bukharin group was bent on total victory. The first fruits of such victory were the expulsion of Trotsky and Kamenev from the Party's executive, the Politburo, and the removal of Zinoviev from the presidency of the International (he was replaced by Bukharin).

After Gramsci's letter, the International secretariat decided to send a representative to Italy to explain the nature of the controversy within the Russian Party. A clandestine meeting was called at Valpolcevera near Genoa, at which this representative – Jules Humbert-Droz – was supposed to address the executive of the Italian Party from 1 to 3 November. But on the very eve of this meeting, 31 October, events were precipitated by still another attempt on Mussolini's life. This one occurred in Bologna, and was attributed to a boy of fifteen, Anteo Zamboni. Again, fascist violence was greatly intensified in the wake of this attempt, with more attacks and punitive expeditions (including one to Benedetto Croce's house in Naples). To move at all became a great risk for Gramsci. He left Rome nevertheless, headed for Valpolcevera. Togliatti learnt something of what happened from information supplied by other comrades close to Gramsci at this time:

> He wanted to get to Genoa via Milan, where some comrades were expecting him. At Milan he could not get off the train. A police inspector appeared and detained him on the train, saying, 'Please return to Rome, sir, for your own good.' And he did so. He took the first train back, saving the comrades in Milan and Genoa from danger, but unable now to attend the Valpolcevera meeting, for which he had done much preparatory work.

Some days later, Gramsci wrote to Julia: 'I've had to return to Rome because of a contretemps.' The meeting near Genoa which was supposed to clear the air had no impact whatever. Ruggero Grieco wrote a report on it for Togliatti on 30 November: 'An uneventful meeting from 31/10 to 2/11! Amadeo [Bordiga], Antonio [Gramsci], Angelo [Tasca] and others were missing. There were very few of us. . . .' There is no indication whatever that Humbert-Droz tried to meet Gramsci separately, after the useless encounter at Valpolcevera, although Gramsci was the leader of the Communist Party of Italy and had inspired the document sent to Moscow. But the rapidly deteriorating internal situation may explain this failure.

On 5 November the fascist council of ministers dealt the final blow to the little that remained of democratic freedom in Italy, using the Bologna incident as a pretext. The government intended to cancel all passports, to order that anyone crossing the frontier illegally be fired upon, and finally to suppress all anti-fascist papers and dissolve all parties and organizations in any way opposed to the regime. They also had a law ready to reinstitute the death penalty and set up special courts. The Chamber was to discuss and approve the new laws on 9 November.

> For some time [wrote Camilla Ravera in a report to Togliatti later in November] we had been insisting that Antonio should go 'outside' and set up an office abroad which would have special tasks and work in close conjunction with our centre here. Antonio was generally opposed to the idea: he remarked that such a step should only be taken when the workers could see for themselves that it was absolutely justified and necessary; that leaders ought to remain in Italy until it became quite impossible for them to do so; and many other things as well, all different and all worth considering.

One important motive in Gramsci's mind was his desire not to miss the parliamentary session of 9 November. But he probably also thought himself still protected by the rules of parliamentary immunity. Certain recent developments had encouraged him in a false optimism on this score. On 6 November the fascist daily *Il Tevere* published a front-page declaration by Roberto Farinacci proposing that the opposition deputies should be expelled from parliament; the reason advanced was their systematic 'neglect of parliamentary duties' since the Aventine secession. However, this reason could not apply to the communist deputies, who had reoccupied their seats at Montecitorio some time ago – and in fact, they did not figure in the list of names in *Il Tevere*. Gramsci's confidence probably derived from this fact. He gathered together some colleagues at Montecitorio on the evening of 8 November, and Ezio Riboldi was briefed to speak on the group's behalf next day, against the return of the death penalty and against Farinacci's motion to unseat the Aventine deputies. That same evening, the blow fell.

'About 8 o'clock [recalls Riboldi] Mussolini called Farinacci and Augusto Turati to Palazzo Chigi, and informed them that the names of the communist deputies should be added to the list. Farinacci pointed out that his motion justified the expulsion in terms of the Aventine's abandonment of parliamentary work, while the communists had in fact been participating in the work. Mussolini replied that the King wanted it.' The King had implicated himself in the *coup* and was willing to support it, but only on this condition. Later, knowing nothing of this last-minute development, Gramsci left Montecitorio for the house where he was now living, just outside Porta Pia. At 10.30 that evening he was arrested, though still legally covered by parliamentary immunity.

He wrote to Julia immediately afterwards:

You used to say that we are both still young enough to hope we shall see our children grow up together. Now you must hold fast to this idea, and think it every time you think of me, or of me and the children. I am sure you will be strong and courageous, as you have always been. You will have to be so more than in the past, so that the children grow up properly and become worthy of you in every way.

To his mother, he wrote:

I've thought of you a great deal these last days. I've thought of the new pain I was about to bring you, of your age, and of all the sufferings you have endured already. You will have to be strong in spite of it all, not less strong than me, and you will have to forgive me, with all the tenderness of your great love and goodness. To know that you are enduring your suffering with patience and strength will be enough to give me added strength. . . . I am calm and serene. Inwardly I was prepared for anything. I will try and bear up physically to whatever difficulties may be in store for me and not lose my composure. . . . Dear mother, dear ones, my heart feels especially heavy at this moment, when I reflect that I have not always been good and affectionate towards you all, as I certainly should have been, and as you quite certainly deserved. Love me all the same, if you can, and remember me.

The long calvary of Antonio Gramsci was beginning.

23

Any idea that Gramsci let himself be arrested out of a desire for martyr-dom, when he could have escaped, has a romanticism quite out of keeping with all we know of his personality. He was not in the least inclined to make rhetorical gestures, either large or small. He wrote later to Tatiana, with irony and a touch of bitterness:

> On the whole you like to picture me as a man insisting on his right to suffer, to be a martyr, unwilling to be defrauded of one single second or nuance of his punishment. You see me as another Gandhi desirous of bearing universal witness to the torments of the Indian people, or as another Jeremiah or Elijah (or whatever the Hebrew prophet was called) deliberately eating unclean things in public to draw the wrath of the gods down upon him. . . .

In reality, Gramsci was extremely conscious of the practical result and meaning of all forms of action, and had always felt repugnance for inconclusive gestures. The rhetoric of self-sacrifice was a sentimental trap he was unlikely to fall into. Hence his constant attitude throughout the prison years: he would never put up with one unnecessary suffering or inconvenience, if it might be avoided by appealing to legal rights or prison regulations (the right to have writing materials and books, for instance, or to be sent to a special penitentiary for the sick, or to have a cell on his own, or to demand a retrial, or release on bail). Neither, on the other hand, would he ever ask for any facility which was not guaranteed by law, and which might therefore appear as a personal act of clemency by the regime. He would get all he was entitled to, but never do anything that might cast the slightest doubt on his stance as an uncompromising and combative opponent. We read in a letter to his brother Carlo:

> The procedures for obtaining recognition of my right to write are now under way. They ought to work. . . . I see that Tatiana has been making up fairy tales again, all about how imprisonment could be changed to house arrest for health reasons – all quite possible and normal and accord-

ing to the book, naturally. In fact, this would be possible only as a personal concession to me, and the concession would be made only if I wrote an official request, giving as reason that I had changed my views, now recognized this, that and the other, and so on. Tatiana never thinks about all this. Her absolute ingenuousness terrifies me sometimes, because I have no intention of getting down on my knees for anyone or anything, or changing my conduct in any respect whatever. I am enough of a stoic to face up calmly to whatever consequences follow from this premise. I knew for some time what might happen to me. The reality of it has only strengthened my resolution, it has not shaken me in the least. Given that this is the case, Tatiana must be told that it's wrong even to mention such fairy tales, because the very mention of them might suggest to somebody that I myself envisaged them as possibilities.

This last idea irritated him 'to the point of frenzy', and made him positively rude to Tatiana: 'Every one of your interferences has done nothing except throw a shadow of doubt over the crystal-clear position I have taken up (on that of others as well, but specially on mine). Why can't you understand that you're quite incapable, utterly incapable of appreciating the importance of my honour and my dignity in matters of this kind? . . . I only want to point out the objective impossibility for someone like yourself – a foreigner – of reliving the grim and ruthless climate through which I have had to pass.' The point was simply that he refused to ask for more than the little that laws and regulations permitted him. 'On the whole I believe that in my situation,' he explained to Carlo, discussing the possibility of obtaining a retrial, 'one has a duty to take every step legally open to one, though without entertaining any illusions about it. I will know then that I have done everything legally possible to demonstrate that I was arrested and imprisoned without legal justification.'

After the arrest, he was sent first of all to forced residence on the small island of Ustica. Of the 1,600 inhabitants on its eight square kilometres, five or six hundred were non-political prisoners. Gramsci found himself living with five other 'politicos': two ex-socialist deputies, Giuseppe Sbaraglini of Perugia and Paolo Conca of Verona, two communists from Abruzzi, and his own old opponent from the internal struggles of the Communist Party, Amadeo Bordiga. In spite of their differing ideas and the memory of recent furious polemics, they got on very well together. They had to look after themselves, and Gramsci willingly undertook his share of the chores: 'I have to play my part in our eating arrangements, and today it's my turn to be waiter and kitchen-boy: I don't know yet whether I'll have to peel the potatoes, clean the lentils, or wash the salad, before serving it all up at table. My début is awaited with much curiosity: several good friends have volunteered to take my place, but I've been quite unshakeable in my desire to play my part.'

He had enough to read. For this, he had turned to a friend of his Turin days, Piero Sraffa, who was now teaching economics at the University of Cagliari. Sraffa was the son of a professor at the Bocconi University in Milan, and had managed to open an unlimited credit account for Gramsci at Sperling & Kupfer's, the Milan bookshop. The books he got from there were also used in the school organized on Ustica among the political prisoners. Gramsci was both teacher and student: he taught history and geography, and took lessons in German. Bordiga took care of the science subjects. In the evenings they played cards ('I'd never played before; Bordiga assures me I have the makings of a good player at *scopone scientifico*'). The political prisoners had to pay for their keep out of the government's allowance of ten lire per day. Gramsci said he had no need of help, and wrote to Tatiana: 'I *absolutely forbid* you to make any *personal* sacrifices for me: if you can, send it to Julia, who certainly needs it more than I do.' The stay on Ustica was not too disagreeable, but soon came to an end. On 20 January 1927, after forty-four days on the island, Gramsci left to be taken to the San Vittore prison in Milan.

He arrived there on 7 February. The nineteen-day journey had been a painful one, with innumerable stops on the way in different prisons:

I would like to give you an overall impression of the journey. . . . One arrives tired out, dirty, unshaven, hair uncombed, wrists sore after wearing manacles all day, eyes sunken and bright with the feverish effort of trying to stay awake. One collapses on palliasses of unimaginable age, keeping on all one's clothes to avoid contact with the filth, covering face and hands with towels and the rest with thin blankets to avoid being frozen. Then one is moved on again, still filthy and tired, until the next stopping-place, where one's wrists will be still more livid from the cold, chafing iron and heavy chains, and the strain of carrying all one's own luggage at the same time.

San Vittore appeared almost a haven after this journey. Two days after his arrival there he was questioned by an examining magistrate, Enrico Macis. He was not worried. Instead of seeking comfort, he wrote to his mother to comfort her:

Patience is required, and fortunately I have plenty of it, tons of it, wagon-loads of it, housefuls of it (you remember how when Carlo was very little and there was some particularly nice sweet he liked, he would say, 'I'd like a hundred housefuls of that!', well I have that much patience, *kentu domos e prus*, a hundred houses and more). But you too require patience and goodness. Your letter seems to show you in a very different frame of mind. You write that you're feeling old, etc. Well, I'm sure that you're still very strong and tough, in spite of your age and all the sorrows and misfortunes you have had to suffer.

He reminded her of a familiar play on words, 'Corrias' (his mother's family name) and the Sardinian *corriàzu*, strong, tough as leather:

'Corrias, corriàzu.' Do you remember? I'm quite sure we'll see them again all together, children, grandchildren and – why not! – great-grandchildren, and we'll have a marvellous feast, with *kulurzones* and *pardulas* and *zippulas* and *pippias de zuccuru*. Do you think Delio will like *pirichittos* and the *pippias de zuccuru*?[1] I think so, and he'll ask for a hundred housefuls of them too. You can't imagine how closely he resembles Carlo and Mario when they were children, particularly Carlo (except for the nose, Carlo's was very rudimentary at that age). I think sometimes of all these things, and like recalling events and scenes from my childhood. There was a lot of sorrow and suffering, I know, but also something cheerful and fine about it all. And then there was always you, dear mother, your hands always busy doing something for us, making things easier for us, turning everything to a good use. Do you remember my shifty manoeuvres to get decent coffee, without barley or other such rubbish in it?

On 20 February, he wrote to his sister Teresina:

I'm very worried by the state mother seems to be in, but don't know how to console or reassure her. I would like to make her feel that I'm well in myself, as in fact I am, but obviously I'm not succeeding. . . . There's a whole area of feeling, a whole way of thinking that lies like an abyss between us. While for me this is one episode in a political struggle which was being fought and will continue to be fought not only in Italy but all over the world, for her it is a terrible tragedy whose complex causes and effects she doesn't understand. I got caught, just as during the war one might have been made a prisoner, knowing quite well that it was liable to happen, and also that much worse might happen.

In May, Tatiana moved to Milan, to be nearer her brother-in-law; but soon she fell ill and was forced to spend some time in a clinic. She was the only member of the family Antonio could rely on for help, and

---

[1] *Kulurzones*: ravioli filled with soft cheese; *pardulas*: sweet made of cheese, pasta and honey; *zippulas*: fritters; *pippias de zuccuru*: sweet (literally, 'sugar babies'); *pirichittos*: sweet of egg and vanilla. (T.N.)

her prolonged illness depressed him. At the same time other links were being broken off.

He had been quite out of touch with his brother Mario since visiting him at Varese in 1921. Mario was no longer active politically, or certainly not to the same extent as previously, when he had been secretary of the local fascist federation. But he still held to the same ideas. He had been attacked by communists, at about the same time that his brother Gennaro was beaten up by the Turin fascists. Then he had left his party job, and devoted himself to his business. Antonio received some news of him in May, and wrote to his mother: 'I'd like to have Mario's exact address – though we've been out of touch since 1921, I've learned that he's done something for me, and would like to write and thank him.' Then there was a letter 'full of lamentations' about Antonio, to Ghilarza from Mario's wife, Anna Maffei Parravicini, which Signora Peppina at once reported to Antonio who wrote to his brother, asking him to come to the prison. Mario came towards the end of August. Antonio though he seemed 'very embarrassed', but did not give too much weight to what might have been a mere impression. On 29 August 1927 he wrote to Tatiana:

> My brother Mario came to see me on Thursday, and he reassured me about your health. . . . He told me he'd invited you to spend a few days in Varese with him. Why don't you? The heat is over now, but the country-side will still be very pleasant and the Lombardy lakes region is well worth seeing. My brother's a good fellow, I'm sure you would be *à ton aise* in his house. I hardly know his wife: I only met her once, years ago, when she was on the point of giving birth – not the most opportune moment to make a lady's acquaintance.

The same day, he wrote to his mother:

> Mario came here on Thursday, and we spoke for about a quarter of an hour. He's very well. He mentioned his business, now doing very well too. I think he's showing signs of getting fat, like father. Before coming here he went to visit my sister-in-law at the hospital, and this put my mind at rest. He promised me he would write to you right away, to tell you he had found me in very good health.

But Mario's letter to Ghilarza was quite different in tone, and Antonio was dismayed by its effects: 'Carlo has written to me as if he thought I had one foot in the grave already; he's talking about coming to Milan, and even about bringing mother with him, a woman of seventy who's hardly been outside her village and never made a rail journey longer than forty kilometres. It's all sheer lunacy, and has hurt me very much and made me feel very annoyed with Mario, who could at least have been frank with me and not terrorized the old lady in this way.' He concluded bitterly: 'I can no longer count on my brother Mario.'

Other bonds appeared to be slackening too. He was very upset by a feeling that Julia might be beginning to forget him. On 26 February 1927 he had written home: 'I've had no news of Julia and the two children for about a month and a half now; so I can tell you nothing about them.' Then to Tatiana, on 20 March: 'I have seen Julia's handwriting once more: but how little the girl writes, and how well she justifies herself with the racket the children are making around her!' To Tatiana again, on 25 April:

> You write to me and say a letter is coming from Julia; then you write again saying that another one is on the way; then I receive still another letter from you (and your letters are very dear to me) but nothing from Julia, none of hers have arrived. You simply cannot imagine what existence is like here in prison. You cannot imagine how, when one is told something is coming, one expects it each day, and each day becomes a fresh deception which affects every hour, every minute of every day.

On 1 August, to his mother: 'I've had no news from Julia for some time; no news of her or the children for nearly three months. My sister-in-law is still in hospital.' This may be why he said in a letter to Giuseppe Berti (a party colleague) on 4 July: 'I am undergoing a period of great moral stress, to do with developments in the family.'

Tatiana came out of the clinic early in September, to Antonio's relief. Not only did she remind him of Julia.[2] She was actually a more outgoing personality than Julia, less subdued, more lyrical, more emphatic, more romantic in her feelings. She felt a strong need to mother Antonio, to look after him like a nurse; and she loved him. The sacrifices she made to help him exalted rather than tired her, and clearly derived from some inner impulse of participation in the suffering of others: during Antonio's ten years in prison, she would go to the greatest lengths to ease his lot, and was to be his most precious ally. Gramsci's feeling for her is well conveyed in the first letter he wrote her after being arrested: 'I embrace you tenderly, my dearest, because through you I embrace all those most dear to me.' Tatiana was the only

[2] He said once: 'I've often said you are very like one another, in spite of certain very distinct personality traits. In any case, don't you remember how one afternoon in Rome I once turned to speak to you thinking you *were* Julia?'

member of the family constantly close to him, and very like a real
sister: 'You see that I write to you as my own sister now, and all this
time you have been more than a sister to me. So I have upset you from
time to time – but doesn't one always upset those to whom one is
closest? I want you to do all that is necessary in order to get well and
stay well, so that you can write to me, keep me informed about Julia
and the children, and console me with your affection.' To his mother,
on 3 October 1927, he said:

> My sister-in-law is out of hospital now and comes to see me quite often.
> She is still convalescing, and makes great sacrifices for me. She comes
> every day to the prison and has some choice tit-bit sent up to me: fruit,
> chocolate, or fresh milk or cheese. Poor thing, I can't persuade her to take
> less trouble on my account and think more of her own health. I even feel
> a bit humiliated by such self-sacrifice, which one wouldn't often find in a
> real sister.

He was now awaiting his trial, and entertained no illusions whatever
about its outcome. He expected a very stiff sentence. But the thought
did not perturb him unduly:

> My morale is very high, whatever people may say or think. I have no
> desire to be either a martyr or a hero. I believe I am simply an average man,
> who happens to have deeply-rooted convictions and will not give them up
> for anything in the world. . . . In my first months here at Milan, one of the
> guards asked me naïvely if it was true that I could have become a Minister
> if only I'd been willing to change sides. I laughed and told him that a
> Minister was rather much, but I might well have been Under-Secretary
> at the Post Office or the Public Works Department, since that was the kind
> of job governments gave deputies from Sardinia. He shrugged his shoulders,
> and asked me why I hadn't changed sides then, touching his temple with
> one forefinger. He had taken me quite seriously, and thought I was crazy.

The preliminary investigation was lasting a long time. It was not
proving easy to produce adequate proof of the allegations against
Gramsci, based as they were mainly on police reports which were
prolific in judgements ('subversive', 'dangerous to public order',
'trouble-maker', etc., etc.) but thin in concrete evidence.[3] As the
investigation went ahead, several attempts were made to trap him by
the use of *agents provocateurs*.

[3] One report from the Rome carabinieri stated that he had been 'found in possession of
arms and explosives in November 1922'. By November 1922 he had been in Moscow for
some six months and was at the Serebranyi Bor sanatorium.

The original warrant for his arrest was dated 14 January 1927. During the journey from Ustica to Milan there was a stop at Bologna, and in the prison there Gramsci was approached by someone calling himself Dante Romani. He claimed to be an anarcho-syndicalist and an engine-driver by trade, and said he had been arrested for his part in the riots at Ancona in 1920; he was now on his way back to Ancona after serving his sentence at Portolongone prison. However, he appeared singularly well-informed for someone who had spent years in prison, and Gramsci was on his guard at once. He did not fall into the trap.

After the preliminary inquiry at San Vittore (from 9 February to 20 March) Judge Macis sent his report to Rome, to the 'Special Tribunal for the Defence of the State' which had been functioning since 1 February that year. The report was not good enough. At this point 'Dante Romani' reappeared on the scene. Till then, Gramsci's prison regime had been a strict one: solitary confinement, exercise by himself, no communication with other prisoners. Now everything changed. Romani was permitted to approach him, and even to spend many hours at a stretch in his cell. He would regularly offer to take letters, messages, orders to the outside; he said that the communist movement was in a bad way, and urged Gramsci to put things right by re-establishing contact with the Party's underground organization.

This crude police trick failed again; but the trial machinery continued functioning. A new warrant was issued on 20 May, accusing Gramsci of provoking civil war and destroying property and life; and a new preliminary investigation was started on 2 June. It was still proving hard to find evidence. In the first half of October, a certain Corrado Melani appeared in the yard where Gramsci was habitually taken for exercise. This man claimed to be the lover of the sister-in-law of the secretary of the Milan fascist federation, Mario Giampaoli. Melani claimed he was being persecuted by Giampaoli: the reason for this was that the attempt on Mussolini's life at Bologna on 31 October 1926 had in reality been a trick, a put-up job organized from Milan by Giampaoli. A militiaman had shot in the air, and Giampaoli had promptly thrown himself on the young Anteo Zamboni and cut his throat. Melani said he had documents proving this, and others proving Giampaoli's connexion with brothels and gambling, and still others proving that certain fascist deputies were homosexuals. If these were published there could be another crisis for the regime, worse than the Matteotti affair. Hence Giampaoli's wish to liquidate the dangerous possessor of such papers. Corrado Melani offered them to Gramsci, in exchange for a suitable permanent monthly allowance from the Communist Party.

Again, the trap was an ingenuous one, and Gramsci was not tempted for an instant. His dossier remained innocent of the sensational accusations the police would have dearly liked to include. But the trial could no longer be deferred; after several postponements, it was finally fixed for 28 May 1928, in Rome.

Gramsci left Milan ıor Rome on 11 May 1928. The hearing lasted from 28 May until 4 June. It was precisely the kind of grand occasion for which Mussolini had set up his new political court, the Special Tribunal for the Defence of the State, to replace the ordinary judicial system (guilty of some resistance to the fascist take-over of all State organs).

Initially it had been dealing with somewhat more modest cases, like the two Roman workmen who – according to the indictment – had been heard insulting the Head of State in public: one had shouted 'Damn his eyes, the rotten bastard!', and the other (upon hearing of still another failed assassination attempt) 'My God, haven't they killed the bastard yet!' Now however the judges confronted twenty-two of the regime's most stubborn opponents, men hated by Mussolini for the genuine threat they represented. They included Antonio Gramsci, Umberto Terracini, Mauro Scoccimarro, Giovanni Roveda, and the ex-deputies Luigi Alfoni, Igino Borin, Enrico Ferrari and Ezio Riboldi. It was designed as a great show trial, and framed by every sort of fascist pomp and circumstance: a double cordon of militiamen with black helmets, daggers, and rifles with fixed bayonets, judges dressed to the eyes, and a complex and sinister court-martial ritual.[1] Correspondents of the *Manchester Guardian*, the *Petit Parisien* and Tass were admitted to the press table. Gramsci's brother Carlo was also permitted to attend, as were the brothers of Terracini and Scoccimarro.

The twenty-two accused sat in the dock 'in military custody but free in their persons', as the minutes of the hearing put it (i.e. unshackled). They had agreed on a common position – to admit their activity in the ranks of the Communist Party, but deny they were leaders – and appeared calm and collected. Antonio Gramsci was the first to be questioned, at the hearing of 30 May. One of the defence lawyers, Giuseppe Sardo, has reconstructed what happened:

[1] The president of the tribunal was a general, and the jurymen were five colonels from the fascist militia.

PRESIDENT: You are accused of conspiracy, of instigation to civil war, of justifying criminal acts, and of fomenting class hatred. What have you to say in your defence?

GRAMSCI: I confirm the statement already made to the police. I was arrested in spite of being a parliamentary deputy in the exercise of my functions. I am a communist, and my political activity is well-known and has been explained publicly by me both as a deputy and as a writer in *L'Unità*. I have never undertaken clandestine activities of any kind, and even had I wished to it would have been quite impossible. For years now six police agents have followed me about everywhere, with the avowed aim of keeping me under surveillance, both at home and away from it. I was never left alone, therefore. Supposedly to protect my person, a close watch was maintained on me which now becomes my best possible defence. I demand that the Prefect and the Chief of Police of Turin be called as witnesses, in confirmation of what I have stated. Apart from this, I accept entirely whatever responsibility is entailed in the fact of being a communist.

PRESIDENT: In the writings seized there is much talk of war, and of the taking over of power by the proletariat. What is the meaning of such writings?

GRAMSCI: I believe, General, that all dictatorships of a military sort end sooner or later by being overthrown in war. When that happens, it seems quite clear to me that the proletariat should replace the ruling class, take over the reins of power, and try to build the nation up again.

He spoke quietly, and lost patience only towards the end of the interrogation. Some of the prosecutor's interruptions annoyed him, and he turned towards the judges and said with great vehemence: 'You will lead Italy to ruin, then it is we communists who will have to save her.'

Sometimes the other accused counter-attacked as well. One of the items on Ferrari's criminal record was an old sentence for the Modena strikes of 1913. When this was mentioned, Ferrari objected at once: 'Mr President, the fact is that my actions on that occasion won me the highest praise from the editor of *Avanti!*, and the same gentleman is now our Head of State.' Riboldi (himself a lawyer, and on the Communist Party's legal commission) said: 'I have defended more than three hundred communists, every one of them declared innocent and acquitted by their judges. Why should I be condemned today, for having defended them?'

The prosecutor spoke at the hearing of 2 June. It was a violent tirade. Referring to Gramsci's case, he stated: 'We must prevent this brain from functioning for twenty years.'

Finally, before the Tribunal retired to consider its verdict, the accused were allowed to speak in their defence. Terracini spoke for all of them.

TERRACINI: Each one of us has made clear in his individual statement what his position was in the organization of our party. Nothing any of us said has been seriously challenged by the numerous police witnesses who conveniently concealed their sources of information behind the 'Official Secrets Act', that principle of official irresponsibility, and declared that every one of us, without exception, was a leader of the party. And anyway, what if this *were* true?

PRESIDENT: Very well, this will go down on the record.

TERRACINI: Thank you, Your Honour, but I trust that what I am now about to say will also go down on the record. I remember I was once awarded the title of 'lawyer' myself, and I would dearly like to show off my jurisprudence. No, not the old jurisprudence dealing with old judgements handed down under old regimes – the *new* jurisprudence, I mean, that being established by tribunals drawing their inspiration from our new ethical and political truths. Not so long ago a judgement was made by a court very much higher than the present one. . . .

PRESIDENT: What? What?

TERRACINI: . . . by a court which, unlike the present one, was constitutional . . .

PRESIDENT: Mind what you are saying.

TERRACINI: You can scarcely fail to agree with me, Your Honour. I refer of course to the Senate, in its function as a judicial High Court, the Supreme Court of the land, whose being and functions are laid down by the Constitution of our State. Very well: this judgement it made – which the government did all in its power to make known to the whole population, by way of warning – was to the effect that no leader or officer of a party or other organization may be held responsible for actions committed by members or followers of such parties or organizations, unless concrete proof is forthcoming of their personal involvement in the actions in question. You cannot fail to grasp the point, gentlemen of the Tribunal: I refer of course to the pronouncement made by the Supreme Court's committee of investigation, in the proceedings against General Luigi De Bono, accused of complicity in the murder of Matteotti and subsequently acquitted for lack of proof. Now I ask you – does this jurisprudence apply to us as well? In his summing-up the public prosecutor implicitly denied this was so. And, quite frankly, I myself have little doubt what this Tribunal's answer will be. Nevertheless, even though it is a foregone conclusion, even though the sentences passed upon us are certain to be stiff ones, I cannot conceal a certain pleasure. You should not be surprised by this. If we take all these arguments, formulated so far only in juridical language, and translate them into political language, what is their true meaning?

PRESIDENT: Leave politics out of this, keep to the substance of the matter in hand.

TERRACINI: But Your Honour, I must ask to be allowed to do what we have been prevented from doing for six days in this trial, whose whole origin and *raison d'être* lies entirely in the field of politics – that is, to speak politically. I was saying – what is the *political* sense of the public prosecutor's conclusions? Simply this: that the mere fact of the existence of the Communist Party is in itself a grave and immediate threat to the regime. So here is our powerful, well-defended State, our totalitarian State armed to the teeth – threatened in all its solid strength and security by this tiny, despised, persecuted party, this party which has seen all the best of its militants killed or imprisoned, and been forced into a secret existence in order to preserve its links with those toiling masses for whom it lives and struggles! Is it so surprising that I should declare my whole-hearted agreement with the public prosecutor's conclusions?

PRESIDENT: Enough of all this. Have you anything more to say?

TERRACINI: I would have concluded already, did I not feel obliged to follow up the public prosecutor's observations concerning the future. Not his more sentimental forecasts, to be sure, where it would be too easy to score off him. I am quite certain that our condemnation will be greeted with grief and sadness, not joyful applause. Once again, Your Honour, it is a political forecast which I would like to make: we are about to be found guilty and condemned for exciting class hatred and inciting civil war. But tomorrow, nobody who reads the list of ferocious sentences waiting to be delivered will see these proceedings as other than an episode of civil war, and a formidable act of incitement to hatred among the social classes . . . (*The President interrupts and tries to stop him speaking.*)

TERRACINI: One may not say such things? In that case, Your Honour, let me end on a lighter note. You are well aware, learned gentlemen, that this hearing has been beyond any doubt the most typical and worthy act of commemoration of the eightieth anniversary of the constitution of our State, which you yourselves celebrated yesterday to the sound of gunfire and the blaring of brass bands throughout the streets of this capital city . . . (*The President finally succeeds in stopping him.*)

Maximum sentences rained down on the accused, as Terracini had predicted. Gramsci was given twenty years, four months and five days. Roveda and Scoccimarro got the same, while Terracini was awarded twenty-two years, nine months and five days.

At first it was thought Gramsci would be sent to Portolongone prison. On 8 June 1928 Teresina wrote a personal letter to Mussolini from Ghilarza, asking him to authorize a 'careful medical examination' of her brother, and to have him sent to a 'prison hospital where he can receive the proper food and care his weak constitution requires, and endure his punishment more humanely'. A medical examination did take place. We learn from a report sent on 6 July by a secretary at the Ministry of Justice to the Ministry of the Interior that Gramsci had recently lost twelve teeth, and was suffering from 'gingivitis, with abscess formation, caused by uricemic disturbance and accompanied by nervous exhaustion'. He was not after all sent to Portolongone.

Instead, they sent him to the prison at Turi, a small town about thirty kilometres from Bari. He arrived there on 19 July, after a twelve-day journey:

> The trip from Rome to Turi was dreadful. The pain I'd felt in Rome, which I thought at the time was a liver upset, turned out to be the beginning of a very bad fever. I was incredibly ill. I spent two hellish days and nights at Benevento, writhing about like a worm, unable to stay still either standing, or sitting, or even lying down. The doctor told me it was only St Anthony's fire, and nothing could be done about it.

On arrival he was almost helpless. Another of the prisoners, Giuseppe Ceresa, says: 'He was suffering from skin eruptions caused by a urinary disorder, his digestive system was completely upset, he was breathing with great difficulty, and unable to walk more than a step at a time without leaning on someone.'

Gramsci was at once made aware of the rigour and inhumanity of the prison administration at Turi. Another of the political prisoners, Aurelio Fontana, remembers his words to the prison governor: 'I was arrested while still a parliamentary deputy, and theoretically protected by my office. I ought therefore to be treated more or less like a Cardinal who happens to have been arrested. But I can see that here you intend to treat me less well than a parish clerk.' The prison's medical service was provided by a certain Dr Cisternino, of whom another writer, Domenico Zucàro, was able to record without fear of contradiction or legal action:

> Gramsci is in need of medical care, and his living conditions should be drastically improved. . . . Dr Cisternino leaves him alone; indeed he informs him one day that, as a good fascist, he would like nothing better than to see him dead. One ought not to be too surprised at the cynicism of this ignoble coward and liar. . . . People in the village say that when he is

called out at night, it is his custom to look down from his window first, and establish the fee before descending. . . . He asks whether the customer is willing to pay for a 5,000 lire visit, or a 10,000 lire visit.

Other members of the prison staff were more humane. However, Gramsci's cell was next door to the guardroom and the noise often kept him from sleeping.

Early in February 1929, after two years and four months in prison, Gramsci was finally granted what he needed to work in his cell.[1] He had already outlined his plan of work to Tatiana, four months after being arrested:

> I am spurred on by this idea: that I ought to do something *für ewig*, to use Goethe's rather complex conception, which I remember once greatly worried our own Pascoli – that is, I would like to work intensively and systematically, according to a predetermined plan, on certain subjects which could absorb me totally and give focus and direction to my inner life.

At that time he was thinking in terms of four topics: (1) research into Italian intellectuals, their origins, their groupings in accordance with cultural trends, and their varying modes of thought; (2) a study of comparative linguistics; (3) a study of Pirandello's theatre, and of the transformation of Italian theatrical taste which Pirandello had represented and helped to bring about; (4) an essay on the serial novel, and popular taste in literature more generally.

When finally given pen and paper, however, he did not turn immediately to these or other subjects: he did some translation from the German. 'For the moment I'm only doing translation, to get my hand in; and in the meanwhile, trying to introduce some order into my thoughts' (9 February 1929). The day before, in fact, he had drawn up a preliminary scheme of work, on the title page of a notebook manufactured by Giuseppe Laterza & Sons (two hundred pages, with a black-and-red marbled cover):

First Notebook (8 February 1929) – Notes and Comments – Main Subjects – (1) Theory of history and historiography; (2) Development of the Italian bourgeoisie up to 1870; (3) The formation of Italian intellectual groups:

---

[1] Letter dated 14 January 1929: 'I shall soon have the wherewithal for writing in my cell, and so my greatest aspiration as a prisoner will be satisfied.' On 9 February: 'Now that I am able to take notes properly, I want to read according to some plan and develop definite themes, instead of just "devouring" books one after another.'

development, attitudes; (4) Popular literature, as in serialized novels, and the reasons for its persistent popularity; (5) Cavalcanti[2] – his position in the structure and the art of the *Divine Comedy*; (6) Origin and development of Catholic Action in Italy and Europe; (7) The concept of folklore; (8) Experiences of prison life; (9) The Southern Question and the question of the islands; (10) Observations on the population of Italy: its composition, the function of emigration; (11) Americanism and Fordism; (12) The question of language in Italy: Manzoni and G. I. Ascoli;[3] (13) 'Common sense'; (14) Reviews, for instance: theoretical, critical-historical, reviews of general culture (divulgation); (15) Neo-grammarians and neo-linguists ('this round table is square'); (16) The disciples of Padre Bresciani.[4]

Right from the start, then, Gramsci had clear in his mind at least the outline of his plan of work. He clarified it further in a letter to Tatiana on 25 March 1929: 'I have decided to concentrate and take notes on three principal topics: – (1st) Italian history of the nineteenth century, with special reference to the formation and evolution of intellectual groups; – (2nd) The theory of history and historiography; – (3rd) Americanism and Fordism.'

His working conditions were difficult. The prison governor had a well-developed bureaucratic taste for refusal and minor harassment, and his books arrived irregularly from the outside. Prison companions remember him as absorbed in work for long periods. He used to write without sitting down. He would walk to and fro plunged deep in thought; then when he had worked out what he wished to say he would go over to his table, and bend over it with one knee on a little stool, to write down the note. Once it was written he would straighten up at once and resume his walking. He had never been a fluent or easy writer, in spite of his considerable experience of daily journalism. However, after each bout of thought the little he had to set down would be written straight off, without deletions or further polishing.

Year after year, he managed with exemplary tenacity to overcome all the unfavourable conditions of his prison environment, and spend

---

[2] *Guido Cavalcanti* (*c*. 1255–1300): One of Florence's greatest early poets, along with his close friend Dante. He was the head of what was called the 'stil nuovo' school of poetry (T.N.)

[3] *Graziadio Isaia Ascoli* (1829–1907): The first great modern Italian linguist. Appointed Professor of Linguistics and Oriental Languages at Milan in 1861, to a new chair specially instituted for him. Hostile to the influence of Manzoni on the Italian language. (T.N.)

[4] *Padre Bresciani's disciples*: Padre Antonio Bresciani Borsa (1798–1862), was one of the first editors of the review *Civiltà Cattolica*, and author of a number of novels which were serialized there. (T.N.)

at least a couple of hours each day in this fashion. He wrote on, in spite of the impossibility of properly consulting the wide range of books and documents required by his chosen themes, in spite of his progressive physical degeneration, and in spite of the depression arising from the difficulty and discontinuity of his correspondence with Julia. For Gramsci, this work became life itself: these memoranda and brief notes, these sketches of the first germ of ideas, these tentative ideas left open for endless development and elaboration, were all his way of continuing the revolutionary struggle, his way of remaining related to the world and active in the society of men.

In the end, there would be 32 notebooks, of which 21 were either wholly composed or started at Turi: 2,848 pages, equivalent to approximately 4,000 typewritten quarto sheets. The first impression received by anyone handling the originals is of their fragmentary character. The themes are closely interwoven with one another, and always condensed into the form of short notes and observations. Side by side one finds the précis of some article he had just read, a jotted-down recollection of an idea someone else once had, the first rough sketch of an argument, indications for the framework of an essay, or remarks on the part the essay might play in some wider argument – an accumulation of minute raw materials, as it were, to which organic form and development should have been given at a later date. Then, months or years later, Gramsci would return to these first notes, and work them up, or add others, rewriting and amplifying earlier suggestions and connecting groups of notes. At this second stage they become more solid and meaningful, though still requiring a great deal of further work and correlation, still far from being fused into a finished structure of any kind. In only a few cases was Gramsci able to arrive at the last stage, and make his notes into something approaching a final draft. On the whole they remain fragmented to the end.

And yet they undoubtedly exhibit one central idea, to which all these innumerable, scattered fragments of thought can be related.

It was already present and partially developed in his essay on the Southern Question.[5] He had begun there by posing the question of class alliances: the proletariat can be victorious and guarantee the stability of its new order only to the extent to which it wins over the other exploited classes to its cause, and above all the peasant class. But the

---

[5] Letter to Tatiana, 19 March 1927: 'Do you remember that very quick and very superficial thing I did on southern Italy and the importance of Benedetto Croce? Well, I would like to develop much more fully the argument outlined in it. . . .'

peasant class is integrated into an historical 'bloc' where middle-class intellectuals have the function of disseminating a bourgeois *Weltanschauung*, a conception of life elaborated by the great intellectuals of the ruling class. In order to detach the peasants from the landowners within this structure, therefore, it is necessary to encourage the formation of a new stratum of intellectuals who reject the bourgeois *Weltanschauung* (like Gobetti or Dorso).

Gramsci's 'Notebooks' are essentially the continuation and development of this essay on the Southern Question. They contain studies on the function of the intellectuals in Italian history up to the formation of the nation-state in 1870; a critique of the philosophies which supply the basis for bourgeois domination; and Gramsci's own ideas on the construction of the new proletarian *Weltanschauung*, the new conception of life opposed to the old bourgeois one, and which must replace the latter in the minds of the exploited masses. Such are the three main avenues of thought explored by Gramsci in the prison writings. They are, more succinctly: the historical analysis of past cultural movements and trends; a critique of the philosophy of Croce; and Gramsci's battle against economistic, mechanistic, and fatalistic deformations of Marxist thought.

Gramsci's originality as a Marxist lay partly in his conception of the nature of bourgeois rule (and indeed of any previous established social order), in his argument that the system's real strength does not lie in the violence of the ruling class or the coercive power of its state apparatus, but in the acceptance by the ruled of a 'conception of the world' which belongs to the rulers. The philosophy of the ruling class passes through a whole tissue of complex vulgarizations to emerge as 'common sense': that is, the philosophy of the masses, who accept the morality, the customs, the institutionalized rules of behaviour of the society they live in. The problem for Gramsci then is to understand *how* the ruling class has managed to win the consent of the subordinate classes in this way; and then, to see how the latter will manage to overthrow the old order and bring about a new one of universal freedom. This is no abstract analysis of capitalism in general, or of the general meaning of exploitation, however. Gramsci is principally concerned with the much more concrete reality of Italy and Italian history: he is trying to see how the Italian bourgeois state was formed, and what part the intellectuals played in the process.

Why was it that the popular masses had played so limited and secondary a part in the Italian Risorgimento of the nineteenth century?

Why had it assumed the character, therefore, of a 'regal conquest' something imposed from above rather than a popular movement from below? Because, Gramsci answers, the people of that time had no national consciousness. They could not, because the culture and literature of the period did not impart it – culture and literature were not 'national-popular' in character, they were still bound up with a tradition of cosmopolitanism, a tradition of intellectuals whose mentality reflected the needs of two great supranational institutions, the Church and the Empire. It was precisely this void, this vacuum of consciousness, which estranged the people from the unification movements, and enabled Cavour and his moderates to direct these movements so easily, shaping them to their own ends and eventually producing a new State markedly inclined towards forms of bourgeois dictatorship. Here was the original sin of the modern Italian State, the root cause of its weakness and its constant tendency towards reaction. This could also be put in another way: the movement which had given birth to contemporary Italy was lacking in 'Jacobin' spirit and direction, in truly revolutionary meaning.

After unification, the first great theorist of the bourgeois-democratic *Weltanschauung* was Benedetto Croce. He had the merit, Gramsci stresses, of energetically drawing attention to the importance of the ethical-political element in historical development. His historical idealism was therefore a valuable attack upon current versions of Marxism, which were mostly crudely mechanistic or positivistic, or influenced by evolutionism. For Croce, man was the unique protagonist of history. His thought stimulates action – concrete 'ethical-political' action – which is the creation of new history. Croce's philosophy reinstated man's active role in the unfolding of reality, as against the determinism in vogue. It should consequently be seen as one of the models for the renovation of Marxist thought, as the latter struggles to free itself from the confusions of economism and fatalistic determinism.

But on the other hand, what 'man' is Croce speaking of? Of historically determined man, existing in a very concrete reality of objective conditions, at a determinate time and in a determinate place? No, Crocean philosophy deals with Man in general, with a metaphysical entity, rather than with the social creature whose personality and way of thought are determined by his relationship to himself, to other men in society, and to nature. Croce thinks in terms of the Spirit, the Idea (his major work is entitled *La Filosofia dello Spirito*), the abstract essence of real men moving and working within the circumstances of social evolution. Hence, though he makes man the creator of history, he also errs (in effect) by removing him from history altogether. Crocean historicism remains 'theological and speculative' in character, whereas the philosophy of praxis (Gramsci's term for Marxism in the 'Notebooks') contains a historicist vision of reality which is in principle capable of liberating thought from all such traces of the transcendental.

Gramsci defined Croce as the national leader of liberal-democratic culture. Crocean historicism, he went on, is nothing but a form of political moderatism: it sees the only proper form of political action as that which produces 'progress' – the unfolding of a historic dialectic whose poles are, respectively, 'conservation' and 'innovation'. In contemporary language, Gramsci observes, this is another way of saying 'reformism'. But this historicism for moderates and reformists is no scientific theory, it is not identical with 'true' reformism – it is only the intellectual reflection of a form of political practice, an 'ideology' in the most destructive sense. In fact, why should the first term of the dialectic, 'conservation' – the 'thesis' – be this or that particular conserved form, one given element of past history rather than another? The past is complex, an interwoven tapestry of the live and the dead, and the choice cannot be made arbitrarily or in an *a priori* fashion, by an individual or a political movement. If the choice is made this way (at least on paper) then we are not dealing with historicism but with the arbitrary will, the unilateral decision of some political tendency. And this cannot be the foundation of a science, but only a short-term political ideology. Croce wants to dictate *a priori* the rules of the dialectical process. He wants to establish himself what the synthesis must finally retain of the thesis (the past), once the latter has been subjected to the antithesis (innovation). In addition, he demands that the whole process be channelled within the forms of the liberal State. But how can one demand that the real forces active in such a process 'moderate' their struggle within certain limits (the limits of the liberal State's conservatism) without falling into arbitrariness, or into some preconceived design?

In historical reality, Gramsci points out, the antithesis has to posit itself *as the radical antagonist* of the thesis, and tend towards its complete *destruction* in order to take its place. The synthesis is indeed the overcoming, the resolution of this conflict; but no one can say *a priori* what of the original thesis will be conserved in this synthesis. It is not possible to 'measure' the blows exchanged, like a boxing judge.

To see historical evolution as some sort of sport or game, with a referee and rules, is merely one of the many ways of rewriting history to suit oneself. And what this particular way suits is, naturally, the interests of the dominant class: Croce's moderate, reformist historicism became its ideology when the bourgeois dictatorship of the decades after unification had to give way (around 1900) to a new bourgeois-democratic power-bloc. Croce was the leader of the cultural movements which sprang up to renovate the older political forms, and his leadership signified the creation of a new cultural climate, the offering of a new *Weltanschauung* to the governed. The new, more democratic form of bourgeois hegemony could then function because of the acceptance by its citizens of this new conception of the world.

Gramsci's references to Croce are constant, because, first, Gramsci believed that no revival of Marxism was possible which did not incorporate the Crocean conception of the identity of history and philosophy; and second, because Croce's influence obliged one to reflect on the function of great intellectuals in the organic life of civil society and the State, and on the meaning of hegemony and consensus as the necessary inward form of any epoch of social history.

On the first point, Gramsci was explicit:

Just as the philosophy of praxis was the translation of Hegelianism into true historicist language, so today the philosophy of Croce is to a considerable extent the retranslation into speculative language of the realist historicism developed by the philosophy of praxis. . . . It is necessary to treat Croce's philosophy now in the same way as the founders of the philosophy of praxis, Marx and Engels, treated the theories of Hegel. This is the only historically valid way of ensuring an adequate revival of the philosophy of praxis, which has become progressively 'vulgarized' by the pressures of practical life. Only in this way can it be developed and enriched, and made capable of solving the more complex tasks posed by the struggles of our own day: that is, the task of creating an integral new culture which will have both the mass character of the Protestant Reformation or the French Enlightenment and the classical cultural character of Greek civilization or the Italian Renaissance – a culture which (to use Carducci's terms) synthesizes Maximilien Robespierre and Immanuel Kant, politics and philosophy, in a dialectical unity which belongs no longer to one particular French or German social class, but to Europe and the world. The heritage of German classical philosophy must be not simply passed under review but made to live again; and for us, this means coming to terms with Croce, because his philosophy is the present-day world form which this heritage has assumed.

Gramsci's fundamental problem was the creation of the new proletarian *Weltanschauung* which should first of all penetrate the minds of
the governed and limit popular consent to the reigning liberalism of the
State (thus making the conquest of power possible); and then, when
power is won, secure the widest possible active consent for the new
State. The proletariat will have to be both the *dominant* class and
the *ruling* class. It must 'dominate' to overcome and liquidate capitalist
groups; and it must 'rule', in the sense of assume the moral and intellectual direction of society, in order to win over to socialism all the
groups which have some reason to oppose capitalism. He writes: 'A
social group can, and indeed must be *ruling* before it conquers the
power of government (and this is itself one of the principal conditions
for the take-over of power); afterwards, when it is exercising power, it
becomes the *dominant* group as well, but it must strive to remain the
ruling group.'

The conquest of power: Gramsci believed that the Russian revolutionary experience could never be repeated anywhere in the West.
In Russia, open warfare followed by a rapid and decisive assault had
been possible, because civil society had been 'primordial and gelatin-
ous', because the Tsarist State was not founded upon a consensus of its
subjects. But in the West, the intellectual and moral rule of the bourgeoisie had won the consent of great masses of citizens to a liberal
State form, so that here 'the State is merely a frontal trench, an
advanced line of defence, and behind it there is a powerful fortress of
concrete pillboxes'. This 'fortress' consists of the ways of living and
thinking, the ambitions, morality and habits which most people have
absorbed as they adapt themselves to the prevalent *Weltanschauung*
diffused by the bourgeois ruling class; and this is what makes civil
society 'resistant to catastrophic eruptions arising out of immediate
economic causes (crises, depressions, etc.)'. Hence, in western liberal-
bourgeois States, open warfare must give way to a war of positions, the
Bolshevik strategy must give way to a new strategy which is not aimed
simply at the conquest of state power (the 'frontal trench') but concen-
trates on the capture and possession of the 'powerful fortress' behind as
a pre-condition of political domination.

> I think that Ilici [Lenin] had understood that a change was necessary from
> the open warfare which won in the East to the positional warfare which
> alone makes sense in the West. . . . But he had no time to develop his
> formula further, and in any case one must remember he could have done
> so only theoretically, for the basic task to be accomplished was a national

one, that is, *it required an exploration of the real terrain and a charting of all the elements of the different civil societies* [G.F.'s italics].

In the 'Notebooks', Gramsci (as he had already started to do in the essay on the South) carries out such an exploration of the terrain, the Italian terrain: he charts the 'trenches and fortresses' which control the bourgeois State. In order to do so, he studies the development of Italian history from the end of the Roman Republic, through the medieval communes, to the Reformation, the Renaissance, the Counter-Reformation, and the attainment of national unity in the nineteenth century. He interprets these past facts with his historicist method, seeking to define the real forces at work in Italian society, the forces which led to the formation of the modern nation-state. And after considering the historic meaning of all other main Italian cultural trends, he treats Croce's philosophy in the same way, attributing to it in the last analysis the function of constructing the cultural emplacements – so to speak – of contemporary bourgeois society.

But is it enough to chart the 'trenches and fortresses', in this positional warfare? This is an indispensable preliminary; but once it is achieved, the attacking army must also have the means to carry out its assault. That is, the proletarian army must be ideologically equipped, it must be armed with a new *Weltanschauung*, new ways of living and thinking, a new morality, new ideas, to oppose to the bourgeois vision of existence. Only thus will the emplacements fall, will the liberal consensus be weakened, and a new proletarian State sustained by the active consent of its future subjects be born.

After the conquest of power, the exercise of power: Lenin himself, Gramsci points out, stressed the importance of the cultural struggle, in opposition to the various 'economist' trends. He developed the theory of 'hegemony' (domination plus intellectual and moral direction) as the complement to his theory of the State as force (the dictatorship of the proletariat), and as the contemporary form of Marx's doctrine. Its significance was clear: domination (coercion) is one form of power, and historically necessary at a given moment; rule by intellectual and moral hegemony is the form of power which guarantees stability, and founds power upon wide-ranging consent and acquiescence. 'From the moment in which a subordinate social group becomes really autonomous and hegemonic, and calls forth a new type of State, there arises the concrete need for a new intellectual and moral order, that is, a new type of society, and hence *a need for the most universal concepts, the most refined and decisive ideological weapons*' [G.F.'s italics].

Much of Gramsci's work in prison was devoted to a consideration of such concepts. One of his principal concerns was the reinstatement of the concept of 'dialectic' in its Hegelian-Marxist sense. This was partly expressed in his attack on Crocean idealism: he claimed that it was a speculative abuse of dialectic which substitutes a dialectic of concepts for the dialectic of reality, a dialectic of ideas for the dialectic of things, so that in Croce 'history becomes formal history, a history of concepts, and in the last analysis a history of intellectuals, or even an autobiographical history of Croce's own thoughts on the subject in question'. But Gramsci also attacked traditional materialism with the same energy, for correcting the error of idealism (the reduction of reality to ideas) with another, opposed error of its own (the reduction of reality to matter), and for denying the dialectic with its evolutionary view of the course of history. In reality historical process is not 'evolution' but total negation, in which the antithesis strives to destroy the thesis and not merely to modify it. The critique was also directed against metaphysical materialism of the kind Gramsci attributed to Bukharin; that is, against the attempt to separate philosophy from praxis, so that philosophy became the science of dialectics (dialectical materialism) as distinct from the theory of history and politics (historical materialism).

In the 'Essay',[6] there is no consideration whatever given to dialectic. . . . This may have two sources, of which the most important is probably that the author supposes there to be a division of the philosophy of praxis into two parts, a theory of history and politics understood as 'sociology' . . . and, on the other hand, a 'philosophy' in the true sense, which would be philosophical, or metaphysical, or vulgar-mechanical materialism. Even after all the great discussion directed against mechanistic thinking, the author does not appear to have altered his own approach in the least. . . . He continues to think that the philosophy of praxis is split in two: the theory of history and politics, and philosophy, which he claims however is dialectical materialism and not the old philosophical materialism. . . . The root of all the errors of the 'Essay' and its author lies here, in this division of the philosophy of praxis into two parts: a 'sociology' and a systematic philosophy. Separated from the theory of history and politics, philosophy can be nothing but metaphysics.

[6] The reference is to *La Teoria del materialismo storico: Manuale popolare di sociologia marxista* ('The Theory of Historical Materialism: a Popular Handbook of Marxist Sociology'), published in Moscow in 1921. An English edition was published in 1926, *Historical Materialism: a System of Sociology*. (T.N.)

How is the new proletarian *Weltanschauung* to be diffused? The task of the intellectuals organically associated with the working class is to win over the traditional intellectuals to socialism; then they must together transform the new conception of the world into 'common sense'. It is in this way that the 'fortress' (cultural dominance) can pass into the hands of the working class, to be followed by the front-line 'trench' (political dominance), and the hegemony of the proletariat be established.

The 'collective intellectual' of the working class is the revolutionary political party, which Gramsci also calls the 'Modern Prince':

> The Modern Prince, or mythical 'Prince' cannot be (like the 'Prince' Machiavelli hoped for, in his famous treatise of that title) a real person, an individual. He can only be an organism: a complex social body, in which a collective will has already begun to take shape, after asserting itself and coming to consciousness of itself in action. Such an organism has already been produced by history, it is the political party: the primary cell where the seeds of collective will accumulate, and strive to become universal and total. . . . The Modern Prince must be, and cannot fail to be, the protagonist and organizer of intellectual and moral reform – that is, he proposes the terrain for a further development of the collective, national-popular will towards the construction of a superior, all-embracing form of modern civilization. These two fundamental points: formation of a collective national-popular will (of which the Modern Prince is both expression and creator), and intellectual and moral reform, should constitute the structure of the work.

Such was the grand plan of the 'Notebooks', those foundations for a great inquiry into the reality of Italy, and for another into the realm of theory. Not all the problems were solved – nor could they possibly have found more than an approximate solution, given Gramsci's precarious conditions of work (and Gramsci himself was the first to recognize this). But the plan was a grand and original one, and its leading notions were propounded with such precision and with such a wealth of references that it is often possible to see clearly how they would have been developed further.

The 'Notebooks' were numbered by Tatiana Schucht after Gramsci's death, but her numbers do not correspond to the order in which they were composed. However, three criteria enable one to fix their true order· references to them in Gramsci's letters from prison; the dating on certain of the notebooks themselves, 'written in November 1930', 'notebook begun in 1933', etc.; and the dates of the reviews and periodicals from which he quotes. It appears that notebooks 16, 20, 9 and 13 belong to his first period of activity, from 1929 to 1930. In them he wrote the essay on the tenth Canto of Dante's *Inferno*, the essay on the intellectuals and education, and notes (much amplified later on) on historical materialism, on the philosophy of Benedetto Croce, and on Bukharin's *Historical Materialism*. Notebooks 15, 19, and 26 probably also belong to this period: they contain translations from the German – the Grimm brothers' fairy tales, the first part of *Linguistic Families of the World* by Franz Nikolaus Fink, a special number of the review *Die Literarische Welt* devoted to the United States, the conversations of Eckermann and Goethe, and some extracts from Goethe's prose and poetry.

He was now receiving few letters from his wife; coming months apart, they were obviously scribbled hastily, in pencil, on whatever odd scrap of paper was at hand. Their tone varied greatly: sometimes formal and bureaucratic, sometimes affectionate. Gramsci was very dismayed:

> I see that Julia still has not written, after all this time. I'm very hurt. It can't be a question of shortage of time. She hasn't written to me for nearly four months, and in this time I have written to her twice without any answer. . . . I don't think I could write again, unless I got some direct news from her first. . . . I am not easily offended by petty personal considerations, but I can't help thinking sometimes that if she no longer writes to me, it may be because she no longer particularly enjoys hearing from me.

Julia would occasionally interrupt these inexplicable long silences with messages which were anything but distant – indeed, full of feeling. There seemed no logic to it, and he asked Tatiana: 'How do you think I should interpret the letter in which she says that after my letter of 30 July she felt much closer to me, when the next four months went by without a single word from her? I haven't yet found the synthesis to resolve this particular contradiction, and doubt if I ever shall.' He had come across a book by Silvio Spaventa, *Dal 1848 al 1861: Lettere, scritti, documenti* ('From 1848 to 1861: Letters, Writings, Documents'), published by Croce in 1923, and in it there was a passage which mirrored his own state of mind. It was from a letter written by an Abruzzi patriot to his father, while in prison:

> From you I have had no news for two months; from my sisters, not for four months or more; and from Bertrando, not for some time. . . . I do not think I am less loved than formerly by my family. But misfortune commonly has two effects: the first is the extinction of all feeling for those who endure it, while the second – no less common – is the extinction in the latter of all feeling for those who do not endure it. I fear the second of these effects in myself more than the first in you.

He stopped writing to Julia. Naturally, Tatiana invented any number of hypothetical excuses for her sister (although she herself had had no word from Julia), but Gramsci countered them brusquely:

I beg of you, don't keep asking me to write to Julia, or I think I shall have to stop writing to you too. Don't think I'm angry; I was, four months ago, and I vented my anger in the letters I wrote you then. Now I have become indifferent. It seems impossible to me that I should be reduced to such a state, but there it is, and I don't feel it's my fault, if one may talk of fault in such matters. I've been through a crisis which lasted more than a year (much more), and had many black days in it; now, as it happens, I have become insensible and I do not wish to feel sour with rage again or go through more weeks of migraine. I must ask you not even to mention this subject again, when you write to me. Let me have whatever news you receive, but don't exhort me and don't preach at me.

In the year from July 1929 to July 1930 he received only one letter from Julia. He felt that he was enduring more than one form of imprisonment:

There is the prison regime which consists of the four walls, the grating, the spy-hole, etc., etc.; I foresaw all this and indeed discounted it, since from 1921 up to November 1926 the strongest probability was not even prison, it was losing one's life. What I did not foresee was this other prison added to the first, which consists of being cut off not only from social life in general, but even from one's own family, etc., etc. I was able to foresee the blows of the enemies I was fighting against, but not these blows struck from a different direction altogether, from where I had least reason to expect them.

Writing this, he felt sure that Tatiana would object. She, in fact, was making many sacrifices to render his double imprisonment easier: the long trip to Turi, the lengthy stays there which aggravated her own poor health, the anxiety and expense. She did all this with great enthusiasm, so devoted to Gramsci that she gave the impression of having lost all taste for life on her own, and of entertaining no purpose other than her brother-in-law's health and peace of mind. Gramsci was certainly aware of this self-abnegation and deeply grateful for it. But he had been and still was in love with Julia: Tatiana's nearness could make prison less of a trial for him, it could scarcely remove the grief he felt at Julia's silence. So, concluding his remarks to Tatiana on the two sorts of imprisonment, he wrote: 'But there's always you, you are bound to say. It is true, you are very good, and I love you greatly. Only, there are some things for which one person can simply never take another's place.'

Two letters did finally come from Julia, in August and September 1930. He replied to them:

What you wrote gave me great pleasure: you say that on re-reading my letters of '28 and '29 you noticed we had the same thoughts. However, I would like to know on which subjects and in what circumstances you observed this identity of views. In our correspondence what was always missing was precisely any real, effective 'correspondence': we never managed to get a 'dialogue' going – our letters are so many 'monologues' which don't always agree even on the most general things.

He thought that their relationship had become very like the one among the giants in the popular Scandinavian story: 'Once there were three giants who lived in Scandinavia, on three distant mountain tops. After thousands of years of silence, the first giant shouts to the other two "I can hear a herd of cattle mooing!" Three hundred years later the second giant answers: "I hear it too!" Then three hundred years later still, the third giant tells both of them: "If you don't stop this row, I'm going!" '

Gramsci had also lost many political contacts, and suffered as a result. His political isolation was not only a matter of being excluded from practical activity, detached from his old comrades, and receiving belated and summary accounts of political developments in the International and the different parties. It was now aggravated by something much worse. After its Sixth Congress (7 July–1 September 1928), and the Tenth Plenum of its executive committee (July 1929), the Comintern had settled on a new political line which no longer corresponded to Gramsci's views.

In his last report to the Italian Party's central committee a few months before his arrest, Gramsci had maintained that:

While it is true that fascism might be succeeded by a dictatorship of the proletariat – since no other party or coalition of parties could give even minimal satisfaction to the economic demands of the working classes which would erupt violently on to the scene the moment the existing structure was smashed – *nevertheless it is by no means certain, or even likely, that the transition from fascism to the dictatorship of the proletariat would be immediate* [G.F.'s italics].

Gramsci judged that some bourgeois-democratic solution was a more probable immediate alternative to fascism. And such a diagnosis implied that a popular front strategy embracing all working-class and even republican forces was necessary for the overthrow of fascism, preferably under the hegemony of the working class and guided by the communists.

The International's Sixth Congress, on the other hand, had declared that the 'rightist' phase was now over and done with, and that the 'single united front' should be no more. This abrupt swerve reflected further fierce struggles within the Russian Bolshevik party. Stalin had liquidated the left opposition (Zinoviev, Trotsky, Kamenev) with Bukharin's help; but he now found himself confronting a 'right opposition', in which Bukharin had formed an alliance with Tomsky and Rykov. Since 1926 Bukharin had been president of the International in succession to Zinoviev. The Sixth Congress abolished the post altogether. Then on 23 April 1929 the central committee expelled Bukharin from the Soviet party executive and the praesidium of the International.

From this debate on Russian issues and the power-struggle accompanying it (fought by Stalin with the utmost intransigence) there derived a whole new orientation of the Third International. Its main points were: the capitalist regimes are on the edge of catastrophe, and everywhere proletarian protest is tending to become more radical and revolutionary; the overthrow of the bourgeoisie must be followed *immediately* by the dictatorship of the proletariat, without any intermediate bourgeois-democratic phases; social democracy is not a revolutionary force, and the bourgeoisie employs it merely to block revolutionary advance – it is a form of social reaction, or 'social-fascism'. Hence a new series of directives were sent to the national parties: they must henceforth carry out 'autonomous' action *without regard to any system of alliances,* to overthrow capitalism; they must fight the social democrats tooth and nail; and internally they must strive to keep the party safe from 'opportunism' (as all deviations from this new line were described).

This policy was sectarian in its equation of fascism with democratic socialism and politically unrealistic because unfounded on any correct analysis of the situations it was supposed to deal with. In Italy it was simply absurd: fascism had destroyed the organized proletariat, mown down its leadership, and broken its organization and means of communication to the point where it was incapable of serious action against the regime without seeking allies among the rural semi-proletariat and those sections of the bourgeoisie hostile to fascism. The Italian Party's move over to the new line was naturally slow and hesitant. Togliatti had been given the job of explaining and engineering the change, and he found many leaders and a considerable proportion of the rank and file deaf to his arguments. He admitted on 3 March 1929, in *State Operaio* ('Worker's State', the monthly he now edited on behalf of the Party in Paris): 'The discussion on international questions which took place at the last meeting of our central committee revealed the existence of divergent points of view, broadly similar to the divergences which have transpired in nearly all other parties of the International regarding the acceptance and interpretation of the theses of the Sixth World Congress.' This article was entitled 'The Peril of Opportunism in our Party'. It insisted that: 'The proletariat must put forward its candidature for the succession to fascism, because the historic dilemma confronting Italian society is not between a progressive capitalism (bourgeois democracy) and a regressive capitalism seeking to put the clock back to the middle ages (fascism); it is between the dictatorship of capital and the dictatorship of the proletariat.'

The Tenth Plenum of the Comintern executive increased the pressure on the Italian Party. The removal from power of Bukharin and Humbert-Droz was to be taken as a model – as *Stato Operaio* instantly explained in its July-August issue:

Without a rigorous purge of our ranks, without ridding ourselves of whoever has shown the influence of an ideology other than our own, and of whoever is likely to sow doubt, hesitation and confusion in our ranks, we cannot conduct the struggle to win over the majority. The leadership of our Party must draw a series of most important conclusions from the decisions of the Tenth Plenum. . . . *The battle against opportunism in our ranks must take on the same severity which has been shown in the other parties of the International, that is, it must be carried on unflinchingly and without giving quarter* [G.F.'s italics].

We also learn from *Stato Operaio* that the Tenth Plenum had criticized the Italian Party for not laying down a clear enough line in conformity with International policy, for not giving sufficient emphasis to this policy, and for failing to promote a sufficiently open and ruthless struggle against backsliders in the leadership and elsewhere. Angelo Tasca was expelled from the Party in September. But still resistance to the change continued. Then in March 1930 the Italian Party's executive split wide open. The motion which provoked the split argued:

The strong pressures exerted by fascism tend to lead certain sectors of the working class to think that, because the proletariat cannot speedily destroy fascism, the best tactic would be to support bourgeois and petty-bourgeois movements aiming at the elimination of fascism without a proletarian revolution.

This conception was then denounced as 'radically false': 'The idea of a bourgeois-democratic regime following upon fascism is only intended to distract the worker and peasant masses from revolutionary struggle, from their preparation for insurrection and civil war.' Togliatti, Luigi Longo and Camilla Ravera voted for this motion; it was opposed by Alfonso Leonetti (in charge of the underground press), Paolo Ravazzoli (leader of the trade union movement), and Pietro Tresso (organizing secretary). Ruggero Grieco and Ignazio Silone were absent. The deciding vote in favour of the motion was cast by the representative of the Young Communist federation, Pietro Secchia (although actually he had only an advisory vote). Some months later Leonetti, Tresso and Ravazzoli were expelled from the executive and the central committee. A violent campaign of vilification was begun against them, and everybody was made to condemn them publicly. Pressure was also put upon Silone to denounce them, though he had in fact disapproved of their stand.[1]

Did Gramsci know? What was he thinking of all this? Gennaro Gramsci was now the only one who could still enter Italy legally and visit his brother at Turi. Togliatti sought him out where he was working in Paris, and asked him to go and inform Antonio of all that happened and bring back his point of view. The expulsion of Leonetti, Tresso and Ravazzoli was announced on 9 June 1930. One week later, Gennaro saw his brother in prison.

Marcella and Maurizio Ferrara state in their report on their interview with Togliatti that: 'Although he knew only the overall character of the conflict and not its details, Gramsci gave from prison his consent to the most stringent measures.' The truth was quite different. Even if subsequently (for reasons which will become clear) Gennaro felt obliged to convey a false report to Togliatti in Paris.

'We were able to speak freely,' Gennaro told me. The interview was watched over by a Sardinian warder from Paulilàtino, a village near Ghilarza. In the short time available, Gennaro outlined to his brother what had happened. Antonio was very shaken. He supported the attitude of Leonetti, Tresso and Ravazzoli, would not concede that their

---

[1] Silone's last book *Uscita di Sicurezza* gives an account of these important days, and of his meeting with Togliatti in Switzerland before his own expulsion from the Communist Party. (*Uscita di Sicurezza* was published under the title *Emergency Exit* by Gollancz, London, 1969.)

expulsion was justifiable, and rejected the International's new policy. He said he thought Togliatti had agreed to it too hastily.

Later in the month Gennaro spoke to Antonio again, after paying a visit to Ghilarza to see the family. But now he was under surveillance by a whole swarm of plain-clothes men. Even in the restaurant where he went to eat with Tatiana, he could see they were being spied upon. At the prison he was accompanied by the prison secretary instead of an ordinary guard, on express orders from the governor. The two brothers were forced to confine themselves to family affairs. Gennaro returned to Paris.

'I went to see Togliatti,' he said to me, 'and I told him Nino was in complete agreement with him.' I had scarcely expected this conclusion, and betrayed my surprise as I asked him why he had done this. He looked blank at first, as if failing to grasp why anyone should be puzzled. Then he went on to explain patiently that, of course, this was the only logical and possible thing to do in the circumstances. He had realized that if his brother's true position were known in Paris and Moscow, he too would be accused of 'opportunism'. Togliatti and the group around him were quite determined to repress any form of dissidence. So he covered up. 'Had I told a different story,' he concluded, 'not even Nino would have been saved from expulsion.'

Meanwhile, back in prison, Gramsci was anxiously turning over the news in his mind. On the day of Gennaro's first visit he had written to Tatiana: 'My brother came to visit me a short while ago; since then my thoughts have been zig-zagging wildly.' After more mature reflection on this wide range of problems and events, however, Gramsci would not change his mind. Indeed, he decided later that year to start up a new political education class among his prison comrades, and began to hold discussions during their exercise hour together in the courtyard. We know from a report written by Athos Lisa for Party headquarters when he was released from Turi prison in March 1933, that the aim of Gramsci's education programme was the formation of new, non-sectarian cadres:

> Gramsci never tired of repeating that the Party had been infected by maximalism, and that the purpose of his political education was (among other things) to create a nucleus of militants capable of propagating a saner ideology within the Party. Too often in our Party (he would say) there is a fear of any and every idea not sanctified by inclusion in the old maximalist dictionary of clichés. . . . Any and every tactic which does not correspond nicely to the visions of this dream-world is considered an error.

a deviation from proper revolutionary tactics and strategy. Then one ends up talking revolution with no exact idea of what has to be done to bring it about, of the means which might realize the end. One is left unable to adapt means and methods to differing historical situations. In general, there is a tendency to prefer words to political actions, or to confuse the one with the other.

Another witness to Gramsci's attitudes at this time is Giuseppe Ceresa, who wrote in 1938:

He was offended by the superficiality of certain comrades who, in 1930, would habitually assert that fascism was on the point of collapse (two or three months more . . . by winter at the latest, these glib prophets used to say) and that there would be an inevitable and immediate passage from fascist dictatorship to a dictatorship of the proletariat. Gramsci fought against these mechanical, abstract, anti-Marxist positions, mostly founded on the idea that economic 'misery' would be the decisive factor in propelling the masses into a proletarian revolution. He used to point out that misery and hunger can provoke uprisings, revolts, which may even shatter the existing equilibrium of the social order, but that many other conditions must be fulfilled before capitalism will be destroyed.

Togliatti had declared at the Comintern Sixth Congress: 'We say that the fascist take-over and the total reactionary transformation which it has inflicted upon bourgeois society do not open the way to a second bourgeois-democratic revolution, but demonstrate that the time is ripe for proletarian revolution; we say that we are now in the period of political preparation for the proletarian revolution, and not in the period of preparation for a bourgeois-democratic revolution.' Gramsci, on the other hand (in Ceresa's words) '. . . kept intact all his faith in the capacity of the masses, but did not pretend that the leaden tyranny of fascism had not profoundly disoriented them, and weakened their combative power; under such conditions, he said, the masses certainly longed for democracy.'

A further series of comparisons can easily be made, to illustrate and amplify this profound political divergence.

Stato Operaio, the organ of Togliatti's group, had said:

We exclude the possibility of any so-called 'transitional phase', that is, any period of bourgeois-democratic revolution before the development of the proletarian revolution. This means that we cannot and must not work on the assumption that any period of legality or semi-legality will be allowed the working masses and their vanguard . . . in which they can reorganize their forces free of daily attack and harassment by the enemy. Such a period was allowed the Bolsheviks after the triumph of the bourgeois revolution in March 1917, but it will not be given to us.

Gramsci's opinion was (again in Ceresa's words):

Fascism has driven the proletariat and the entire Italian people back into retrograde positions; hence, the class struggle in Italy is bound to develop along the lines of the freedoms which fascism has destroyed. . . . Mass pressure may reach and influence even that sector of the fascist leadership which lives in closest contact with the workers. At the same time there will be a reanimation of the bourgeois anti-fascist movements and many of fascism's 'fellow-travellers' will go over to the opposition and try to exploit the revival of mass consciousness and activity while containing them within the limits of the bourgeois State. Is it legitimate, then, to speak of a direct transition from fascist dictatorship to the dictatorship of the proletariat? No: to predict this is to fall into mere abstract schematism.

Stato Operaio:

It is often asserted that as the economic and political crisis of Italian society grows more acute, we shall see the bourgeoisie withdraw from fascism and – driven by the very pressures of the situation itself – become 'anti-fascist', undoing much of the work, institutions, forms of government, etc., in which the present reactionary regime consists. The policy of the Coalition [of republican parties] and other 'democrats' is based on this assumption. But similar ideas, or at any rate echoes of them, are undoubtedly present in certain sectors of the Italian working class and even in the ranks of our own Party. . . . We must certainly admit that as the crisis becomes more acute, parts of the ruling class will be affected by panic and will lose confidence in their own powers. . . . But though this is true, it is on the other hand truer still that we should commit the gravest error were we to base our policy and work upon this assumption, were we to believe that panic and uncertainty will of themselves lead to the formation of a 'bourgeois anti-fascist' front and turn the ruling orders against fascism. . . . The organization of fascism has become such that it cannot be defeated except by a mass movement which assumes the character of an insurrection; and there is no stratum of the bourgeoisie or of the petty bourgeoisie which wants this or would be willing to do anything that might unleash such a movement.

Gramsci (from Lisa's report):

It is possible for the Party to undertake action in common with the other parties struggling against fascism in Italy. . . . The outlook for revolution in Italy must be a double one, one must consider both what is most likely to happen and what is less likely to happen. Personally I believe that what is most likely is a period of transition. Consequently, the Party must adapt its tactics to this eventuality without fear of appearing unrevolutionary.

Stato Operaio:

The Coalition and the social democratic parties talk of 'plutocracy' instead of 'capitalism' and 'imperialism', they talk of a 'paternalist regime' rather than of 'state capitalism', of 'obscurantism' and the 'triumph of medievalism' rather than of reaction and the dictatorship of capital. Their language is designed to make the workers forget that the fight for proletarian dictatorship, the fight to overthrow the capitalist system, the fight for socialism, are together the one task history has assigned to the working class, *and form the only possible content of the struggle against fascism*. Each and every concession which we make on this crucial point to the political and historical arguments of the Coalition, and to their equivocal and soothing slogans, each such concession is opportunism, and constitutes a substantial deviation from our political line.

Gramsci (from the Lisa report):

The formation of alliances has become an extremely delicate and difficult operation for the proletariat. But on the other hand, *if it fails to form such alliances the proletariat cannot hope to undertake serious revolutionary action*. If one takes account of the particular historical conditions within which the political evolution of the Italian peasantry and petty bourgeoisie must be understood, it is easy to see that any political approach to these strata by the Party must be carefully thought out, and must seek to win them over in gradual stages. . . . Thus, it is easy nowadays to persuade a peasant of the Mezzogiorno or any other region that the King is socially useless, but not so easy to make him understand that the workers could take his place, as he doesn't see in general how the boss could ever be got rid of. The petty bourgeois – the lower ranks of the army officer class, for instance, discontented about lack of promotion and precarious conditions of life, etc. – is more likely to think that his conditions will improve under a republican regime than under a soviet one. The first step such strata must be led into making is a formulation of their attitude towards the Constitution, and other institutional problems. The futility of the Crown is now grasped by all workers, even the most backward peasants of Sardinia or the Basilicata. The Party can work in conjunction with the other antifascist parties on this terrain [G.F.'s italics].

In essence, Gramsci's argument was based on three main points: (1) even under the most favourable conditions, the Party could not count on more than about six thousand activists; (2) the most suitable tactic was therefore not sectarian isolation, but a search for class alliances; (3) the backward peasantry and discontented lower middle classes could be won over to alliance with the working class, but only if the purpose of the alliance was an intermediate one: the restoration of the freedoms destroyed by fascism. It was necessary to promote and try to lead a wide, popular, anti-fascist movement. 'The Party,' Gramsci concluded, according to Ceresa, 'will have to find the ideas and words capable of mobilizing all anti-fascist forces behind such a movement.'

Gramsci's new educational programme for his fellow-prisoners lasted only a few weeks. Not everyone agreed with Gramsci's theses. Angelo Scucchia and Lisa himself embraced different positions, for instance. When these divergences came to light – according to Lisa – 'all those present were asked to think the problem over again, and say what they thought about it after a fortnight. This re-examination was not possible because in the meantime Gramsci had been misled by false information into believing that the comrades were discussing the problems in a sectarian fashion'.

In fact, Gramsci had not been misled; the information was not false, as Giovanni Lay makes clear in his account:

The truth is that the debate comrades carried on in their cells was not always kept on a proper political level. Often – much too often, I thought – they sank to the level of mere gossip, or even downright slander, with quite inexcusable personal remarks about Gramsci. I was in the same cell as Bruno Spadoni and Angelo Scucchia. Scucchia went so far as to assert that Gramsci's position was social-democratic, that he was no longer a communist, that he had become a Crocean out of opportunism, that we should denounce his disruptive influence on the Party, and that we ought to begin by excluding him from our own company and driving him out of the exercise-yard. Spadoni and I put up with it patiently to begin with, in the hope of making our comrade see reason, though we made it clear we would not countenance such shameful actions. When it became obvious he was beyond redemption, we discussed the situation with Gramsci. He told us at once that in other cells too, debate had often degenerated to the same absurd level, and done nothing except foster division and enmity among comrades.

The tension was extreme. When Gramsci tried to dissuade his comrades from arguing too violently with the warders, who were ex-peasants not directly responsible for the harshness of the prison regime, he found himself accused of excessive regard for legality and even of 'being afraid to lose the privileges he enjoyed, like being able to write, and receive books'.[2]

He withdrew into isolation. Once, he said to Lay: 'The thankless task of scratching the surface to see what lies underneath it has fallen to me more than once in the past. There are people – and lots of them in our own ranks – who give the impression of being important and serious, and are really nothing but windbags.'

[2] In a letter of 28 March 1931 to his brother Carlo, Gramsci wrote: 'In order to stick rigidly to my absolutely correct behaviour in accordance with the necessities of prison life, I've come into conflict with some other prisoners and been forced to break off personal relationships.'

In an outburst of 3 September 1933, we find Gramsci writing: 'When Inspector Saporiti came to examine me he said (and I don't know from what source he can have drawn his information) there were other than physical reasons for my state of health, and that I was affected by psychological factors, especially the feeling of having been abandoned by my family (not in a material sense, but in certain more intimate ways which matter a great deal to an intellectual).' Gramsci had undergone two and a half difficult years, from mid-1930 to the end of 1932, and they had undoubtedly been made more difficult by the irregularity of his correspondence.

Julia was suffering from a very serious nervous breakdown. Antonio had learnt what was wrong about the end of 1930, from various hints which gradually built up into a full picture; but the hints had not come from Julia herself. On 13 January 1931 he wrote to her:

> I have only just been informed – reliably, I think – about your state of health. It seems to me this way of going about things will end by making our relationship quite conventional and byzantine, and take all the spontaneity out of it; so many barbed-wire fences are bound to breed sickness and exasperation. Once, we promised each other we would always be frank and truthful in our relationship – do you remember? Why haven't we kept our promise? . . . Naturally I am always very happy to have a letter from you, it helps occupy my empty, meaningless hours, and breaks my isolation from life and the world. But I think you ought to write for your own sake too, as I feel that you too must be rather isolated and cut off from things and might feel less lost if you wrote to me.

Julia's illness helped him to understand the long silences, and his tone became more tender again:

> I feel very impatient at being unable to do anything real and positive to help you; I'm torn between feeling immense tenderness towards you, feeling I must console your weakness at once by holding you in my arms, and the uncomfortable recognition that at this distance all I can do is make a great effort of will and try to persuade you in cold, insipid words that

you are really strong, that you can and must get over this breakdown. . . . I think that what was wrong was our never being together for long enough, and always under abnormal conditions, cut off from ordinary things and everyday life. Let's do our best to make up for the lack now, in spite of these circumstances neither of us can help. Let's try and hold our relationship together and save from the ruins the things which were truly beautiful, the things which will live on in our children.

About the middle of May 1931 he had a long letter from Julia. It was different from the others. It seemed to show signs of recovery from the breakdown, and helped clear up some of the bad feeling there had been between them. Gramsci replied: 'I think this letter marks a new beginning in our relationship, and I'm very happy, for I must confess that I'd begun to retreat very much into my own corner and was getting pricklier than a porcupine. Now you will be able to help me get back to normal again.'

But there were to be no more such letters from Julia. Instead, further lengthy silences, broken only by hastily scribbled notes empty of real news or feeling. On 31 November of that year he wrote to her:

Judging by your last letter you too seem to feel there's something wrong with the way we write to each other, in dribs and drabs, with months of silence in between. The worst thing is, I don't seem able to do anything about it. During your months of silence I brood a good deal about this, and think how different it is from what I expected five years ago when I was arrested. I believed then that our life in common could still to some extent continue, and that you would help me keep in touch with life and the world outside; or at least with your own life and that of the children. At the risk of hurting you greatly, I must say that you've done just the opposite, you have aggravated my isolation and made me feel it even more painfully. You often insist in your letters that 'we are closer together, stronger', but it seems to me this is less and less true, and that you know it very well, and are fighting off the knowledge even as you write the words. . . . In fact I know nothing about you – not even if you've gone back to work. Your letters are extremely vague. I can't succeed in imagining anything of your life. I've tried so many times to start a real dialogue with you, I've asked you so many questions and indicated the kind of thing it would interest me very much to know. All this has produced nothing; and so I've fallen back into this state of mind, which makes it very hard and painful for me to write to you at all. The present letter is one more attempt to make contact; I believe it is still possible, and that we may still be in time.

However, there were serious psychological difficulties on both sides which could not be so easily resolved. The feeling of having been left alone at a difficult period of her life (when Tatiana might have come back to Moscow to help her, for instance) obviously made Julia feel some bitterness, just as the sensation of being forgotten tormented Antonio. Their relationship went on deteriorating in this vicious circle.

The rest of the family was by no means assiduous in its correspondence either. There had been the break with Mario in 1928, after which no more letters came from Varese. When he visited Turi in 1930 Gennaro had promised to write often; there was one heavily censored letter from Namur not long after the visit, and then nothing more. Carlo was having serious troubles of his own. He had been forced to close down his shoe shop in Ghilarza, and had gone to work in the co-operative dairy at Macomer. But the first time there was a reduction of staff he had to go, and became unemployed. He visited Antonio at Turi in September–October 1930; and he too failed to write, when he returned to Ghilarza: 'Carlo hasn't written to me since his trip to Turi (or at any rate I haven't received the letters)' (17 November 1930). 'Dearest mother, I don't understand what's going on. Carlo hasn't written for more than three months. . . . I did think that Carlo might have got into some kind of trouble because of me, and doesn't want or doesn't know how to say that he is upset and uncertain' (15 December 1930).

Gramsci set about trying to find Carlo a job. The man who might be able to help him was Piero Sraffa, who had been lecturing in economics at Cambridge University for some time. Sraffa had already proved his devotion to Gramsci more than once. Delio used to receive toys from him, and the books Gramsci got through the Milan bookshop were paid for by him. Given his connexions, it would be easy for him to find Carlo a post. Antonio suggested the idea and wrote to his brother on 26 January 1931:

> I thought for a while that you had settled in Milan, and so didn't understand Tatiana's references to your being in Rome at a certain stage. I only realized by chance that you had gone back to Ghilarza (from a letter of Grazietta's, I think). All this seemed quite mysterious for a time, and I was rather worried. Why the move? I was afraid the Milan police had been getting at you because of your name, in spite of all your papers and your different ideas, and the information they could have got from Cagliari. I know what I'm talking about, having suffered from the zealous persecution of the Milan police myself.

But in fact Carlo did settle in Milan that winter, and was found a job with the Snia Viscosa textile firm. In March he went to see Antonio again. And on the 28th of that month, was urged once more to write regularly: 'For the reasons I mentioned during your visit, I'd like you to write as often as you can during your stay in Milan, and tell me about your life there and what you're doing.' There was no answer for a long time: 'Carlo hasn't written yet; if you have his address, write and tell him how upset I am by his behaviour; he won't even write to mother, though he knows the state of health she is in [4 May 1931].

Antonio expected that the women would write regularly from home, at least. When they did not, he could at least try to understand why by imagining what things were like for his mother, now elderly and in poor health; for Teresina, caught up in her work at the post office, and for Grazietta:

They haven't written from home either, for at least a month. Mother is unable to write, and my sisters are very busy; and anyway I lived alongside them long enough to know their life and imagine what's going on. Every day my mother complains because nobody's writing to me: everybody promises at once to write to me... next day, but everyone thinks that one of the others will actually do it, and things will drag on in this way for long enough. It's a funny, rather Chinese pattern of behaviour, and I remember very well I used to do exactly the same myself [to Tatiana, 1 June 1931].

Occasionally he would complain about it to his mother:

Why do you leave me without news for so long? Even someone struck down with malaria can usually manage a line or two, and I would be perfectly happy with a few picture post-cards. I too am getting old, don't you understand? And with it, more irritable and more impatient. Here is what I tell myself: people don't write to someone in prison either because they don't care, or because they lack imagination. In the case of you and the others at home, I will not believe it can be because you don't care. So it must be a case of lack of imagination: you just cannot visualize what life in prison is like, and how utterly essential letters become, how they fill up one's day and give some flavour and meaning to one's existence. I never say much about the negative side of my life here, mostly because I do not wish to be pitied. I was a fighter who had bad luck at a certain moment of the battle, and fighters cannot and should not be pitied when they fight out of a conscious choice, and not because they have to. Still, this doesn't mean that the negative side isn't there, or that those dear to me shouldn't at least try not to make it worse.

But the reproach was in fact aimed more at Teresina, Grazietta, and the eleven-year-old Edmea, than at his mother. He knew that much of the time she was in no condition to write to him. A letter which she had dictated to Teresina had greatly moved him:

> I received the letter which Teresina wrote down for you. I think you ought to write that way more often; I felt all your spirit and way of thinking in the letter – it was really yours, not Teresina's. Do you know what it brought back to my mind? I remember as if it were yesterday how you used to correct my homework when I was in my first or second year at school: I remember very clearly that I never managed to spell 'uccello' correctly, with two 'cs', you must have corrected me ten times at least. So, since you helped us learn to write . . . it's only right that one of us should write for you, when you don't feel up to it. . . . You can't guess how many scenes I recall in which you appear as a wholly helpful, tender influence upon us. If you think about it, all these problems about the soul and the soul's immortality, or about paradise and hell, are only so many ways of looking at one simple fact: the fact that each one of our actions impresses others according to its value, according to our own goodness or badness, from father to son and from one generation to the next, in an unbroken chain. And since all the memories we have of you are of goodness and strength and you gave of yourself to bring us up, that means that you are already in paradise, the only real paradise there is, which for a mother I think must lie in the hearts of her own children. You see what I've written to you?

Though the letters from Sardinia were few enough, Gramsci knew much more about his relatives there than those in Moscow: 'I certainly know Teresina's children much better; they've written to me several times and Teresina tells me about them so that I can write back – I'm able to because I know what the background of their life is like from my own experience. But for Delio and Giuliano I imagine I must be some sort of Flying Dutchman.' He felt very attached to all the children; he tried to follow their development and keep in touch with them as best he could. He had once written to Teresina:

> Franco looks very lively and intelligent: I expect he's speaking well already. I hope you'll let him speak Sardinian and not pester him to speak 'properly'. I thought it was a big mistake not to let Edmea speak Sardinian freely when she was small. It damaged her intellectual development and put a straightjacket on her imagination. . . . I really do entreat you not to make the same mistake, please let your own children pick up all the 'sardisms' they want, and develop spontaneously in the natural environment they were born into.

He would often spend long hours in his cell looking at and comparing the photos of the various children, studying the differences and resemblances between Delio and Giuliano and Teresina's family (Franco, Mimma and Diddi) and Gennaro's girl, Edmea.[1]

He was very ill, and usually slept very little. In October 1930: 'I slept for five hours on only two nights, for nine whole nights I didn't sleep a wink, and less than five hours on all the rest, which makes an average of less than two and a half hours per night'. His sleep was, moreover, frequently interrupted. Giovanni Lay recalls that 'Gramsci occupied the first cell on the first floor corridor, where there was coming and going all night long to the infirmary and other parts of the prison. The traffic was less intense – and Gramsci's degree of disturbance less – only if there happened to be a less zealous lot of guards on duty'. Sometimes he felt utterly drained: 'I hardly sleep at all, and feel overcome by a terrible lethargy; not even reading appeals to me. As they say in Sardinia, I walk up and down the cell like a fly that doesn't know where to go and die' (20 July 1931).

> For some months now I've been suffering very badly from absent-mindedness. I haven't been having the very bad headaches which once plagued me (I think of them as 'absolute' headaches), but in exchange for that find myself even more plagued by a seemingly permanent condition which I can only sum up as a sort of evaporation of the mental faculties: general fatigue, stupefaction, inability to concentrate, loss of memory, etc. [27 July 1931].

Seven days after writing this letter, on 3 August, he suddenly spat up blood one morning. He described what happened coldly to Tatiana, much later, like someone writing a clinical report:

[1] 'I got a letter from my sister Teresina with a picture of her son Franco, born a few months after Delio. I don't think they're like one another in the least, while on the other hand Delio is very like Edmea. Franco's hair isn't curly, and I think it must be dark brown; and anyway, Delio is certainly much more handsome'. 'I was very struck by how little Franco resembles our family, at least in the picture: I suppose he's like Paolo [Paulesu, Teresina's husband] and his Campidano stock – or might it even be *maureddina* [Moorish]? What about Mimì, who is she like?' 'Tatiana sent me some very nice pictures of Teresina's children a few weeks ago. It's true Mimì is very like Edmea when she was a baby. For the rest, it's marvellous how these children all have the family features (so do Delio and Giuliano, very markedly): they make me think of faces seen long ago, faces which suddenly surface in one's memory after so many years of oblivion. Diddi looks to me like Teresina at the time when we still lived in Sòrgono and went to the nuns' nursery school together; except that she isn't fair and curly-headed like Teresina. The last picture of Delio was like seeing Mario when he was eight years old; Giuliano's features make me think of Nannaro, and even more of Uncle Alfredo.'

It was not a haemorrhage in the proper sense of the word, not the irresistible discharge I've heard other people describe: I heard a gurgle in my breathing – as when one has catarrh – then there was a cough, and my mouth filled with blood. The coughing was not particularly violent – it was like the cough one gets when something sticks in one's throat, single coughs, not a fit or a spasm of coughing. It lasted until about four o'clock and in this time I coughed up 250 to 300 grammes of blood.

After giving some more details, he concluded in the same detached tone: 'I believe I've given you all the essential information. I should add that it does not appear to have weakened me noticeably, or produced unfortunate psychological side-effects. . . . So you see, there's no reason to worry although, as doctors are fond of saying, we shall have to "watch it".' At this stage, bodily accidents did not affect his state of mind too badly: he was rather inclined to take physical failings for granted.

Personal suffering was another matter. Writing to Tatiana on 3 August he had not even mentioned the bleeding of the night before. Something else entirely was obsessing him, something worse than the physical pain:

> Don't think that the feeling of being personally isolated is making me desperate, or inducing in me any other such tragic state of mind. The fact is that I've never felt the need of moral support from outside to live my own life, even in the worst conditions; I require it even less today, when my will-power has become even stronger and more highly developed. *The difference is, that whereas I used to feel almost proud of my isolation, now I feel all the meanness, all the aridity and narrowness of a life based exclusively on such efforts of will* [G.F.'s italics].

In the same letter he also referred to his work. He was not discouraged, he said, but the difficulties in the way of pursuing his chosen lines of inquiry grew greater all the time. He had written on 17 November 1930 to Tatiana:

> I've fixed on three or four main subjects, of which one is the cosmopolitan function of Italian intellectuals up to the eighteenth century. There are so many sides to it, the Renaissance and Machiavelli, etc. If only I had the chance to look up the necessary material, I think that a really interesting book could come of it, a book nobody has done as yet. I say 'book', but it would be more like an introduction to a certain number of monographs, since the question is different at different periods of history, and I believe it would be necessary to go right back to the Roman Empire. In the

meantime I write notes: reading what little material I have reminds me of other things I read in the past.

In the letter of 3 August he returned to the difficulties affecting his researches:

> One might say that I don't have a real work programme any longer, and naturally this was bound to happen. I decided to think about a certain series of problems, but it was inevitable that at a certain point my reflections should need documentation and require to be substantiated by a period of work and rethinking in a big library. This doesn't mean I'm wasting my time; but there we are, I am less curious about certain general themes, at least for now.... It should also be borne in mind that the rigorous scholarly habits I picked up doing philology at the university have left me with a (perhaps) excessive load of methodological scruples.

Tatiana's reply was not long in coming: 'Of course it's true that to write a perfect history of the intellectuals one would need a great library to work in. But why not do it imperfectly for the moment, and complete it later when you have access to what you need?' (28 August 1931). But Gramsci was not really too discouraged by the objective difficulties of his work in prison. On 7 September he answered Tatiana:

> You must not think I'm not going on with my studies, or that I am downcast because I can't get beyond a certain point with them. I haven't yet lost a certain inventive power, in the sense that everything important I read leads me to think for myself, and to ask: how could I write an article on this subject? To amuse myself, I imagine a racy beginning and ending, and a chain of irresistible arguments in between, like so many straight lefts in my opponent's eye. But I don't write down such irresponsible outbursts, of course. I confine myself to putting down weighty philological and philosophical discourses, the sort of thing of which Heine wrote: they were so boring that I fell asleep, but that proved so boring I just had to wake up again.

When lack of books did prevent him going on with his work, he tried to pass the time translating from the Russian: Gogol, Turgenev, Dostoyevsky, Tolstoy. But his work on the intellectuals was not so easy to put aside. He grew tired of waiting for the books he needed, and decided to make a formal request to the head of the government, a draft of which is found in Notebook 14:

> The undersigned, in full accordance with prison regulations and discipline, and with the proper authorization, has been attempting to make good use of his enforced idleness by preparing a history of the formation and development of Italian intellectual groups. Since difficulties of an obscure

nature appear to have been in the way of this work recently, and cannot be dealt with as things stand, the undersigned begs Your Excellency to grant him direct authorization for the prosecution of this work.

He went on accumulating notes and observations as best he could for the essays he could only hope to complete later on. On pages 1 and 2 of Notebook 28 (written in 1932) we find under the heading 'Assorted notes and remarks for a history of Italian intellectuals' a foreword which indicates clearly the scope and intention of this study:

> (1st) Provisional, memorandum character of all such notes and remarks; (2nd) They might lead to a number of separate essays, rather than one single, coherent work; (3rd) Not yet possible to distinguish between the main body of the argument and secondary developments, the 'text' and the 'notes' on it; (4th) There are often unconfirmed statements, 'first approximations' one might call them – some might be abandoned later after more thorough research, and the very opposite might even turn out to be true; (5th) The vast scope and undefined limits of the subject ought not to be misinterpreted in the light of the above remarks: I have not the slightest intention of compiling a jumbled-up commonplace-book, an encyclopedic monster touching briefly on anything and everything. *Principal Essays*; *General Introduction*: Development of Italian intellectuals up to 1870; the different periods – Popular literature in the serialized novel – Folklore and common sense – The problem of literary language and the dialects – the offspring of Padre Bresciani – Reformation and Renaissance – Machiavelli – The school and national education – The place of B. Croce in Italian culture up to the World War – The Risorgimento and the Partito d'Azione – Ugo Foscolo and the origins of the national rhetoric – Italian theatre – History of Catholic Action – Catholics: integral, Jesuit, and modernist – The medieval commune as the economic-corporative phase of the State – Cosmopolitan function of the Italian intellectuals up to the eighteenth century – Reaction to the absence of national-popular culture in Italy: the Futurists – The single comprehensive school and what it would mean for the whole organization of national culture – 'Lorianism' as one of the characteristics of Italian intellectuals[2] – Absence of 'Jacobinism' in the Italian Risorgimento – Machiavelli as political technologist

---

[2] *Lorianism* was Gramsci's category for a certain type of intellectual absurdity, chronicled in the last section of *Gli Intellettuali e l'organizzazione della cultura* (see Bibliography), and associated by him with the name of the positivist economist *Achille Loria* (1857–1943). Typical of Loria's fancies were the idea that in the future the capitalist order might collapse because of the invention of the aeroplane, for the workers would escape from their servitude in planes or balloons; that morality and civilization were directly proportional to height above sea-level, so that criminals could be reformed by building mountain-top jails. Gramsci's contention was that this kind of bizarre notion was not chance, but the expression of one aspect of the national culture; each country has its own 'Lorianism'. (T.N.)

and political man of action. *Re-ordering of material*: (1) Intellectuals, scholarly problems; (2) Machiavelli; (3) Leading notions and cultural themes; (4) Introduction to the study of philosophy and critical notes on a popular essay on sociology; (5) History of Catholic Action, integral, Jesuit, modernist; (6) Miscellaneous assorted scholarly notes (past and present); (7) Italian Risorgimento (in the sense of Omodeo's age of the Italian Risorgimento, but focusing on the more strictly Italian aspects)[3]; (8) The disciples of Padre Bresciani and popular literature (literary notes); (9) Lorianism; (10) Notes on journalism.

So Gramsci went on, in spite of his declining physical powers, and his great dejection over the relationships which had been broken off or obscured by mutual incomprehension.

Perhaps he was now asking too much of his body, afflicted and ill-cared-for as it was. Finally the collapse came:

> I have reached a point where my powers of resistance are near to complete collapse. I don't know what the result will be. These last few days I've felt more ill than ever before in my life; for more than eight days now I have not slept more than three quarters of an hour a night, and sometimes I haven't closed my eyes. Insomnia may not cause particular ills, but it certainly aggravates all those one has already and creates so much concomitant misery that the whole of one's existence becomes intolerable [29 August 1932].

He became bad-tempered with the strain. Some ideas deriving from Tatiana's incorrigible 'romanticism' he found especially exasperating.[4] He wanted her to go to Moscow for good.[5] Two other new developments added to his nervousness at the same time. He heard from Grazietta that his mother might be dying; and he heard from Carlo that there was a possibility of his being freed from prison.

Signora Peppina had been ill in bed for many months. On 7 October 1932 Grazietta wrote with very bad news: their mother had already

---

[3] *Adolfo Omodeo* (1889–1946): a liberal historian, author of an important study of the Risorgimento published in 1932.

[4] 'Thinking over the past again more recently, I've become convinced that when Julia used to write me two or three letters a year, all the same, quite stereotyped and full of obvious embarrassment and effort, this was only partly due to her illness. It must have been due also to something you told her about me, something dishonourable for me which she quite reasonably thought must have come from me and been passed on to her in this way. How else can one explain some recent sibylline remarks of hers about having judged me unfairly in the past?'

[5] 'Julia believes you are staying on in Rome and can't decide to go back to your parents because you can't decide to break off your (relatively) close relationship to me. I don't know if this is right, or if this is the only reason, or the one that is keeping you here. If it is, then you ought to come to a decision, and leave right away.'

expressed her dying wishes, and there was no hope for her. A note from Edmea two days later was more reassuring, but the shock of the letter remained:

> The idea that mother might be dying while I know nothing about what's going on and might never see her again haunts and obsesses me all the time, night and day. I remember her as full of energy and vitality, and so many vivid memories of our old family life come crowding back that I can scarcely believe she's in the state you have described, and herself feels she is on the point of leaving us. I don't know if you [Grazietta] can make her feel how much I have always loved her, and how one of the great sorrows of my life – and one of the things which has had most effect on my character – was seeing how her existence never had one single moment of repose in it, how she lived without doing anything to please herself and without finding any enduring peace (17 October 1932).

He was still in this frame of mind when, at the end of the month, a telegram came from Carlo: 'Have learned of amnesty concession, with you in spirit, please telegraph my presence necessary or otherwise.' In fact there had been some measures of amnesty and remissions of sentence (including political prisoners) on the tenth anniversary of the March on Rome. But though Gramsci's sentence was duly reduced, there was no question of his being released immediately. Carlo's telegram made him believe 'for seven or eight hours' that his sufferings in prison might be almost over, and the truth came as a bitter disappointment. All the more so, because he could no longer place hope in certain other possibilities of escape.

At the beginning of 1932 he had heard of a high-level initiative for the exchange of political prisoners between the Vatican and the Soviet Union (represented by the historian and diplomat Platon Michailovich Kerzhentsev and another diplomat called Makar). Since the failure of the Genoa conference (April–May 1922), Soviet-Vatican relationships had deteriorated, but they still found it possible to reach understandings on specific questions of mutual interest. Thus, the Pope had obtained the release of Cheplak, the archbishop of Mogilev who had been condemned to death in 1923, and the possibility of Gramsci's release was part of a scheme involving exchanges for other imprisoned prelates. Monsignor Giuseppe Pizzardo (later a Cardinal) had visited Turi prison in his capacity as deputy Foreign Minister of the Vatican. He had not been able to meet Gramsci, but left a card for him.[6]

[6] The card is preserved at the Gramsci Institute in Rome. It reads: 'Mons. Giuseppe Pizzardo, Deputy to the Secretary of State to His Holiness' and (handwritten) 'Regards'.

Then the negotiations were suspended. When, and at whose initiative? Had Gramsci's deviation from the new Stalinist line become known outside prison, in spite of Gennaro's attempt at concealment, and before the Lisa report (March 1933)? Or was Mussolini personally opposed to the deal?

In September 1932 Carlo Gramsci spent ten days holiday at Ghilarza, mainly to see his mother, who was now declining rapidly. When he got back to the mainland he went to Turi. He was forced to spend almost a week in the little town. Antonio wanted to discuss certain rather delicate matters with him, but could not manage to get the warder he trusted at any of the sessions, so that they could speak freely. Finally the right man was there, and Antonio was able to tell his brother about the Vatican operation, and Pizzardo's visit. He was furious with Tatiana, who had not kept him informed of the manoeuvre. He could have given her some useful suggestions, but she had not been at Turi for some time. On his way home, Carlo went to see Tatiana in Rome and told her of his conversation with Antonio, and she in turn told him what she had been able to gather from Soviet embassy circles. Litvinov had officially proposed an exchange through the Italian ambassador in Moscow, and Mussolini had intervened personally and curtly rejected the proposal. So any hope of liberation from a move of this sort had vanished. Now there seemed no other possible chance.

Embittered and exhausted by his physical collapse, Gramsci was pondering ways of resolving his relationship with Julia once and for all, so as to be rid of the equivocation it now represented. She was better, or at least appeared to be over the worst of her breakdown. Gramsci thought her progress was obvious: 'Your thought-processes have become limpid and clear again, free from all those doubts, regrets, and uncertainties' (1 August 1932). 'You are obviously making great strides from one week to the next, towards complete recovery and good all-round health' (2 August 1932). And yet again, on 9 August, in a letter to Tatiana: 'It seems to me we can now say with some certainty that Julia has come through the worst of it and is beginning a new life.'

But more than this was needed to undo the harm which had been caused. Perhaps a trip to Italy by Julia and the children might restore something of its old freshness to their relationship? Antonio hoped so. One glimpses an echo of this wish in a letter from Tatiana to Grazietta, on 30 November 1932: 'I had news of Julia and the children not long ago, they're all fine. Giuliano wanted to write to his Daddy, and asked for a photo of him. We must hope that before too long the child will be able to know his own father, mustn't we? Let's go on hoping.'

But Julia never came. Antonio had long given up trying to understand his wife's attitude: 'I'm just a simple uncomplicated Sardinian and it wears me out coping with the complications of others.' Now inclined to analyse his own past ruthlessly, he was persuaded he had been at fault with Julia. The fault had been egoism: not the commonplace egoism 'which consists in using other people as instruments in the service of one's own pleasure or happiness', however, but a more unusual sort, intimately connected with his life as a political combatant:

> When one has devoted one's life to a single end and focused on this the whole sum of one's energies and will-power, is it not inevitable that one's personal account should be overdrawn (heavily, not so heavily, but at least a little)? One doesn't always realize this at the time. But at a certain point the account falls due and must be paid. One discovers that one seemed an egoist to those whom it seemed impossible should see one in this way. And one discovers the source of one's mistakes in weakness, the weakness of having been unable to risk remaining alone, unable to avoid creating bonds, affection, relationships, etc.

Was there any remedy? Was it now possible to make up for this old 'weakness'? Gramsci thought the answer was a return to solitude, and that he should give Julia her freedom. She was thirty-six, young enough to make a less tormented existence for herself. Antonio first told Tatiana of his plan on 14 November 1932:

> This is a difficult subject to tackle, but I must try. Listen. I heard some time ago about several women married to men serving long prison sentences, who considered that the bond was no longer morally valid under such circumstances and set about making a new life for themselves. According to what I heard this happened unilaterally. One might pass all sorts of judgements on this, from many different points of view. Personally, after thinking it over more than once, I've come round to seeing it as wholly explicable and justifiable. I don't mean it's simple, naturally, or that it can be done without hurting feelings and causing conflicts. But even so, it can be done, if it has to be. . . . Why should a living being remain tied to someone as good as dead? . . . As I say, it isn't simple, it means a real break, a painful wound, and one would have to put up with a period of remorse and doubt after any such decision; but one would at least know that this would pass, with time, and that a new life would be created out of it. I'm telling you all this so persuasively (I hope), so that you can tell

Julia – or else advise me to tell her myself, directly. I am quite serious:
I've thought it over for a long time, perhaps even from the day of my
arrest onwards, jokingly at first, then later more and more seriously and
deeply. I haven't overlooked the possibility of such a gesture appearing
romantic. I'm quite aware it might be seen as a very clever dodge, a sort
of sentimental blackmail ('I offer you this, so that you'll be overwhelmed
by my magnanimity, and so compelled to refuse ...'). But the initiative
must come from me, I'm sure of that. . . . I believe that though Julia is
no girl any longer, she could still easily make a new life for herself. She
can give a new meaning and direction to her existence – radically, if need
be. This would solve a whole series of closely related problems. I would
retreat into my Sardinian shell. I don't mean that I would not suffer. But
I do get more hardened and adaptable with each day that passes. I could
stand it, I'd get used to it. . . . On this matter you yourself must be very
strong-minded and absolutely impartial. You must reflect very coolly and
calmly on what I've been saying, and think primarily of Julia's life and
future.

Gramsci's decision was certainly no sudden or moody one. A week
later he wrote to Tatiana (21 November):

I am still waiting for the letter you say is on the way, replying to my last
one to you; but I don't like the hints you are dropping one bit. I do not
understand what it means to say that 'my feelings are inadequate to the
circumstances'. Anyway it's not a question of 'feeling' in this immediate
sense, but of something which takes a very wide range of factors into
account, and in which it is hard to separate feeling from reason. It is
a feeling, if you like; but the conditions of this feeling are not emotive
impulses or instinctive passions, but a long and very calm and collected
meditation on the problem.

And 5 December:

Dear Tania, I must beg you with all my heart not to discuss, analyse or try
to disprove my letter of 14 November. . . . Just answer me one thing: are
you willing to act as go-between with Julia on what I wrote to you about,
or not? A yes or a no, that's all I want. I will be very annoyed by any further
attempt to get round the issue. It's like a surgical operation – or a decapi-
tation, in a certain sense – and can be justified only if done firmly, with one
clean cut. Otherwise it would become a sort of Chinese torture. I would
have liked you to answer at once. You couldn't. *Pazienza!* But at least you
must not start twisting the knife in the wound.

On 30 December 1932, Signora Peppina passed away at Ghilarza.

His family thought that Antonio might be unable to stand the shock
and did not tell him. Three months afterwards, on 3 April 1933,
Antonio was writing to Teresina: 'Before I forget, you must remember
to give all my best wishes to mother for Easter. I forgot to wish her a
happy name-day this year and felt very bad about it.'

28

When 1933 dawned, Gramsci had undergone one whole year of torment, and the new year looked equally black. He expressed his foreboding in a few lines written on 2 January 1933:

> The old year wasn't exactly full of pleasant memories for me; it was the worst of my years in prison. Nor does the new year look particularly enticing from where I am now. If '32 was bad, '33 is almost bound to be worse. I'm very run down and the load I have to drag along gets heavier all the time. The relationship between the forces I can call on and the efforts I have to make gets more and more unfavourable. I am not demoralized though: on the contrary, my will-power draws new sustenance from the realism with which I force myself to analyse the facts of the situation, and my resistance to it.

The truth was that in the absence of proper care and medical treatment, Gramsci was already slowly dying. His insomnia continued, and he felt at times – 'as if I'm suspended in mid-air with no physical balance, a condition rather like an attack of vertigo or dizziness, or being very drunk'. His teeth had all fallen out. He was afflicted by the most painful gastric disorders, and he had begun to suffer from tuberculosis, arterio-sclerosis, and Pott's Disease (a tubercular infection in which the vertebrae are eaten away and abcesses form in the back muscles).

However, his critical faculties and will-power were still intact, at least in the earlier months of 1933. It was as if they stood apart from his disintegrating body, unaffected by its sickness and retaining all their lucidity and tension: 'I've gone through many ugly moments, and felt physically feeble so often, but I've never given in to this weakness and – in so far as one can predict such things – I don't believe I shall in the future. The more I am conscious of suffering and weakness, the more I key myself up and keep going by summoning up every ounce of will-power' (30 January 1933). The result was a life of torture, 'hateful' and intolerable in the extreme. But Gramsci desired to live it, none the less:

For some time now, about a year and a half, I have been undergoing what one can only define as a kind of continuous catastrophe. I am not managing to react so well to physical illness now, I feel my energy slowly draining away from me. I won't give up, though, and take the line of least resistance. I will not overlook anything, however remote or unlikely, which offers the smallest chance of curtailing or ending my sufferings. I think that to overlook the smallest thing would be like committing suicide, in a sense. I know I've become full of contradictions; but not so full that I can't grasp elementary things like this [to Tatiana, 13 February 1933].

But Gramsci was made of flesh and blood, not pure thought, and a recurrent nightmare tortured him: so far, he had managed to resist fascist terrorism, he had refused to be blackmailed into making an appeal for clemency. What might happen to him later, if he became completely broken by physical suffering and his mind gave way under the strain? He wrote in one of his notebooks:

One hears people say: 'He stood it for five years, why not for six? He could surely have held out for one more year, and come out on top?' Sometimes this is merely a matter of wisdom after the event, because the person in question didn't know in his fifth year that he had *only* one more year of suffering to endure. But apart from this, the fact is that a man in his fifth year is not the same as in his fourth, his third, his second, or his first year: he is a new personality, completely new, someone in whom the passing years have eaten away those moral restraints, those powers of resistance which he had to start with. A typical example is cannibalism.

He gave a fuller account of this example in a letter to Tatiana:

Imagine a shipwreck and a number of people who have escaped in a small boat with no idea of where or when or after what ordeals they are likely to be saved. Naturally, none of them ever thought of being shipwrecked before the shipwreck happened . . . still less did they ever think of what actions they might be led into committing under the conditions of shipwreck, such as, for instance, turning to . . . cannibalism. If you had inquired of each of them beforehand whether they would prefer to become cannibals or die, they would have answered in complete good faith that – if such really were the alternatives – they would choose to die. Then there's the shipwreck, the escape in the small boat, etc. After some days without food, the concept of cannibalism appears in a somewhat different light . . . and finally, at a certain point, some of those present do become cannibals. But are they truly the same people as before? In between these two points, the time when it was a purely hypothetical, academic question and the time when the choice forced itself upon them in all its practical immediacy, there had occurred a kind of 'molecular' transformation . . . and one may say that they are not the same people, except in a purely legal or bureaucratic sense.

The point was that Gramsci thought he could feel a similar mutation taking place within himself:

> One's personality becomes double: one part observes the process and the other part undergoes it, but the observing part (as long as this part exists it means one has some self-control and the possibility of getting a grip on oneself) feels the precariousness of its own position, and knows that at a certain point it will function no longer, so that there will be no more self-control and the entire personality will be swallowed up in some new 'individual' with quite different impulses, different desires, different ways of thinking. . . .

These words were written on Monday, 6 March 1933. Some days before, the other prisoners had seen Gramsci staggering from side to side in the courtyard. Tatiana had also become aware of his extremely weak condition (she was living in a Turi boarding-house at this time). On 1 March she had written to Teresina: 'I think it is vitally necessary to come and see him as often as possible, for he is without doubt going through a very bad time just now, so bad that it really frightens one.' She had not had the courage to tell him about the death of his mother, and was terrified at the prospect of having to do so: 'To think that one day he's bound to find out about the loss he and his brothers have suffered – I can't imagine how he'll take the news.' On the morning of Tuesday, 7 March – the day after the letter about the shipwreck – Gramsci fell to the floor shortly after getting out of bed, and found he was unable to get up again by himself.

He was delirious. Two comrades took turns looking after him in his cell, and he learned from them later – the Bolognese Gustavo Trombetti and a worker from Grosseto – that he had held forth on the immortality of the soul, sometimes interrupting his speech with long tirades in Sardinian dialect. 'It appears I spent a whole night discoursing about the immortality of the soul, in a realistic and historical sense, that is as the survival of all our useful and necessary acts, and their incorporation into the universal historic process regardless of our own wishes, etc. My audience was a Grosseto workman dropping with sleep, who I'm quite sure thought I was going round the bend, as did the prison officer on duty.' This was the effect of the arterio-sclerosis. The most acute symptoms lasted several days:

I spoke at some length in a language nobody could understand, and which was certainly Sardinian dialect, because up to a few days ago I noticed that I was quite unintentionally slipping Sardinian words and phrases into my Italian. The windows and walls appeared peopled by figures and faces, particularly faces, not frightening, rather the opposite – smiling, in all sorts of poses, etc. Every so often it also seemed as if compact yet fluid masses were forming out of the air in front of me, gradually accumulating and then falling over on top of me, making me fall back on the bed with a thud. My retinas were persistently retaining past images and superimposing them on more recent ones, etc. I had auditory hallucinations too. Every time I shut my eyes to get some peace I would hear voices saying very clearly, 'Are you there?', 'Are you asleep?', etc., or other detached words.

So Gramsci's 'observing part' had not disappeared, and he could still follow critically what was happening to him. From the very start of his arterio-sclerotic attack he had dreaded that the change he feared might be under way, that his old personality might be caving in before the new one free of moral scruples, and capable of 'cannibalism'. But in fact his character was not dragged down by his body's defeat.

Tatiana went to see him:

At one point, when Antonio had been trying to convince me that he really had done everything possible to obtain decent conditions, and that nothing more could be done for his health as long as he remained in prison . . . the guard who was present turned to me and said that I should tell Nino what to do: 'Since he says he's done everything he can to help himself, now he ought to do the biggest thing of the lot.' You can imagine how bad I felt when the guard went on (after I'd indicated that I had not followed him): 'You ought to tell your brother-in-law about what we were discussing in the office, Signorina. . . .' Then without any anger, in a calm way that really surprised me, Nino said to him in turn: 'Ah, I see; but it isn't a new thing, it's a very old thing – you mean make an appeal for mercy, don't you? Well, that's a form of suicide as far as I'm concerned. I suppose if it's a question of which form of suicide to choose, a quick one is best. But that's an old story.' Then I said that in the village everybody except the prison staff was suggesting the same thing to me, and that this wasn't a sign of ill-will on the part of these poor people – on the contrary, it was a sign of their sympathy. He admitted that it was blindness and ignorance rather than ill-will. . . . Quite frankly, I sometimes can't understand how it is that Nino should be so afraid of suffering an intellectual breakdown. . . .

She had sent an appeal for his better treatment to the Head of State on 15 September 1932, and asked that an outside doctor be allowed to examine him. On 20 March 1933, Professor Umberto Arcangeli was permitted to see him in prison. In his view, any improvement in Gramsci's condition depended upon a radical change in his living conditions, possible only if he was granted a pardon. Gramsci refused to ask for this, and reference to it was deleted from the certificate, which stated:

> Antonio Gramsci is suffering from Pott's Disease. He has tubercular lesions in the upper lobe of the right lung, which have given rise to two discharges of blood, one of which was serious and accompanied by fever lasting several days. He is also suffering from arterio-sclerosis, with hypertension of the arteries. He has suffered several collapses, with loss of consciousness and partial aphasia lasting several days. Since October 1932 he has lost seven kilos in weight.

And Professor Arcangeli concluded: 'Gramsci cannot survive for long under his present conditions. I consider his transference to a hospital or clinic absolutely necessary, unless he can be granted conditional freedom.' For some time, however, there were to be no appreciable changes in Gramsci's prison regime.

The physical strain made him irritable. His tone of voice to those dear to him was often resentful; he became impatient and easily angered. But Tatiana and Carlo were fully aware of how eminently forgivable these outbursts were and did not slacken in their devotion. After his plan for a legal separation from Julia, he had veered back and forth on the subject, sometimes regretting the move, sometimes making further demands for a clean break. He still loved her; all his indecisiveness derived from this simple fact. On 27 March, twenty days after his attack of arterio-sclerosis, he wrote to her: 'I have had no letter from you and no news of the children for some time. In the same period I've written several times to you. I believe that Tatiana has had no news or letters either. Please write and reassure me.' He was also becoming anxious about the lack of news from his mother. The general silence about her had not made him suspicious enough to guess the truth yet, but he was worried. He wrote to Teresina on 30 April: 'I've had two postcards with best wishes from yourself, Grazietta, and all the children. You've sent me no more news of mother, and there was nothing from her on the cards. Please tell me about her, and ask Grazietta to write too.'

For a few weeks Gramsci's condition was relatively comfortable; but then the sharp decline continued. The medical attention at Turi remained quite inadequate for his many ailments. He should quite clearly have benefited from Clause 176 of the Italian penal code, which established that conditional freedom should be granted to prisoners seriously ill. Or at least – since this was not applied in his case – from very much better medical care. He was forced to remain in his narrow prison bunk most of the time ('In bed I can lie with my eyes closed and avoid seeing the walls spinning round'). On 29 May he wrote, mentioning again the words of Romain Rolland ('Pessimism of the intelligence, optimism of the will') which had become something of a motto for him:

> Until recently I used to be, so to speak, a pessimist of the intelligence and an optimist of the will. That is, though I saw very clearly all the extremely unfavourable conditions likely to prevent any improvement in my situation (either legally, or as regards my health), I believe none the less that by a rationally guided effort, with much patience and adroitness, and making the most of the few favourable circumstances, it might be possible to achieve something – to keep alive physically, and stop this terrible slipping away of vitality which is getting the better of me. I do not believe this any longer. This doesn't mean I'm going to give up. But it does mean that I can no longer see any possible way out or forward, and that I no longer have any reserve of vitality to draw upon.

A response from the Ministry to his request for a transfer to a prison hospital was slow in coming. On 15 June Tatiana went to see him again ('I found that his face was all swollen up by his infection of the gums'). Some days later, her suspicions of Gramsci's worsening state were confirmed. She wrote to Nilde Perilli on 21 June: 'Nino has written that he is worse again, like when he collapsed on 7 March. . . . He has returned to the subject of Julia again in the letter, just like last November. I feel quite desperate.' Then she heard the news from Moscow: her father had died on 29 May. It is not hard to imagine her state of mind when she visited Antonio again on 1 July. She found a man drained of all vitality, a mere shadow of his former self. And the following day she received a letter from him:

> I feel immensely tired. I feel cut off from everyone and everything. Yesterday's meeting only confirmed this. I must tell you that it was sheer torture, and I was longing for it to be over. I must tell you the truth quite frankly, or brutally, if that's the word that fits. I have nothing to say to you or to anybody else. I'm completely finished. My last effort at living, the last spasm of life inside me, was back in last January. You didn't understand. Or I didn't make myself understood, given the conditions under which I have to live and talk. There's nothing to be done about it now. Believe me, should you happen to have any other experience like

this one with me in your life, time is the only thing that counts: it is simply another word for life.

Now it was Tatiana's turn to be stubborn. She too was unwell, and at an age (nearly fifty) which did not allow her to support the strains of such an existence without some ill effects. Life in a village like Turi did little to help her health. But she would not go back to Rome, even after this letter. Another one arrived four days later, on 6 July:

I've asked to be allowed to write you an extra letter. You must have received the other one I wrote on Sunday by now, and it must have hurt you very much. I've become half-mad, and am not at all sure I won't go completely crazy before long. . . . I beg you to believe that I cannot put up with this any longer. The pain in my skull and at the back of my head is shattering me. The difficulty in using my hands is worse, and keeps getting worse; it can't be due only to the arterio-sclerosis. . . . Today a prison inspector came to see me and gave the most solemn assurances that I shall be better looked after from now on. . . . The inspector assured me that the Ministry intends doing something about my case. So I trust that something as simple as a transfer to a modern prison infirmary won't be too difficult to obtain. It happens all the time. I can't say more than this, for I know nothing: I've heard talk about the infirmaries at Rome and Civitavecchia, but I'm not too concerned about the place. All that matters is to get out of this hell in which I am slowly dying.

They ended by transferring him from one cell to another. The new cell was half-underground, and damp, as well as being next door to the punishment block. However, it was at least quieter. Gramsci now also had a permanent cell companion, Gustavo Trombetti. Away from the insupportable noise he had endured for so long, he enjoyed something of a brief respite. Some days after the move, on 24 July, he could write to Tatiana:

I think I can tell you – but you know how hazardous such judgements can be – that I'm a little better. The change of cell has helped me at least in the sense that I'm now able to sleep, or anyway, the conditions are no longer there which used to prevent me sleeping even when very tired, or wake me up with a start and leave me restless and upset. I'm not sleeping regularly yet, but I *could* sleep; and even when I don't, I'm not too restless.

He was able to study and write a little again. Notebooks 1 (notes on various topics), 2 (introduction to politics), 4 and 22 (miscellaneous notes) all belong to 1933.

The change of cell was a quite inadequate provision, however. Serious treatment was required, not a change of floors. He had a long time to wait yet before the Ministry would make up its mind to transfer him to some place where he could be looked after; and in the meantime, his diseases got worse. He had been condemned to prison, not death. Yet the sentence he actually found himself serving was worse than death: without proper care, he was dying a little each day in the most atrocious suffering.

Some doubt had arisen that the Ministry of the Interior might be actively obstructing the transference, and Carlo decided to ask Mussolini directly to authorize it. On 23 August 1933 he went to Rome and presented the request. In order to make sure it got to Mussolini, Carlo confided it to the doctor who, with a first-aid unit, usually accompanied the dictator on his journeyings. But still the answer was delayed. In the meantime, a committee for the liberation of Gramsci and other victims of fascism had been set up in Paris and included a number of well-known names, from Romain Rolland to Henri Barbusse. Professor Arcangeli's statement had been given to the press by Piero Sraffa and published by *L'Humanité* in May and by *Soccorso rosso* (organ of an organization for helping left-wingers persecuted by the fascists) in June. The effect on international public opinion was considerable. Influenced by this, the fascist government finally had to unbend slightly, and agree at least not to let Gramsci die without some further care.

On 1 September 1933 a message went from the Ministry of the Interior to the Prefects of Viterbo, Terni, Rieti, Frosinone and Rome, asking for details of a possible location, not by the sea, and with a clinic 'suitable for reception of important political prisoner suffering tuberculosis and other grave diseases needing special treatment. Location chosen must be easily watched and guarded'.

Critical months and years had been lost by this long delay – from Gramsci's first discharge of blood in August 1931, to the first arteriosclerotic attack of March 1933. His new residence was decided upon at the end of October: it was to be in Formia (a small town near Gaeta, about half-way between Rome and Naples), at the clinic of Dr Giuseppe Cusumano, provided Gramsci agreed to pay the fees – 120 lire per day plus the cost of the necessary security measures (bars on windows, etc.). On 13 November Carlo went to Formia to draw up the contract with the clinic. The departure order arrived in Turi on the 18th. Gustavo Trombetti remembers the leave-taking:

Accompanied by the warder who looked after the prison storehouse, Gramsci and I went there to get his luggage ready. As we had agreed beforehand, he engaged the warder in conversation while I slipped the 18 manuscript notebooks into his trunk along with the other stuff [there were in fact 21]. Once we were back in the cell Gramsci couldn't sleep the rest of that night. . . . Around 6 next morning, when it was still pitch dark, an armed escort came for him. . . . They made him climb up on to a cart, put his luggage beside him, and we said goodbye.

On the way he stopped in the prison hospital of Civitavecchia. 'I felt a terrible sensation of shock in the train, after six years of seeing nothing but the same roofs, the same high walls, the same grim faces. Now I saw that all this time the great world outside had gone on existing: its fields, its woods, its ordinary people, crowds of boys, these trees here, those orchards over there. . . . But this was nothing, compared to the shock of seeing my own face in a mirror again after so many years.' He arrived at Civitavecchia on the evening of the same day, 19 November. There were many 'politicos' there: Terracini, Scoccimarro, Negarville, Pajetta. But steps were taken to make sure that Gramsci did not see any of them. 'Only one comrade saw him,' says Celeste Negarville, 'by the purest chance. He was taken to see the prison doctor at the same time as Gramsci and told us later that Gramsci was walking very slowly and appeared to be in a feverish state, huddled in his long convict's coat with the collar turned right up.'

He reached Formia on 7 December 1933. There, one carabinieri always guarded his room and as many as twenty at a time would patrol the corridors and garden of the clinic. But though police surveillance was maintained with great severity, Gramsci was at least receiving better medical treatment. The clinic was a modest one without specialist doctors or facilities, and the treatment was belated; however, Gramsci was soon responding. Once a week he was allowed to stroll in the garden. Dr Cusumano had said this was desirable, and the Ministry had accorded its permission on 19 December. Tatiana and Carlo came for Christmas:

> On Christmas Day [Carlo wrote to Teresina] they wouldn't let us see him, so we passed the time with a trip to Gaeta. Next day we spent an hour with Nino in the morning, and a couple of hours in the afternoon. . . . Nino has a lesion at the top of his right lung (keep this to yourself). He has got very small and thin. He was in good humour on Tuesday and greeted us very cordially. He is less feverish in the evening and his blood-pressure goes down. I left the clinic less grief-stricken than when I used to leave him in prison – indeed, feeling almost light-hearted. I had begun to hope again.

Tatiana said: 'Little by little he is recovering his old confidence and courage, and for this reason one may hope to see his physical condition improve too. And in fact his intestinal disturbance is already less bad, he manages to digest things with less effort and pain.' She still did not feel able to disclose the news of his mother's death, however. Teresina had made up and sent the usual Christmas parcel. Carlo got the carabinieri captain to open it on Boxing Day: 'As he was opening the packet of biscuits to let the carabinieri see what was inside, Nino said, "Mother must have made these," and I agreed with him.' In a letter of 14 January 1934, Tatiana commented:

> Naturally Carlo didn't have the heart to say anything else. It is better he should be kept from knowing of the family's loss just now, while he is

still in such a bad way and in need of such careful treatment; but all the same, it will certainly create grave problems for us when we have to tell him the truth. Let's hope it can be put off as long as possible, and cushioned by whatever falsehoods are needed to prevent him realizing it in a way that might cause another relapse – he has had enough upsets already.

On 8 March 1934, as his mother's name-day drew near – St Joseph's Day, 19 March – Gramsci still knew nothing of her death nearly a year and a half ago. He wrote to her:

Dearest Mother, I couldn't send you name-day greetings last year because I was critically ill at just this time. I wouldn't like this year to go by as well without reminding you of how much I care for you. Tatiana has kept Teresina informed about my new conditions of life here – still far from ideal, but incomparably better than those of a year ago. I haven't written so far because I've been unwell for so long, and more or less incapable of it; and anyway, I knew that Tatiana (who comes to see me every Sunday) was keeping you up to date. I'm not quite back in full possession of my faculties yet, either physically or mentally. During the last period at Turi I had fallen into a really shocking state, and my recovery is proving slow, with relapses and very uncertain progress. . . . I know little about how you are.

He had written no other letters since arriving at Formia, and on 13 April Tatiana wrote to Teresina: 'Nino hasn't sent any word to Julia, nor even to me, his only letter has been the one he sent home to his poor mother, for her name-day. He isn't strong enough to write, I think, and you can imagine how much Julia is suffering – she's had no word from him for over a year now.'

Though Gramsci had rallied a little in his new environment, compared to the disastrous years at Turi, his condition remained very precarious. He would like to have been transferred again, to a clinic specializing in nervous disorders at Fiesole, near Florence. A request to this effect was made in April. On 12 July 1934 he was examined by Professor Vittorio Puccinelli of the Quisisana (literally, 'Be-healed-here') clinic in Rome. Three days later, another request for transfer was put in. On 22 July he wrote to Tatiana:

I decided to write to you this morning, because I was feeling even worse than usual. Now I'm beginning the letter again from bed. I've had another long spell of fever, and my temperature went up to 39·4. It's 38·4 at the moment. . . . Please do your best to obtain the interview with Commendatore Leto [a Ministry official] as I think it's more important than ever. I believe it might be useful to explain to him why this particular

clinic at Fiesole was chosen, and how we have tried to take police require-
ments into account; I am a realist and do not wish to ignore the problems
or play at blind-man's buff with them. . . . If there is likely to be delay in
answering the request, you might also ask if there's any chance of my being
allowed to change residence within Formia itself. If I feel so unwell today,
it's largely due to the fact that I didn't sleep: the Cusumano family has
arrived, and there is constant coming and going right over my head, from
five in the morning until midnight. They've repeatedly assured me that it
will stop; but the truth is that I am extremely ill, and the slightest murmur
is enough to upset me badly.

There was in fact another lengthy delay while his request for a move
was being considered. At the end of the summer, since his condition
still corresponded to the definition laid down in Clause 176 of the penal
code, he made another request. This time, he asked for a conditional
discharge from prison, and to be allowed to choose his subsequent
place of residence in consultation with appropriate medical authorities ('since I can scarcely avoid residing in a specialist clinic, or near
one').

Abroad, the campaign to help Gramsci had intensified. The November issue of *Soccorso rosso* said: 'In Italy Mussolini intends to assassinate
Gramsci by refusing to apply in his case the norms laid down in the
fascist penal code itself. According to the code's provisions, Gramsci
should have been freed already.' Romain Rolland also published a
pamphlet with the story of Gramsci's martyrdom.

In October 1934, his last request was formally complied with. But in
practice the 'provisional liberty' specified was to mean very little change
in his way of life. The guard was taken away from his room, but not
from the building and garden; he was permitted to move outside the
clinic; and the window-grills were taken down. But he was now
scarcely strong enough to go out. He made only a few brief excursions
outside, on foot or in a cab, accompanied by Tatiana, Carlo, and his
devoted friend through all his years of suffering, Piero Sraffa.

His situation had become highly paradoxical: he had been formally
'liberated' from prison but was not in practice free to move elsewhere
and seek treatment at some more specialized clinic. Any such move was
opposed by Rome, where there were periodic suspicions that Gramsci
might be bent on flight. Thus, on 12 February 1935 a memo was sent
from the Roman police to the police at Littoria: 'Tatiana Schucht has
made arrangements with Antonio Gramsci concerning escape financed
by anti-fascists resident in New York.' Next day four motor-cycle guards

arrived in Formia. In this climate of suspicion, a move to Fiesole or any other place less easily watched than the Cusumano clinic appeared inopportune to the government. Consequently, the 'provisional discharge' granted in October 1934 ended by changing next to nothing in the life of the 'beneficiary'.

Gramsci still succeeded in doing a little reading and writing. The will-power of this man, driven almost insane by suffering, certainly bordered on the superhuman at this stage of his life. Even now, he could still react to the remorseless disintegration of his physique and the exhaustion of all his energies by withdrawing into a still centre: instead of giving up, or despairing, he concentrated the last of his resources on severe intellectual work. To the Formia period (1934–35) belong five notebooks begun at Turi, and another eleven composed entirely in the Cusumano clinic. He was now chiefly concerned with revising earlier work, correcting, enlarging, and transcribing his notes. The overall framework of his thought became clearer at this stage, as his great chain of related themes was further developed. But his sense of intellectual probity still drove him to write on the inside front page of Notebook 18 (mostly a reworking of the material in notebook 28):

> Like those in the other books, the notes in this one have been written straight down without revision and are intended as memoranda. They all need to be revised and checked minutely, as they contain imprecise statements, false comparisons, and anachronisms. Since they were written in the absence of the works referred to, it is possible that after such a check they may have to be radically altered, and the very opposite of what is asserted here may well turn out to be the case.

These are the five notebooks begun at Turi and continued at Formia. Notebook 18 contains the essay on Bukharin's *Historical Materialism*, studies on 'the logical instruments of thought', on 'the translatability of scientific languages', and on various philosophical problems; also notes on Antonio Labriola, Alessandro Levi, Alessandro Chiappelli, Luciano Herr, Giovanni Gentile, Antonio Rosmini, Antonio Lovecchio, Ettore Ciccotti, Giuseppe Rensi, Corrado Barbagallo, Georges Sorel, Pierre-Joseph Proudhon, Henri De Man, and G. A. Borgese. In Notebook 29 (containing only 24 written pages), some previous work on the history of the intellectuals and the organization of schools and culture is taken further. Notebook 30, which Gramsci entitled *Noterelle sulla politica di Machiavelli* ('Brief notes on the politics of Machiavelli') contains studies on parties, on the political analysis of situations and

forces, on economics, Caesarism, politico-cultural hegemony, voluntarism, and the social masses. All his notes on Croce's philosophy are
transcribed in Notebook III (Gramsci's own Roman number for it). In
Notebook 31 there are only two pages written, the beginning of a translation of a Grimm brothers' fairy tale which he had tackled once before
in an earlier book.

However, Gramsci did not confine himself to revision and thematic
re-ordering of his previous work. The Formia notebooks also contain
many new studies. Notably Notebook 6 (on problems of literary criticism) and Notebook 10 ('Notes on the Risorgimento'). Towards the
end his hand-writing becomes very unsteady and clearly betrays his
dwindling physical powers. In the summer of 1935 Gramsci was
forced to break off his work for good, without having had the chance to
revise systematically or re-order a considerable part of his notes.

Ten months after he had been formally granted provisional freedom, he was allowed to move to another clinic. On 2 August 1935,
he left Formia for the Quisisana clinic in Rome.

30

On 26 August 1935 Gramsci was examined by Professor Cesare Frugoni. His plight was desperate: Pott's Disease, pulmonary tuberculosis, high blood pressure, plus attacks of angina and gout. Still he fought on.

He thought a great deal about Julia. He wrote to her again. On 25 November he told her: 'I feel much calmer since I started writing to you again.' Then on 14 December he proposed that she come to Italy:

> I believe you would do very well to come to Italy, from every point of view. For your health, which might finally recover here, and for me, because I need to feel you near me more than ever, I need to renew those bonds which have always held us together, though they have tended to become rather abstract and arbitrary with the passing of years. My darling, I have always waited for you, and you have always been quite essential to my life, even when I wasn't hearing from you or was receiving only rare and superficial letters, even when I wasn't writing to you because I didn't know what to say and was afraid you no longer wished to keep in contact at all. I believe the time has come to put an end to this state of affairs, and we could do that if you came to me, as I am unable to come to you. I am certainly very run down, and I think it scarcely likely I shall ever recover all my old energy; nevertheless, I think you could do a great deal for me, and perhaps I might be able to do something for you, not much I'm afraid, but something. . . . Darling, I am trying to put into this letter all my great feeling for you, even should it not appear clearly in the words I put down. In any case, you will remember that back in 1923 I was not very eloquent either, but I know that you could feel all the depth of my tenderness for you then, and it has not grown less. My feelings have only become stronger, and more serene, because now we have our two sons alongside us.

Again, on 25 January, he pressed the invitation: 'After so long a time, after so many events whose real significance has passed me by, after so many dark years of wretched oppression and misery, simply to be able to talk to you as one friend to another would do me a great deal of good. . . . So I'm quite persuaded that from all points of view a trip here would be very good for both of us. . . .'

Julia did not come. Slowly, he began to pass away:

His heart is very weak [wrote Tatiana in April 1936] and although in some respects his physical condition may seem better, it is not really so. I am afraid that Nino has become a complete invalid. He has suffered too much over the years, and now his organism is too worn out to be able to recover from the very exhausted state into which he has lapsed. Too many vital organs have been too badly affected, and are now scarcely functioning.

He appeared to be – and perhaps really was – detached from everything. We have no evidence of any attempt to re-establish contact with Togliatti, or other leaders or Party functionaries. At the Quisisana he was left relatively free, although an external watch was kept on the building. Had he wished, he could certainly have contacted the Party through the friends and relations who visited him, if only with a note, a few lines of greeting to be handed on. But there is no trace of any such step.

Gramsci seemed to be thinking only of Julia, and his distant sons. He had never known Giuliano except through photographs. Delio was now twelve years old. They wrote to one another, overcoming the great distance between them in a simple dialogue of the utmost tenderness:

Dear Délio . . . thank you for embracing Mummy so hard for me: I think you ought to do so every day, every morning. I am always thinking of you; so I'll imagine you doing it every morning, and say to myself, 'Julia and my two boys are thinking of me now, this very instant.' You're the older brother, but you should tell Julik about this too: so every day you will have 'five minutes with Daddy'. What d'you think of the idea? [2 December 1936].

He now had very little energy left. The only thing which kept him from slipping away was the prospect of soon being definitively freed from prison: his sentence was due to expire on 21 April 1937. He was thinking of returning to Sardinia and living in complete isolation. He wrote home.

When his father learnt of the plan, he became feverish with emotion. Francesco Gramsci was ill himself and now in his seventy-ninth year. He had not seen Nino since 1924. His other sons were also far from home: Gennaro in Spain, fighting Franco with the republican army at Bilbao; Mario in Africa, where he had remained with the Italian army after fighting in the Abyssinian campaign; and Carlo, in Milan. He had seemed likely to die without one of them being near him. Now, with the news of Nino's imminent return, he took on a new lease of life. Edmea Gramsci remembers what happened:

> When his prison sentence was nearly up, Uncle Nino wrote to us. He wanted us to find him a room at Santulussurgiu. He had been there as a student, and the climate was suitable. I went there with Teresina and a friend, Peppina Montaldo. We found a room, a very nice room. Then we waited for Uncle Nino to come, from one day to the next. He was supposed to come on the 27th of April, and we waited for him that day, expecting him at any moment. The day ended, nothing had happened. We were disappointed. Grandad had been longing for his son to arrive on that day. But we told ourselves, he'll come tomorrow all right. Then the next day a woman came to the house and asked: 'Is it true that Nino is dead?' We were struck dumb. 'The wireless said so, I heard it on the wireless,' said the woman. Then people started to come in, everyone turned up with their condolences. Grandad wasn't well, and no one had the courage to tell him, so somebody had to stay in his room near the door and stop people coming in and telling him about it. I stayed with him mostly, I was only a girl then, seventeen years old. Then at one moment I went out and left him, I can't remember why. I was in the kitchen, I heard this shriek, we all ran to him, and there was Grandad screaming: 'Assassins, murderers, they've killed my boy, killed my boy.' I remember that so clearly He kept on saying: 'They've killed my boy', and tearing his hair and his beard and hitting himself. It really was a dreadful scene, you know. . . .

Nino had died at 4.10 a.m. on 27 April. He was forty-six. Next day, in the afternoon, he was taken to be cremated. Tatiana and Carlo were in the one car which followed behind his coffin, through a sudden thunderstorm which had burst over Rome.

Francesco Gramsci died just over a fortnight later, on 16 May 1937. On his death bed he read many times, over and over again, the words that Nino had written to his mother on 10 May 1928, just before his trial:

> For the sake of my own peace of mind I would like you not to be too frightened or upset, whatever the sentence they mean to hand out. I would like you to understand, and to feel, that I am a political prisoner and that I have nothing to be ashamed of, and never will have anything to be ashamed of. I would like you to understand that in a certain sense I have myself wished to be imprisoned and condemned, because I would not change my opinions, and indeed would be willing to give up my life for them, not only to go to jail. I would like you to understand that for this

reason I am bound to be at peace with myself, and not unhappy at what I have done. Dearest Mother, I really would like to hold you very close to me now, so that you could feel how much I love you, and how much I would like to console you for this great grief which I've caused you. But I could not do otherwise. Life is like this, very hard; and sons must sometimes cause great grief to their mothers if they wish to preserve their honour and their dignity as men.

Bibliography

The Works of Gramsci

The Letters

A first collection of 218 of the prison letters was published by Giulio Einaudi (Turin) in 1947. Not all the letters were complete. Cuts had been made for three sorts of reasons: (1) the letters from Ustica had been cut to conceal the friendly personal relationship between Bordiga and Gramsci, for political reasons; (2) certain references to other members of Gramsci's family had been omitted, to avoid offending the living members of the family; (3) an attempt was made to reduce each letter to its essential points, and exclude matters of marginal interest. In spite of these cuts, and the incompleteness of the edition, it presented a clear enough intellectual and moral portrait of Gramsci and it is still worth reading today by anyone looking for an outline sketch of his personality. (An excellent English translation of this edition of the *Lettere* was made by Hamish Henderson of Edinburgh University not long after it appeared: in the twenty intervening years, it has never found an English or American publisher.)

A selection from these letters was published by Editori Riuniti (Rome) in 1961, prefaced by the outstanding lecture given by Luigi Russo at the Scuola Normale Superiore in Pisa on 27 April 1947, the tenth anniversary of Gramsci's death.

Other letters continued to appear, as they were found or released by members of the family and other correspondents, and published by various newspapers or reviews. Giansiro Ferrata and Niccolò Gallo collected these together with some from the original Einaudi edition and others hitherto unpublished, in the second volume of *2000 pagine di Gramsci* (Il Saggiatore, Milan 1964). This volume contains 64 letters of the period 1912–26 and 268 prison letters; the notes are useful. Also extremely important is the collection of letters exchanged by Gramsci and other future PCI leaders before Bordiga's displacement in 1923–24, published in 1962 as *La Formazione del Gruppo Dirigente del PCI* (Editore Riuniti, Rome).

Finally a complete collection of the prison letters was published by Einaudi in 1965: (*Lettere dal carcere*, ed. Caprioglio and Fubini, NEU Giulio Einaudi, Turin). This contains 428 letters, mostly checked against the originals. The editors have included information on Gramsci's various correspondents (though the data on the Schucht family are not entirely correct) and a very precise chronology of Gramsci's life. There is also an index of all the books and periodicals referred to in the letters. The notes are excellent, and contain much new and original information relating to Gramsci's life.

The rest of Gramsci's writings can be divided under two headings: articles and essays published in various newspapers and reviews between 1914 and 1926; and the Prison Notebooks, the *Quaderni del carcere*.

Writings of the period 1914-26

Einaudi has published so far the articles from *Il Grido del popolo, La Città futura* and *Avanti!* (1914-18) in a volume entitled *Scritti giovanili* ('Early Writings') 1958. A selection from *Sotto la Mole*, Gramsci's daily rubric in *Avanti!*, appeared under the same title in 1960. His articles from the weekly *L'Ordine Nuovo* were published in *L'Ordine Nuovo 1919-20* (1954). In 1963 Einaudi also published an *Ordine Nuovo* anthology, edited with an excellent introductory essay by Paolo Spriano (reprinted by Editori Riuniti in 1965 under the title *Gramsci e L'Ordine Nuovo*). Additional articles from the period 1915-21 were collected by Sergio Caprioglio in a special issue of the review *Il Corpo* in 1968. Gramsci's articles from *L'Ordine Nuovo*, 1921-2 were published by Einaudi in 1966. Some writings of the period before Gramsci's arrest appear in *2000 pagine di Gramsci* mentioned above. In this Ferrata and Gallo have included, as well as selections from writings previously published by Einaudi, articles of the period 1921-26 drawn from both the daily and the fortnightly *L'Ordine Nuovo*, from *Stato Operaio* and from *L'Unità*. Their anthology also contained Gramsci's speech in parliament of 16 May 1925, the letter to the Soviet Communist Party leadership of October 1926, and the uncompleted essay *Alcuni temi della questione meridionale* ('Some aspects of the Southern Question'), first published in Paris in 1930, in *Stato Operaio*. *2000 pagine di Gramsci* has a very lucid introduction by Ferrata, and good prefatory notes to each section of the anthology.

Elsa Fubini is currently preparing editions of the writings of the periods 1921-22 and 1923-26, for Einaudi.

Some articles from *L'Ordine Nuovo* were published by *New Left Review*, no. 51, London 1968, under the title 'Antonio Gramsci: Soviets in Italy'.

The Prison Notebooks

The 2,848 pages of the thirty-two prison notebooks constitute the great heritage Gramsci bequeathed to future generations. Felice Platone, the first editor of the notebooks, wrote: 'The 2,848 pages of the original correspond to about 4,000 type-written sheets. As soon as she came into possession of the notebooks, Tatiana Schucht numbered them by sticking a label on the front and back covers of each one, but paid no heed to the order in which they had been written (thus, the first notebook, dated 8 February 1929, bears the number 16). One of the notebooks was given the number 'III' by Gramsci himself and entitled *La Filosofia di Benedetto Croce*; it was not numbered along with the others; we do not know why. Twenty-one notebooks were written (or at least started) at Turi prison, near Bari, and bear the prison stamp on each page; each page is also numbered by the prison authorities and the cover and inside front page carry written statements to the effect that 'This notebook contains pages numbered from 1 to . . . belonging to prisoner No. 7047 Gramsci Antonio'. Sometimes this statement is para- phrased into the formula 'No. 7047 pages . . .', and followed by the governor's signature. The eleven other notebooks, numbered as 3, 5, 6, 10, 11, 12, 17, 31, 23, 25 and 27, bear no official stamp or other prison marking; they must therefore have been composed during the years 1934–35, after Gramsci's transference to the clinic at Formia. In 1935, Gramsci's work was broken off for good: his lucidity and intellectual vigour remained unimpaired, according to those who visited him in the last months of his life, but his physical energy was exhausted.

The dating of the notebooks themselves presents considerable problems. Einaudi published them in six volumes, in the following order: *Il Material- ismo storico e la filosofia di Benedetto Croce* ('Historical Materialism and the Philosophy of Benedetto Croce'), 1948; *Gli Intellettuali e l'organizzazione della cultura* ('The Intellectuals and the Organization of Culture'), 1949; *Il Risorgimento*, 1949; *Note sul Machiavelli, sulla politica e sullo Stato moderno* ('Notes on Machiavelli, on Politics and on the Modern State'), 1949; *Letteratura e vita nazionale* ('Literature and National Life'), 1950, containing in addition Gramsci's theatre criticism of the period 1916–20 from *Avanti!*; and lastly, *Passato e presente* ('Past and Present'), 1951, which has a useful subject-index to all six volumes. An anthology of Gramsci's writings was published by Editori Riuniti in 1963, edited by Carlo Salinari and Mario Spinella. The same publisher brought out another selection edited by Mario Spinella in 1964, with the title *Elementi di Politica* ('Elements of Politics'). An English translation of the selected writings of Gramsci was published by Lawrence & Wishart (London 1957) under the title *The Modern Prince* (selection and translation by Louis Marks). The same publisher will shortly bring out a much more comprehensive selection of Gramsci's writings, translated and introduced by Quintin Hoare and Geoffrey Nowell-Smith (Spring 1970). One of Gramsci's writings on education – 'In Search of Education', translated with an introduction by Quintin Hoare, was published in *New Left Review*, no. 32, 1965. *The Open Marxism of Antonio Gramsci* (Cameron Associates, New York 1957) is a short selection from *Il Material- ismo storico*, translated and annotated by Carlo Marzoni, relating Gramsci to 'American problems'.

Works on Gramsci's Life and Thought

Critical Studies

There is a vast critical literature on Gramsci's thought, and (as yet) no adequate general bibliography. In the absence of this, it is however worth mentioning the following: Nicola Matteucci, *Antonio Gramsci e la filosofia della prassi* ('Antonio Gramsci and Marxism'), Giuffrè, Milan 1951; Carlo Leopoldo Ottino, *Concetti fondamentali nella teoria politica di Antonio Gramsci* ('Basic Concepts of Gramsci's Political Theory'), Feltrinelli, Milan 1956; the two volumes of essays entitled *Studi Gramsciani*, Rome 1958, and *La Città Futura*, Milan 1959; Giuseppe Tamburrano, *Antonio Gramsci: La vita, il pensiero, l'azione* ('Antonio Gramsci: His Life Thought, and Action') Lacaita, Manduria 1963; Silverio Corvisieri, *Trotsky e il comunismo italiano* (Samonà & Savelli, 1969). Useful articles on Gramsci are those in *La Rivista storica del socialismo* (nos. 17–31, Milan) from a more pro-Bordiga position; and the special number of the PCI review *Critica marxistia* (Rome, 'Quaderni', no. 3, 1967), entitled *Prassi rivoluzionaria e storicismo in Gramsci*.

In English, specially worthy of note are John M. Cammett, *Antonio Gramsci and the Origins of Italian Communism* (Stanford University Press, 1967), and John Merrington's 'Theory and Practice in Gramsci's Marxism' (*The Socialist Register*, London and New York 1969).

Biographies

The first attempt at a biography was by Lucio Lombardo-Radice and Giuseppe Carbone, who published their *Vita di Antonio Gramsci* in 1952 (Edizioni di Cultura Sociale, Rome). Later research showed up the limitations of this work – admitted in any case by the authors in their own preface. Giuseppe Tamburrano's *Antonio Gramsci: La vita, il pensiero, cazione*, mentioned in the above section, contains a somewhat schematic biographical outline, and some of his judgements have provoked much dissent and controversy. Salvatore Francesco Romano's large study *Antonio Gramsci* (Einaudi, Turin 1967) contains no new material, but the chapters on the Turin years are exhaustive. Two outstanding studies on different periods of Gramsci's life have been made by Domenico Zucàro: 'Antonio Gramsci all'Università di Torino 1911–15', in the review *Società*, December 1957; and *Vita del Carcere di Antonio Gramsci* (Edizioni Avanti!, Milan-Rome, 1954). Both essays contain much original and useful information. Most valuable for understanding the background of Gramsci's political life are the two volumes which have so far appeared of Paolo Spriano's *Storia del Partito Comunista Italiano* (Einaudi): volume I 'From Bordiga to Gramsci'

(1967), and volume II 'The Years of Clandestinity' (1969). There is also a useful collection of documents on the early history of the PCI, *I primi dieci anni di vita del PCI* (Feltrinelli, Milan 1962), with an introduction by G. Berti.

Index

Because Antonio Gramsci's name occurs throughout the book there is no entry for him in this index.

Agnelli, Giovanni, 138, 151
Alagon, Leonardo, 31
Alfoni, Luigi, 229
Alfieri, Vittorio, 71
Alfredo (Gramsci's uncle), 264
Amendola, Giovanni, 176, 188, 204
Amoretti, Giuseppe, 117, 173
Angioy, Giovanni Maria, 30-1
Angius (Sardinian bandit), 31
Angius, Vittorio, 10n, 33
Arborea, Eleonora d', 31
Arcangeli, Umberto, 278, 281
Arrullani, Vittorio Amedeo, 67-8
Ascoli, Graziadio Isaia, 236
Azuni, Domenico Alberto, 71

Bacaredda, Ottone, 47-8
Bacci, Giovanni, 144
Balabanov, Angelica, 164
Baldussi, Celestino, 18
Baratono, Adelchi, 144
Barbusse, Henri, 118, 281
Barrili, Anton Giulio, 56
Bartoli, Matteo, 73, 75, 80, 83, 92-3, 97
Battelli, Alcibiade, 35-6, 56
Bava-Beccaris, Fiorenzo, 33
Bellieni, Camillo, 13, 30, 32
Belloni, Ambrogio, 147
Berger, Cesare, 76
Bergson, Henri, 91n
Bernolfo, Giacomo, 148
Berra, (Camillo's mother, Gramsci's land-lady in Turin), 89
Berra, Camillo, 76, 89
Berra, Perrone Clementina, 120
Berrini, Nino, 116
Berti, Giuseppe, 225
Bianchi, Giuseppe, 101-2
Bianco, Vincenzo, 132, 169, 179 and n, 180

Bibolotti, Aladino, 200
Boccardo, Carlo, 113
Boero, Giovanni, 116, 120, 124-5, 132
Bolivar, Simon, 181
Bombacci, Nicola, 111, 142, 147
Bonomi, Ivanoe, 135
Bordiga, Amadeo, 76, 103, 111, 123-4, 130, 133, 136, 140, 142-4, 146-7, 149, 151-4, 159-60, 162-3, 166-7, 168, 170, 175, 183, 198, 201, 203, 217, 221
Borin, Igino, 229
Boscolo, Alberto, 46
Bourbons, 41-2
Bousquet (captain), 58
Bovio, Giovanni, 54
Boyl di Putifigari, 83
Bresciani, Antonio, 236 and n, 267-8
Bruno, Giordano, 32, 54
Bruno, Nino, 182
Bukharin, Nicolai Ivanovich, 123, 158, 212-13, 216, 244, 246, 250-1, 286
Buozzi, Bruno, 82, 106, 113

Camedda, Ezio, 28
Cantù, Cesare, 74 and n
Cao, Umberto, 47-8
Carducci, Giosuè, 11, 200, 241
Carta, Patrizio, 27
Carta Ledda, Pietro Paolo, 38
Casalini, Armando, 182
Castagno, Gino, 76, 82
Cattaneo, 66 and n
Cavallera, Giuseppe, 33, 34-6, 56, 62, 85-7
Cavallotti, Felice, 32, 33n
Carena, Attilio, 106, 113
Carena, Pia, 106, 113, 118, 148, 170
Carlini, Armando, 106
Cavalcanti, Cavalcante, 236
Cecchi, Emilio, 57 and n

Ceresa, Giuseppe, 233, 254-5
Cheplak (archbishop), 269
Chernov, Victor, 109
Chironi, Giovanni, 75, 83
Cialdini, Enrico, 10 and n, 42
Cisternino (doctor), 233
Ciuffo, Piero (Cip), 76 and n
Cocco Ortu, Francesco, 13, 51, 57, 61
Codevilla, Mario, 164
Conca, Paolo, 221
Consolo, Gaetano, 201
Conti, Ettore, 194
Contini, Antonio, 121
Corona (wine expert of the Co-operative Alliance), 106
Corradetti, Gino, 84, 86-7
Corradini, Enrico, 77
Corrias (the family), 10, 223
Corrias, Ignazio, 18
Corrias, Maria Domenica, 20
Corsi, Angelo, 36
Corvi, Giovanni, 181
Cosmo, Umberto, 74-5, 93, 97n, 104, 113
Cossu, Luigi, 18
Costa, Enrico, 31
Crispi, Francesco, 13, 32
Croce, Benedetto, 51, 74, 91 and n, 106, 113, 211, 217, 239-41, 243-4, 246-7, 267, 287
Cromwell, Oliver, 181
Cuba, Nennetta, 16, 20, 26
Cugusi, Claudio, 53
Cusumano Giuseppe, 281, 283, 285

D'Annunzio, Gabriele, 77, 151
D'Aragona, Ludovico, 140
Darwin, Charles Robert, 76
De Bono, Emilio, 204, 231
De Felice, Renzo, 7, 134n
Deffenu, Attilio, 84
Degott, V., 134, 150
Deledda, Grazia, 31, 56, 94
De Leon, Daniel, 122
Delka see Gramsci, Delio
Delogu, (Sardinian bandit), 31
Delogu, Achille, 70
Delogu, Delio, 69-70, 179
Delogu, Grazia, 11, 184
Delogu, Serafino, 70, 179
Delogu, Zaccaria (Gramsci's uncle), 70
De Man, Henri, 286
Derosas (Sardinian bandit), 31

De Sanctis, Francesco, 74-5
Dezzani, Carlo, 98
Donati, Giuseppe, 204
Dore, Francesco, 84, 86, 88
Dorso, Guido, 211, 238
Dostoyevsky, Fyodor Mikhailovich, 266

Eastman, Max, 117
Eckermann, Johann Peter, 246
Einaudi, Luigi, 75, 83
Engels, Friedrich, 241

Fancello, Nicolò, 84
Farina, Giovanni, 199
Farina, Salvatore, 94
Farinacci, Roberto, 194
Farinelli, Arturo, 75
Ferrara, Marcella, 77, 92, 96, 252
Ferrara, Maurizio, 77, 92, 96, 252
Ferrari, Enrico, 229-30
Ferraris, Erminio, 45
Ferrata, Giansiro, 217
Ferri, Enrico, 79
Figàri, Renato, 51, 53, 56
Filippelli, Filippo, 181
Finck, Franz Nikolaus, 246
Finzi, Aldo, 181
Fontana, Aurelio, 233
Fortichiari, Bruno, 142, 147, 162
Fortunato, Giustino, 211
Foscolo, Niccolò Ugo, 54, 71, 267
Fournière, Joseph-Eugène, 122
Francesco II (Bourbon king of the Two Sicilies), 42
Frau, Dino, 51
Frau, Sebastiano, 12
Frey, Joseph, 164
Frongia, Gildo, 46n
Frugoni, Cesare, 288
Fubini, Elsa, 7

Galetto, Leo, 111
Gana, Remundu, 184
Gandhi, Mohandas Karamchand, 220
Garibaldi, Giuseppe, 181
Garzìa, Raffa, 55, 57-9, 67
Gay (lieutenant in the carabinieri), 59
Gay, Pilade, 94
Gennari, Egidio, 147, 163, 172
Gentile, Giovanni, 286
Germonio (prefect of Cagliari), 59, 64
Gerosa, Pietro Paolo, 74

Giampaoli, Mario, 227
Gibson, Violet, 204
Gilodi, Giovanni, 116
Giolitti, Giovanni, 35, 61 and n, 138, 141, 195, 209
Giudice, Maria, 101, 103, 114
Gobetti, Piero, 93, 102, 114, 116–18, 138, 181, 193, 204, 238
Goethe, Johann Wolfgang, 235
Gogol, Nicolai Vasilievich, 266
Goldenberg, Joseph Petrovich, 109
Gonzales, Teresa, 10, 22, 42
Gramatica, Emma, 122
Gramsci, Carlo,[1] 7, 13, 20, 37, 69, 89, 100, 115, 183–4, 220–21, 224, 229, 258n, 261, 262, 268–70, 278, 281, 283, 285, 290
Gramsci, Delio, 22, 43, 185, 191–2, 197, 199–200, 202, 205, 223, 261, 263–4, 289
Gramsci, Edmea, 7, 11, 183, 185, 264, 269
Gramsci, Emma, 11, 24, 37, 115, 142 and n, 183
Gramsci, Francesco, 7, 9–15, 17, 22, 28, 37, 41–2, 64–5, 72, 89, 100, 115, 183, 290
Gramsci, Gennaro,[2] 7, 10, 11, 15–16, 20, 22 and n, 24–25, 33, 100, 115, 137, 150, 176, 185, 224, 252, 253, 261, 264 and n, 270, 289
Gramsci, Gennaro (Francesco's father), 10, 41
Gramsci, Giuliano,[3] 205, 263, 264 and n, 270, 289
Gramsci, Grazia,[4] 12, 16, 24, 37, 72, 91, 98, 261–2, 268, 270, 278
Gramsci, Mario,[5] 13, 20, 27, 37, 42, 69, 89, 100, 115, 150, 223–5, 261, 289

Gramsci, Nicola, 10, 14, 22n, 42
Gramsci, Teresina,[6] 7, 16, 17, 19 and n, 24, 27, 56–7, 66, 81, 115, 183, 185, 223, 233, 263, 264 and n, 273, 276, 278, 283–4, 290
Gramsci, Marcias Giuseppina, 9, 10, 13, 15–17, 22, 26, 28, 37, 65, 106, 115, 142, 183, 185–6, 224, 273, 278
Graziadei, Antonio, 84, 159, 166
Grieco, Ruggero, 78, 147, 162, 217, 252
Grimm, Jakob, 246, 287
Grimm, Wilhelm, 246, 287
Guiso, Luciano, 18, 98

Hebbel, Friedrich, 107
Heine, Heinrich, 266
Horthy di Nagybanya, Miklos, 133
Humbert-Droz, Jules, 123, 217, 251–2

Invernizio, Carolina, 56

Kalinin, Michail Ivanovich, 212
Kamenev, Leo Borisovich, 144, 213–16, 250
Kant, Immanuel, 241
Kerensky, Alexander, 109–11
Kerzhentsev Platon Michailovich, 269
Kun, Béla, 123

Labriola, Antonio, 92, 286
Labriola, Arturo, 176
Lamarmora, Alberto, 83
Lambert, Édouard, 77
Lay, Giovanni, 183, 257–8, 264
Lazzari, Costantino, 111, 124, 149

[1] Now over 70, he works in the publicity department of the Italian Communist weekly *Unita*.

[2] Died in Rome, aged 81, in a car crash in October 1965. He had kept the till in a chemist shop in the Garbatella quarter of the city. His daughter, Edmea, married a doctor and is a primary school teacher in Sardinia.

[3] Giuliano and Delio visited Italy in 1947 and have made other visits since. Giuliano lives in Moscow and is a professional violinist. Delio is a captain in the Russian navy and lives in Leningrad.

[4] Died in 1962 aged 75.

[5] Enlisted in the army during the Abyssinian war, and later fought in North Africa. He was captured and spent several years in an Australian P.O.W. camp. Died in 1945 aged 52 immediately after his return from Australia from a serious illness contracted during imprisonment. He left two children, Gianfranco and Cesarina.

[6] Now over 70, she used to work in the post office at Ghilarza. She has four children: Franco, a doctor at Bargos; Mimma, a primary school teacher in Milan; Diddi and Marco who teach in the secondary school at Ghilarza.

Lenin, Vladimir Ilych, 109, 114, 117, 122, 134, 135, 136–7, 143–6, 149, 153, 166, 180, 212, 214–15
Leonetti, Alfonso, 7, 91, 113, 117, 151, 167–8, 252
Licheri, Michele, 24n
Liebknecht, Karl, 131
Lisa, Athos, 253, 255–7, 270
Lombardo-Radice, Giuseppe, 113
Longo, Luigi, 252
Loria, Achille, 75, 267n
Loriga, Giovanni, 45
Lucatelli, Luigi, 49, 50
Lussu, Emilio, 189
Luxemburg, Rosa, 133
Luzzatti, Luigi, 57, 61, 64

Maccarone, Francesco, 55, 68
Machiavelli, Niccolò, 245, 265, 267
Macis, Enrico, 222, 227
Maffei, Parravicini Anna, 115, 150, 224
Maffi, Fabrizio, 161
Makar (soviet diplomat), 269
Mameli, Peppino, 80, 183
Manca, Giomaria, 39
Mannu, Francesco Ignazio, 55
Mannu, Giuseppe, 83
Manzini, Vincenzo, 75
Manzoni, Alessandro, 236
Marabini, Anselmo, 147
Marcello (mayor of Cagliari), 62
Marcias (the family), 10
Martinet, Marcel, 118
Marx, Karl, 56, 66, 76, 85, 92, 112, 113n, 241
Marzullo (brothers), 51, 89
Massida, Marco, 40
Mastino, Pietro, 84
Matteotti, Giacomo, 172–3, 175, 180–2, 187, 198, 204, 227
Melani, Corrado, 227
Miglioli, Guido, 152
Milyutin, Vladimir Pavlovich, 144
Misiano, Fortunato, 142, 147, 150
Modigliani, Giuseppe Emanuele, 118, 138
Molotov, Vyacheslav Michailovich Scriabin, 212
Mondolfo, Ugo Guido, 113
Monicelli, Tomaso, 56
Montagnana, Mario, 96, 117, 121, 132, 172
Montaldo, Peppina, 290
Motta (industrialist), 194

Mura (Gramsci's Sardinian friend in Turin), 106
Mussolini, Benito, 47 and n, 91 and n, 96–7, 158 and n, 159, 171n, 173n, 174–5, 181, 188, 192, 193, 194–6, 201, 203–4, 218, 227, 229, 233, 270, 281, 285

Negarville, Celeste, 185, 282
Nenni, Pietro, 126 and n, 174
Nessi, Vittore, 17
Niceforo, Alfredo, 14n, 79
Nicolini (a Bolshevik), 134
Nitti, Francesco Saverio, 126n
Nogin, Victor Pavlovich, 144

Obinu, Giulia, 40
Oddone, Costante, 55
Omodeo, Adolfo, 268
Onnis, Giuseppe, 85
Oppo, Francesco, 70
Orano, Efisio, 35, 49, 56
Orano, Paolo, 79

Pacchioni, Giovanni, 75, 77
Pais, Ettore, 77
Pais, Serra Francesco, 13, 14, 30
Pajetta, Gian Carlo, 282
Papini, Giovanni, 57
Parini, Giuseppe, 55
Parodi, Giovanni, 116, 124–5, 132, 138, 140, 147
Pascoli, Giovanni, 56, 235
Pasolini, Pier Paolo, 101
Passarge (the family), 172
Pastore, Angelo, 113
Pastore, Annibale, 75, 92–3
Pastore, Ottavio, 95, 101–2, 122, 129, 148
Paulesu, Diddi, 264 and n
Paulesu, Franco, 264 and n
Paulesu, Mimma, 264 and n
Paulesu, Paolo, 19, 183
Pelloux, Luigi Girolamo, 36
Perilli, Leonilde, 7, 156, 190, 202, 279
Pesci, Gino, 56, 62, 64
Pilati, Gaetano, 201
Pirandello, Luigi, 104, 235
Pirisi, Pirione di Bolotana, 21
Pizzardo, Giuseppe, 269 and n, 270
Platone, Felice, 117, 172, 189
Podrecca, Guido, 61 and n, 62–3, 135
Polano, Luigi, 142, 147

Porcella, Felice, 59, 86, 88
Porcu, Antioco, 9, 12
Porcu, Doloretta, 53
Porcu, Francesco, 38
Prezzolini, Giuseppe, 56, 76, 84, 211
Prospero, Ada, 138
Proudhon, Pierre-Joseph, 286
Puccinelli, Vittorio, 284
Puxeddu, Francesco, 12

Rabezzana, Pietro, 116, 150
Rákosi, Mátyás, 160
Ransome, Arthur, 123
Ravazzoli, Paolo, 252
Ravera, Camilla, 218, 252
Renier, Rodolfo, 75
Reed, John, 122
Riboldi, Ezio, 218, 229-30
Riccio (Gramsci's uncle), 10
Robespierre, Maximilien François Isidore de, 241
Rolland, Romain, 104, 118, 279, 281, 285
Romani, Dante, 227
Romita, Giuseppe, 76
Rossi, Cesarino, 181, 188
Rousseau, Jean-Jacques, 180
Roveda, Giovanni, 132, 229, 232
Rudinì, Antonio Starabba di, 14, 36 and n
Ruffini, Francesco, 75, 83
Rykov, Alexei Ivanovich 144, 212

Saba, Francesco, 85
Saba, Michele, 84
Sacchi, Ettore, 66
Salvemini, Gaetano, 57, 84, 91, 95, 106, 113, 204
Sanna, Giovanni, 84
Sanna, Randaccio Giuseppe, 87
Sanna, Titinu, 148
Santhià, Battista, 105, 132, 139-40
Sardo, Giuseppe, 229
Satta, Sebastiano, 31 and n, 54, 56, 94
Sbaraglini, Giuseppe, 221
Scalas (Communist deputy for Oristano at the clandestine Cagliari Congress), 183
Schiavazzi, Pietro, 58

Schucht, Anna, 155-6, 205
Schucht, Apollo, 155-6, 192, 205
Schucht, Eugenie, 155-7, 161, 192, 201-2, 205
Schucht, Julia,[1] 23, 26, 154-7, 161-5, 169-70, 173, 177-9, 185-7, 189 and n, 190-2, 196-7, 199, 201-3, 205, 217-18, 222, 225 and n, 226, 237, 247-8, 259, 260, 261, 270-2, 278-9, 284, 288-9
Schucht, Nadina Leontieva, 155-6, 205
Schucht, Tatiana,[2] 7, 40, 104, 155-6, 190, 197, 201-2, 205, 220, 221, 223-5, 235-6, 237n, 245, 247-8, 253, 261-2, 264 and n, 265-6, 268, 270-2, 275-6, 278-80, 283-5, 290
Schucht, Vittorio, 155-6, 205
Scoccimarro, Mauro, 161-2, 166-7, 169, 229, 232, 282
Scucchia, Angelo, 257
Secchia, Pietro, 252
Senes, Agostino, 67
Sergi, Giuseppe, 79
Serra, Renato, 99
Serrati, Giancinto Menotti, 123-4, 133-4, 135 and n, 143-6, 153-4, 161, 184
Sessa, Cesare, 147
Settembrini, Luigi, 74
Silone, Ignazio, 252 and n
Siotto, Jago, 35, 57
Smirnov, Ivan, 109
Solari, Gioele, 75
Sorel, Georges, 91, 122, 286
Sotgiu, Pietro, 25, 31
Souvarine, Boris, 111
Spadoni, Bruno, 257
Spano, Velio, 35, 47-8, 115, 172
Spaventa, Silvio, 247
Spencer, Herbert, 76
Sperling & Kupfer, 222
Spiridonova, Maria, 190
Sraffa, Piero, 74, 222, 261, 281, 285
Stalin, Joseph Vissarionovitch, 212, 216, 250
Stampini, Ettore, 75
Stara, Serra Massimo, 38, 84, 86
Stecchetti, Lorenzo (Olindo Guerrini), 54
Sturzo, Luigi Don, 159

[1] Now over 70, she lives in Moscow with her sister Eugenie at 2 Troitskii Per Dom 6 A K V. 14. She has never been back to Italy since her visit in 1925-6.
[2] Left Rome in 1939, two years after Gramsci's death. She suffered from tuberculosis and died in 1941 at Frunze, in Kirghizia.

Tarsia, Ludovico, 147
Tasca, Angelo, 76, 79–80, 88, 91, 94–6, 102, 117–18, 126, 131, 139, 141, 154, 166–7, 171, 181, 217, 251
Terracini, Umberto, 91, 103, 117–18, 120, 131–2, 137, 142, 147, 153, 159, 166–8, 184, 229, 231–2
Tilgher, Adriano, 104
Toesca, Pietro, 75
Togliatti, Palmiro, 9, 30, 71, 75, 77–8, 80, 82–3, 91–2, 96, 102, 113, 117–18, 120, 130–2, 137, 141, 143, 153–4, 159, 162, 166–9, 184, 200–1, 215–17
Tolstoy, Leo Nikolayevich, 61, 266
Tolu, Giovanni, 31
Tomsky, Michail Pavlovich (pseudonym of M. P. Efremov), 212, 252
Toriggia, Felle, 18, 20
Tramatzu (Sardinian bandit), 85
Tresso, Pietro, 252
Treves, Claudio, 108, 118, 126n, 135, 172
Trombetti, Gustavo, 276, 281
Trotsky, Leon, 212–16, 250
Tseretelli, Irakly Georgevich, 109
Tunis, Nicolino, 12
Turati, Augusto, 218

Turati, Filippo, 118, 122, 135–6, 143, 153, 159, 176, 204
Turgenev, Ivan, 266

Umberto I, (King of Italy), 33

Vella, Arturo, 174, 176
Viglongo, Andrea, 106, 113, 117, 122, 132, 152
Victor Emmanuel III (King of Italy), 42, 58–9
Voroshilov, Klementy, 212
Vota (member of the PCI executive), 162, 166

Wizner, Aron, 114, 134

Zabel, Teodoro, 156
Zamboni, Anteo, 217, 227
Zaniboni, Tito, 202, 204
Zannerini, Emilio, 144
Zini, Zino, 141
Zinoviev, Gregory Ovseyevich, 134, 144–5, 146n, 155, 159, 199, 212–13, 214, 216, 250
Zucàro, Domenico, 71, 73, 90, 233